# SEX DISCRIMINATION LAW

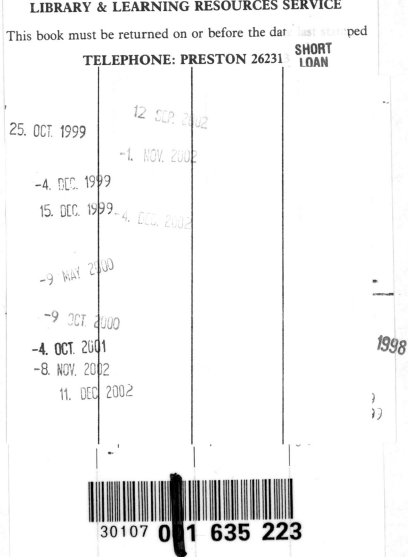

# SEX DISCRIMINATION LAW

EVELYN ELLIS

Gower

Aldershot · Brookfield USA · Hong Kong · Singapore · Sydney

Published by
Gower Publishing Company Limited
Gower House
Croft Road
Aldershot
Hants GU11 3HR
England

Gower Publishing Company
Old Post Road
Brookfield
Vermont 05036
USA

**British Library Cataloguing in Publication Data**

Ellis, Evelyn, *1948–*
    Sex discrimination law.
    1. Great Britain. Women. Sex
    discrimination by society. Law
    I. Title
    344.102'878

    ISBN 0 566 053551

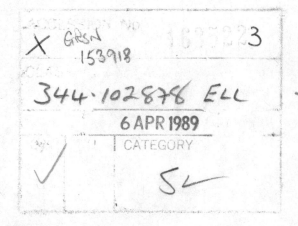
Printed and bound in Great Britain by
Anchor Brendon Ltd, Tiptree, Essex

# Contents

# Abbreviations

AC   Appeal Cases
ACAS   Advisory, Conciliation and Arbitration Service
All ER   All England Law Reports
AG   Advocate General of the European Court of Justice
Bull.   Bulletin of the European Communities
Bull. Supp.   Supplement to the Bulletin of the European
    Communities
Ch.   Chancery Reports
CMLR   Common Market Law Reports
CML Rev.   Common Market Law Review
Cmnd.   Command Paper
COM   Official Paper of the European Commission
CRE   Commission for Racial Equality
CREW Reports   Monthly reports of the Centre for Research on
    European Women
ECJ   European Court of Justice
ECR   European Court Reports
EEC   European Economic Community
ELR   European Law Review
EOC   Equal Opportunities Commission
EOR   Equal Opportunities Review
ESF   European Social Fund
FEP Cases   Fair Employment Practice Cases (USA)
ICLQ   International and Comparative Law Quarterly (journal)
ICR   Industrial Cases Reports
ILJ   Industrial Law Journal
IRLR   Industrial Relations Law Reports
IRRR   Industrial Relations Review and Report
JSWL   Journal of Social Welfare Law
LAG Bulletin   Bulletin of the Legal Action Group
Law Soc. Gaz.   Law Society's Gazette
LIEI   Legal Issues of European Integration (journal)
LQR   Law Quarterly Review
MLR   Modern Law Review
NLJ   New Law Journal

OJ No. C   Official Journal of the European Communities – series
    containing non-normative communications and information
OJ No. L   Official Journal of the European Communities – series
    containing secondary legislation
OJLS   Oxford Journal of Legal Studies
QB   Queen's Bench Division Reports
SI   Statutory Instrument
SLT   Scots Law Times
UNTS   United Nations Treaty Series
US   United States Reports
WLR   Weekly Law Reports

# Table of Cases

# Foreword

The proposition which is central to this book is that the anti-discrimination laws have a vital, although of course not exclusive, part to play in the attainment of equality of opportunity between the sexes. The legislation, as interpreted and applied by tribunals and judges, not only gives tangible form to people's theoretical rights but also provides an unrivalled educative model and authoritative statement of principle. This is why it is so important that judicial decisions on the subject should not be restrictive, technical or blinkered.

Since the main text was completed, there has for the most part been a steady trickle of encouraging decisions from the higher courts. Admittedly the outcome of the appeals in *Aziz* v. *Trinity Street Taxis Ltd* (Chapter 3, p. 73) ([1988] IRLR 204) and *Leverton* v. *Clwyd County Council* (Chapter 2, p. 26) (*The Independent* 7 April 1988) was disappointing. But in *Noone* v. *North West Thames Regional Health Authority* (Chapter 3, p. 146) ([1988] IRLR 195) the Court of Appeal ruled that £1,000 was an insufficient award of compensation for severe injury to feelings in a race discrimination claim, and substituted an award of £3,000; and in *Bromley and others* v. *Quick Ltd* (Chapter 2, p. 29 and n. 141) (*The Independent* 13 April 1988) it overturned the Employment Appeal Tribunal's decision and ruled that a job evaluation scheme which compares jobs on a 'whole job' basis rather than on an analytical basis does not satisfy the requirements of s. 1(5) of the Equal Pay Act 1970. The Court of Appeal has also upheld the decisions in *West Midlands Passenger Transport Executive* v. *Singh* (Chapter 3, p. 155–6) ([1988] IRLR 186) and *R.* v. *Birmingham City Council, Ex p. EOC* (Chapter 3, n. 303 and Chapter 5, p. 265) (unreported).

By far the most significant, however, have been two decisions of the House of Lords. In *Stockton-on-Tees Borough Council* v. *Brown* ([1988] 2 WLR 935) the ruling of the Court of Appeal (Chapter 5, p. 284) was reversed and it was held that s. 60(1) of the Employment Protection (Consolidation) Act 1978 does indeed apply to the selection of an employee for dismissal on the ground of redundancy, where the reason for her selection is connected with the fact that she is pregnant. Lord Griffiths said: '[S. 60] must be seen as a part of social legislation passed for the specific protection of women and to put them on an equal footing with men. I have no doubt that it is often a considerable inconvenience to an employer to have to make the necessary arrangements to keep a woman's job open for her whilst she is absent from work in order to have a baby, but this is a price that has to be paid as a part of the social and legal recognition of the equal status of women in the workplace' (at p. 940). And in *Hayward* v. *Cammell Laird Shipbuilders Ltd (No. 2)* (Chapter 2, pp. 54–6) ([1988] 2 WLR 1134), Ms Hayward finally won her battle to have each and every provision in her contract of employment upgraded to match those of her male comparators doing work of equal value to hers. Both these rulings demonstrate an enormously greater sensitivity on the part of the House of Lords to the underlying issues in sex discrimination cases than the bulk of the cases had shown hitherto. It is very much to be hoped that these clear signals from the House of Lords will be received and understood by the lower courts and tribunals, and that a more purposive and insightful approach can now be anticipated from them.

This book could not have been written without the help and advice of many friends and colleagues. In particular, I should like to thank members of the Women Law Teachers Group, especially Susan Atkins, for providing critical comment and support, my colleague Michael McConville for his helpful suggestions in relation to Chapter 1, the staff of the Equal Opportunities Commission for the information contained in Chapter 5, Jacqui Wootton for (almost) taming the word-processor and producing a typescript, and, last but by no means least, my family for putting up with me during what must often have seemed a never-ending process.

# 1 Introduction

Many societies and many legal systems differentiate between the sexes over the distribution of rights, powers, duties, functions and wealth. It is far from unusual to encounter the attitude, both on the part of individuals and of the legal system, that the rightful place of the female is in the home, bringing up children, and for that purpose a lesser degree of education is required than will be necessary for her brothers; neither will she require independent earning power because her father and, later on, her husband will provide for her in economic terms. Consistently with such views, the law does not have to grant her equal or identical rights with her male peers.[1]

Such attitudes are not confined to the past, nor to distant jurisdictions such as those where Islam is the prevailing religion. As recently as 1974, the UK government remarked in a White Paper:

> Many children are brought up from their earliest years in the belief that the social and economic roles of men and women are radically different. This is reflected in the differences which are common in the curricula for boys and girls. For example, in England and Wales, at A-level, there is a marked difference in the proportionate distribution between boys and girls taking arts and sciences, and at all examination levels from CSE upwards there are fewer subject entries from girls than from boys. One reason for this difference is that more girls than boys leave school at the minimum school-leaving age. There are differences also in the proportion of boys and girls taking the ordinary and higher grade examinations of the Scottish Certificate of Education in certain subjects.
>
> The disparity is more striking in higher education. In 1971–7, 4.2% of girl school leavers and 7.3% of boy school leavers were destined for the Universities; whereas 1.4% of boy school leavers and 5.0% of girl school leavers went to colleges of education. Male students at the Universities outnumbered female students by a ratio of over two to one.
>
> These figures illustrate the extent to which women receive less

education than men during and after school. The gap between the
sexes has tended to narrow and the situation is improving for those
who are now at school or in higher education. However, in the 25–34
age group, some of whom towards the end of the century will be
assuming many of the most responsible positions in our society, only
2.5% of women against 7.5% of men have university degrees or
equivalent qualifications and 59% of women as compared with 48%
of men have no formal qualifications of any kind. And while many
more women are now qualified at some level, there has been little
tendency for them to diversify. In 1971 three quarters of all women
with qualifications at A-level and above were in the health and
education fields while similarly qualified men were in a much wider
range of occupations. About the same number of men and women
were qualified in languages and arts subjects, but in science and
social science men out numbered women by about five to one. These
differences help to explain why, for example, the proportion of
women who are engineers is tiny, by comparison with other
advanced industrial societies.[2]

By 1985, at which time girls represented 49 per cent of the 18-year-
old population, the Equal Opportunities Commission[3] was able to
report:

In 1984 girls gained 53.6% of all CSE Grade I passes, 51.2% of GCE
O-level passes and 47% of GCE A-level passes. In broad terms girls
are disproportionately represented in arts and languages, and boys
in science, technical drawing and computer studies. Nonetheless
girls have been gradually improving their share of passes in most
technical and scientific subjects, the main exception to this trend
being computer studies.[4]

The proportion of female university undergraduates had risen to
41.5 per cent by 1985. Even so, women were, and still are, found
to be heavily concentrated in relatively few occupations, frequently
those with a large demand for part-time labour. They are still
earning only three-quarters of the wages of their adult full-time
male colleagues. They are seriously under-represented in public
life, both in elected office and among public appointments; only 41
women were elected to the House of Commons in the 1987 general
election. And although the number of women studying for the
professions is increasing, women still make up less than half of the
annual new entrants to the professions of medicine, accountancy,
banking and the law.[5]

## THE DIFFERENTIAL LEGAL RIGHTS OF MEN AND WOMEN

Our legal system has, in the main, always reflected through the conferring of differential rights some degree of division of roles between the sexes. In the eighteenth century, Blackstone wrote:

> By marriage, the husband and wife are one person in law: that is, the very being or legal existence of the woman is suspended during the marriage, or at least is incorporated and consolidated into that of the husband.[6]

As a consequence, at common law, most of a wife's property, even her earned income, became vested in her husband. A married woman therefore could not enter into a legally binding contract and her power to leave property by will was extremely limited. Such rules became mitigated for the rich by equity, but the very fact of providing relief in these cases only in effect reinforced the common law for the rest of the population and helped to perpetuate the inequalities inherent in it. Later, statutory reforms, in particular the Married Women's Property Act of 1882, brought separation of the property of spouses, though even this turned out to be very far from the same thing in practice as equality.[7] By 1926, the old common law rules were regarded by some commentators at least as quite out of keeping with then-contemporary social mores, as Professor A. V. Dicey made clear:

> The way in which the rules of the common law might, occasionally at any rate, deprive a rich woman of the whole of her wealth may be seen by the following illustration. A lady is possessed of a large fortune; it consists of household furniture, pictures, a large sum in money and bank notes, as well as £10,000 deposited at her bankers, of leasehold estates in London, and of freehold estates in the country. She is induced, in 1850, to marry, without having made any settlement whatever, an adventurer, such as the Barry Lyndon of fiction, or the Mr Bowes of historical reality, who supplied, it is said, the original for Thackeray's picture of Barry Lyndon's married life. He at once becomes the actual owner of all the goods and money in the possession of his wife. He can, by taking the proper steps, with or without her consent, obtain possession for his own use of the money at her bankers, and exact payment to himself of every debt due to her. He can sell her leaseholds and put the proceeds in his own pocket. Her freehold estate, indeed, he cannot sell out and out, but he can charge it to the extent of his own interest therein at any rate during coverture, and if under the curtesy of England he acquires a life interest in the freehold estate after the death of his wife, he can charge the estate for the term of his natural life. In any case he can spend as he pleases the whole of his wife's income. He turns out a

confirmed gambler. In the course of a few years he has got rid of the whole of his wife's property, except the freehold estate, but though it has not been sold, he has charged it with the payment of all his debts up to the very utmost of his power. If he outlives his wife she will never receive a penny of rent from the estate. He and his wife are in truth penniless; she earns, however, £1,000 a year as a musician or an actress. This is a piece of rare good luck – for her husband. He is master of the money she earns. Let him allow her enough, say £200 a year, to induce her to exert her talents, and he may live in idleness and modest comfort on the remaining £800. Under this state of things, which up to 1870 was possible, though, of course, not common, it is surely substantially true to say that marriage transferred the property of a wife to her husband. Blackstone, indeed, though he knew the common law well enough, tells us that, 'even the disabilities which the wife lies under, are for the most part intended for her protection and benefit. So great a favourite is the female sex of the laws of England.'[8] But this splendid optimism of 1765 is too much for even the complacent toryism of 1809, and at that date, Christian, an editor of Blackstone's Commentaries, feels bound to deny that the law of England has shown any special partiality to women, and protests that he is not so much in love with his subject 'as to be inclined to leave in it possession of a glory which it may not justly deserve.'[9]

Nevertheless, it was not until the mid-1970s that a woman was granted any legal right to demand equal pay with a male colleague, or to complain legally if she was treated less favourably than a male would be by her employer or by an educational institution or by her bank. Even today, our law permits the exploitation of female labour in the many situations which fall outside the confines of the legislative scheme. Women may also still quite lawfully be treated differently from men, for example, in the provision of insurance facilities, in relation to sport, by the taxation system or by a charitable trust, in relation to immigration into this country, and where the security of the state is involved. In short, although our law has moved far from the eighteenth- and nineteenth-century position so graphically described in Dicey, it still discriminates against women. One question that it becomes vital to ask, therefore, is whether any sort of justification can be found to rationalise a continuing legal differential.

## THE JUSTIFICATIONS ADVANCED FOR LEGAL INEQUALITY OF OPPORTUNITY

An almost infinite number of justifications for inequality of opportunity as between the sexes has been advanced over the years and all that can be achieved within the space of a few pages is to draw attention to the most notable. All, it will be seen, are open to grave suspicion and none come anywhere near to providing a rational or fair basis for a system of legal rights and duties. However, even though some of the traditional reasoning sounds unconvincing, even bizarre, to modern ears, it bears repetition in order to put us on our guard when more contemporary but equally noxious arguments are voiced today. The justifications for denying women equal rights with men in the latter part of the twentieth century will sound as hypocritical in a hundred years' time as the words of the nineteenth-century judges on such matters do today.

An early justification which appears to have influenced at least Western thinking is that grounded in the Old Testament. According to the Book of Genesis, God made man first and then later, and in order to provide him with a partner, created woman from one of his ribs. This has sometimes been taken to imply that God intended the male to be the superior sex and the female to be merely his adjunct. If such a premiss were accepted, then it would seem logical for the law to reflect the sex difference. Furthermore, such a philosophy can quickly be seen to generate its own empirical supporting evidence: if women are considered inferior, less effort is expended on educating them and their opportunities for expression and achievement are correspondingly limited. If they are then found to have achieved less than men in tangible terms, measured by their output of, for example, scientific inventions and works of art, literature or music, then some people at least will conclude that this is proof of their inferiority. In the words of Eisenstein:

> Their traditional role prescribed a character structure and a set of values for women that evoked contempt from men towards women, and from women towards themselves. The condition of being subordinated by and to men had turned women into an inferior species. Women had fulfilled their role expectations all too successfully. As a result, they were genuinely ill-fitted for equality with men. By a kind of self-fulfilling prophesy, women had become the poor creatures that men thought they were.[10]

Nevertheless, despite the historically important part that this reasoning has played in the definition of gender-roles and legal rights, it gets nowhere near to providing a justification for unequal rights today. Few people nowadays would accept such a literal interpretation of the Bible and many would deny that its contents ought in any way to influence the design of the law.

Perhaps slightly more convincing than the literal-Biblical explanation for differential legal expectations as between the sexes is the anthropological or cultural explanation, namely, the argument that the human race in practice so organises itself as to allot different roles and functions to the two sexes and this difference needs to be reflected in law. Such a theory easily extends itself to postulating that women are dependent on, and indeed subordinated to, men. Anthropologists have devoted considerable efforts to projecting the image of 'man the hunter' and to establishing that the modern human race owes it existence to him. Others, however, regard this as a gross over-simplification and argue that the survival of the human race depended at least as much on 'woman the horticul-turalist' growing vegetables as on 'man the hunter's' occasional successful efforts at bringing home an animal carcass on which to feed his family.[11] Similarly, Elaine Morgan argues:

> I believe the deeply rooted semantic confusion between 'man' as a male and 'man' as a species has been fed back into and vitiated a great deal of the speculation that goes on about the origins, develop-ment and nature of the human race. A very high proportion of the thinking on these topics is androcentric (male-centred) in the same way as pre-Copernican thinking was geocentric. It's just as hard for man to break the habit of thinking of himself as central to the species as it was to break the habit of thinking of himself as central to the universe. He sees himself quite unconsciously as the main line of evolution, with a female satellite revolving around him as the moon revolves around the earth. This not only causes him to overlook valuable clues to our ancestry, but sometimes leads him into making statements that are arrant and demonstrable nonsense.
>
> The longer I went on reading his own books about himself, the more I longed to find a volume that would begin: 'When the first ancestor of the human race descended from the trees, she had not yet developed the mighty brain that was to distinguish her so sharply from all other species . . .'.
>
> Of course, she was no more the first ancestor than he was – but she was no *less* the first ancestor, either. She was there all along, contributing half the genes to each succeeding generation.[12]

Morgan goes on to explain a number of female biological character-istics as a response to the ecological demands made on early women, rather than as existing in order to gratify the male of the species.[13]

In any event, irrespective of conflicting theories about primitive human beings, it can scarcely be argued that today's society relegates women exclusively to the position of dependency on the male. Nor can it be said any longer that our cultural norm consists of home-making, child-rearing females, provided for throughout their lives in economic terms by wage-earning males. In 1985, women constituted 41.7 per cent of the labour force of this country and in 52 per cent of all married couples both the spouses were in employment. The EOC found around this time that:

> Among young couples without children, the typical pattern was for both partners to work full-time. However, the picture was very different among those with small children; only 25% of mothers with children aged 0–4 were in employment, three quarters of them part-time. And in only 5% of families with children aged 0–4 were both parents working full-time. In families where the youngest child was aged 5–9, more than 50% of wives were back in employment, again three quarters of them part-time. By the time the youngest child was aged 10 or over, two thirds of women were back at work, two thirds of them part-time. Among older married women with no dependent children, full-time working was more common; in fact they divided fairly evenly between full-time work, part-time work and economic inactivity.
>
> The more children there were in a family, the less likely it was that the mother would be in employment, either full-time or part-time. Much the same applied to men; 8% of men with one child were unemployed, 8% of men with two children, 13% of men with three children and 24% of men with four or more children.[14]

The picture which emerges today therefore is of considerable variety in the lifestyles and working habits of women, both at different ages and across the social spectrum. Many women now are clearly playing a very important part in the economic activity of the country and, without their efforts, the income of many families would be insufficient for subsistence. It can no longer be argued, therefore – even if it ever could – that women, since they will not be called upon to earn their living or support their families, do not require rights in the fields of education and employment. Such a justification for differential legal rights can therefore carry no weight; nevertheless, it is most important that the variety of roles in which our society now casts women is taken into consideration by our lawmakers, a matter to which we shall return.

Another explanation which has sometimes been advanced for inequality of legal opportunity as between the sexes is that men derive specific material advantages from limiting the legal rights of their female counterparts. For example, Professor Kahn-Freund suggested that matrimonial community of property régimes developed in order to finance male commercial enterprise, in the days before corporations:

> Since the later Middle Ages the need for providing commerical enterprise with capital resources worked strongly in favour of a community system. Early capitalist enterprise was, of course, much in need of accumulating capital and accumulating income, – and the

matrimonial community system was available as an adequate and probably very necessary instrument for the capitalisation of commercial and later of industrial firms, in a society which knew little of modern forms of corporate enterprise. All the community systems developed in Western Europe serve this purpose of letting the wife's dowry and her inherited wealth work in the husband's business, or at least of making the revenue derived from such wealth available for its growth.[15]

In similar vein is Albie Sachs' and Joan Hoff Wilson's analysis of the attitude of the judiciary to the nineteenth-century 'Persons Cases'. In this series of cases, the judges held that women were not 'persons' for the purpose of the legislation governing enfranchisement. Sachs and Wilson comment:

Women were variously described as refined, delicate and pure, quite as worthy and noble as men, but different. One judge said he shared the widely held view that women were intellectually inferior to men, and in particular were incapable of severe and incessant work, while another judge expressly left open the question of whether women were fickle in judgment and liable to influence. But the general view of those who spoke of the unfitness of women for public life was that their incapacity should be seen as an exemption flowing from respect rather than a disability based on inferiority. Men and women were different but complementary, rather than separate but equal. . . . The vaunted complementarity of the sexes, invariably expressed in semi-mystical terms, had practical roots in a division of labour in respect of which the husband supervised minions at work and the wife supervised minions at home. Different attributes were required for the performance of their respective tasks, and these attributes were given exaggerated reflection in the culture of the times. It is suggested, then, that the main reason why Victorian men resisted the entry of middle-class women into public life and their professions was their interest in ensuring that their wives remained housekeepers. Mill certainly hinted as much, adding that it was a reason that men were ashamed to advance because of its manifest injustice. . . . Whether in the Church, Parliament or the law, then, male protectiveness as proclaimed by the judges was mythical rather than real – what was in truth being protected was the right of upper-middle-class men to have their wives working for them and for them alone.[16]

The same argument is sometimes heard today: in times of high unemployment, men have a material interest in keeping women out of scarce jobs and therefore in limiting their legal rights in relation to employment. Furthermore, some husbands undoubtedly believe that, if their wives went out to work or played a major part in public life, this would be to the husband's disadvantage, since it would place greater demands on him in terms of child-care and domestic responsibility. It seems likely that such material concerns have in the past influenced male attitudes towards sex equality and continue to do so today. However, it must be remembered that we are concerned to discover a justification for differential legal rights as between the sexes. The material advantage of the male sex can never, as Sachs and Wilson point out, provide a justification, since it is patently one-sided and grounded on what have been seen to be the unsupportable assumptions of male superiority and the overwhelming importance of men in economic terms.

Social policy is also sometimes suggested as a justification. For example, it is argued on occasion that mothers should be positively discouraged from going to work outside the home since the physical and psychological well-being of children depends on their mothers' continuous presence in the home. Such discouragement can therefore permissibly take the form of repressive legal rules relating to the employment of mothers. This argument is suspect on a number of grounds. First of all, there is no proof that the psychological well-being of children is related to the continuous presence of the mother in the home. On the contrary, it seems sensible to suppose that such well-being develops from domestic stability, and that this may be wholly unrelated to where the mother spends her time. Secondly, as pointed out already, the economic prosperity of many families in this country today is dependent on the mother's wages; to undermine the earning capability of women by legal device would destabilise such families and itself result in physical and even psychological damage to the children. This argument cannot in any event justify discrimination against women who are not mothers or whose children are grown up. Even if a social policy could be formulated whose effect was beneficial to society in general but discriminatory in relation to one sex, it would require to be articulated, debated and finally accepted in a truly non-discriminatory legislature, and this of course is one of the very things which the existing arrangements and practices make unattainable.

Probably the only sound justification for the law to recognise any differences at all between male and female rights is the biological difference between the two sexes. The problem in this context is how far the argument really goes.[17] Clearly it covers differences in the reproductive roles of the two sexes: only females can become pregnant and bear children, and this fact together with its attendant physical implications must be recognised in law. If our offspring are to thrive and be healthy, the law must, for example, grant pregnant women maternity leave from employment under proper conditions which render it a viable option. But the role of child-bearing must not be confused with that of child-rearing. We must be careful not to over-extend the biological argument; in the words of Barrett,

> Racists who attempt to provide 'scientific' apologias for the oppression of blacks are treated with the contempt they deserve and we should be equally wary of apologias for gender division.[18]

Biology demands that women bear children, but not that they play an exclusive role in rearing them. Any law creating positive rights with respect to child-rearing, such as a right to leave from work or to the custody of the child's person, ought, therefore, to be expressed in a gender-neutral fashion and be equally available to both sexes. But does the biological argument extend at all beyond child-bearing? Are there any other biological differences between the sexes which the law ought to reflect, for instance differential longevity? Women have, of course, traditionally been regarded as the 'weaker' sex (although this expression has been variously applied to different types of supposed weakness, from physical to intellectual). This weakness has been reflected by the law over the years in numerous ways, such as in the rights given in the past to husbands with respect to their wives' property, and in the 'protective' legislation outlawing certain types of employment for women. The approach adopted by the present sex discrimination legislation appears the most rational in this context. There is no scientific or other evidence of women's weaker intellect. As far as physical abilities and characteristics are concerned, it is known that on average women possess less strength in certain physical tests, such as lifting weights, and moreover that women on average are smaller than men. However, these statements ignore individual characteristics: an individual woman may be very much larger and stronger than the average man. Individual ability is therefore what should be examined and the law should not base itself on generalisations which may frequently turn out to be untrue in individual cases.

A more difficult question in this area is whether, because of their different biological make-up, the two sexes are behaviourally different in a way that the law ought to recognise. Ruth Bleier describes the science of sociobiology as follows:

> Sociobiology considers all human behaviours, characteristics, social relationships and forms of social organisation to be biologically, genetically and evolutionarily determined. Human characteristics and relationships are explicitly programmed in our genes, having evolved over millions of years because they were adaptive for survival. The very fact of their existence proves they have to exist, otherwise they would not have evolved. Not only do sociobiologists claim to establish the innateness of racism and wars, but also sex differences in

social roles and position. . . . Sociobiology announces certain characteristics of the female and male 'nature' to be universal and then
explains why they are universal: why women are genetically predis-
posed to be 'attached' to home and nursery and men to business
and professions; why men are hasty, fickle, and promiscuous and
women are faithful and selective; why men are aggressive and dominant and women nurturant and coy.[19]

Bleier goes on to criticise the methodology of sociobiology and thus
to challenge its conclusions:

The universal behaviours, characteristics, and sex differences of
humans that they presume to explain as biological and innate are *not*
universal either within or between cultures; the behaviours of
animals *cannot* be taken to indicate innate behaviours of humans,
'uncontaminated' by culture, since animals learn and have cultures;
nor are the animal behaviours they describe universal. But, most
importantly, it is *not* possible to tease apart genetic and other
biological factors from environmental and learning factors in human
development. This is, in fact, a meaningless way to view the problem,
since, from conception the relationships between the actions of genes
and the environment of fetus are inextricable. The very structure and
functioning of the brain, the organ of mind and mediator of behaviour, are influenced by environmental input both before and after
birth. Thus, whatever the genetic and hormonal influences are on
the development of our fetal and newborn brains, they are inextricable from the influences of the environmental milieu, from sensory
input and learning. . . . No science or discipline can peel off layers
of culture and learning and find an untouched core of biological
*nature*. Rather than biology acting to constrain and limit our potentialities, it is, in fact, the supreme irony that our magnificent brains,
with their nearly limitless structural and functional potentiality for
learning, flexibility, and choice-making, have produced *cultures* that
constrain and limit those potentialities.

Distinctions of human characteristics and temperaments into *innate*
male and female natures have been social, *cultural* constructs and are
not *natural*.[20]

The question of whether there are biological behaviour differences between the sexes is, therefore, highly problematic. However,
it would appear from the diversity of roles played by women both
in our culture and in others, too, that no clear pattern of behavioural
differences emerges. In consequence the matter is not one with
which the law ought to preoccupy itself in the present state of
knowledge.

The picture which emerges, therefore, is one of a plethora of
excuses put forward over the centuries for differential rights and
opportunities to be granted to the two sexes by the law. Almost all

of these excuses can be discounted as irrational, unfair and otherwise unacceptable; but two points of distinction emerge which are
vital and which must be taken into account by a just legislature.
The first is the obvious biological distinction as far as child-bearing
is concerned. The second is that culturally and psychologically we
still force a very different gender role on women from men. For
example, girls continue to be discouraged from studying science
subjects; married women frequently perform both domestic work
and work outside the home as well, and the majority of women
still leave the labour market when their children are very young.
This means that formal equality, the mere conferment of apparently
identical rights by the legal system on the two sexes, will not result
in their actually achieving equality of opportunity. Facially neutral
treatment is not enough, because women do not begin from the
same 'starting-point' as men and therefore cannot be considered to
share equal chances of success. To consider for employment both
a formally well-educated and psychologically career-minded man
and a less educated and less career-minded woman is not, in reality,
to offer them equality of opportunity. The law thus has a difficult
but vital role to play. Above all, its aim must be to provide not
merely equal but the *same* opportunities to both sexes.

To achieve this result the legal system has to perform a balancing
act. It must certainly guarantee identical treatment where there are
genuinely no differences between the sexes as regards the way the
law affects them; but it must also be sensitive to all including the
hidden obstacles and, in particular, contain in-built compensatory
devices to cater for the situations where, for biological, cultural or
other reasons the two sexes are unable to take equal advantage of
theoretically equal chances. And it must achieve this result without
expressly or impliedly reinforcing gender-stereotyping, a particularly difficult task since, in recognising gender divisions at all, it
may appear to give its blessing to them. How successfully or otherwise our existing anti-discrimination laws perform this balancing
act is one question which this book will seek to answer and it will
provide a recurring theme for later chapters.

## EQUALITY OF OPPORTUNITY

The legal system also has another vital decision to make in this
area. It has to decide what it means by 'equality of opportunity'.
How should it go about achieving a 'sameness' of opportunities?
Should it seek to open up to women all the opportunities that
men have traditionally been offered? Should it offer to men those
opportunities which have hitherto been the preserve of women?

Or should it seek some third ideal and, if so, what? This is a matter which our legislators have never directly confronted. Feminist perspectives of the law are of course many and varied.[21] They range from those early feminists who argued for women to be given strictly the same rights as men – thereby pressurising women to operate within the constraints of a male-constructed society – to those 'gynocentrists' whose aim is essentially to replace men by women as the pivot for our social organisation. To adopt the original feminist standpoint and simply to grant women the same rights that men have enjoyed in the past is not the same thing as achieving equality, since men have been dominant in the construction of the existing social fabric; women would thus be being admitted into a milieu in the design of which they had had little or no say. On the other hand, the gynocentrist view is also open to serious doubts and criticisms; it assumes a generalised approach, signifying common needs, demands and desires, for female and male respectively and, most objectionably, it treats one sex as entitled to a sort of supremacy over the other. The perspective of the present writer is therefore midway between the two extremes.

Men and women are both essential to the continuation of human life and society, and both must therefore be equally able to influence and determine the rules upon which that society operates. Instead of rigidly forcing gender roles on people irrespective of their desires, we must aim for a freer environment in which either sex can be expected to play a part in child-rearing, family nurture and outside employment. The law, a potent instrument for social change, plays an important part in achieving this dynamism. It must be constructed so as to achieve this end and the extent to which it satisfies this demand provides a second underlying theme for later chapters.

The present work deals exclusively with the anti-discrimination laws of this country and the European Economic Community (EEC). This topic is selected unashamedly, not because of any naïve supposition that it can provide the whole antidote to our heritage of androcentricity,[22] but because it focuses on the key areas in which law can produce meaningful and practical changes. In particular, the fields of education and employment are critical to the attainment of economic and political power and influence in the present world. Open them up in real terms to women as well as men and the chance of redistributing power more equitably between the two sexes becomes a live possibility. It must be admitted at this point that there are many who would disagree with this as a strategy for social change and who would argue that such an approach not only predicates assumption of the existing political and social structures of this country but also requires women to conform to male values and requirements to sustain the existing patriarchy. However, this is where the design of the legislation has such a significant part to play. If it simply provides for the equal treatment of the sexes, then there is little doubt of the accuracy of this criticism. If, however, it is designed more perceptively and in such a way as to offer real opportunities irrespective of gender stereotypes, then the force of the criticism ebbs away. To give a practical illustration, a law which merely offers women the opportunity of part-time working reinforces existing gender roles and does little to further equality of opportunity. Not so a law which forces employers to look for employees amongst an under-represented section of the population and consequently to question traditional and long-held assumptions, such as that the best workers are those who stay at work for 14 hours a day. This second route is the one which the legislation should pursue and, bearing this in mind, the existing anti-discrimination laws must be analysed, understood, criticised and reformed. Moreover, this approach has a secondary importance too. The exemplary value of this legislation can never be scientifically assessed or demonstrated, but it is undoubtedly there. The express recognition on the statute book of the principle of equality of the sexes raises it above a matter of individual conscience and into a norm on which our social values are founded. The subject matter of the legislation may remain for a few a matter of clandestine mockery, but deliberate disobedience of it carries the risk of legal sanctions and the stigma of being branded a law-breaker.

The anti-discrimination laws of this country in the field of sex are still relatively new. The Equal Pay Act 1970, discussed in Chapter 2, and the Sex Discrimination Act 1975, which provides the subject matter of Chapter 3, contain the essential rules by which equality of opportunity is sought to be achieved. Although some amendments have been made to these statutes, their basic structure and scheme remain unaltered and they therefore represent the legislature's first attempt to regulate this complex area. They are supplemented by the EEC's growing body of rules on the subject, which are legally binding in this country and are discussed in Chapter 4, and by the provisions of, in particular, the Employment Protection (Consolidation) Act 1978 in the field of maternity rights, which is dealt with in Chapter 6. The domestic legislation created the EOC, intended to play an important strategic role with respect to the enforcement and effectiveness of the law, and this is discussed in Chapter 5.

As a first attempt at legislation, it is hardly to be wondered at if these provisions do not wholly achieve the objectives discussed above. It will become apparent from succeeding chapters that there are really four major defects in the present scheme, which require to be remedied as soon as possible. First, the law as presently framed is insensitive in its scrutiny and treatment of the obstacles, both apparent and disguised, which are placed in women's paths. The main vehicles used by the legislation in this area are the concept of indirect discrimination and the rules relating to maternity rights. Both, it will be suggested, are far too narrowly constructed at present.

Secondly, the legislation fails to pay sufficient regard to the need to break down gender stereotyping. In order to achieve this, some form of leverage undoubtedly has to be applied; neither male nor female will normally be brave enough to depart from the usual social expectations and constructs unless some form of inducement is offered to do so. In legal terms, this translates into schemes of 'positive action' by which members of one sex are encouraged to take part in activities traditionally the preserve of the other sex, with a consequent restructuring of the ways in which those activities are performed and the demands which they impose. As will be seen, the legislation is at present very weak in this area and requires considerable bolstering if real equality of opportunity is to be achieved.[23]

Thirdly, the legislation is drafted with extreme narrowness and niggardly technicality. It is riddled with detailed exceptions and the whole corpus of rules is administered, with plenty of scope for the exercise of discretion, by male-dominated tribunals who are unlikely and ill-equipped to abandon legal traditions and sacrifice literal interpretation to the spirit underlying the legislation. Numerous detailed amendments and additions require to be made to the statutes to create meaningful and enforceable legal rights.

A fourth problem which is evident at the moment is that the law governing sex discrimination is too fragmented and distributed amongst too many domestic and EEC instruments. The array of legal provisions is confusing to litigants and to tribunals and, although some measure of congruence is at last beginning to emerge as between UK law and that of the EEC, this development is taking place at the expense of individual complainants. A recasting of the legislation is therefore urgently called for so as to produce a single and unified code of rules for the area.

The aim of the following chapters is thus to provide analysis and constructive criticism of the sex discrimination laws applicable to this country, and to suggest appropriate amendments to them. The present legislative scheme must be sustained, strengthened and then utilised, because in the long run it provides a vital part of the answer to the social inequality which continues to exist today between the sexes.

## NOTES

1. For discussion of the design and effects of the law in particular fields in relation to women, see O'Donovan, *Sexual Divisions in Law* (1985, Weidenfeld and Nicolson) Brophy and Smart, *Women in Law* (1985, RKP) and Smart, *The Ties that Bind* (1984, RKP).
2. 'Equality for Women', Cmnd. 5724 (1974) paras 12–15.
3. Hereafter referred to as the EOC.
4. EOC, *Women and Men in Britain: a Statistical Profile* (1985).
5. Information from EOC, *Women and Men in Britain: a Statistical Profile* (1985 and 1986). See also the Law Society's *Annual Statistical Report 1987*, which shows that 44 per cent of those qualifying as solicitors in 1986–7 were women; nevertheless, women still only constituted one-fifth of the total number of practising solicitors and were only achieving partnership level at half the rate of men.
6. Blackstone, *Commentaries* i, p. 441.
7. See Cretney, *Elements of Family Law* (1987 Sweet and Maxwell) especially Chapter 8, and also the discussion by Lord Denning MR of the history of family property rights in *Williams Glyn's Bank* v. *Boland* [1979] 1 Ch. 312.
8. Blackstone, *Commentaries*, i, p. 445.
9. Dicey, *Law and Public Opinion in England during the Nineteenth Century* (1926, Macmillan).
10. Eisenstein, *Contemporary Feminist Thought* (1984, Unwin).
11. See Lewenhak, *Women and Work* (1980, Fontana).
12. Morgan, *The Descent of Woman* (1973, Corgi).
13. Ibid.
14. EOC, *Women and Men in Britain: a Statistical Profile* (1985).
15. Kahn-Freund, Josef Unger Memorial Lecture: 'Matrimonial Property: Where Do We Go From Here?', delivered at the University of Birmingham in 1971.
16. Sachs and Wilson, *Sexism and the Law* (1978, Martin Robertson).
17. See also Edwards, *Gender, Sex and the Law* (1985, Croom Helm).
18. Barrett, *Women's Oppression Today* (1980, NLB).
19. Bleier, *Science and Gender* (1984, Pergamon).
20. Ibid.
21. See in particular Eisenstein, *Contemporary Feminist Thought* (1984, Unwin); Lacey, 'Legislation Against Sex Discrimination: Questions from a Feminist Perspective', *Journal of Law and Society*, vol. 14, no. 4 (Winter 1987) p. 411; and Rubenstein, *Protecting Whites, Men and Protestants* (1987) 15 EOR 44. In the last two mentioned, the authors argue that the fundamental objective of the anti-discrimination laws is being frustrated by their 'symmetrical' protection of both the oppressed and the privileged. Such a view, although dynamic and realistic, is at odds with the present author's contention that equality of opportunity must be extended to *all*. Any other view is not only morally questionable but fails to get to the heart of the problem. It is not enough for the law to take account of the disadvantages which women experience; it must also take an active part in the *dismantling* of those disadvantages and this necessitates a positive attack on gender stereotyping.
22. Although the changes it can produce may be greater than commonly appreciated; Zabalza and Tzannotos in *Women and Equal Pay* (1985, Cambridge University Press) estimate that the lion's share in the improvement of women's wages after the Equal Pay Act 1970 came into force as the direct result of that Act.
23. See also Gregory, *Sex, Race and the Law* (1987, Sage).

# 2 The Equal Pay Act 1970

## SCOPE OF THE ACT

Until its amendment by the Sex Discrimination Act 1986, the Equal Pay Act[1] attempted to combat sex discrimination on two separate but complementary levels. On the one hand, it contained, and still contains, provisions which confer rights of action on individuals and enable them to obtain legal remedies in respect of their own circumstances.[2] As will be seen, although recently amended, in many respects these provisions fall short of adequate protection for the employee. On the other hand, the Act used also to attempt to provide redress for more widescale discrimination contained in collective agreements, pay structures and wage regulation orders.[3] This two-pronged approach would seem essential; the individual wronged certainly requires her remedy from the point of view of the protection of her essential rights. However, contractual terms are frequently the subject matter of group negotiation so that the provisions of, say, a collective agreement may well prove in reality to be the actual bone of contention. Furthermore, there are bound sometimes to be situations in which discrimination over contractual terms is occurring against a number of workers, yet no one individual is prepared or able to be responsible for an action in respect of it.

Unfortunately, the provisions in the Equal Pay Act governing widescale discrimination, although interpreted liberally by the Central Arbitration Committee, to which they gave the jurisdiction, were eventually construed so restrictively by the Divisional Court as to render them of no practical use.[4] The legislation now provides[5] for the automatic nullity of sexually discriminatory provisions of collective agreements, employers' rules and the rules of trade unions', employers' associations, professional organisations and qualifying bodies. However, no statutory collective remedy is provided for ascertaining the nullity of such a provision or for altering it. The Central Arbitration Committee's power to revise such terms has been removed[6] and not replaced.[7] The lack of a collective remedy amounts to a serious gap in the legislative framework in relation to this far-reaching form of discrimination and it is one, moreover, which is unlikely to be remedied by the EOC's power to launch formal investigations; as will be seen in Chapter 5, this power is hedged about with procedural limitations and has in practice been little utilised, particularly in this field.

The Act's Short Title is misleading, since the statute is actually concerned with all the terms of a contract of employment[8] and is not restricted simply to those terms relating to pay.[9] The Long Title in fact describes the Act as intended 'to prevent discrimination, as regards terms and conditions of employment between men and women'. Even this, however, is not really accurate. The Act is designed to achieve parity in contractual terms between comparable male and female employees, but this is not the same thing as outlawing all contractual discrimination against females since the Act has no effect in the situation where male and female jobs are not comparable. One instance is where the man is accorded disproportionately favourable treatment, for example, where he is paid twice as much as the woman for work which is in reality only slightly more arduous than hers.[10] Neither does the legislation help the female employee who is treated identically with a male colleague even though her work is actually worthy of more reward than his. In *Pointon* v. *University of Sussex*[11] a woman lecturer was placed at the same point on the salary scale as a less qualified male colleague, but failed to establish a ground of complaint under the Act because she was being paid marginally more than him, so that, in the words of Lord Denning MR, 'the terms of her contract were equally favourable to the terms of his'.[12]

The Act is drafted in terms of women and their treatment relative to men, but it applies identically *mutatis mutandis*.[13]


## THE EQUALITY CLAUSE

The device adopted by the Act for safeguarding the individual's position is to imply an 'equality clause' into the terms of every contract under which a woman is employed at an establishment in Great Britain.[14] The equality clause has two effects. First, it ensures that if a term of the woman's contract is or becomes less favourable to the woman than a term of a similar kind contained in the contract of employment of a male colleague with whom she can under the legislation be compared, then that term of the woman's contract is treated as so modified as not to be less favourable.[15] Secondly, if the woman's contract does not include a term corresponding to a term benefiting the male colleague included in the contract under which he is employed, the woman's contract is treated as including such a term.[16]

In order to claim the benefit of an equality clause, the claimant has to be 'employed'.[17] This is defined[18] as meaning 'employed under a contract of service or of apprenticeship or a contract personally to execute any work of labour'. This definition received a wide construction from the Employment Appeal Tribunal in *Quinnen* v. *Hovells*[19] and was held to extend to a self-employed machine operator hired for a limited period and paid on a commission basis. The Tribunal ruled that the statutory definition was intended to enlarge on the ordinary connotation of 'employment' so as to include persons outside the master-servant relationship; the concept of a contract for the engagement of personal work or labour lying outside the scope of a master-servant relationship is a wide and flexible one, said Waite J, and intended by Parliament to be interpreted as such; 'those who engage even cursorily the talents, skill or labour of the self-employed are wise to ensure that the terms are equal between men and women'.[20] However, the Court of Appeal in *Mirror Group Newspapers Ltd* v. *Gunning*[21] ruled that the dominant purpose behind the contract must be personal performance by the claimant of the work or labour in question. The word 'any' in the statutory definition refers to work or labour of any kind rather than to any extent. The Court would not, however, go so far as to accept that the sole purpose of the contract must be the personal performance of the work; otherwise, said Balcombe LJ, 'this would exclude from the definition a contract with a sculptor, where it was contemplated that some of the menial work might be carried out by persons other than the contracting party, a contract with a one man builder, who might be expected to subcontract some of the specialist work, or even a contract with a plumber, who might be expected to have his mate with him on all occasions'.[22] On the facts, the Court held that a contract granting an area distributorship of two Sunday newspapers did not fall within the extended statutory definition of 'employment', since its dominant purpose was not the personal execution of work or labour but rather the efficient distribution of the newspapers in the area in question. This narrowing of the statutory formula is regrettable; discrimination may occur whenever any element of personal execution is involved and the objective behind the legislation ought to be to forbid such discrimination, even where it relates only to a part of the contractual obligation.

A claim under the Act becomes time-barred six months after the employee has left the relevant employment.[23] In practice, this is an extremely short period in which to obtain all the complicated information necessary in order to decide whether to begin legal proceedings.

The equality clause is implied into any contract under which a woman is employed at an establishment in Great Britain,[24] but not to the contract of any woman employed outside Great Britain even if her employer is present or registered here. Employment is to be regarded as being at an establishment in Great Britain unless the employee does her work wholly or mainly outside Great Britain.[25] A slightly different rule applies to employment on board a ship registered in Great Britain, or on board an aircraft or hovercraft registered in the UK and operated by a person who has his principal place of business, or is ordinarily resident, in Great Britain; in such a case, such employment is to be regarded as being at an establishment in Great Britain unless the employee does her work wholly outside Great Britain.[26] It is immaterial whether the proper law of the contract is the law of any part of the UK or not.[27] These rules exclude from the protection of the Equal Pay Act[28] many persons working abroad, and especially those working on board foreign-registered vessels, even where the vessels are owned by UK companies. This position is quite unsatisfactory and requires amendment. There is no logical reason why the legislation should not apply to all contracts made with an employer who, being a person, is ordinarily resident in this country or, being a company or partnership, is either resident here or has a place of business in this country, irrespective of where the contract is to be performed. In all these cases, the British Courts could exercise effective jurisdiction over the employer since either persons or assets will be present in the UK. It will be seen in Chapter 3 that the employer will have a defence to a claim of sex discrimination if he can show that the job in question will have to be performed in a country whose laws or customs preclude the employment of women.

The Act applies, in the main, to employees of the Crown but not to service in the naval, military or air forces of the Crown;[29] however, as regards the armed forces, the Secretary of State or Defence Council may not make any instrument relating to the terms and conditions of service if the instrument has the effect of making a distinction as regards pay, allowances or leave between men and women, unless that distinction is fairly attributable to differences between the obligations undertaken by the men and those undertaken by the women.[30] These special provisions for the armed forces may well constitute a breach by the UK of its obligations under EEC law, in particular Article 3 of the Equal Pay Directive[31] which lays down that 'Member States shall abolish *all* discrimination between men and women arising from laws, regulations or administrative provisions which is contrary to the principle of equal pay',[32] and Article 5(1) of the Equal Treatment Directive[33] which stipulates that 'Application of the principle of equal treatment with regard to working conditions . . . means that men and women shall be guaranteed the same conditions without discrimination on grounds of sex'.[34]

In order to benefit from the equality clause implied into her contract of employment, the woman must be able to compare her work with that of a male colleague. The Act provides that there are three, and only three, situations in which such a comparison may be made. They are where the male and female employee are performing 'like work', where their jobs have been rated as equivalent under a job evaluation scheme and where their work is of equal value.

## Like work

A woman worker may invoke the equality clause implied into her contract of employment where she 'is employed on like work with a man in the same employment' (s.1(2)(a)). The definition of 'like work' is provided by s.1(4):

> A woman is to be regarded as employed on like work with men if, but only if, her work and theirs is of the same or a broadly similar nature, and the difference (if any) between the things she does and the things they do are not of practical importance in relation to terms and conditions of employment; and accordingly in comparing her work with theirs regard shall be had to the frequency or otherwise with which any such differences occur in practice as well as to the nature and extent of the differences.

The legal burden of proving like work is on the applicant but, if she shows that her work is of a broadly similar nature to that of her male comparator, the evidential burden of proving that there are differences of practical importance rests on the employer.[35]

The aim of s.1(4) is clearly to capture the most straightforward of the situations of comparability, namely where the male and female employee perform the same job. However, were the statutory provision drafted in such language, the way would have been open for the unscrupulous employer, eager to save himself the cost of equal contractual terms for male and female, to introduce small differences into the work of his male and female employees. The legislation therefore extends to comparisons between work of a 'broadly similar nature'. This leaves considerable discretion in the hands of the tribunal as to what factors it will regard as creating a significant difference and how it will quantify them. The first case on the point to come before the Employment Appeal Tribunal, *Capper Pass Ltd* v. *Lawton*,[36] gave grounds for optimism that the Courts would take a broad view. Phillips J held that in cases where the work is of a broadly similar nature there will necessarily be differences between the work done by the woman and that done by the man. But

> the definition requires the industrial tribunal to bring to the solution of the question, whether work is of a broadly similar nature, a broad judgment. Because, in such cases, there will be such differences of one sort or another it would be possible in almost every case, by too pedantic an approach, to say that the work was not of a like nature despite the similarity of what was done and the similar kinds of skill and knowledge required to do it. That would be wrong. The intention, we think, is clearly that the industrial tribunal should not be required to undertake too minute an examination, or be constrained to find that work is not like work merely because of insubstantial differences'.[37]

The Employment Appeal Tribunal went on to find that a female cook in a directors' kitchen, providing lunch for 10–20 people a day, performed like work with male chefs providing 350 meals a day, breakfast, lunch and tea, in a factory canteen.[38] McCrudden has argued[39] that this comes close to an 'equal value' approach to the meaning of like work, concentrating as it does on the comparability of the factors of skill and knowledge.[40] The same attitude to the statutory definition can be seen in *Shields* v. *Coomes (Holdings) Ltd*.[41] The company operated a chain of betting shops. At most of them the counterhands were female but there were nine shops in 'trouble' areas where the company, as a matter of policy, insisted on employing a male counterhand 'not only as a possible deterrent to attack or forcible entry or other trouble but also to ensure that if trouble arises, then physical help shall be available on the spot'. The applicant was a female counterhand at a 'trouble' shop and she sought pay parity with the male counterhand who worked alongside her. The Court of Appeal held that she was so entitled since their work was like work; it was of a broadly similar nature and the man's contractual obligations were irrelevant unless they resulted in actual and not infrequent differences in practice from the woman's work, which they did not in the circumstances since the man had never had to deal with any trouble.[42] Lord Denning MR went so far as to say that s.1(4) involves comparison of the woman's and the man's work:

and making an evaluation of each job irrespective of the sex of the worker and of any special personal skill or merit that he or she may have. This evaluation should be made in terms of the 'rate of the job', usually a payment of so much per hour. The rate should represent the value of each job in terms of the demand made on a worker under such headings as effort, skill, responsibility or decision. . . . if the value of the woman's job is equal to the man's job, each should receive the same rate for the job. This principle of 'equal value' is so important that you should ignore differences between the two jobs which are 'not of practical importance'. The employer should not be able to avoid the principle by introducing comparatively small differences in 'job content' between men and women: nor by giving the work a different 'job description'.[43]

Other cases, however, have unfortunately taken a narrower view of like work and have concentrated their attention less on equal value and more on close similarity of job content. 'S.1(4) is primarily concerned with what the woman and man do', said Phillips J in *Waddington* v. *Leicester Voluntary Service*.[44] Needless to say, this more legalistic approach reduces the scope of this part of the Act quite considerably in practice.

Amongst the differences which have been held to be at least potentially of practical importance, so as to preclude a finding of like work, are being in sole charge of an industrial process,[45] having greater discretion in the carrying out of the job,[46] having greater responsibility in the sense of greater possible loss in the event of a mistake by the employee,[47] having an obligation which is actually carried out in practice to supervise or control,[48] and being under training as distinct from being expert at a job.[49] The Employment Appeal Tribunal has said[50] that a practical test is to determine whether the differences are such as to put the two jobs into different grades or categories in an evaluation study.

The time at which the job is carried out is not a difference which of itself can prevent the tribunal from finding like work. The Employment Appeal Tribunal made this clear in *Dugdale* v. *Kraft Foods Ltd*,[51] where the man but not the woman applicants had to work at nights and on some Sunday mornings. Phillips J pointed out that, were this not so, the Equal Pay Act would not have applied to many cases in which it was clearly intended to apply, namely, where men work on factory night shifts but women are or have been forbidden from so doing by the protective legislation.[52] Nevertheless, there will not be pay parity between the male and female employees in such a situation. Phillips J went on to hold that the men can properly be compensated for the extra burden of working at night or on Sundays by a shift payment or premium; all that the legislation requires is that the women employees should have equality of treatment in respect of the basic wage. Is there then a danger of the employer in fact discriminating against his female employees through the device of paying his male workers a disproportionately large premium? In *NCB* v. *Sherwin*,[53] the Employment Appeal Tribunal affirmed its decision in *Dugdale's* case and Phillips J went on to say that the man is not entitled to receive a sum which is greater than that necessary to recognise the fact that he works at an inconvenient time; if he does receive a disproportionately large sum, the woman employee can demand to have her wages increased to the extent of the excess.

Even though the time at which the job is performed is not alone directly relevant to a finding of like work, it is possible for it to be indirectly relevant. In the words of Phillips J in *NCB* v. *Sherwin*,[54] in reality the nature of a job done at night may be different. The fact of working at night may bring with it

> additional duties. Thus one can imagine the case of a teleprinter operator working at night having thrust upon her all sorts of additional duties and responsibilities, including the need to act in emergency, which would make the job different from that of a teleprinter operator working by day, and apparently doing the same work. There have been such cases, and they are a legitimate recognition of the fact that working at a different time has changed the nature of what is done. But such cases need to be considered with care.[55]

If the time at which the job is performed can be 'severed' from the other characteristics that the tribunal will examine, is it also possible to subtract other features of the man's job and say that, without them, his work is broadly similar to the woman's? The Employment Appeal Tribunal (by a majority) took a narrow view on this point in *Maidment* v. *Cooper & Co. Ltd*,[56] where Phillips J said that, 'whereas it is normally right to disregard the time at which the work is done, it is not permissible in ordinary circumstances to disregard any part of the work actually done in practice'. However, he added that there may be unusual cases in which it would be right to proceed otherwise, for instance where

> it can be seen that part of the work, although subsumed under the general description of the tasks of the employee, is in effect a separate and distinct job. For example, when comparing two cleaners, one male and one female, both of whom do identical work during the week, it might be right to ignore work of a quite different kind done by the man coming in, say on Saturdays, in order to cut the grass. Each such case must depend on precise facts.[57]

Unfortunately, this leaves room for considerable differences of opinion as to which facts are material. In the *Maidment* case itself, the majority of the Employment Appeal Tribunal considered that the fact the man's basic wage included an element attributable to working as a storeman did not mean that his activities as storeman could be disregarded. In truth, concluded the majority, 'just as Mrs Maidment might be described . . . as a packer/clerk, he could be described as a packer/storeman'.[58] On the other hand, the dissenting (woman) member of the tribunal pointed out that for 90 per cent of their time Ms Maidment and her male comparator were doing like work – packing. The storeman's element of the man's job was separate, as was shown by the fact that the employers were able to give it a separate job description and that they added on a separate increment to his wages in respect of it. The minority conclusion, therefore, was that Ms Maidment ought to be paid the same wage as the man, but less the increment for working as storeman. This more imaginative construction of the legislation would not only provide redress in a greater number of cases, but would also close a loophole by which an unscrupulous employer can evade the duty to provide equal pay.

As well as showing that she is engaged on like work with a male colleague, the woman employee must also be able to prove that she is 'in the same employment', as him.[59] S.1(6) provides that

> men shall be treated as in the same employment with a woman if they are men employed by her employer or any associated employer at the same establishment or at establishments in Great Britain which include that one and at which common terms and conditions of employment are observed either generally or for employees of the relevant classes.

The legislation does not contain a definition of 'establishment'. S.1(6)(c) states that

> two employees are to be treated as associated if one is a company of which the other (directly or indirectly) has control or if both are companies of which a third person (directly or indirectly) has control.

S.1(6) is essentially an ungenerous provision because it leaves the door open to an employer who wishes to discriminate between his male and female employees to segregate them into different establishments; provided that he ensures that common terms and conditions do not apply to both establishments no comparison between them can be made for the purpose of the Equal Pay Act. The Act would be considerably strengthened if it allowed a comparison between two workers simply on the basis that both were employed by one and the same employer or by associated employers; moreover, such a provision would accord with common sense, since this situation would correspond with what most people would probably regard as being 'in the same employment'. In practice, an industrial tribunal has held that the sort of factors which determine whether or not there are common terms and conditions as between two establishments include whether staff work different hours, whether staff in both establishments are represented by the same union, whether there is interchange between the staff in the two establishments and whether the promotion prospects are the same in both establishments.[60] In the first decision by the Employment Appeal Tribunal on the subsection, *Leverton* v. *Clwyd County Council*,[61] it was held that common terms and conditions did not exist as between two establishments of the County Council because the applicant at one worked 32½ hours per week and had 70 days' annual holiday whereas her comparators at the other worked a 37 hour week and received 20 days' holiday. The Tribunal was not persuaded by the fact that the relevant employees were all covered by the same collective agreement and that many other terms of their contracts of employment were identical. This decision proceeds from an unsound basis, because the Tribunal did not make a comparison between the terms and conditions applied at the two *establishments* concerned. Rather, it asked itself whether there were differences between the terms and conditions applied to the *applicant* and her *comparators*; clearly this test would be satisfied, because otherwise no equal pay claim could begin to be made. The question that the Tribunal ought to have asked itself was whether it would have made any difference to the terms and conditions of each employee involved if he or she had been moved to the other establishment. Since the evidence showed that the terms and conditions in all the County Council's establishments were subject to nationally negotiated terms and conditions, it would appear that the decision ought to have been that this was a case of applicant and comparator being 'in the same employment'.

## Work rated as equivalent

The second instance in which a female employee may invoke the equality clause implied into her contract of employment is 'where she is employed on work rated as equivalent with that of a man in the same employment' s.1(2)(b)). S.1(5) goes on to explain that

A woman is to be regarded as employed on work rated as equivalent with that of any man if, but only if, her job and their job have been given an equal value, in terms of demand made on a worker under various headings (for instance, effort, skill and decision), on a study undertaken with a view to evaluating in those terms the jobs to be done by all or any of the employees in an undertaking or group of undertakings, or would have been given an equal value but for the evaluation being made on a system setting different values for men and women on the same demand under any heading.

It will be observed that this provides very little guidance as to what constitutes proper job evaluation; it attempts no thorough enumeration of the factors which must be considered,[62] nor lays down any minimum procedural standards. Furthermore, it is recognising an extraordinarily difficult concept, that of the innate value of a *job*, divorced logically from the qualities, characteristics and sex of the persons performing it and divorced also from its market worth to the employer. It is, perhaps, not generally appreciated quite what a metaphysical idea this is, nor how prone it is to subjective notions of worth. The risk is thus a live one that an evaluation could itself be carried out in a way which discriminates on the ground of sex, for example, that the types of expertise required to carry out the jobs done predominantly by women in an enterprise are given an unjustifiably lower evaluation than those required for the men's jobs. The EOC reported as long ago as 1981 that it had received complaints of this nature; for instance, in a bank cash centre, heavy lifting was included as a factor whilst mental concentration was not, and complaints in the engineering industry apparently indicated a tendency for high weighting of such factors as experience and physical strength as against low weighting of mental and visual factors.[63] In an attempt to combat such practices, the EOC in 1981 produced a booklet designed to draw attention to the danger of biased schemes and to provide guidance to practitioners.[64]

The chief techniques of the job evaluation are set out, as follows, in an Appendix to the judgment of the Employment Appeal Tribunal in *Eaton Ltd* v. *Nuttall*:[65]

As not all concerned are familiar with job evaluation, we set out below a note on the principal methods (see: ACAS Guide No. 1).

**Job ranking**   This is commonly thought to be the simplest method. Each job is considered as a whole and is then given a ranking in relation to all other jobs. A ranking table is then drawn up and the ranked jobs grouped into grades. Pay levels can then be fixed for each grade.

**Paired comparisons**   This is also a simple method. Each job is compared as a whole with each other job in turn and points (0, 1 or 2) awarded according to whether its overall importance is judged to be less than, equal to or more than the other. Points awarded for each job are then totalled and a ranking order produced.

**Job classification**   This is similar to ranking except that it starts from the opposite end; the grading structure is established first and individual jobs fitted into it. A broad description of each grade is drawn up and individual jobs considered typical of each grade are selected as 'benchmarks'. The other jobs are then compared with these benchmarks and the general description and placed in their appropriate grade.

**Points assessment**   This is the most common system in use. It is an analytical method, which, instead of comparing whole jobs, breaks down each job into a number of factors – for example, skills, responsibility, physical and mental requirements and working conditions. Each of these factors may be analysed further. Points are awarded for each factor according to a predetermined scale and the total points decide a job's place in the ranking order. Usually, the factors are weighted so that, for example, more or less weight may be given to hard physical conditions or to a high degree of skill.

**Factor comparison**   This is also an analytical method, employing the same principles as points assessment but using only a limited number of factors, such as skill, responsibility and working conditions. A number of 'key' jobs are selected because their wage rates are generally agreed to be 'fair'. The proportion of the total wage attributable to each factor is then decided and a scale produced showing the rate for each factor of each key job. The other jobs are then compared with this scale, factor by factor, so that a rate is finally obtained for each factor of each job. The total pay for each job is reached by adding together the rates for its individual factors.

Given the sparseness of the legislative detail, it has been up to the courts to explain what are the necessary ingredients of a job evaluation scheme. In *Eaton Ltd* v. *Nuttall*, Phillips J held that

subsection (5) can only apply to what may be called a valid evaluation study. By that we mean a study satisfying the test of being thorough in analysis and capable of impartial application. It should be possible by applying the study to arrive at the position of a particular employee at a particular point in a particular salary grade without taking other matters into account except those unconnected with the nature of the work. It will be in order to take into account such matters as merit or seniority etc., but any matters concerning the work (for example, responsibility) one would expect to find taken care of in the evaluation study. One which does not satisfy that test, and requires the management to make a subjective judgment concerning the nature of the work before the employee can be fitted into the appropriate place in the appropriate salary grade, would seem to us not to be a valid study for the purpose of subsection (5).[66]

A job evaluation scheme, to fulfil the requirements of s.1(5), does not, however, have to be 'analytical' and may proceed on a 'felt-fair' basis, according to the Employment Appeal Tribunal in *Bromley and others* v. *Quick Ltd*;[67] nevertheless, the Appeal Tribunal did point out that a non-analytical scheme was more vulnerable to sex discrimination and must therefore be scrutinised closely by the tribunal if challenged.

It appears that there is no complete job evaluation study for the purpose of s.1(5) unless and until the parties who have agreed to carry out the study have accepted its validity. This was the ruling of the Employment Appeal Tribunal in *Arnold* v. *Beecham Group Ltd*,[68] which they justified as according with common sense since the attribution of value to work under a job evaluation study is not an exact science. However carefully a study is undertaken, the Tribunal felt that there is always a risk that the results may be unacceptable to those whose relationship it is designed to regulate. It is, however, possible to accept the validity of a study at a stage substantially before it is implemented by being used as the basis of the payment of wages.

> It is not the stage of implementing the study which makes it complete: it is the stage at which it is accepted as a study. If . . . employers and employees were to find themselves subject to the provisions of s.1 of the Act of 1970 without having agreed that the study is a valid one it would, we fear, discourage both employers and employees from entering on such studies.[69]

This ruling offers considerable scope for the perpetuation of discrimination against women employees where the union is dominated by men and the effect of the scheme would be to upgrade the women's rather than the men's wages. It is far from clear whether the Employment Appeal Tribunal's conclusion would be supported by the House of Lords, given the latter's broad statements of principle in *O'Brien* v. *Sim-Chem Ltd*[70] where it was held, after a job evaluation scheme had been accepted, that it needed no further implementation before employees could rely on it. In that case there had been a job evaluation scheme which had been agreed between employer and employees. The women applicants had been told of their new job grade and the salary range for that grade but the employers intended, before implementing the study, to introduce a merit assessment scheme. In the event, a government pay-pause intervened and the employers decided that they could not implement the new pay scheme. The applicants claimed that they were entitled to equal pay on the basis of the job evaluation scheme which had been completed and under which they were rated as equivalent to male colleagues who were being paid more. The Court of Appeal held[71] that their claims could not succeed because until the pay of the workforce was being determined by reference to the job evaluation scheme that had taken place the terms of the woman's contract and the man's contract were not 'determined by the rating of the work' as required by s.1(2)(b). The House of Lords reversed this very technical decision, holding that once the job evaluation scheme had resulted in a conclusion that the job of the woman was of equal value with the job of the man, the comparison between the respective terms of their contracts became feasible, so that thereafter the applicants could rely on the job evaluation scheme even though it had never been implemented. Lord Russell, with whose speech all other Members of the House agreed, said that he

> would expect that at that stage when comparison first becomes feasible, and discrimination can first be detected, that the provisions of paragraph (b) would be intended to bite, and bite at once. Comparison of terms and conditions of employment must be at the heart of the legislation: and I cannot imagine any reason why Parliament should postpone to a later stage the operation of paragraph (b). . . . It seems to me emininently sensible that Parliament should impose the requirements of paragraph (b) at the moment when the evaluation study and exercise has made available a comparison which can show discrimination.[72]

For the purposes of s.1(2)(b) as well as for s.1(2)(a), the woman employee must be able to compare her work with that of a male colleague 'in the same employment' as herself.[73]

## Work of equal value

A right to claim equal pay with a man whose work is of equal value, although dissimilar in content, to that of a woman is clearly essential to any legislative scheme which seriously seeks to promote equality of opportunity. Without such a right, the traditional undervaluing of women's work will continue more or less unrestricted and attempts to break down gender stereotyping will be doomed to failure since economic factors will deter men from applying for 'women's' jobs. This third situation in which a woman employee can invoke the equality clause implied into her contract of employment was incorporated into the legislation by the Equal Pay (Amendment) Regulations 1983.[74]

Widespread criticism had been voiced of the ambit of the pre-existing legislation, on the ground that the many women employed in sex-segregated occupations[75] were effectively debarred from demanding equal pay: since there were no men doing the same job as themselves, they could not rely on the 'like work' provision, but neither could they demand job evaluation so as to demonstrate that their work was of equal value because job evaluation could not, under the legislation, be undertaken without the employer's consent.[76]

In the forefront of this criticism was the EOC which, in 1980, had recommended to the Home Secretary that the Equal Pay Act be amended so as to admit equal pay for work of equal value and to provide for the value of the work in an individual case to be assessed by the Central Arbitration Committee, following a reference of the case to it by an industrial tribunal.[77] The government took no immediate steps to heed this advice and the following year the EOC reported that

> the extent to which individual women and men see the Equal Pay Act as providing a remedy worth seeking has reached an all-time low. The Commission remains convinced that the effect of the Equal Pay Act 1970 has been exhausted, and that any further progress towards equality requires, as an essential pre-condition, amendments to the two Acts along the lines which this Commission has proposed.[78]

In fact, the tribunal statistics for the following year showed an even further decline in the numbers bringing proceedings under the Equal Pay Act. The figures in Table 2.1 are from the Commission's Seventh Annual Report (1982).

**Table 2.1:  Applications to tribunals where action had been completed**

| Equal Pay Act | |
| --- | --- |
| 1976 | 1742 |
| 1977 | 751 |
| 1978 | 343 |
| 1979 | 263 |
| 1980 | 91 |
| 1981 | 54 |
| 1982 | 39 |

In the meantime, the wind of change was blowing from another direction. An EEC Directive had been passed in 1975 'on the approximation of the laws of the Member States relating to the application of the principle of equal pay for men and women'[79] (usually known as the Equal Pay Directive). In Article 1, it lays down that

> the principle of equal pay for men and women outlined in Article 119 of the Treaty . . . means for the same work or for work to which equal value is attributed, the elimination of all discrimination on grounds of sex with regard to all aspects and conditions of remuneration.[80]

The Directive cast an obligation on each Member State to attain the principles set out in it by February 1976. The European Commission considered that the UK had not properly fulfilled this obligation, in that there was no way for a woman not doing like work with a man in the same employment to demand equal pay for work of equal value. Having delivered a reasoned opinion to this effect in 1980, the Commission brought infringement proceedings before the European Court of Justice under Article 169 of the EEC Treaty in 1981. The main argument for the UK focused on the wording of Article 1 of the Directive and was to the effect that equal pay cannot be demanded unless and until equal value 'is attributed'; in other words, it is not until equal value has been established, either by showing that the applicant is performing like work with a man or through a job evaluation scheme, that the Directive begins to bite. Since the Equal Pay Act entitled the applicant to equal pay in both of these situations, the government maintained that it was not contravening the Directive. It also maintained that, in view of the cost of compulsory job evaluation, its was the only practical interpretation to put on the Directive. However, the European Court did not agree. It held that the UK's interpretation amounted

> to a denial of the very existence of a right to equal pay for work of equal value where no [job] classification has been made. Such a position is not consonant with the general scheme and provisions of Directive 75/117. . . . a worker must be entitled to claim before an appropriate authority that his work has the same value as other work and, if that is found to be the case, to have his rights under the Treaty and the Directive acknowledged by a binding decision. Any method which excludes that option prevents the aims of the Directive being achieved.[81]

It went on to rule that

> the implementation of the Directive implies that the assessment of the 'equal value' to be 'attributed' to particular work may be effected notwithstanding the employer's wishes, if necessary in the context of

adversary proceedings. The Member States must endow an authority with the requisite jurisdiction to decide whether work has the same value as other work, after obtaining such information as may be required.[82]

The European Court's judgment came in July 1982. The following month the Department of Employment produced proposals for amending the Equal Pay Act to give effect to the judgment. After considerable political wrangling and alterations to the draft Regulations,[83] they were eventually approved by Parliament at the end of 1983, although the House of Lords took the unusual step of adding the rider that 'This House believes that the Regulations do not adequately reflect the 1982 decision of the European Court of Justice and Article 1 of the Equal Pay Directive of 1975'.[84]

S.1(2)(c) of the Equal Pay Act, having been added to the statute by these Regulations, now provides that an equality clause is effective 'where a woman is employed on work which, not being work in relation to which paragraph (a) or (b) applies, is, in terms of demands made on her (for instance under such headings as effort, skill and decision), of equal value to that of a man in the same employment'.[85] The effect of this provision is to make s.1(2)(c) claims a residual category, to be relied on only where the applicant cannot prove like work or a valid job evaluation scheme. From the outset, the EOC protested vigorously against this, saying that equal value should, as a result of EEC law, be treated as the generic concept, of which like work and equal value demonstrated by a job evaluation scheme are merely specific examples; it should certainly not be treated as a remedy of last resort. Furthermore, it follows from the form of words adopted in the legislation that, if a woman employee is paid the same as a man doing like work to herself, she cannot demand comparison with a higher paid man in the same employment whom she alleges is in fact doing work of equal value to hers; this offers scope for evasion of the Act by employers through the device of employing a few token males doing like work in a predominantly female job. The Court of Appeal however confirmed this view in *Pickstone and others* v. *Freemans plc*.[86] They rejected the possibility of any ambiguity in s.1(2)(c) or of any alternative construction which might be put on it. (In particular, it had been argued for the applicants that the words 'not being work in relation to which paragraph (a) or (b) applies' are intended to relate *only* to a comparison of the woman's work with that of her *chosen* comparator; they are not intended to mean that, *whenever* there is a man in the same employment engaged on like work with the woman, this is to preclude her claim.[87]) However, the Court of Appeal mitigated the harshness of the decision by going on to hold that the applicants in such circumstances had a direct claim under EEC law.[88]

Two problems remain however. The first is to what extent the jurisdiction of the industrial tribunals[89] and the British procedure for equal value claims[90] is to apply to a claim under EEC law; the Court of Appeal did not elaborate on this point. Secondly, it would appear that the UK, through not having provided a domestic remedy in the *Pickstone* situation, remains in breach of EEC law; it is no answer as a matter of EEC law that a remedy exists as a result of the direct effect of EEC law. In the words of Nicholls LJ,

> Even when the national legislation does no more than reproduce the Community right, explicit national legislation, with appropriate procedural rules and regulations, can have a practical usefulness for claimants and their advisers not possessed by a directly enforceable Community right which lacks that convenient clothing.[91]

Another significant feature of the drafting is its lack of detail with respect to the meaning of the elusive expression 'equal value'[92] Does it mean that the value of the work to be examined is the value of the work to the particular employer or, its value on the open market, or is it to be assessed in some other way?[93] It would appear that it is job content which is to be regarded as the main determinant of value, since the subsection refers, in the same wording as s.1(5), to 'demands made on [the employee] (for instance under such headings as effort, skill and decision)'. However, as McCrudden has pointed out,[94] the notions of market value and value to the employer are indirectly relevant as a result of the material factor defence provided by s.1(3).[95] As with s.1(5), remarkably little guidance is provided as to what factors are to be regarded as relevant, or how they are to be assessed.[96]

Even more problematic is the fact that there can be no accurate parallel between non-compulsory and compulsory job evaluation. In non-compulsory evaluations, a large number of jobs are usually compared, which of course provides the opportunity for the cross-matching of results. The process is achieved not exclusively by mathematical formulae but also through negotiation and bargaining with employers and employees involved. These aspects cannot be present in a s.1(2)(c) evaluation. Only two jobs are compared, the woman's and her comparator's; not only does this carry the risk that if the wrong comparator is chosen the woman's case fails, but it also introduces the possibility of the evaluation reaching an idiosyncratic result which might in turn generate many more claims from other employees. Without the opportunity for multilateral negotiations, the chances of such consequences are even further magnified. In short, the s.1(2)(c) assessment of equal value is dangerously pseudo-scientific.

It appears from the decisions of some industrial tribunals that the meaning of 'equal' also requires some clarification. The greater is usually accepted by courts and tribunals as including the lesser, so that it was without much difficulty that the industrial tribunal in *Wells and others* v. *Smales Ltd*[97] held that nine out of 14 applicants were doing work of equal value to that of their male comparator even though their work had actually been evaluated as being of greater value than his. This is just as well, since if tribunals were not prepared to interpret the legislation in this way the equal value claim would lose much of its potential. However, a problem does manifest itself where the applicants' work turns out to be of slightly *less* value than that of the comparator, especially given the imprecise basis of the evaluation. In *Wells and others* v. *Smales Ltd*,[98] the work of the remaining five applicants was evaluated at between 79 per cent and 95 per cent of that of the comparator. The tribunal nevertheless held that they had scored so closely as to be doing work of 'equal value', because the differences between them and the comparator were not 'relevant' or 'real material differences'. However, in *Brown and Royle* v. *Cearns and Brown Ltd*[99] another industrial tribunal declined to take this 'broad brush' approach and ruled that the applicant's work was not of equal value to that of the comparator where it had been evaluated at 95 per cent of his work. Guidance on this point is necessary from a higher court, if great variations between the rulings of different tribunals are to be avoided.

A major restriction on the ambit of the equal value claim is the fact that it can only be used where the woman employee can show her work to be of equal value to that of a man 'in the same employment',[100] consistently with claims made on the basis of like work and job evaluations. This means that, where there is no man in the enterprise performing work of comparable value to the woman's, she will have no claim; of course the chances of this are greatest in small businesses and also in those many sectors of activity with a high concentration of female employees. The European Court's judgment[101] does not mention expressly whether an equal value claim is restricted under EEC law to comparisons with colleagues. However, in certain passages in which it would have been possible so to restrict the concept, the Court's statements are noticeably broadly expressed; for example, as was seen earlier, it held that 'a worker must be entitled to claim before an appropriate authority that his work has the same value as *other work*'[102] and later it was said that the UK was in breach of EEC law because it had not introduced a measure 'to enable *all* employees who consider themselves wronged by failure to apply the principle of equal pay for men and women' to obtain redress.[103] If EEC law does indeed require the comparison of a worker's wages with those of a member of the opposite sex working for a different employer then the UK is again in breach of its Community obligations; the argument that comparison with employees in other enterprises is impracticable would easily be met since such comparisons are made under both Dutch and Irish law.[104]

A further shortcoming of s.1(2)(c) is that it deals only with individual contracts of employment and gives no power to remedy collective agreements which fail to grant equal contractual terms for work of equal value.[105] Although such discriminatory terms of collective agreements are automatically invalid,[106] as the EOC commented when the Equal Pay (Amendment) Regulations were in the process of being drafted.

> it would be wise and prudent to establish adequate machinery . . . for the orderly resolution of the anomalies in existing collective agreements and job evaluated pay structures which are certain to arise as a result of individual equal value awards.[107]

## The necessity for a comparator of the opposite sex

It has been seen that, for each of the three situations in which an equality clause operates, a woman applicant must be able to point to an actual male colleague to use as a comparator. This is not the case with extra-contractual discrimination which is governed by the Sex Discrimination Act 1975.[108] This non-congruence between the two statutes was well illustrated by *Meeks* v. *National Union of Agricultural and Allied Workers*.[109] The applicant complained that, as a part-time secretarial worker, she was being paid a lower hourly rate than full-timers, for substantially identical work. The industrial tribunal held that her employers had committed an act of indirect discrimination against her within the meaning of the Sex Discrimination Act 1975, but that it was excluded from the ambit of that Act since the discrimination related to the payment of money under a contract of employment.[110] Her difficulty was that the employer's actions were not unlawful under the Equal Pay Act either because there was no male colleague whom she could use as a comparator. In *Shields* v. *Coomes (Holdings) Ltd*[111] Lord Denning MR aptly described the task of construing the Equal Pay and Sex Discrimination Acts as

> like fitting together a jig-saw puzzle. The pieces are all jumbled up together in two boxes. One is labelled the Sex Discrimination Act

1975. The other the Equal Pay Act 1970. You pick up a piece from one box and try to fit it in. It does not. So you try a piece from the other box.[112]

The necessity for a male comparator in practice represents a very serious limitation on the usefulness of the Act on account of the prevalence of occupational segregation of the sexes.[113] As well as reducing the scope of the Act, the comparator requirement also poses the danger that, should the applicant mistakenly choose the wrong colleague with whom to compare her work, the tribunal possesses no jurisdiction to substitute another comparator.[114]

Critics of the legislation have therefore argued in favour of amendment so as to allow a 'hypothetical man' test: what contractual terms would this woman be getting if she were a man?[115] Included amongst the EOC's proposals for reform in 1980 was the suggestion that s.1(2) of the Equal Pay Act be amended so as to 'enable a woman to compare her work with that of a hypothetical male counterpart as well as an actual male'.[116] More recently, it has lucidly summed up the arguments in favour of such a position as follows:

> The limitation of a person's rights to equal pay for equal work to circumstances in which an actual comparator exists is considered to be both unfair and unnecessary. If an employee can satisfy an industrial tribunal on the balance of probabilities that had she been a man (or vice versa) she would have received a higher rate of pay for doing the work, she should have the right to present her claim free of this jurisidictional limitation. This might even involve comparisons with the treatment of employees of different employers, but the relevance and validity (if any) of such a comparison in the particular case, would be a matter of evidence. It should not be ruled out, as at present, as a matter of principle.[117]

The requirement for a comparator of the opposite sex poses special difficulties in equal value cases. The applicant may not have sufficient information to be able to choose a comparator, particularly if the organisation for which she works is a large one. (In like work claims, the problem is less severe because the applicant and her comparator often work in fairly close proximity to one another.) The Employment Appeal Tribunal has, however, held that, provided that the applicant can make out a prima facie case of disparity, then she may obtain an order for discovery of the relevant documents.[118] What precisely is meant by a prima facie case in this context is not made clear by the judgment (nor by succeeding cases), but the Tribunal did rule that fishing expeditions, seeking discovery to enable the applicant to hunt around amongst the employers' documents and contracts in order to construct a prima facie case, was not permissible.

Despite the use of 'comparator' in the singular by the legislation, in practice an applicant is not prevented from comparing her position with that of several comparators.[119]

## THE CLAIM

A claim under the Equal Pay Act is, in the first instance, to an industrial tribunal.[120] There is no specialist division of industrial tribunals to deal with discrimination cases. The Commission for Racial Equality (CRE) has advocated such a reform on the ground that, since there are relatively few discrimination cases, the average industrial tribunal has at the moment little opportunity to acquire expertise in the complicated legislation involved.[121] The EOC, whilst agreeing that there is a lack of expertise in tribunals (sex discrimination and equal pay cases currently account for only about 2 per cent of cases heard by industrial tribunals), considers that the real difficulty springs from the apparent random assignment of cases to tribunals in England and Wales; it reports that most tribunal members hear only one or two sex discrimination cases a year.[122] In research carried out by Dr Alice Leonard for the EOC between 1980 and 1982, it was found that the 215 sex discrimination and equal pay cases examined were distributed among 116 different tribunal chairpersons; 48 per cent of the chairpersons heard one sex discrimination or equal pay case only and 46 per cent heard only two or three cases. Only 6 per cent of the chairpersons heard more than three cases.[123] The EOC's conclusion is therefore that it is unnecesary to create a specialist division for discrimination cases, since the objective of greater expertise could be achieved within the existing system by a greater specialisation among existing tribunal members. Such tribunal members should also receive considerably more training than at present in the details of the legislation. On balance, these seem sensible suggestions. If a specialist division of the industrial tribunals were created, there would be a significant risk of its becoming regarded as a 'special court', appearing to apply different rules to women and ethnic minorities from those applying to the rest of the population and thereby conferring some sort of advantage on those groups.

Industrial tribunals consist of a legally qualified chairperson and two lay members who are chosen for their industrial relations experience, one from a list of TUC nominees and the other from a panel of nominees of the CBI, local authorities, Health Service and the Retail Consortium. There is inherent in this system the danger that the lay members, although well-versed in current industrial relations practice, will be insensitive to complaints of discrimination: what is being challenged may frequently turn out to be a practice which they personally have accepted for years. Despite not being legally qualified, the lay members are expected to act as independent members of the bench and are full members of the tribunal, which can decide cases by majority vote if necessary. There is an urgent need, as the EOC has pointed out, for greater training for tribunal members, to ensure that they are properly aware of the subtle issues arising in discrimination cases and to acquaint them thoroughly with the details of the complex law in this area.

As might be expected considering their composition, industrial tribunals have a minority female membership, as Table 2.2 indicates.

**Table 2.2:   Composition of Industrial Tribunals: February 1987[124]**

|                                  | Male | Female |
|----------------------------------|------|--------|
| Employees' representatives       | 719  | 197    |
| Employers' etc. representatives  | 767  | 213    |
| Full-time chairpersons           | 60   | 6      |
| Part-time chairpersons           | 113  | 9      |

There is no statutory requirement (although there ought to be) in sex discrimination or equal pay cases of any female representation on the tribunal; in practice, the aim is always for there to be at least one woman member of the tribunal in all equal pay and sex discrimination cases but this aim is by no means invariably achieved in fact.[125]

The parties may either represent themselves or be represented by a solicitor, barrister, trade union, employers' association or any other person of their choice. However, legal aid is available only for advice under the Green Form scheme and not for representation before an industrial tribunal. This means that, unless the woman can obtain funding from an agency such as the EOC[126] or a union, she has to pay for the proceedings herself, a very serious obstacle when it is remembered that women do most of the low paid jobs in the community and that, indeed, this fact will often be the essence of the woman's complaint. Research has shown that fear of the financial cost is the reason most often given by women to explain their withdrawal of sex discrimination claims.[127] It hardly needs to be pointed out that the employer may well be able to afford the most skilled legal representation. The position can only be exacerbated from the applicant's point of view if the government proceeds with its proposal to introduce a fee of £25 for all persons bringing claims before an industrial tribunal.[128]

There is appeal on a point of law only from industrial tribunals to the Employment Appeal Tribunal,[129] which consists of High Court judges nominated by the Lord Chancellor, together with other persons who have special experience of industrial relations. Appeals are heard by a judge and either two or four appointed members but there must always be an equal number of appointees representing employers and employees respectively.[130] There is no regular practice (although there should be) in the Employment Appeal Tribunal of having a woman member to hear an appeal in a discrimination case. A party can appear in person before the Employment Appeal Tribunal, or else be represented, and legal aid is available for this stage in the proceedings. Further appeal lies from decisions of the Employment Appeal Tribunal to the Court of Appeal and thence to the House of Lords.

An industrial tribunal may become seised of a case under the Equal Pay Act either as a result of a complaint by the employee,[131] or because the employer has requested an order declaring the rights of himself and the employee,[132] or as a result of a reference by the Secretary of State where it appears to him that there may be a question whether a particular employer has been contravening the Act but it is not reasonable to expect his employees to bring an action.[133] In addition, where in proceedings before any court a question arises as to the operation of an equality clause, the court can on the application of a party or otherwise refer that question to an industrial tribunal.[134]

## The special procedure in equal value cases

A special procedure for equal value cases is provided by s.2A of the Equal Pay Act, which was inserted by the Equal Pay (Amendment) Regulations 1983. The Regulations were described in Parliament as 'of Byzantine complexity', 'legal gobbledegook' and 'incomprehensible'[135] and nowhere would these epithets appear to be more apt than in describing s.2A.[136] The seriously detrimental consequences of this for the promotion of equality of opportunity cannot be overstated: the equal value concept has got to be fully recognised if equality is ever going to become anything like a reality, and any procedure which frustrates it strikes at the very heart of the legislative scheme. Substantial reform of the design and procedure for equal value claims will ultimately be seen as inevitable, and it is a great pity that this fact was not appreciated by the government at the time the new Regulations were being proposed.

Subsection (1) presents an industrial tribunal[137] facing an equal value case with the choice of dismissing the application in a preliminary screening hearing, or allowing it to proceed for evidence to be gathered. It may dismiss the case at the outset if it is satisfied that there are no reasonable grounds for considering the work to be of equal value; this is a sweeping power to reach summary judgment about a matter which, in the nature of things, inevitably involves complicated comparisons. Unfortunately, tribunals appear to be construing the provision as placing a burden on the complainant to show a prima facie case that she is employed on work of equal value with her comparator, although this case does not have to be disclosed in the originating application and can emerge from evidence given at the screening hearing.[138] It has been commented that this is a particularly dangerous provision since many equal value claims appear unreasonable at first sight because they involve a challenge to traditional views as to what a woman's job is worth.[139] In addition, the power seems unnecessary since the industrial tribunal can already strike out a claim if it considers it to be frivolous or vexatious and, in a pre-hearing assessment, it can order that a party be made to pay the costs if unsuccessful. As Lester has pointed out,[140] if the tribunal decides that there are no reasonable grounds for considering the work to be of equal value, this decision being within the discretion of the tribunal, it is only appealable in the very extreme case in which it amounts to an error of law.

There is one situation in which the legislation lays down that there are no reasonable grounds for finding equal value; this is where the woman's work has already been given a different value from that of her chosen male comparator in a job evaluation scheme and there are no reasonable grounds for considering the job evaluation scheme was itself discriminatory on the ground of sex.[141] It follows from this that an existing job evaluation scheme does not constitute a barrier to making an equal value claim where the woman employee can show that the scheme is discriminatory;[142] it is laid down that a job evaluation scheme will be found to be made on a system which discriminates on grounds of sex 'where a difference, or coincidence, between values set by that system on different demands under the same or different headings is not justifiable irrespective of the sex of the person on whom those demands are made'.[143] This avenue of attack on a pre-existing job evaluation scheme, which is presumably intended to allow challenge to a scheme on the ground of its being either directly or indirectly discriminatory,[144] was thought to be a necessary element of the new legislation because of EEC law; Article 1(2) of the Equal Pay Directive[145] lays down that 'where a job classification system is used for determining pay, it must be based on the same criteria for both men and women and so drawn up as to exclude any discrimination on grounds of sex'. Under the Equal Pay Act, before it was amended by the 1983 Regulations, it appeared that the scope for challenging the validity of a job evaluation scheme was extremely limited and there was therefore a risk of further proceedings against the UK in the European Court of Justice for inadequate implementation of this part of the Directive.[146] However, even with the legislative amendments the task facing the applicant seeking to challenge a job evaluation scheme has been described as 'herculean', especially where she is without legal, trade union or EOC support, and the employer is well-advised to lead expert evidence in defence of his study at the preliminary stage.[147] It has been suggested that, to remove the danger of discrimination being contained in a job evaluation scheme, there should be instituted a general system of approving and monitoring job evaluations under the auspices of the EOC, with rights to appeal to independent chairpersons,[148] but unfortunately such a system has not been adopted in practice.

If the tribunal faced with an equal value case does not decide to dismiss it at the outset, it must require a member of 'the panel of independent experts' to prepare a report on the question of equal value; it may not determine the case until it has received that report.[149] The independent experts are persons designated by ACAS, who are not members of the ACAS Council nor its officers or servants.[150] The government's discussion paper published with the original draft Order said that the experts would be approved for their wide experience of industrial relations, but the legislation lays down no particular qualifications for them. This system for determining equal value was subjected to considerable criticism when the legislation was at the preparatory stage. In particular, the EOC recommended that there should be full-time equality officers[151] 'so as to ensure a continuity of experience and expertise and a consistency of approach in the entirely unprecedented task of analysing and establishing the value of potentially vastly dissimilar jobs'; the Commission considered that the panel system would 'ensure that there is no consistent or coherent body of experience to draw upon in this essential and difficult task and [would] potentially . . . lead to a series of inconsistent recommendations and awards which in turn [would] give rise to further unnecessary, time-consuming and costly litigation'.[152] In addition, the allegation has been made that ACAS is an organisation biased in favour of men and their claims and has in the past actively discouraged women from pursuing claims based on sex discrimination.[153]

It has been observed earlier that the legislation makes no real attempt at a systematic or analytical definition of equal value. This means that there is little or nothing to guide the independent expert when the assessment is made, and is a further reason to suspect a lack of consistency between awards.[154] A serious lacuna in the provision is the lack of any reference to indirect discrimination, which may well not be at once obvious to the expert. The extent to which the expert's report is challengeable, and other practical considerations relevant at this point, are governed by the Industrial Tribunals (Rules of Procedure) (Equal Value Amendment) Regulations 1983,[155] adopted at the same time as the substantive Regulations (and henceforth referred to as the 'Procedure Regulations')

In order to prepare his report, the expert will require access to documents and other types of information; he is enabled to demand information if he first makes application to the industrial tribunal.[156] When the tribunal requires the expert to prepare his report, it must stipulate that the expert must take account of all the information he has received which has a bearing on the case, that he must send a written summary of his draft report to the parties and invite their representations, that he must inform the tribunal of what those representations were and what his conclusions are, and that he must take no account of the difference of sex and at all times act fairly.[157] If the expert does not comply with any of these stipulations, or if the tribunal considers that the expert has reached a conclusion which, taking due account of the information supplied and the representations made to the expert, could not reasonably have been reached,[158] or if the tribunal thinks that for some other reason (apart from disagreement with the expert's conclusion) the report is unsatisfactory, the tribunal can refuse to accept the report and must then commission another.[159] In forming its views on these matters, the tribunal must listen to the representations of the parties and hear relevant witnesses.[160] It is to be hoped that this provision enables the expert's report to be challenged on the ground that it is itself directly or indirectly discriminatory. Such a conclusion is arguably to be presumed since (as seen earlier) Article 1(2) of Equal Pay Directive[161] forbids discrimination in any job classification system. The tribunal itself can require the expert to explain any matter contained in his report[162] and the parties are entitled to cross-examine the expert. If either party wishes to cast further doubt on the expert's report, he or she may call one witness to give expert evidence on the question of equal value (but not on any matter of fact upon which a conclusion in the expert's report is based), and the other side can cross-examine that witness.[163]

The period within which the expert is expected to report appears to be extremely short compared to voluntary job evaluation which often takes months or even years to complete.[164] Not less than six weeks after the tribunal has asked for the expert's report, if the tribunal considers that there has been or is likely to be undue delay in receiving the report, then it can demand reasons for the delay from the expert and may even commission another report from another expert.[165] The parties must be given at least two weeks after the report has been produced in which to digest it before the hearing before the industrial tribunal can be resumed.[166]

The Regulations do not spell out precisely the weight to be attached by the tribunal to an expert's report; in other words, they do not state whether, where doubt has been cast on the expert's report by evidence adduced before the tribunal, the tribunal can simply refuse to follow the expert's report and reach its own conclusion. It would appear that it can since the report is described by the Regulations merely as 'evidence in the case'.[167]

The Procedure Regulations go some way towards ensuring that the expert acts fairly in the preparation of his report. However, there remain serious defects. Like the substantive Regulations, the Procedure Regulations do not state whether or not the expert is required to have regard to indirect indiscrimination in the fixing of contractual terms. It is also very difficult in practice to adduce evidence which casts doubt on the expert's report without possessing a power corresponding to the expert's power to subpoena information.

The procedure in these cases is unfortunately extremely cumbersome and long drawn-out. In the House of Lords debate on the Regulations, Lord Wedderburn pointed out that there could be a possible 10 or 11 stages in an equal value case[168] and it was estimated around the time that the new Regulations were coming into effect that each claim would take a minimum time of six to eight months.[169] In actual fact, claims are occupying an average of almost 13 months and ACAS has commented[170] that equal value cases in this country are 'taking very much longer to complete than those in other jurisidictions'.[171]

## DEFENCES

### The material factor defence

According to s.1(3) of the Equal Pay Act, 'an equality clause shall not operate in relation to a variation between the woman's contract and the man's contract if the employer proves that the variation is genuinely due to a material factor which is not the difference of sex'. In the case of a claim in respect of like work or work rated as equivalent under a voluntary job evaluation scheme, the material factor must also be a 'material difference between the woman's case and the man's', whereas in an equal value claim it may, but need not, be such a material difference. This subsection was substantially amended by the Equal Pay (Amendment) Regulations 1983.[172] The pre-existing law had referred only to the material difference defence and there was a considerable amount of litigation in which its scope was defined.

*The meaning of 'material difference'*

In *NAAFI* v. *Varley*[173] Phillips J pointed out that

> it is not altogether clear what is the extent of the meaning of the word 'material' in this context, but we think it is put in to emphasise the fact that it must be a real difference: just as the word 'genuine' has been put in. Those words have been included to emphasise the fact that the subsection is not to be used to deprive claimants of the benefit of the equality clause to which prima facie they are entitled, except in the clearest possible case where it is established that the difference is not one of sex, but is a genuine and material or real difference between her case and his.[174]

And in *Rainey* v. *Greater Glasgow Health Board*,[175] Lord Keith said: 'the difference must be "material", which I would construe as meaning "significant and relevant." '[176]

The burden of proving the s.1(3) defence rests on the employer,[177] although he need only discharge it on the balance of probabilities;[178] some early decisions of the Employment Appeal Tribunal suggested that this burden of proof was a particularly heavy one but the Court of Appeal in *National Vulcan Insurance* v. *Wade*,[179] unfortunately for the applicant, rejected this view. Lord Denning MR, perhaps revealing the fundamental attitude of other members of the judiciary, too, to the subject of sex discrimination, said that

> the burden of proof required depends upon the nature and gravity of the subject matter. It depends on whether it is a grave offence or a minor one. In a civil case the burden is usually on the balance of probabilities. In these cases, under s.1(3), it seems to me that this court must say that the burden of proof on the employer is not a very heavy burden of proof. It is the ordinary burden of proof in a civil case. It is on the balance of probabilities.[180]

In a practice, very weak evidence from the employer has been held to satisfy the burden of proof as, for example, in *Boyle* v. *Tennent Caledonian Breweries Ltd*,[181] where the Employment Appeal Tribunal accepted that a sum paid to the woman applicant with the *intention* of equalising her rate of basic pay with that of a male colleague was sufficient. This was so despite the fact that the man continued to receive some £300 a year more than the woman, ostensibly because of the material difference between his case and the applicant's, and despite the fact that the employer did not produce precise evidence to explain how he quantified the equalisation payment. Lord McDonald said:

> a tribunal does not require to be satisfied in every case that such an increase eliminated [the discriminatory] element with mathematical precision. That is a matter for negotiation between employers and unions.[182]

In an influential series of cases, now over-ruled, the courts held that the material difference defence involved only the 'personal equation' of the two employees; it was not concerned with the nature of the jobs performed since *ex hypothesi* that had already been found to be comparable within the meaning of the statute.[183] For example, Lord Denning MR said in *Shields* v. *Coomes Holdings Ltd*[184] that the subsection dealt only with cases where the woman and the man were doing like work (or work rated as equivalent) but the personal equation of the man was such that he deserved to be paid at a higher rate than the woman; even though the two jobs, viewed as jobs, were evaluated equally, nevertheless, there could quite genuinely be 'material differences between the two people . . . doing them – which merit a variation in pay – irrespective of whether it is a man or a woman doing the job'.[185] In *Clay Cross Ltd* v. *Fletcher*[186] this principle was reiterated and the riders added that the employer's intentions were irrelevant (in other words, it made no difference that he did not intend to discriminate) and that the tribunal was not to have regard to any 'extrinsic forces' which led to the man being paid more. Lord Denning MR ruled that

> an employer cannot avoid his obligations under the Act by saying: 'I paid him more because he asked for more', or 'I paid her less because she was willing to come for less'. If any such excuse were permitted, the Act would be a dead letter. Those are the very reasons why there was unequal pay before the statute. They are the very circumstances in which the statute was intended to operate. Nor can the employer avoid his obligations by giving the reasons why he submitted to the extrinsic forces. As for instance by saying: 'He asked for that sum because it was what he was getting in his previous job',

or 'He was the only applicant for the job, so I had no option'. In such cases the employer may beat his breast, and say: 'I did not pay him more because he was a man. I paid it because he was the only suitable person who applied for the job. Man or woman made no difference to me'. Those are reasons personal to the employer. If any such reasons were permitted as an excuse, the door would be wide open. Every employer who wished to avoid the statute would walk straight through it.[187]

The first inroad as far as the 'personal equation' was concerned came with *Jenkins* v. *Kingsgate (Clothing Productions) Ltd (No. 2)*,[188] in which a woman part-time worker sought to compare her rate of pay with a male full-time colleague. Earlier British cases had held that the fact of one worker being part-time and the other full-time was sufficient to constitute a 'material difference'.[189] A reference was made to the European Court of Justice in the *Jenkins* case, which resulted in a ruling that a basic rate of pay differential between part-time and full-time workers is contrary to EEC law where it is in reality an indirect way of discriminating against women; the Court accepted that, for domestic reasons, women are often unable to work more than part-time.[190] The importance of this judgment lay in the fact that the British equal pay legislation had hitherto been interpreted as extending only to *direct* discrimination over contractual terms;[191] henceforth, it had to be interpreted so as to cover *indirect* discrimination (at least as far as pay was concerned), in other words the situation where conditions are attached for entitlement which are considerably easier for men to fulfil than women. The material difference defence had therefore to be construed so as not to permit indirect discrimination by the employer. When the case returned to the Employment Appeal Tribunal, the European Court's judgment was found to be ambivalent on the question of whether all such indirect discrimination was outlawed, or whether it was only intentional indirect discrimination that was forbidden. Browne-Wilkinson J held that he would construe the Equal Pay Act and the Sex Discrimination Act in like fashion, since they are intended to form parts of a single 'code'; as the latter precludes unintentional indirect discrimination,[192] so should the Equal Pay Act. In the end, he held (applying the European Court's judgment) that, if the factual situation in the case really were indirectly discriminatory against women, then the only defence for the employer under s.1(3) would be to show that the difference in pay between full-time and part-time workers was in fact reasonably necessary in order to obtain some result (other than cheap female labour) which the employer desired for economic or other reasons. Construed strictly, such a test sets up a formidable barrier to the employer; he must prove that the greater sum paid to male employees actually *achieves* a bona fide business objective. The Employment Appeal Tribunal's ruling, although entirely consistent with that of the European Court, was, of course, out of line with the *Clay Cross* formula and raised a doubt as to whether different defences applied in EEC and domestic law.[193]

The precise nature of the defence allowed in EEC law was later clarified in *Bilka-Kaufhaus GmbH* v. *Weber von Hartz*,[194] where the European Court held that

> If the national court finds that the measures chosen by Bilka correspond to a real need on the part of the undertaking, are appropriate with a view to achieving the objectives pursued and are necessary to that end, the fact that the measures affect a far greater number of women than men is not sufficent to show that they constitute an infringement [of EEC law] . . . a . . . company may justify the adoption of a pay policy excluding part-time workers, irrespective of their sex, from its occupational pension scheme on the ground that it seeks to employ as few part-time workers as possible, where it is found that the means chosen for achieving that objective correspond to a real need on the part of the undertaking, are appropriate with a view to achieving the objective in question and are necessary to that end.[195]

The European Court thus made it clear that some economic reasons, extrinsic to the personal equation between applicant and comparator, are acceptable in EEC law and the House of Lords was quick to adopt that less stringent standard for the purposes of domestic law too. The case in which it did so was *Rainey* v. *Greater Glasgow Health Board*,[196] which concerned the decision by the Secretary of State for Scotland in 1979 to establish a prosthetic fitting service within the National Health Service in Scotland. To get the scheme off the ground, it was necessary to recruit a number of qualified prosthetists to the National Health Service and the only prosthetists then available were employed in the private sector. It was decided that, in general, the pay of employees in the new prosthetic service should be related to the Whitley Council scale but, since it was appreciated that this might not be attractive to prosthetists in the private sector, they exceptionally were given the option of remaining on the rates of pay and conditions of service that they were then receiving, subject to any future alterations negotiated by their trade union. The action arose out of a claim for equal pay brought by a female prosthetist who had entered the National Health prosthetic service directly, not having been previously employed in the private sector. Her claim was to pay parity with a male Health Service prosthetist, who had been employed in the private sector before and who consequently was earning some £2,790 per annum than more than her. The industrial tribunal held that the applicant and her comparator were performing like work, but that there was a material difference between their two cases because they were being paid on different scales negotiated by different unions, which was a consequence of their having entered the service in different ways. The case proceeded to the House of Lords, after the Employment Appeal Tribunal and the Court of Session both rejected appeals by the applicant. It was argued for the applicant that the only difference between her situation and that of her comparator was in reality an economic one and that it therefore could not constitute a material difference for the purpose of s.1(3). The House of Lords rejected this argument and, in doing so, disapproved of Lord Denning's remarks in the *Clay Cross* case; Lord Keith said, in particular, that

> consideration of a person's case must necessarily involve consideration of all the circumstances of that case. These may well go beyond what is not very happily described as 'the personal equation', *i.e.* the personal qualities by way of skill, experience or training which the individual brings to the job. Some circumstances may on examination prove to be not significant or not relevant, but others may do so, though not relating to the personal qualities of the employee. In particular, where there is no question of intentional sex discrimination whether direct or indirect (and there is none here) a difference which is connected with economic factors affecting the efficient carrying on of the employer's business or other activity may well be relevant.[197]

The House was strongly influenced by the rulings of the European Court in the *Jenkins* and *Bilka-Kaufhaus* cases and concluded that 'a relevant difference for the purposes of s.1(3) may relate to circumstances other than the personal qualifications or merits of the male and female workers who are the subject of comparison'[198] The test is whether or not there are 'objectively justified grounds of difference', and here it was held that there were because of the necessity when the National Health prosthetic service was set up to attract qualified prosthetists to it.

In some ways, this ruling of the House of Lords makes a positive contribution to the case law in this area. In strictly logical terms, it does away with the need to ask what factors are included within 'the personal equation'; in particular, it was difficult to explain why the amount of pay a person had been earning in a previous post, and thus the amount he or she was now demanding, was not a part of that equation. In addition, from the point of view of the certainty of the legal process, it seems wholly desirable to harmonise as far as possible the provisions of EEC law and of domestic law. Furthermore, the House of Lords was at pains to point out that the market forces at work in this case were not being used to downgrade the female employee's pay, but rather to inflate that which would ordinarily be paid to her male comparator.[199] However, as against these factors, there must be weighed one very important negative one: it is very hard to be completely 'objective' in determining the existence of 'objectively justified grounds'. Lord Denning in the *Clay Cross* case demonstrated that he was sensitive to the fact that, in general, women do not yet possess as much economic clout as their male colleagues. There is a spiral of economic deprivation out of which women have not yet emerged (evidenced by the continuing differential between their rates of pay and those of men).[200] The social facts which underlie the stark economic figures are not always immediately obvious to a court and many will not investigate in sufficient depth to uncover them. In *Rainey* itself, for example, the House of Lords observed, but paid no further attention to the fact, that all of the private sector prosthetists recruited at the higher rate into the National Health Service were male. Grounds for differential pay will only truly be 'objectively justified' if they are not rooted in any way in past discrimination, but the new test enables Courts to pay mere lip service to this principle. Applicants and their representatives must now be very much more watchful than hitherto, to ensure that the 'material difference' relied on by the employer, although facially neutral, is not itself a consequence of inequality of opportunity as between the sexes or a disguised form of continuing discrimination.[201]

The legislation contains no list of permissible material differences other than sex, although it has been argued that such differences require to be exhaustively enumerated.[202] Amongst the matters which have been held in the past to constitute such material differences are the protection or 'red circling' of an employee's wages where the red circling itself is not grounded on earlier acts of sex discrimination,[203] different places of work carrying with them different customs as to the hours worked,[204] long service,[205] superior skills or qualifications or bigger output,[206] widely negotiated and different pay scales[207] and a properly operated grading scheme according to ability, skill and experience.[208] However, the tribunal must be careful to ensure that it looks at all the circumstances of the case; it must in particular ask itself whether the circumstances are such that the passage of time means that what was initially a justifiable reason for a variation has ceased to be so.[209]

A problem not yet addressed in any detail by the courts is what should happen in a situation where there was shown to be a material difference between the two cases, but it was not such as to account for the whole of the variation in contractual terms. It is suggested that the tribunal should intervene to the extent of the unjustified variation since the whole of the variation in such a case would not be 'genuinely due' to the material difference.[210]

*The scope of the defence in equal value claims*

In equal value claims (that is to say, those not in respect of like work or work rated as equivalent), all the employer has to establish by way of a defence under s.1(3) is, as has been seen, that the variation in contractual terms is genuinely due to a material factor which is not the difference of sex. The legislature expressly opted for this new defence in equal value cases and, in particular, it appeared to wish to confine the (later-discredited) 'personal equation' rule to like work and work rated as equivalent since it is only in those cases that the material factor must also be a material difference 'between the woman's case and the man's'. In the House of Commons, in introducing the Equal Pay (Amendment) Regulations, Mr Alan Clark stated that the new defence would cover 'circumstances where the difference in pay is not due to personal factors between the man and the woman, but rather to skill shortages or other market forces'.[211] Lord Gowrie, in the House of Lords, went rather further and explained that the new subsection was not intended to allow the employer to argue market forces as a general justification for paying a woman less than a man but that 'an employer should be able to argue that market forces account for the pay differential between the two jobs provided . . . that there is no direct or indirect discrimination on grounds of sex'.[212]

The problem faced by the legislature was certainly a difficult one. On the one hand, as the Court of Appeal recognised in *Clay Cross Ltd* v. *Fletcher*,[213] the value of women's services has traditionally been underrated; indeed this very fact provided the *raison d'être* for the equal pay legislation. If it were enough, therefore, for an employer to justify a differential on the basis that he could obtain women to work for lower wages than men, the right to equal pay for work of equal value would become meaningless. On the other hand, there clearly are other economic factors which affect the value of work performed for employers and which can operate quite irrespective of sex. Skill shortages provide an example of such a factor. It would be unfair to employers to exclude the possibility of this type of argument when presenting a s.1(3) defence. The obvious answer would have been for the legislation to have provided a great deal more detail in this area, and perhaps to have indicated, at least illustratively, the types of economic factors or market forces which might ground the defence. Unfortunately, the legislature did not choose this course and left it to the tribunals, courts and commentators to work out the circumstances in which such economic factors can be relied upon by employers.

Until authoritative guidance is obtained from the higher courts as to the relevance of market forces to the material factor defence, it is only possible to speculate about their role.[214] However, on the authority of *Jenkins* v. *Kingsgate (Clothing Productions) Ltd*,[215] it would appear that a market forces defence would not be acceptable if its effect were either directly or indirectly discriminatory. By analogy with the reasoning of Browne-Wilkinson J in the *Jenkins* case in the Employment Appeal Tribunal,[216] this would extend not merely to a situation where the defence resulted in intentional discrimination but also to unintentional discrimination. In addition, it seems more than likely that, as with the material difference defence, a material factor would not constitute an acceptable excuse where it has its roots in prior acts of discrimination;[217] this may, in practice, prove a very important brake on the scope of market forces as a defence.

Despite the apparent desire of the legislature in 1983 to differentiate between the material factor and the material difference defences, the upshot of the House of Lords' decision in *Rainey* v. *Greater Glasgow Health Board*[218] has been to reduce any such distinction to vanishing point. Relevant economic issues or market forces may now ground either defence, provided only that they do not operate in a discriminatory fashion. The only real point of difference remaining is probably that different sorts of economic factors will be relevant to the different cases. However, this leaves the courts with the difficulty of explaining the construction of s.1(3); the material factor defence is expressed to be wider than the material difference defence, and moreover, a material difference must be 'between the woman's case and the man's'. With the over-ruling of the 'personal equation' cases, this phrase appears to be redundant and it is going to require a considerable exercise of imagination on the part of the judges to ascribe a meaning to it.

The material factor defence was used to justify a very serious inroad into the scope of equal value claims by an industrial tribunal in *Clark and others* v. *Bexley Health Authority*.[219] Some women National Health Service speech therapists claimed that their work was of equal value to that of male clinical psychologists. The employers argued that health authorities are statutorily required to pay their employees according to the salary scales agreed by the Whitley Councils and approved by the Secretary of State under the National Health Service (Remuneration and Conditions of Service) Regulations 1974. Thus, even if the work in question was of equal value, any variation in pay was attributable to a material factor other than sex, in other words, to the obligation of the employers to pay the approved salaries. The tribunal upheld this argument, saying that under English law the employers had no choice other than to comply with the approved scales. They went on to say that whether the 1974 Regulations or the Secretary of State's approval conflicted with EEC law (by denying the right to demand equal pay for work of equal value) would have to be determined by judicial review proceedings. The Divisional Court later quashed the tribunal's decision[220] and sent the case back for decision on the merits. Its outcome is of enormous practical importance because of the large number of women employees of the Health Service affected by it.[221]

In an equal value claim, the tribunal has a discretion where it considers it appropriate to receive evidence on the material factor defence before it requires the expert to prepare a report;[222] if it takes this course, it may still reconsider the issue after it has received the expert's report.[223] Although at first sight this appears a curious inversion of the normal logical pattern, in which the employer might be expected to produce his defence after the case against him has been made out, it was introduced in order to reduce public expense by minimising the number of cases referred to independent experts. However, this rationale cannot explain why the employer is allowed two bites at the cherry; if injustice is to be avoided, tribunals must be careful not to allow employers to rehearse arguments that they have already run after the expert's report has been received.

## Protective and maternity legislation

By virtue of s.6(1) of the Equal Pay Act,[224] the equality clause does not operate in relation to terms which are affected by the law regulating the employment of women,[225] or which afford special treatment to women in connection with pregnancy or child birth.[226] Theoretically, the expression 'special treatment' could be taken to extend to unfavourable as well as favourable treatment. However, an industrial tribunal in *Coyne* v. *Export Credits Guarantee Department*[227] roundly rejected such an approach for two reasons. First, 'the expression "special treatment" should be construed in the same sense in the 1970 Act as it is used in s.2(2) of the Sex Discrimination Act 1975. In that context it is perfectly clear that the expression means specially favourable treatment'. Secondly, 'if we were to construe "special treatment" in the wider sense, the result would be that an employer would be entitled to put a provision in a woman's contract providing that if she became pregnant her pay would immediately be reduced by, say, 50%, and the 1970 Act would be powerless to prevent that. That is a result from which this Tribunal recoils'.[228] On the facts of the case, the tribunal deleted a clause in the Civil Service Regulations which reduced the normal contractual entitlement to sick leave where the sick leave followed maternity leave and the sickness was a consequence of the confinement.

### Provisions related to death and retirement

The Equal Pay Act and the Sex Discrimination Act both contain exceptions in relation to death and retirement. Since these exceptions are closely linked, they will be dealt with together in Chapter 3 (p. 108 *et seq.*).

## REMEDIES

It has been seen that the technique adopted by the Equal Pay Act is to insert an equality clause into every contract of employment by which a person is employed at an establishment in Great Britain.[229] When operative, the clause modifies any inequality in contractual terms between a man's and a woman's contract. The claimant thus has essentially only to apply to the tribunal for a declaration to confirm such modification. However, the award of a remedy via the device of the equality clause is ill-adapted for the resolution of equal value cases, because there is often little congruence between the terms of the applicant's contract and those of her comparator's; this was demonstrated by *Hayward* v. *Cammell Laird Shipbuilders Ltd (No. 2)*.[230] Ms Hayward, a cook, had proved that her work was of equal value to that of some skilled shipyard workmen who were also employed by Cammell Laird. Her employers argued, however, that they did not have to pay her the same basic wage and overtime rates as her male comparators because, looked at as a whole, her terms and conditions of employment were not less favourable than theirs; although she received lower basic pay and overtime rates, she had a paid meal break, longer holidays and better sickness benefits. The issue before the Court of Appeal thus became whether each aspect of the pay package had to be compared individually, or whether the packages as a whole were to be compared. In favour of Ms Hayward's point that individual items of the contract should be compared is the actual wording of the legislation, which provides that if '*any* term of a woman's contract is or becomes less favourable to the woman than a term of a similar kind in the contract under which [the] man is employed, *that term* of the woman's contract shall be treated as so modified as not to be less favourable'.[231] On the other hand, the Court of Appeal pointed out that this approach would involve a serious risk of leap-frogging claims.

> Take the case of a man and a woman who are doing the same work, or work of equal value. The woman's salary is lower than the man's, but unlike the man she is provided with a car by her employer. On the applicant's argument, the woman is entitled to have her salary increased to the same level as the man's regardless of the extra benefit she receives in the form of a car. But the matter would not stop there. The equality provisions in s.1 of the Equal Pay Act 1970 apply to men just as much as to women: s.1(13). So, after the woman's pay had been increased to match the man's, he could make a complaint in respect of the failure of the employer to provide him with a car. Thus, by pointing out and relying on the differences in each other's contract, each would be able to obtain an improvement in his or her contractual terms to match the most favourable parts of the other's contract.[232]

The Court of Appeal therefore opted in favour of the employer's approach, pointing out that everything depends on what the Act means by 'term'. They held that the 'term' relating to pay must include all the consideration, both in money and in kind, received by the employee; 'the complainant cannot, by limiting her claim . . . elevate to the status of a term what is, in the context of the statutory comparison, only part of the relevant term'.[233]

The problem with this solution to what must be admitted is a difficulty in the working of the legislation is that it leaves far too large a discretion in the hands of the tribunal, for it is the tribunal which ultimately has to quantify the value of all the 'remuneration' benefits in the applicant's contract and that of her comparator. There is unquestionably great scope for paternalism here. The instances discussed by the Court of Appeal are relatively gender-neutral, but this will not invariably be the case; what, for example, of the situation where the woman is paid considerably less than her male comparator but her contract of employment allows her occasional time off work when her child is absent from school through illness? How in reality is the latter advantage to be quantified? There is a real risk of the sum being done to the woman's detriment, but this will be well-nigh impossible to prove. In the present writer's submission, the Court of Appeal also attached undue weight to the leap-frogging argument. Whilst it is undoubtedly true that, adopting Ms Hayward's argument, a male comparator would be entitled to claim any advantages appearing in her contract which were not also contained in his, this would be as far as the matter could go and further leap-frogging would be impossible. Whilst such claims would have an inflationary effect for a time, in the long run the legislation would encourage the negotiation of new contracts of employment with much more regard for the principle of equality of treatment and simplicity of terms.

It is sometimes suggested that s.1(3) might provide an escape from the dilemma in which the Court of Appeal found itself, in other words that it might be argued that a material factor other than sex (paid meal breaks, longer holidays and better sickness benefits) justified Ms Hayward's lower pay rates. However, again this is an undesirable course for the courts to take. The very important principle was established in *Ministry of Defence* v. *Jeremiah*[234] that sex discrimination cannot be 'bought off' by making a money payment to the victim: precisely the same principle applies here and no item with a money value (such as paid meal breaks and so on) should be permitted to 'purchase' the discrimination over pay.

Where the discrimination has been going on for some time, no payment by way of arrears of remuneration or damages can be awarded in respect of a time earlier than two years before the date on which the proceedings were instituted.[235] The practical effect of this is that the threat of a claim under the Equal Pay Act is rarely a highly efficient sanction against a recalcitrant employer. It is frequently argued that it would be otherwise if an employer could be faced with a class claim, on behalf of all his employees affected, as is the case in the USA where enormous sums by way of damages have now been awarded under the Equal Pay legislation. Equal pay, perhaps more than any other issue in the field of discrimination law, is usually in essence a group concern and it is a very serious defect in our present legislative scheme that there is really no group remedy available for it.

Claims in respect of work of equal value under s.1(2)(c) have only been possible since 1 January 1984, and no arrears of back-pay were claimable in respect of a period before this date; in other words, it was not until January 1986 that the full two years' arrears in an equal value case could be claimed. This was arguably a breach by the UK of its obligations under EEC law, since Directive 75/117,[236] which s.1(2)(c) is designed to implement, has cast an obligation on the Member States since 1976.[237] The rest of the Act has been effective since 29 December 1975. The five-year gap between the passing of the Act and its coming into effect was said to be to enable employers to make the necessary administrative and other arrangements to ensure compliance with the new legislation. A more sceptical view is that the time-lag gave them an opportunity to devise ways of by-passing its provisions.[238] The Act is not retrospective and claims to a full two years' arrears of pay could not be made until 29 December 1977.[239]

## NOTES

1. The Equal Pay Act, as originally enacted in 1970, has also been substantially amended by the Sex Discrimination Act 1975, the Equal Pay (Amendment) Regulations 1983, the Armed Forces Act 1981, the Employment Protection Act 1975, the Employment Protection (Consolidation) Act 1978 and the Wages Councils Act 1979. Unless otherwise stated, the notes in this chapter making reference to statutory sections refer to the Equal Pay Act 1970, as amended.
2. Ss.1 and 2.
3. This was the effect of ss.3, 4 and 5.
4. *R.* v. *CAC, Exp.Hy-Mac Ltd* [1979] IRLR 461. See Davies, 'The CAC and Equal Pay' (1980) *Current Legal Problems* 165. In an ironic decision, on the eve of the repeal of its jurisdiction, the Central Arbitration Committee ruled that the effect of the *Hy-Mac* decision was mitigated by EEC law: see (1987) 12 *EOR* 32.
5. Sex Discrimination Act 1986, s.6.
6. By the Sex Discrimination Act 1986, s.9(2).
7. S.77(2) of the Sex Discrimination Act 1975 provides that where the victim of the discrimination is a party to the contract, the discriminatory term is not void but unenforceable against that party, and s.77(5) provides for a county court, on application by any person 'interested in a contract to which subsection (2) applies', to make an order removing or modifying any term made unenforceable by that subsection. These provisions will not usually be of use where the discrimination is contained in a collective agreement, because the parties to the collective agreement (employer and trade union) are not themselves the victims of the discrimination.
8. Other than those specifically excepted by later sections.
9. S.1(2). The Act extends, for example, to rest allowances stipulated in the contract of employment: *Tremlett* v. *Freemans Ltd* [1976] IRLR 292, and to the right to leave the employer's premises early if that is a term of the contract: *Peake* v. *Automative Products Ltd* [1977] ICR 480 and 968.
10. See Phillips J in *Electrolux* v. *Hutchinson* [1977] ICR 252, 259.
11. *Pointon* v. *University of Sussex* [1979] IRLR 119.
12. Ibid., at p. 120.
13. S.1(13) The present chapter proceeds on the same basis.
14. S.1(1).
15. S.1(2)(a)(i), s.1(2)(b)(i) and s.1(2)(c)(i).
16. S.1(2)(a)(ii), s.1(2)(b)(ii) and s.1(2)(c)(ii).
17. S.1(1).
18. By s.1(6)(a). The definition of 'employment' is the same for the purposes of the Sex Discrimination Act 1975: see s.82(1) of that Act.
19. *Quinnen* v. *Hovells* [1984] IRLR 227. See also *Hugh-Jones* v. *St John's College, Cambridge* [1979] ICR 848; *Knight* v. *Attorney General* [1979] ICR 194; and *Tanna* v. *PO* [1981] ICR 374. Cf. *Alexander* v. *Home Office* (1987) 15 *EOR* 36 and the *Independent*, 17 February 1988.
20. *Quinnen* v. *Hovells* [1984] IRLR 227, at p. 229. Cf. *Mcnulty* v. *Greenall Whitley*

*Ltd* (19 March 1981, unreported) in which it was held in the county court that the tenancy of a brewery is not 'employment' for this purpose.

21. *Mirror Group Newspapers Ltd* v. *Gunning* [1986] 1 WLR 546.
22. Ibid., at p. 556. It is to be hoped that the gender-specific terminology adopted by the judge in no way influenced his reasoning.
23. S.2(4).
24. Including such of the territorial waters of the UK as are adjacent to Great Britain: s.1(12). The continental shelf was brought within the ambit of the legislation from November 1987 by the Sex Discrimination and Equal Pay (Offshore Employment) Order 1987 (SI 1987 No. 930) after considerable criticism from the EOC and others that important career opportunities in the offshore oil and gas industries were being denied to women. The place at which the employee's work is done should be construed by reference to what was in the contemplation of the parties at the time of the agreement, rather than where the work is actually done in practice, according to the Court of Appeal in a case on the equivalent provisions of the Race Relations Act 1976: *Deria and others* v. *General Council of British Shipping* [1986] ICR 172. Northern Ireland possesses its own separate legislation regarding equal pay and sex discrimination.
25. Sex Discrimination Act 1975, s.10(1). So, for example, the Act does not cover the case of a travel-representative, employed abroad by a British tour-operator.
26. Sex Discrimination Act 1975, s.10(2).
27. S.1(11).
28. And also from the protection of the Sex Discrimination Act 1975, see Chapter 3. See also *Haughton* v. *Olau Line (UK) Ltd* [1986] 1 CMLR 730 and the commentary thereon by Arnull in 'The Incoming Tide: Responding to *Marshall* (1987) *Public Law* 383.
29. Ss.1(8) and 1(9).
30. S.7(1). S.7(2) provides that the Secretary of State or Defence Council may refer to the Central Arbitration Committee for their advice any question as to whether a provision in such an instrument is to be regarded as making a distinction not permitted by the section.
31. EEC Directive 75/117, OJ 1975 No. L 45/19.
32. Italics supplied.
33. EEC Directive 76/207, OJ 1976 No. L 39/40.
34. For further discussion of both Directives, see Chapter 4.
35. Per Bridge LJ in *Coomes* v. *Shields (Holdings) Ltd* [1978] ICR 1159, at p. 1179.
36. *Capper Pass Ltd* v. *Lawton* [1977] ICR 83.
37. Ibid., at p. 87.
38. See also *Berrett* v. *May and Baker Ltd* [1976] IRLR 243.
39. McCrudden, 'Equal Pay for Work of Equal Value: the Equal Pay (Amendment) Regulations 1983' (1983) 12 *ILJ* 197.
40. For criticism of such an approach see Simpson, 'Equal Pay in the Court of Appeal' (1980) 43 *MLR* 209.
41. *Shields* v. *Coomes (Holdings) Ltd* [1978] ICR 1159. Bridge LJ there expressly approved of Phillips J's comments in *Capper Pass Ltd* v. *Lawton*.
42. See also *Redland Roof Tiles Ltd* v. *Harper* [1977] ICR 349; and *Dance* v. *Dorothy Perkins Ltd* [1978] ICR 760. Cf. *Sorbie* v. *Trust House Forte Hotels Ltd* [1977] ICR 55.
43. *Shields* v. *Coomes (Holdings) Ltd* [1978] ICR 1159, at p. 1169.
44. *Waddington* v. *Leicester Voluntary Service* [1977] ICR 266, at p. 269. To the same effect, see also his remarks in *Dugdale* v. *Kraft Foods Ltd* [1977] ICR 48,

especially at p. 54, and *Eaton Ltd* v. *Nuttall* [1977] ICR 272, especially at p. 276.

45. *Brodie* v. *Startrite Engineering Ltd* [1976] IRLR 101.
46. *Peskett* v. *Robinson Ltd* [1976] IRLR 134.
47. *Eaton Ltd* v. *Nuttall* [1977] ICR 272; *Capper Pass Ltd* v. *Allan* [1980] ICR 194.
48. *Waddington* v. *Leicester Voluntary Service* [1977] ICR 266; *Edmonds* v. *Computer Services Ltd* [1977] IRLR 359.
49. *De Brito* v. *Standard Chartered Bank* [1978] ICR 650.
50. In *BL Ltd* v. *Powell* [1979] IRLR 57, at p. 59.
51. *Dugdale* v. *Kraft Foods Ltd* [1977] ICR 48.
52. As to which, see Chapter 3, p. 119. Much of the protective legislation is repealed by the Sex Discrimination Act 1986, ss.7 and 8.
53. *NCB* v. *Sherwin* [1978] ICR 700.
54. Ibid.
55. Ibid., at p. 704. See also *Thomas* v. *NCB* (1987) 14 EOR 37.
56. *Maidment* v. *Cooper & Co. Ltd* [1978] ICR 1094.
57. Ibid., at p. 1099.
58. Ibid., also at p. 1099.
59. S.1(2)(a).
60. *Rice* v. *Scottish Legal Life Assurance Society* [1976] IRLR 330.
61. *Leverton* v. *Clwyd County Council* [1987] 1 WLR 65. At the time of writing, an appeal against this decision had been heard by the Court of Appeal but the judgment was not yet available.
62. Cf. the slightly wider list of relevant factors in the Irish Anti-Discrimination (Pay) Act 1974: 'skill, physical or mental effort, responsibility and working conditions'.
63. See EOC, *Sixth Annual Report* (1981). Also Simpson, 'Job Evaluation and Equal Pay' (1981) 44 *MLR* 334.
64. EOC, *Job Evaluation Schemes Free of Sex Bias* (1981; later revised). For criticism of this guide, see Rubenstein, *Equal Pay for Equal Value: the New Regulations and their Implications* (1984, Macmillan) especially Chapter 6. As to the possibility of legal challenge to a sexually discriminatory job evaluation scheme, see *infra*, p. 41 *et seq*.
65. *Eaton Ltd* v. *Nuttall* [1977] ICR 272.
66. Ibid., at p. 278.
67. *Bromley and others* v. *Quick Ltd*, *The Times*, 24 August 1987.
68. *Arnold* v. *Beecham Group Ltd* [1982] IRLR 307, following *England* v. *Bromley Council* [1978] ICR 1 and *Hebbes* v. *Rank Precision Industries* [1978] ICR 489. Cf. *Greene* v. *Broxtowe DC* [1977] IRLR 34.
69. *Arnold* v. *Beecham Group Ltd* [1982] IRLR 307, at p. 310.
70. *O'Brien* v. *Sim-Chem Ltd* [1980] IRLR 373.
71. *O'Brien* v. *Sim-Chem Ltd* [1980] IRLR 151.
72. *O'Brien* v. *Sim-Chem Ltd* [1980] IRLR 373, at pp. 374-5.
73. For the definition of 'same employment' in this context, see *supra*, p. 25 *et seq*
74. Equal Pay (Amendment) Regulations (S1 1983 No. 1794) passed by virtue of the power conferred by the European Communities Act 1972, s.2(2). S.2(4) of that Act permits delegated legislation made to implement the UK's EEC obligations to amend existing parliamentary legislation. For further discussion of the Regulations see Hepple, *Equal Pay and the Industrial Tribunals* (1984, Sweet and Maxwell); Rubenstein, *Equal Pay for Equal Value: the New Regulations and their Implications* (1984, Macmillan); McCrudden, 'Equal Pay for Work of Equal Value: the Equal Pay (Amendment) Regulations

1983' (1983) 12 *ILJ* 197; and Szyszczak, 'Pay Inequalities and Equal Value Claims' (1985) 48 *MLR* 139.

75. The evidence to support the existence of considerable sex-segregation in employment was overwhelming. The segregation was both 'horizontal' (in other words, different types of jobs being performed by men and women) and 'vertical' (the two sexes working in the same job categories but the men doing more skilled, responsible or better paid work). Hakim concluded in 1979 ('Occupational Segregation', Department of Employment Research Paper no. 9) that, though segregation existed at a national level, it was much more marked in individual establishments; for example, 18 per cent of the establishments she surveyed in 1973 did not employ men and women on the same work, which suggested that complete occupational segregation could still be found in about 1/5 of all establishments. The occupations of manager, supervisor and foreman were completely segregated (with no women at all employed in the category) in about half of all establishments, and in 4/5 of establishments skilled manual jobs were similarly completely segregated. It was also concluded that segregation was more marked in some regions than others. A survey in 1980 (conducted by McIntosh for IFF Research Ltd, 'Women at Work: a Survey of Employers' (*Employment Gazette* (November 1980) vol. 88 no. 11 p. 1142) found that only 17 per cent of jobs and 31 per cent of women were truly integrated, in the sense that not more than 75 per cent of the workforce in their job was of one sex. 45 per cent of women were found to work in totally segregated jobs and the degree to which women were excluded from senior, responsible, prestigious and better-paid jobs was 'very clear'. Particularly in the skilled manual category it was found (as Hakim) that there were few completely desegregated jobs and that half the jobs were male only. Snell, Glucklich and Povall (*Equal Pay and Opportunities* Department of Employment Research Paper no. 20 (April 1981)) found that there were groups of women in 15 of the 26 organisations they surveyed who fell outside the Equal Pay Act. In most cases this was because job segregation had ensured that there was no man doing like work with them and they were not covered by a job evaluation scheme or collective agreement. They concluded that, while the total number of women not entitled to equal pay in the organisations studied was small, the incidence of such cases was high and suggested that large numbers of women on a national scale 'may fall completely outside the terms of the Act' (p. 13). In its *Seventh Annual Report* (1982) the EOC stated: 'All the available information about women's position in the labour force points to their being concentrated in industries and occupations which are very largely female. In manual employment this concentration is increasing; 60% of all female manual workers are employed in catering, cleaning, hairdressing or other personal services compared with 46.7% in 1975. In non-manual employment 52.5% of all female workers are in clerical and related occupations compared with 58.2% in 1975. The proportion of female workers in professional and related occupations in education, welfare and health increased during this period, from 22.4% in 1975 to 26.5% in 1982. For very much more detailed analysis of the position of women in the labour market, see Sloane, *Women and Low Pay* (1980, Macmillan) and Rubenstein, *Equal Pay for Work of Equal Value* (1984, Macmillan) especially pp. 18–26.

76. Cf. Perrins, 'Equal Pay for Equal Worth?' (1981) 131 *NLJ* 1226.

77. EOC, *Fifth Annual Report* (1980).

78. EOC, *Sixth Annual Report* (1981).

79. EEC Directive 75/117, OJ No. L 45/19. See also Chapter 4, p. 199 *et seq.*

80. The UK has also ratified another international instrument, International

Labour Organisation Convention no. 100 of 1951, 165 UNTS 303. This provides that 'the principle of equal pay means equal pay for the same work or for work of equal value and the elimination of all discrimination from all aspects and conditions of employment which are related either directly or indirectly to the sex of the workers concerned'.

81. *Commission* v. *UK*: Case 61/81 [1982] 3 CMLR 284, at p. 298. See also Wallace, 'Equal Pay for Men and Women: UK's Failure to Conform to EEC Rules' (1983) 133 *NLJ* 227.

82. Ibid., at p. 299.

83. It is significant that the government relied on delegated legislation for responding to the European Court's judgment. This procedure guaranteed only 90 minutes of debate and no opportunity for amendment in Parliament.

84. Parliamentary Debates (Hansard) HL, 5 December 1983, vol. 445, col. 890. See also Clarke, 'Proposed Amendments to the Equal Pay Act 1970' (1983) 133 *NLJ* 1129.

85. For a very different suggestion as to how the UK should have acted by way of legislative response to the European Court, see Atkins, 'Equal Pay for Work of Equal Value' (1983) *Public Law*, 19. The writer there advocates the repeal of the Equal Pay Act and the amendment of the Sex Discrimination Act 1975 so as to cover discrimination over contractual terms.

86. *Pickstone and others* v. *Freemans plc* [1987] IRLR 218. At the time of writing, an appeal against this decision was pending before the House of Lords.

87. Such an argument certainly makes practical sense, since it would be extremely wasteful to engage an independent expert to determine whether the work is of equal value if the simpler alternative of like work is applicable: see *infra* for discussion of assessment by independent experts, and see also *Scott* v. *Beam* (1985) 3 *EOR* 38.

88. As to which, see Chapter 4, p. 199.

89. See *Albion Shipping Agency* v. *Arnold* [1981] IRLR 525, discussed in Chapter 4.

90. As to which, see *infra*, p. 40 *et seq*..

91. *Pickstone and others* v. *Freemans plc* [1987] IRLR 218, at p. 223.

92. This is especially ironic in view of the government's argument before the European Court that the criterion of work of equal value was too abstract to be applied by the courts. Consistently with this point, one would have expected detailed criteria for the assessment to be set out in the new legislation.

93. See further McCrudden, 'Comparable Worth: a Common Dilemma' (1986) *Yale Journal of International Law*, vol. 11, p. 396.

94. McCrudden, 'Equal Pay for Work of Equal Value: the Equal Pay (Amendments) Regulations 1983' (1983) 12 *ILJ* 197.

95. Discussed *infra*, p. 51 *et seq*.

96. In *Hayward* v. *Cammell Laird Shipbuilders Ltd* [1985] ICR 71, the jobs being compared were analysed under five factors (physical demands, environmental demands, planning and decision-making demands, skill and knowledge demands, and responsibility demands) and each demand was ranked low, moderate and high. The employer tried to attack this method as crude and imprecise, but the industrial tribunal rejected this argument and said that it would only interfere if the comparison had gone 'badly wrong'.

97. *Wells and others* v. *Smales Ltd* (1985) 2 *EOR* 24. The European Court of Justice reached the same conclusion on the basis of EEC law in *Murphy* v. *Bord Telecom Eireann* Case 157/86. Unreported at the time of writing.

98. Ibid.

99. *Brown and Royle* v. *Cearns and Brown Ltd* (1986) 6 *EOR* 27.

100. S.1(2)(c). See *supra*, p. 25 *et seq.*. for discussion of the meaning of 'in the same employment'.
101. In *Commission* v. *UK*: Case 61/81 [1982] 3 CMLR 284.
102. Ibid., at p. 298; italics supplied.
103. Ibid., at p. 299; italics again supplied.
104. Under the Irish Anti-Discrimination (Pay) Act 1974, a woman can claim equal pay with a man in the same firm or city, town or locality, even where his work and working conditions are totally different from hers. See also 'Equal Value in Ireland' (1986) 9 *EOR* 12. In the Netherlands, the comparison can be made with an employee of the opposite sex working in another undertaking but in the same business sector.
105. Cf. The Irish Anti-Discrimination (Pay) Act 1974 and Employment Equality Act 1977, under which a claim can be made by a group of employees or their union for an investigation into an equal value claim. In practice, groups of applicants who find themselves all in the same position *are* relying on the equal value legislation: see for example *Wells and others* v. *Smales Ltd* (1985) 2 *EOR* 24. The EOC also reports in its *Tenth Annual Report* (1985) that the majority of equal value applications are from groups of women who are supported by their trades unions. After the *Wells* case, the EOC reported that the TGWU estmimated that 200–300 women in the Hull area were likely to have their pay up-rated as an incidental result of the decision: *EOC News Release*, 20 May 1985.
106. Sex Discrimination Act 1986, s.6, discussed *supra*, p. 17.
107. EOC, *Response to the Draft Order to amend the Equal Pay Act 1970* (February 1983).
108. See Chapter 3. Nor is it the case with respect ot discrimination over pay on racial grounds under the Race Relations Act 1976.
109. *Meeks* v. *National Union of Agricultural and Allied Workers* [1976] IRLR 198.
110. See, in particular, the Sex Discrimination Act 1975, s.6(6) See also Chapter 3, p. 80 *et seq.*, for discussion of the meaning of 'indirect discrimination'.
111. *Shields* v. *Coomes (Holdings) Ltd* [1978] ICR 1159.
112. Ibid., at p. 1168.
113. See *supra*, p. 31.
114. *Ainsworth* v. *Glass Tubes and Components Ltd* [1977] ICR 347.
115. See, for example, Atkins, 'Equal Pay for Work for Equal Value' (1983) *Public Law*, 19. As the writer there points out, the adoption of the hypothetical man test would enable the Tribunal to tackle unfair differentials between male and female work of admittedly different values, as to which see the discussion *supra* p. 18. For an application of the 'hypothetical man' test in the USA, see *City of Washington* v. *Gunther*, 452 US 161 (1981).
116. EOC, *Fifth Annual Report* (1980).
117. EOC, *Legislating for Change? Review of the Sex Discrimination Legislation* (1986).
118. *Clwyd County Council* v. *Leverton* [1985] IRLR 197. For further discussion of discovery in anti-discrimination claims, see Chapter 3, p. 157 *et seq.*.
119. For example, see *Hayward* v. *Cammell Laird Shipbuilders Ltd* [1985] ICR 71 and *Leverton* v. *Clwyd County Council* [1987] 1 WLR 65. In *Langley and others* v. *Beecham Proprietaries*, unreported but discussed in relation to this point briefly in (1986) 6 *EOR* 7, the industrial tribunal pointed out that s.6(c) of the Interpretation Act 1978 provides that 'in any Act unless the contrary intention appears words in the singular include the plural'. However, the tribunal did warn that 'procedural means' would be used if applicants abused the system by relying on too many comparators.
120. S.2(1). The principle of issue estoppel applies to such a claim so that, unless some appreciable difference in the facts develops, a comparison once adjudi-

cated on cannot be made the subject of a further claim: *McLoughlin* v. *Gordons Ltd* [1978] ICR 561.

121.  Commission for Racial Equality, *Review of the Race Relations Act 1976: Proposals for change* (1985).

122.  This is not the case in Northern Ireland and Scotland, where discrimination cases are in practice assigned to a small group of Tribunal personnel.

123.  EOC *Legislating for change? Review of the sex discrimination legislation* (1986). See also Leonard, *Judging Inequality* (1987, Cobden Trust).

124.  Figures supplied by the Central Office on Industrial Tribunals.

125.  See Leonard, *Judging Inequality* (1987, Cobden Trust). Note in particular that Leonard found that panels with a woman member decided in the applicant's favour more often than all-male panels.

126.  Under s.75 of the Sex Discrimination Act 1975, as to which see Chapter 5, p. 273 *et seq.*. See also Leonard, *Pyrrhic Victories* (1987, HMSO), on the actual cost of proceedings to successful litigants.

127.  See Sedley, 'Equal Rights: Now You Have Them – Now You Don't' (January 1984) Legal Action, 9. In practice, even unsuccessful applicants are not required to pay the respondent's costs in industrial tribunal proceedings, unless they have acted 'frivolously, vexatiously or otherwise unreasonably'.

128.  See the White Paper, 'Building Businesses . . . Not Barriers', Cmnd. 9794 (1986). The fee would be refundable only if the claim was successful.

129.  Other than in Northern Ireland.

130.  For criticism of the structure, expertise and approach of the Employment Appeal Tribunal, see Rubenstein, 'Why the EAT gets Discrimination Law Wrong' (1986) 9 *EOR* 40. See also the very interesting analysis of the role played by the Employment Appeal Tribunal in influencing the development of anti-discrimination laws in Gregory, *Sex, Race and the Law* (1987, Sage).

131.  S.2(1).

132.  S.2(1A). The National Council for Civil Liberties has urged the repeal of this provision which they argue is unjustified and has no parallel in other employment legislation: see Scorer and Sedley, *Amending the Equality Laws* (1983, NCCL). The subsection was used in *Trico Folberth Ltd* v. *Groves* [1976] IRLR 327.

133.  S.2(2).

134.  S.2(3).

135.  Parliamentary Debates (Hansard) HC, 20 July 1983 vol. 46, cols 488 and 494, Barry Jones MP, Jo Richardson MP and Greville Janner MP.

136.  Jo Richardson MP remarked that 'it is difficult or impossible to find one's way through the negatives and double-negatives. I defy anyone, including the Minister, who appears to be no longer listening, to make any sense out of [the Regulations]', ibid., col. 494. The off-putting effect of the complexity of the Regulations, as far as would-be applicants are concerned, is hard to quantify. However, by the end of 1985, only 16 equal value cases had been decided by the industrial tribunals and 1986 saw a number of very narrow interpretations of the legislation by the higher courts, which can only have contributed further to the reluctance of would-be litigants to bring proceedings.

137.  The TUC opposed the adjudication of equal value cases by industrial tribunals, preferring that they be handled by the Central Arbitration Committee since it has experience of handling sectional claims with a regard for the wider industrial relations implications. The National Council for Civil Liberties agreed: see Scorer and Sedley, *Amending the Equality Laws* (1983).

138.  *Dennehy* v. *Sealink UK Ltd* [1987] IRLR 120.

139.  See Baroness Seear in Parliamentary Debates (Hansard) HL, 5 December

1983, vol. 445, col. 896, and Sedley, 'Equal Pay for Work of Equal Value' (April 1983) *LAG Bulletin* 52.

140. Lester, 'Unequal Pay – Unequal Justice' (1983) 133 *NLJ* 961.

141. S.2A(2). Query whether the woman is precluded from bringing an equal value claim where a job evaluation study has been carried out and has given different values to the man's and woman's jobs but has not been accepted by employer and employees. Clarke points out in 'Proposed Amendments to the Equal Pay Act 1970 – ɪɪ' (1983) 133 *NLJ* 1129) that this is technically within the wording of s.2A(2), though contrary to the spirit of the legislation. Rubenstein argues in *Equal Pay for Work of Equal Value: the New Regulations and their Implications* (1984, Macmillan), especially Chapter 6, that this provision does not cover non-analytical job evaluation schemes; the Act refers to evaluation of 'the demand made on a worker under various headings (for instance effort, skill, decision)' and, since a non-analytical evaluation contains no such assessment, it is therefore not a bar to making an equal value claim. However, this view was rejected by the Employment Appeal Tribunal in *Bromley and others* v. *Quick Ltd, The Times*, 24 August 1987, in which a non-analytical study, which could not be shown to discriminate on the ground of sex and which awarded the women concerned less pay than their male comparators, was held to preclude an equal value claim.

142. An industrial tribunal confirmed in *Neil* v. *Ford Motor Co.* [1984] IRLR 339, that the burden of proving that the scheme is discriminatory rests with the applicant. In *Langley and others* v. *Beecham Proprietaries* (unreported, but discussed in relation to this point in (1985) 4 *EOR* 45) the industrial tribunal refused to dismiss the case at this preliminary stage on the basis of a job evaluation conducted for the management by consultants, which concluded that the jobs were not of equal value; the tribunal considered the evaluation to be defective because it was based entirely on information supplied by the management and involved no contact at all with the job holders.

143. S.2A(3).

144. But see Rubenstein, 'Discriminatory Job Evaluation Schemes and the Equal Pay (Amendment) Regulations 1983' (1983) 133 *NLJ* 1021; Rubenstein there trenchantly criticises the drafting of this part of the Regulations and argues that the sub-section contains no standard other than 'justifiability' for determining whether a job evaluation scheme is sexually discriminatory. It ought, he maintains, to provide expressly that the job evaluation scheme must be shown to discriminate directly or indirectly on grounds of sex. Szyszczak in 'Pay Inequalities and Equal Value Claims' (1985) 48 *MLR* 139, comments that, whilst this formula seems to cover discrimination occurring as a result of unequal value being attached to different but comparable skills, it is not so clear whether a scheme can be challenged where a woman alleges that aspects of her skill have been overlooked in the evaluation process. See Chapter 3, p. 80 *et seq.*. for discussion of the meaning of 'indirect' discrimination.

145. EEC Directive 75/117, OJ No. L45/19.

146. S.1(5) of the Act itself permits the tribunal to 'amend' a scheme where the woman's work would have been given an equal value to that of her male comparator but for the evaluation being made on a system setting different values for men and women on the same demand under any heading. However, this blatant form of discrimination has never been in issue in a decided case. In *Greene* v. *Broxtow DC* [1977] IRLR 34, Kilner Brown J spoke of a general right to challenge a job evaluation scheme on the ground of its containing a 'fundamental error. . . . or where . . . there is a plain error on the face of the record' (at p. 35), though in *Hebbes* v. *Rank Precision Ltd* [1978]

ICR 489 he claimed that the principle he had earlier stated had been 'slightly modified . . . by recognising that there be instances where a job evaluation scheme may not have binding effect. In general, once there is a job evaluation exercise properly carried out and accepted in principle, it must govern the position' (at p. 492). In *Eaton Ltd* v. *Nuttall* [1977] ICR 272, as has been seen, Phillips J referred to 'valid' job evaluation schemes, by which he meant those 'thorough in analysis and capable of impartial application'. However, in *Arnold* v. *Beecham Group Ltd* [1982] IRLR 307, Browne-Wilkinson J expressed 'doubts as to the extent of the right to challenge the validity of a study before the industrial tribunal', although for the purposes of argument he accepted Kilner Brown J's statement in *Greene* v. *Broxtowe DC*. Even had such a challenge been allowed, there was no provision under the unamended legislation by which the woman employee could have compelled the employer to carry out another evaluation with a view to establishing equal value for her work; cf. Perrins, 'Equal Pay for Equal Worth?' (1981) *NLJ* 1226.

147. See Townshend-Smith, 'The Equal Pay (Amendment) Regulations 1983' (1984) 47 *MLR* 201.

148. Lang, 'The New Equal Pay Regulations' (March 1984) *Legal Action* 30.

149. S.2A(1).

150. S.2A(4).

151. As there are in Ireland, where the applicant simply draws up the job descriptions, makes out her arguments based on those descriptions and the equality officer then adjudicates. No formal job evaluation takes place.

152. EOC, *Response to the Draft Order to Amend the Equal Pay Act 1970* (February 1983). It is perhaps not unduly sceptical to suggest that the term 'expert' was adopted by the legislation in order to create an impression of expertise where otherwise there may be none. For criticism of the methodology so far adopted by independent experts, see Beddoe, 'Independent Experts?' (1986) 6 *EOR* 13.

153. Scorer and Sedley, *Amending the Equality Law* (1983, NCCL); Sedley, 'Equal Rights: Now You Have Them – Now You Don't'. (January 1984) Legal Action, 9; Gregory, 'Equal Pay and Sex Discrimination: Why Women are Giving Up the Fight', *Feminist Review*, no. 10 (February 1982) p. 75. Gregory, 'The Great Conciliation Fraud', *New Statesman* (3 July 1981) p. 6. Cf. Graham and Lewis, *The Role of ACAS Conciliation in Equal Pay and Sex Discrimination Cases* (1985, EOC).

154. Several commentators have suggested that a Code of Practice should be issued, perhaps by the EOC, giving guidance on methods of assessing equal value. For example, see Scorer, 'Equal Pay for Work of Equal Value' *Link*, no. 40 (Spring 1983), and Clarke, 'Proposed Amendments to the Equal Pay Act' (1983) 133 *NLJ* 1129.

155. Industrial Tribunals (Rules of Procedure) (Equal Value Amendment) Regulations. (SI 1983 No. 1807).

156. Ibid., Schedule I, Part II, paragraph 1(1). The Regulations do not specifically grant the independent expert access to the employer's premises however.

157. Ibid., paragraph 2(3).

158. This ground for challenge to the expert's report was included after criticism that, without it, the expert's report was almost sacrosanct and this did not comply with the European Court's ruling that the woman must be able to have her claim determined by judicial process: see for example Lester, 'Unequal Pay – Unequal Justice' (1983) 133 *NLJ* 961.

159. Procedure Regulations, paragraph 2(8). This occurred in *Davis* v. *Francis Shaw & Co.* unreported but discussed briefly in (1986) 9 *EOR* 2. The industrial tribunal found the expert's report to be deficient in a number of respects,

in particular, in that he had failed to take proper account of representations made to him and had failed to give any reasons for his conclusion.

160. Procedure Regulations, paragraph 2(9).
161. EEC Directive 75/117, OJ No. L 45/19.
162. Procedure Regulations, paragraph 2(10).
163. Ibid., paragraph 3(3). In *Whitmore and Alcock* v. *Frayling Furniture Ltd* (1986) 5 *EOR* 22, the applicants sought an interlocutory order from the tribunal chairman directing that their expert should be given access to the employer's premises in order that he might prepare a report on the applicants' behalf. The tribunal granted this order on reliance on Rule 8(1) of the Industrial Tribunals (Rules of Procedure) Regulations 1980, which provided: 'The tribunal shall conduct the hearing in such manner as it considers most suitable to the clarification of the issues before it, and generally to the just handling of the proceedings'. (See now Rule 8(1) of the Industrial Tribunals (Rules of Procedure) Regulations 1985.) The chairman commented that the natural interpretation of this rule would indicate that it is limited to the specific conduct of the hearing and not to matters *preliminary* to the hearing. However, he opted for a more purposive interpretation, on the ground that if the applicant is to be able to cross-examine the independent expert, then she must be granted the facilities on which to base an attack. Nevertheless, he conceded that this was a matter which might well have to be decided by a higher court. (Presumably, if the applicants' expert is granted access to the employer's premises, *a fortiori* the independent expert should be granted such access too.)
164. A 1981 survey found that 2/3 of firms took six months or more to conduct job evaluation schemes: see 'Job Evaluation: Part 1. Selecting a Method for Manual Workers', *Industrial Relations Review and Report*, no. 249 (June 1981) p. 2'.
165. Procedure Regulations, paragraph 2(5). At the time of writing, no expert had actually produced his report within the statutory six weeks.
166. Ibid., paragraph 2(6).
167. Ibid., paragraph 2(7). Differing views have been expressed on this point. Some argue that, if the tribunal disagrees with the expert's conclusion, all it can do is refuse to admit the report in evidence and commission another one. Conversely, Rubenstein, in *Equal Pay for Work of Equal Value: the New Regulations and their Implications* (1984, Macmillan), argues that the tribunal is entitled to admit the expert's report as factual evidence but reach a conclusion contrary to that of the expert. An industrial tribunal adopted this course in *Wells and Others* v. *Swales Ltd* (1985) 2 *EOR* 24, and, whilst agreeing with the factual basis of the expert's report, disagreed with his conclusion that five of the applicants were not engaged in work of equal value to that of the comparator.
168. Parliamentary Debates (Hansard) HL, 5 December 1983, vol. 445, col. 910.
169. Lang, 'The New Equal Pay Regulations' (March 1984) *Legal Action*, 30.
170. In ACAS, *Annual Report*, 1986.
171. By the time the new legislation had been in force for four years, only 12 cases had completed the full equal value procedure: see 'Equal value update' (1988) 18 *EOR* 8.
172. Equal Pay (Amendment) Regulations (S.I. 1983 No. 1794).
173. *NAAFI* v. *Varley* [1977] ICR 11.
174. Ibid., at p. 15.
175. *Rainey* v. *Greater Glasgow Health Board* [1986] 3 WLR 1017.
176. Ibid., at p. 1023.
177. Under the original draft Order, in equal value cases the employer had only

to prove that there was a material difference between the woman's case and the man's and then the burden of proof shifted to the woman. She then had to prove that the variation was in fact due to the difference in sex. However, there was so much criticism of this proposal that the final draft put the burden of proving the defence wholly on the employer.

178. *National Vulcan Insurance* v. *Wade* [1978] ICR 800, at p. 808; *Shields* v. *Coomes Holdings Ltd* [1978] ICR 1159, at p. 1171; and *Methven* v. *Cow Industries Ltd* [1980] ICR 463, at p. 466.

179. *National Vulcan Insurance* v. *Wade* [1978] ICR 800.

180. Ibid., at p. 808.

181. *Boyle* v. *Tennent Caledonian Breweries Ltd* [1978] IRLR 321.

182. Ibid., at p. 322.

183. *ARW Transformers Ltd* v. *Cupples* [1977] IRLR 228.

184. *Shields* v. *Coomes Holdings Ltd* [1978] ICR 1159.

185. Ibid., at p. 1170.

186. *Clay Cross Ltd* v. *Fletcher* [1979] ICR 1.

187. Ibid., at p. 5.

188. *Jenkins* v. *Kingsgate (Clothing Productions) Ltd (No. 2)* [1981] IRLR 388.

189. See especially *Kearns* v. *Trust House Forte* (unreported); *Handley* v. *Mono Ltd* [1978] IRLR 534; and *Durrant* v. *N. Yorks Area Health Authority* [1979] IRLR 401. This was of great practical importance since it has been estimated that about one-third of all women workers work for less than 30 hours a week and, according to the European Court of Justice in *Commission* v. *UK*: Case 61/81 [1982] 3 CMLR 284, in the UK 93 per cent of all part-timers are women. See further Khan, 'Part-time Work and Equal Pay' (November 1982) *LAG Bulletin*, 128; and also 'Part-Time Workers' (1987) 16 *EOR* 6.

190. *Jenkins* v. *Kingsgate (Clothing Productions) Ltd* Case 96/80 [1981] IRLR 228. For further discussion of the European Court's judgment in this case, see Chapter 4, p. 187.

191. See, for example, *Durrant* v. *N. Yorks Area Health Authority* [1979] IRLR 401.

192. See Chapter 3, p. 81.

193. In theory, such a position might be possible, since EEC law merely sets minimum standards and a Member State may, if it wishes, confer more extensive right on individuals. However, there would nevertheless be serious problems resulting from such an approach: see Thomson and Wooldridge, 'Equal Pay, Part-time Workers and European Law' (1982) 98 *LQR* 186; and *Albion Shipping* v. *Arnold* [1981] IRLR 525, discussed further in Chapter 4.

194. *Bilka – Kaufhaus GmbH* v. *Weber von Hartz*: Case 170/84 [1986] IRLR 317, also discussed in Chapter 4, particularly at p. 193 *et seq.*.

195. Ibid., at pp. 320–1.

196. *Rainey* v. *Greater Glasgow Health Board* [1986] 3 WLR 1017.

197. Ibid., at p. 1023.

198. Ibid., at p. 1026.

199. Ibid., see especially p. 1027.

200. See EOC *Women and Men in Britain: a Statistical Profile* (1985), particularly Part 4.

201. This issue is discussed further in the following section. It could be argued that the House of Lords' ruling in *Rainey* was inconsistent with the intention of Parliament: in expressly retaining the defence of 'a material difference between the woman's case and the man's' when the Act was amended in 1983, Parliament appeared to give legislative blessing to the 'personal equation' test for cases of like work and work rated as equivalent.

202. See, for example, Scorer and Sedley, *Amending the Equality Laws*. (1983, NCCL).
203. *Charles Early and Marriott (Witney) Ltd* v. *Smith* [1977] ICR 700. Cf. in *Sun Alliance Ltd* v. *Dudman* [1978] ICR 551, Philips J slightly modified the principle saying that 'it can *seldom* be the case that an employer can make out an answer under s.1(3) when it can be seen that the material difference put forward to justify the variation between the woman's contract and the man's contract has its roots in sex discrimination, albeit sex discrimination occurring before December 29, 1975' (at p. 557; italics supplied). See also *MOD* v. *Farthing* [1980] ICR 705; *Steel* v. *UPW* [1978] ICR 181; and *Thompson* v. *Salts of Saltaire Ltd* (1986) 8 EOR 39.
204. *NAAFI* v. *Varley* [1977] ICR 11.
205. Ibid.
206. *Clay Cross Ltd* v. *Fletcher* [1979] ICR 1.
207. *Waddington* v. *Leicester Voluntary Service* [1977] ICR 266. The logic underlying this material difference is hard to see; it appears in reality to provide an apparently respectable disguise for discriminatory rates of pay. It is probably explicable on the practical ground of seeking to minimize the repercussions of a successful equal pay claim. See also *Clark and others* v. *Bexley Health Authority* (1987) 12 EOR 37, discussed *infra*, p. 52.
208. *National Vulcan Insurance Ltd* v. *Wade* [1978] ICR 800; and *Pointon* v. *University of Sussex* [1979] IRLR 119.
209. *Methven* v. *Cow Industrial Ltd* [1980] ICR 463; and *Avon Police* v. *Emery* [1981] ICR 229.
210. See *NCB* v. *Sherwin* [1978] IRLR 122.
211. Parliamentary Debates (Hansard) HC, 20 July 1983 vol. 46, col. 486.
212. Ibid., HL, 5 December 1983, vol. 445, no. 1233, col. 925.
213. *Clay Cross* v. *Fletcher* [1979] ICR 1.
214. See for example 'Market Forces and the Equal Value Material Factor Defence' (1986) 5 *EOR* 9.
215. *Jenkins* v. *Kingsgate (Clothing Productions) Ltd* Case 96/80 [1981] IRLR 228.
216. *Jenkins* v. *Kingsgate (Clothing Productions) Ltd (No. 2)* [1981] IRLR 388, discussed *supra*, p. 47 et seq..
217. The subsection expressly states that the material factor must *not* be the difference of sex.
218. *Rainey* v. *Greater Glasgow Health Board* [1986] 3 WLR 1017, discussed *supra*, p. 48 *et seq.*.
219. *Clark and others* v. *Bexley Health Authority* (1987) 12 EOR 37.
220. *The Independent*, 5 November 1987.
221. For forceful criticism of the industrial tribunal's decision, see the comment of the editors of the Equal Opportunities Review in (1987) 12 *EOR* 37.
222. The use of this discretion was upheld by the Employment Appeal Tribunal in *Forex Neptune (Overseas) Ltd* v. *Miller* [1987] ICR 170 and *McGregor* v. *GMBATU* [1987] ICR 505. However, in the latter case, the Appeal Tribunal also said that when the 'material difference defence is that a difference in pay is genuinely due to particular experience and skills over and above the basic demands of the job, it is inappropriate for an industrial tribunal to reach a conclusion on that defence before it has had the benefit of an expert's evaluation of the jobs in question. Industrial tribunals are not equipped and were not intended to make ad hoc assessments of sophisticated job evaluation. . . . In the present case the s.1(3) defence was inextricably connected with the jobs themselves and the tribunal were wrong in law in determining it' (at p. 517).
223. Procedure Regulations 1983, paragraph 3(3).

224. As amended by the Sex Discrimination Act 1986.
225. Much of which was repealed by the Sex Discrimination Act 1986; see Chapter 3, p. 119.
226. See Chapter 6.
227. *Coyne* v. *Export Credits Guarantee Department* [1981] IRLR 51.
228. Ibid., at p. 54.
229. S.1(1).
230. *Haywood* v. *Cammell Laird Shipbuilders Ltd (No. 2)* [1987] 3 WLR 20. At the time of writing, an appeal against this decision had been heard by the House of Lords but the judgment was not yet available.
231. S.1(2)(c)(i); italics supplied.
232. *Hayward* v. *Cammell Laird Shipbuilders Ltd (No. 2)* [1987] 3 WLR 20, at p. 26.
233. Ibid., at p. 28.
234. *Ministry of Defence* v. *Jeremiah* [1979] 3 All ER 833. See Chapter 3, especially p. 77.
235. S.2(5).
236. OJ No. L45/19.
237. However, the situation was at least an improvement on the proposal under the draft Regulations that they should not come into force until 12 months after having been made.
238. Snell, Glucklich and Povall in *Equal Pay and Opportunities* Department of Employment, Research Paper no. 20, April 1981) found that in over half of the 26 organisations they surveyed, action was taken which reduced the employers' obligations under the Equal Pay Act and resulted in women receiving less benefit than they otherwise would have done. Such actions included the tightening of women's piece-work rates to offset increases in basic rates, the introduction or restructuring of grading systems so that women ended up on lower rates or grades, increased job segregation to prevent equal pay comparisons and the comparative under-grading of women in job evaluation schemes.
239. *Snoxell* v. *Vauxhall Motors Ltd* [1977] ICR 700; *De Brito* v. *Standard Chartered Bank* [1978] ICR 650.

# 3 The Sex Discrimination Act 1975

## SCOPE OF THE ACT

Like the Equal Pay Act before its recent amendment, the Sex Discrimination Act seeks to confer both individual rights of action and more broadly-based remedies in respect of discrimination. Individuals are enabled to bring claims in the industrial tribunals for redress of grievances sustained personally by them and power is also given to the EOC to initiate enforcement action where an individual claim would not be available or would be impractical or otherwise inappropriate, for example, on account of the large numbers of people involved. The present chapter will be largely devoted to the individual's claim, although some mention will be made where relevant of the EOC's powers.[1]

It has been seen that the Equal Pay Act is aimed at the elimination of discrimination from contractual terms. The Sex Discrimination Act deals in the main with extra-contractual discrimination. But although intended to be legislative bedfellows,[2] the precise relationship between the two Acts is, in fact, exceedingly complicated and this has provided one of the arguments expressed by those in favour of their repeal and the enactment of a single integrated piece of legislation.[3] The Sex Discrimination Act, as a general rule, operates whenever an employer makes a job offer to a prospective employee; if the terms that he offers are discriminatory on the ground of sex, then he contravenes the Act. However, if the offer contains provisions which would be governed by contract if the woman were to accept, then the Sex Discrimination Act does not apply to a condition concerned with the payment of money unless that term would fall to be modified, or any additional term would fall to be included, by virtue of an equality clause.[4] If the term would not be affected by an equality clause then the woman has no remedy at all under the anti-discrimination legislation. This meant, for example, in *Meeks* v. *NUAAW*,[5] that a woman complaining of indirect discrimination over pay for part-time workers had no remedy under the legislation; since her complaint related to the discriminatory offer of money, it was excluded from the scope of the Sex Discrimination Act unless it was covered by an equality clause. In fact, no equality clause operated in the circumstances because there were no men doing like work with the complainant.[6]

The legislation contains similar rules once the contract of employment is on foot. If discrimination is encountered once the woman has become an employee, then the Sex Discrimination Act applies in so far as the discrimination is concerned with extra-contractual provisions. If it is concerned with contractual provisions, then the remedy essentially lies under the Equal Pay Act: the woman cannot rely on the Sex Discrimination Act if an equality clause operates, or would have operated but for the fact that the defence under s.1(3) of the Equal Pay Act applies.[7] However, if the Equal Pay Act does not apply, the Sex Discrimination Act can be used to prohibit the discriminatory provision of benefits by the employer unless the benefit concerned consists of the payment of money and is regulated by the woman's contract of employment.[8] Here the woman is again left without a remedy, even though she may well be encountering *de facto* discrimination.

Lest the erroneous impression be created that the Sex Discrimination Act is concerned only with employment, it must at once be pointed out that employment is only one out of several fields of activity regulated by the Act; it also contains provisions outlawing discrimination in education, and in the provision of goods, facilities, services and premises.[9] The Act is not confined either merely to discrimination on the ground of sex[10] but extends also to discrimination against a married person on the ground of marital status.[11] This latter provision was successfully invoked by a waitress who was dismissed by her employer when he discovered that she had young children; since married people are more likely than unmarried ones to have children, the employer's action constituted indirect discrimination on the ground of marital status.[12] This category of unlawful discrimination is, however, narrowly defined and does not extend to discrimination against single persons (for example, divorcees) on the ground of their marital status.[13] Such discrimination ought to be outlawed, since it is equally as arbitrary and unfair in its operation as discrimination against married persons.

Unlawful marital discrimination is also confined to the context of employment and does not apply to the other activities regulated by the sex discrimination legislation. The EOC has considered[14] the possibility of extension of the proscription of marital discrimination to the fields of education, the provision of goods, facilities and services, and the disposal or management of premises; however, it has rejected the idea of such extension on the grounds that numerous exceptions would have to be made by the legislation to cover cases where marital status is, in their view, quite sensibly taken into account, for example, in relation to the allocation of appropriate housing. In reality, however, such a situation would appear not to involve discrimination on the ground of marital status at all, but rather 'discrimination' on the ground of family size or age-profile; it therefore does not fall within the ambit of the suggested extended legislative provision anyway and does not therefore detract from the argument in favour of such extension. There is, moreover, an irrefutable case for proscribing discrimination on the basis of marital status in relation to such matters as admission to education and the grant of credit facilities.

Two further defects are also evident in the marital discrimination provision made by the Sex Discrimination Act. First, it does not cover situations within the scope of the equal pay legislation. It is, therefore, quite permissible, although wholly illogical to be allowed to do so, to discriminate with respect to the terms of a person's contract of employment on account of that person's married status, although it would be illegal not to employ the person at all on that ground. Secondly, the domestic legislation may not extend as far as EEC Law requires, since Article 2(1) of the Equal Treatment Directive[15] prohibits direct and indirect discrimination on the ground of sex 'by reference in particular to marital or family status'; the inclusion of the term 'family status' seems to imply that discrimi-nation against unmarried persons on the ground, for example, of their being parents would be caught and the use of the general phrase 'marital status' would seem to extend to discrimination against the unmarried as well as those who are married. However, the wording of the Directive is admittedly obscure; the words 'by reference in particular' may indicate that marital and family status discrimination are only prohibited under EEC law where they also constitute sex discrimination, in which case of course, the Directive is actually less extensive than the Sex Discrimination Act.[16] Never-theless, despite the obscurity of the EEC drafting, it is strongly arguable from the point of view of logic and consistency that the present marital status provision in the Sex Discrimination Act requires amendment so as to ensure that it covers discrimination on the ground of any marital or family status, and so that it applies to all situations in which discrimination is proscribed either by the Sex Discrimination Act or the Equal Pay Act.[17]

The Sex Discrimination Act outlaws not only the original act of discrimination but also any subsequent victimisation. That is to say, the concept of unlawful discrimination extends to the situation where someone treats another less favourably than he treats or would treat other persons, 'in any circumstances relevant for the purposes of any provision of' the Sex Discrimination Act, on the ground that the victim has brought proceedings under the Sex Discrimination or Equal Pay Acts, that he has given evidence or information in such proceedings, that he has otherwise done anything under or by reference to the legislation, that he has made allegations in good faith of a breach of the legislation, or that he intends to do any of these things.[18]

The race relations legislation contains an identical provision and the Commission for Racial Equality (CRE) has complained [19] that in practice the section is far too narrow in two respects. First, it is arguable that its whole conceptual basis is misconceived in that the act of victimisation, to be unlawful, must fall within the framework of the anti-discrimination legislation; it does not therefore provide protection against acts which constitute harassment but do not take place in 'circumstances relevant for the purposes of any provision of' the anti-discrimination legislation.[20] A second inadequacy of the section arises from the nature of the comparison that the Tribunal is required to make in determining whether an act of victimisation has occurred. In *Kirkby* v. *MSC*,[21] where the complainant was moved to another job because he disclosed information to the local community relations council about alleged racial discrimination, the Employment Appeal Tribunal held that he had not been victimised because any disclosure of confidential information by an employee would have been treated in the same way and therefore he had not been treated less favourably than any other employee. The same approach is to be found in *Aziz* v. *Trinity Street Taxis Ltd*,[22] where the Employment Appeal Tribunal ruled that 'what has to be looked at is the reason given by the employer for the dismissal or removal and to ask whether other persons who committed an act of a similar kind would be treated in the same way or less favourably'.[23] This comparison in reality produces a very limited amount of protection for the victim's acts and certainly does not capture every situation in which the victim sustains a detriment as a result of resort to the anti-discrimination legislation. The Court of Appeal has further narrowed the scope of victimisation by holding, in *Cornelius* v. *University College of Swansea*,[24] that the victim must prove not only that she has been victimised on account of bringing legal proceedings but also that the basis for the victimisation was that those proceedings were under the anti-discrimination legislation. The CRE has recommended the redefinition of victimisation, so as to enable a person to be protected from suffering any detriment whatsoever as a result of bringing proceedings, giving evidence, making allegations or doing anything else by reference to the anti-discrimination legislation.

The EOC, however, disagrees.[25] Without explaining how it has reached this conclusion, it has stated that, on the face of it, the victimisation section 'appears able to deal with the variety of forms that victimisation can take' and therefore it recommends no change to the substance of the section. Nevertheless, it points out that three separate research projects[26] have shown that victimisation, or fear of it, are experienced by many women bringing claims under the anti-discrimination legislation; in addition, comparatively few actual cases have involved claims of victimisation. It therefore suggests procedural and administrative changes designed to relieve some of the applicant's anxiety, in particular, that all official documentation sent to the parties, and the tribunal itself at the hearing, should draw attention to the victimisation section, that in successful victimisation cases there should be a substantial prescribed minimum level of compensation and that, once the applicant has proved less favourable treatment in circumstances consistent with victimisation, a presumption of discrimination should arise requiring the respondent to prove non-victimisation grounds for that treatment.

The effective proscription of victimisation is essential to the efficacy fo the anti-discrimination legislation. Especially in the light of the *Kirby*, *Aziz* and *Cornelius* cases, the EOC appears over-optimistic about the usefulness of the present provisions. An ideal solution would be to combine the recommendations of both the CRE and EOC, and to amend both the substance of the legislative provision and the attendant procedure.[27]

As to the temporal scope of the Act, the bulk of its provisions became effective on 29 December 1975. It is not retrospective in its operation[28] but, as is the case with the Equal Pay Act 1970, the courts have held that it can be relied upon to prohibit discrimination occurring after its commencement date but which has its roots in earlier discriminatory conduct. In the words of Phillips J in *Steel* v. *Union of Post Office Workers*,[29] 'some acts of discrimination may be of a continuing nature and it would seem to us to be in accordance with the spirit of the Act if it applied as far as possible to remove the continuing effects of past discrimination'.[30]

Part I of the Act contains the statutory definition of 'discrimination' but discrimination is only rendered unlawful in the circumstances listed in Parts II to IV.[31]

## THE MEANING OF DISCRIMINATION

Dictionary definitions of the word 'discriminate' make clear that we accept two significantly different meanings for it in popular speech. The first is the neutral meaning: to differentiate or to make a choice between rivals. The second and value-laden meaning is: to make an adverse distinction or to act to the detriment of somebody. It is beyond doubt from the wording of s.1 of the Sex Discrimination Act that the legislation has adopted the second of these meanings,[32] giving to the tribunal the task of ruling on the component of adversity. This is a highly subjective area which is likely to be perceived very differently by women and by men, so that it is particularly unfortunate that the legislation should have cast this duty on a predominantly male group, that is to say, the judges and members of industrial tribunals.[33]

To import the element of adversity into the matter at this stage often also results in duplication. The Sex Discrimination Act is so designed that discrimination is made unlawful only when it occurs in certain particular factual situations.[34] Most of these situations are defined in terms conveying adversity to the victim and it makes little sense for the tribunal to have to examine this issue twice. In addition, it was argued in Chapter 1 that the identical treatment of the sexes, except where this is impossible because of their biological differences or where it is unjust because it fails to take account of the continuing effects of inequality of opportunity, is a fundamental principle underlying the legislation. The test for whether discrimination has occurred should therefore focus on whether men and women have been treated *differently*, not on whether one group has been treated worse than the other. Thus perceived, there is a basic flaw in the design of the legislation, which can only be cured by statutory amendment; the definition of discrimination requires redrafting so as to embrace all situations in which male and female are treated differently, or where the effect of conduct is for them to be treated differently.

The present s.1 defines the two forms which discrimination can take and with which the Act is concerned: direct and indirect. These are treated by the courts and tribunals as logically separate bases for a claim and the applicant has to choose which she will rely on, or whether she should rely on both in the alternative. The EEC Treaty does not make such a distinction, although it appears in EEC secondary legislation and the European Court accepts that there are various sub-species of discrimination. Occasionally, cases have failed because both types of discrimination have not been pleaded in the alternative, and the legislation ought to require the tribunal to investigate this issue more fully; if only one type of discrimination has been pleaded and that is unsuccessful, the tribunal should be obliged to consider the matter again from the perspective of the other type.[35] In particular, where a claim begins on the basis of direct discrimination, the respondent will almost invariably proffer a seemingly sex-neutral excuse for his conduct. The first task for the tribunal will be to ascertain whether this excuse is genuine, or whether it is merely a pretext for what was actually sex-motivated action. Even if the excuse turns out to be genuine (that is, the direct discrimination claim fails), the tribunal ought to be required by the legislation to investigate whether there was indirect discrimination, in other words, whether the apparently neutral excuse in fact had an unjustifiable adverse impact on women.

### Direct discrimination

Direct discrimination occurs where a person treats a woman, on the ground of her sex, less favourably than he treats or would treat a man;[36] unlike the position under the Equal Pay Act, the Sex Discrimination Act explicitly permits comparison with a theoretical, as well as an actual, man. Direct discrimination is, of course, the most obvious and blatant form that discrimination can take. The first Court of Appeal case on the Sex Discrimination Act, *Peake* v. *Automotive Products Ltd*,[37] did not bode well for a broad and purposive interpretation of this part of the legislation by the judges. The company employed some 3500 men and 400 women in a factory and allowed the women to leave work five minutes earlier than the men, apparently to avoid them being jostled in the general rush at the end of the day. A male employee[38] complained of this practice, saying that it was discrimination and unlawful under the Act. The Court of Appeal disagreed with him. They gave three basic reasons for this conclusion. First, in the words of Lord Denning MR, it would be very wrong

> if this statute were thought to obliterate the differences between men and women or to do away with the chivalry and courtesy which we expect mankind to give to womankind. The natural differences of sex must be regarded even in the interpretation of an Act of Parliament. . . . Instances were put before us in the course of argument, such as a cruise liner which employs both men and women. Would it be wrong to have a regulation 'Women and children first'? Or in the case of a factory in case of fire? As soon as such instances are considered the answer is clear. It is not discrimination for mankind to treat womankind with the courtesy and chivalry which we have been taught to believe is right conduct in our society.[39]

If generally accepted, this argument could, of course, drive a coach and horses through the Sex Discrimination Act, since all kinds of disadvantage might be excused on the basis of 'consideration for the weaker sex'.[40] It is also illustrative of the point made earlier that men's and women's perceptions of disadvantage are liable to vary radically from one another. The second reason that the Court of Appeal gave for considering that Mr Peake had not suffered discrimination was that arrangements made in the interests of safety or in the interests of good administration are not infringements of the law even though they may be more favourable to women than men. Again, this argument is extremely suspect; as will be seen, the Sex Discrimination Act boasts a plethora of exceptions. It is unlikely that further exceptions need to be implied into it, and this one, especially 'good administration', could again be expanded so as to rob the legislation of much practical effect. Thirdly, even in the event that the preceding two reasons were inadequate, the Court would nevertheless have rejected Mr Peake's claim on the principle *de minimis non curat lex;* again quoting Lord Denning MR, 'this discrimination is perfectly harmless'.[41] And, again, this excuse represents a serious threat to the utility of the Sex Discrimination Act, for who is to decide where the dividing line lies between harmful and harmless discrimination? How is its gravity to be measured, and is it the breach or the damage which has to be examined? Where the tribunal considers that no real issue is at stake, its remedy should lie in the striking out of the claim as an abuse of process; in all other cases, the words of the statute should be applied and the seriousness or otherwise of the harm inflicted reflected in the measure of damages awarded. Shaw LJ in *Peake's* case also commented specifically on the statutory definition of discrimination, pointing out that the phase used is 'discrimination against'. This, he said, 'involves an element of something which is inherently adverse or hostile to the interests of the persons of the sex which is said to be discriminated against'. And later he added: 'some acts of differentiation or discrimination are not adverse to either sex and are not designed to be so'.[42] Whilst it is undoubtedly true that this is the general meaning adopted by the legislation, s.1 contains its own test for determining the adversity required for discrimination; the effect of Shaw LJ's dictum is to try to reword that test in stronger terms.[43]

This and other parts of the *Peake* judgment were later disapproved in *Ministry of Defence* v. *Jeremiah*.[44] At a Ministry of Defence ordnance factory, male employees but not female who volunteered for overtime were required periodically to work in a process which was dusty and dirty. A male employee complained that this constituted unlawful discrimination against him and the Court of Appeal this

time held that it did. The majority held that even the fact that the
employers made an extra payment for the unpleasant work did not
exempt the situation, since the legislation does not allow an
employer to buy the right to discriminate. All the members of the
Court were agreed that Mr Jeremiah was being treated less favourably than the women and Lord Denning MR expressly disapproved
of part of the reasoning in *Peake* v. *Automotive Products Ltd*. He
explained that Mr Peake had appeared in person and the Court
was therefore not referred to some relevant parts of the legislation.
On reconsideration, he concluded that the only sound ground for
the decision was *de minimis*, and that the other grounds about
chivalry and administrative practice should no longer be relied on.[45]
Brandon LJ also disapproved of Shaw LJ's restrictive definition of
discrimination in the earlier case; he did not think it was right to
interpret the expression in quite such a forceful way and said that
the correct test was simply: were the men put under a disadvantage
by comparison with the women?

The more recent decision in *Gill and Coote* v. *El Vinos Co. Ltd*[46]
happily takes a broader line still than either of its predecessors. The
Fleet Street wine bar, El Vinos, refused to serve female customers
standing at the bar, unlike their male counterparts, and would
serve them only if they sat at a table. Holding that this constituted
unlawful discrimination,[47] all the members of the Court of Appeal
agreed that this was undoubtedly less favourable treatment of
women since they were being denied an option that they might
wish for on various grounds. Eveleigh LJ disapproved in particular
of judicial substitutions for the language of a statute, saying that it
is

> desirable to avoid looking at cases where substituted phraseology
> has been evoked, because the next step is that one goes on to
> rephrase the substituted phraseology, and on and on one goes and
> departs further and further from the approach which the statute
> indicates. Now this is not a technical statute, and, therefore, is not
> of a kind where one should or need go for the meaning of words to
> other decided cases.[48]

Furthermore, he considered that the *de minimis* doctrine was out of
place in this context; it seemed to him that it involved saying

> 'Well, she was less favourably treated but only very slightly.' I find
> it very difficult to evoke the maxim *de minimis no curat lex* in a situation
> where that which has been denied to the plaintiff is the very thing
> that Parliament seeks to provide.[49]

It is to be hoped that this clear statement marks the demise of the *de minimis* doctrine in sex discrimination law.

Direct discrimination against women is usually rationalised in terms of an assumption of some kind about the characteristics of women in general. The EOC, for example, frequently encounters the assertion by employers that women have not as much stamina as men, and that married women are not prepared to be mobile in their jobs or to work unsocial hours. It is clear from the decided cases that such general assumptions, unrelated to the circumstances and qualities of a particular individual, do constitute discrimination. An industrial tribunal has held that the assumption by a firm of estate agents that some of their clients would not deal with a woman was discriminatory.[50] Similarly, the Employment Appeal Tribunal has rejected the assumption that women with small children make unreliable employees[51] and that a wife will automatically move her place of residence to that of her husband.[52] The Court of Appeal has rejected the assumption that the husband is always the breadwinner in a marriage, and ruled that it was unlawful for a firm of travel agents to dismiss a woman employee when she married an employee of a rival firm and the possibility therefore arose of the leakage of business information from one to the other.[53]

The part played by intention in cases of direct discrimination was clarified by *R v. CRE, Ex p. Westminster City Council*,[54] which was concerned with the parallel provisions in the Race Relations Act 1976. The CRE had served a non-discrimination notice[55] on the Council in consequence of the Council's withdrawal of the appointment of a black dustman; the reason given by the Council for the withdrawal was their fear of industrial action by white dustmen if the black dustman continued with the job. It was undisputed that the Council official who withdrew the appointment was not himself motivated by racial prejudice. In proceedings to challenge the validity of the non-discrimination notice, Woolf J held in the Divisional Court that there can be discrimination on racial grounds without there being an intention to discriminate, so that the CRE was entitled to find that the Council official had acted unlawfully in withdrawing the black dustman's appointment.[56] The majority of the Court of Appeal, although not commenting specifically on this point, agreed with Woolf J. This is a very important decision because it makes it clear that a racially or sexually prejudiced motive is not a necessary constituent of direct discrimination.[57] The alternative construction would have resulted in many cases escaping the net of direct discrimination, on the basis that the reason for the discrimination was an innocent one. The CRE believes that this is such a significant point that the legislation should be amended so as to make it quite clear, without the need for reference to caselaw, that direct discrimination does not require a discriminatory motive[58] and the present author believes that precisely the same reasoning applies in the case of the Sex Discrimination Act.

Discrimination on the ground of sexual orientation is not covered by the legislation, provided that a person of the opposite sex would be treated in the same fashion.[59] Neither is all discrimination on the ground of sex covered, since the statute refers specifically to discrimination against a woman on the ground of 'her' sex; it does not extend to discrimination on the ground of somebody else's sex. This means, for example, that it is not unlawfully discriminatory to dismiss a person for refusing to carry out his or her employer's instructions to discriminate against women; such a dismissal could be said to be 'on the ground of sex', but not on the ground of the dismissed employee's sex.[60]

## Indirect discrimination[61]

Indirect discrimination occurs where a person applies to a woman a requirement or condition which he applies or would apply equally to a man but:

   (i)   which is such that the proportion of women who can comply with it is considerably smaller than the proportion of men who can comply with it and
   (ii)  which he cannot show to be justifiable irrespective of the sex of the person to whom it is applied, and
   (iii) which is to her detriment because she cannot comply with it.[62]

The situation is thus indirectly discriminatory where, for example, an employer attaches to the qualification for a job some physical element which is irrelevant to the task to be performed and which many women are unable to satisfy; an instance would be provided by an employer seeking a clerical worker, but requiring somebody capable of lifting heavy weights. In many ways, this is the more dangerous of the two forms of discrimination since it can be subtle in its operation and difficult to perceive.

Partly on account of the fact that the government of the day saw the Sex Discrimination and Race Relations Acts as logically interlinked, and that the forerunner of the 1976 Race Relations Act dealt only with direct discrimination, the original proposals for the sex discrimination legislation made no mention of indirect discrimination and it was only included after attention had been drawn to American anti-discrimination law[63] and, in particular, to the jurisprudence of the American courts.[64] Nevertheless, despite its somewhat haphazard evolution, the indirect discrimination provision constitutes one of the most significant parts of the Sex Discrimination Act. Not only is indirect discrimination factually important because it embraces a great variety of highly prevalent practices, but its inclusion in the statute represents the acceptance by the legislature of the principle discussed in Chapter 1 (especially p. 12) which underpins the whole legislative structure, namely that equality of opportunity cannot be attained unless it is recognised that society does not allow all its members to compete from an identical base. The concept of indirect discrimination recognises that men and women are subjected to very different experiences educationally, economically, culturally, psychologically and no doubt in a number of other ways. Without such a recognition, the anti-discrimination legislation would achieve little more than the reinforcement of existing differentials. But the very importance of the concept of indirect discrimination means, of course, that its definition and interpretation by the courts are crucial, and must be examined in detail.

Indirect discrimination can be either intentional or unintentional. This is really implicit in the wording of s.1(1)(b), but is anyway confirmed by s.66(3), which provides that there can be no award of damages in a case of unintentional indirect discrimination, thereby acknowledging that the category does exist.[65]

The individual constituents of indirect discrimination all merit some explanation and discussion. In what follows, mention will be made of a number of decisions made under the Race Relations Act 1976 (as well of sex discrimination cases) since its drafting is in all material respects identical in this area to that of the Sex Discrimination Act.

### 'Requirement or condition'

Indirect discrimination as presently defined involves the application to the victim of a 'requirement or condition'. The narrowness of this statutory formula was highlighted by the Court of Appeal decision in *Perera* v. *Civil Service Commission*.[66] Mr Perera, a Sri Lankan, had applied but been rejected for a post of legal assistant in the Civil Service. Candidates had to be members of the English Bar or qualified solicitors here and this requirement Mr Perera was able to satisfy. However, the selection board also took into account both personal qualities and four other factors: whether the applicant had experience in the UK, whether he had a good command of English, whether he had British nationality or intended to apply for it, and his age. These factors Mr Perera alleged to be indirectly discriminatory on the ground of race. He argued that they really amounted to the application of a requirement or condition (which it would be more difficult for a non-British person to satisfy than for a British person), since failure to satisfy the board on all four factors would be an effective bar to a candidate. The Court of Appeal would have agreed with this formulation, had Mr Perera been able to prove it. They held that what the present legislative formula demands is the application of a requirement or condition, 'a "must"; something which has to be complied with',[67] but in the circumstances it had not been demonstrated that a candidate who was unsatisfactory under the four headings but possessed excellent personal qualities would necessarily be rejected. This technical view of the legislation means that if a mere preference is expressed or applied for a particular group, but it is not invariably required, then the situation will not be within the scope of the concept of indirect discrimination. This is of critical importance to the practical efficacy of the section, and an important instance of it happening is where an employer frequently, but not always, relies on word-of-mouth recruitment. The practical outcome of such a preference can, of course, be discriminatory but yet it will not be caught by the legislation. The CRE has therefore recommended a new definition of indirect discrimination, which would embrace any policy, practice or situation which is continued, allowed or introduced and which has a significant adverse impact on a particular racial group and cannot be demonstrated to be necessary.[68] A similar amendment to the Sex Discrimination Act is vital in view of the objectives of this part of the legislation in order to remove this serious loophole and the EOC has suggested the introduction of the phrase 'practice or policy'.[69]

Provided that the requirement or condition is a necessary criterion, the fact that it appears to be a fundamental feature of the job does not prevent it from being indirectly discriminatory. This emerges from the robust decision of the Employment Appeal Tribunal in Home Office v. Holmes[70] in which a woman executive officer in the Civil Service successfully contended that the Home Office's refusal to allow her to transfer from full-time to part-time employment constituted unlawful indirect discrimination. The industrial tribunal had held that Ms Holmes's contractual duty of full-time service was a requirement or condition of her job. It was argued for the Home Office that having to work full-time was not a term of the job; it was a fundamental element of the job itself. The Employment Appeal Tribunal disagreed, saying that:

> words like 'requirement' and 'condition' are plain, clear words of wide import fully capable of including any obligation of service whether for full or part-time, and we see no basis for giving them a

restrictive interpretation in the light of the policy underlying the Act, or in the light of public policy.[71]

*'The proportion of women who can comply with it is considerably smaller than the proportion of men who can comply with it'*

In order to amount to indirect discrimination, the requirement or condition must be such that the proportion of women who can comply with it is considerably smaller than the proportion of men who can comply with it. This is another critically important part of the definition. In *Wong* v. *GLC*,[72] a race case, the Employment Appeal Tribunal appeared to take the view that this element of indirect discrimination would not be satisfied where no persons at all of the racial group in question were able to comply with the requirement or condition since nil is not a 'proportion'. However, in *Greencroft Social Club and Institute* v. *Mullen*[73] the issue arose in the context of the Sex Discrimination Act and the Employment Appeal Tribunal held that the fact that no women could comply with the requirement or condition in question was not a bar to a claim of indirect discrimination. The Tribunal stated:

> It would, in our view, run counter to the whole spirit and purpose of the Sex Discrimination legislation if a requirement or condition which otherwise fell within the definition in s.1(1)(b) because a negligible proportion of women as against men could comply with it was held to lie outside the legislation if the proportion was so negligible as to amount to no women at all.[74]

In such a situation, the dividing line between direct and indirect discrimination becomes somewhat blurred; the imposition of a requirement which no women can satisfy may well disguise direct discrimination. There is unlikely to be any advantage to the discriminator if the situation is presented as one of indirect discrimination, since the requirement will not be 'justifiable irrespective of the sex of the person to whom it is applied'.[75]

The meaning of 'considerably smaller' has unfortunately not received much consideration by the British courts and is, of course, not elucidated by the legislation itself. Waite J pointed out in the Employment Appeal Tribunal in *Kidd* v. *DRG (UK) Ltd*[76] that 'the question of how large a proportion must be before it can be called "considerable" is very much a matter of personal opinion on which views are likely to vary over a wide field.'[77] In the USA, courts accept a 'four-fifths' rule, to the effect that sufficient adverse impact will be established if there is a 20 per cent difference between the two groups being compared. The CRE considers that such a rule of thumb would make a sensible addition to the British race relations law,[78] but the EOC disagrees for the purposes of the Sex Discrimination Act, pointing out that 'the effects on women of many requirements and conditions will vary according to the point in a woman's life-cycle at which they are applied. This dynamic relationship is less likely to hold good for racial groups.'[79] At first sight, it does seem attractive to adopt the four-fifths rule, in particular, since it would eradicate some of the uncertainty associated with the proof of indirect discrimination. On balance, however, the EOC's approach is preferable in the sex discrimination field and not only for the reason put forward by that Commission; too great a concentration on statistics is undesirable from the female claimant's point of view since statistics relating to the sexes are often difficult to obtain.[80] If tribunals are encouraged to demand detailed numerical data in every case, there is a substantial risk of cases being lost which might otherwise have been won.

An even more important point in practice relates to the composition of the pools which are to be compared for this purpose. The legislation does not attempt to provide any guidance. It simply provides that the requirement or condition must be one that a considerably smaller proportion of women than of men can comply with, and it adds that, in making comparisons, the relevant circumstances of one group must not be materially different from those of the other.[81] It would be helpful if the EOC could produce some published guidelines to help applicants to construct their cases. That the choice of pools can be critical to the outcome of a case was demonstrated by *Kidd* v. *DRG (UK) Ltd*,[82] which concerned an allegation by a part-time employee, who was a married woman with two young children, that her dismissal was unlawfully discriminatory on the grounds both of sex and of marital status; the dismissal took place in pursuance of an agreement that part-time employees would be made redundant before full-timers. Ms Kidd argued that this agreement resulted in discrimination because women were less able than men, and married women less able than single women, to work full-time because of child-care responsibilities. The Employment Appeal Tribunal agreed with the industrial tribunal that the complaint failed. The Employment Appeal Tribunal ruled that the choice of pools is a question of fact for the industrial tribunal (usually to be determined at an interlocutory hearing; it might sometimes even be necessary to allow an adjournment for parties to reconsider the evidence in the light of the choice made by the tribunal); the tribunal's decision can therefore only be interfered with by an appellate court if it is found to be perverse. In this case, it had been argued for Ms Kidd that the correct pools for comparison were sections of the population as a whole: in other words, she should have succeeded on this issue if she could have proved that women in general are more often forced into part-time work than men, or that this is true of more married women than single women. The tribunal, however, chose just to look at households where there was a need to provide home care for children to an extent normally incompatible with the acceptance of full-time employment by the person providing the care. They held that, in changing social times, they were unprepared to accept without evidence that, within this section of society, fewer married than unmarried persons, or fewer women than men, could comply with a requirement to work full-time, and with this judgment the Appeal Tribunal refused to interfere.

One point clearly illustrated by the *Kidd* case is that the further the Tribunal departs from the language of the statute – which requires a comparison between the impact of the requirement on 'men' and 'women' generally – even if through the imposition of apparently relevant criteria, the more chance there is of importing discrimination into the very test for indirect discrimination. This danger was adverted to by Schiemann J in *R* v. *Secretary of State for Education, Ex p. Schaffter*.[83] He stated there that there is prima facie discrimination where,

in a situation where there is an equal number of men and women in the population, one sees a practice working in reality in such a way that many more women than men are adversely affected by it. . . . Looked at on its own, [s.1(1)(b) of the Sex Discrimination Act] would seem to indicate that what you should do is establish: firstly, the proportion of all women who can comply with the requirement – I shall call this X%; secondly, the proportion of all men who can comply with the requirement – I shall call this Y%; thirdly, compare X and Y and determine whether one is considerably smaller than the other. In most cases, both X and Y will be very small percentages, but since one is comparing X with Y the difference between 1% and 2% is no less significant than the difference between 30% and 60%. In consequence, if the pool of which the percentages are taken includes all humanity it does not matter if the practice under attack has no impact on the vast bulk of humanity. You may land up comparing two small percentages, but looked at in terms of each other rather than in terms of the whole, the difference between them is significant. However, if one . . . reduces the size of the pool under consideration to a very small size there is . . . a very real risk that you have incorporated an act of discrimination into your definition.[84]

Happily, the courts have generally adopted a benevolent construction of the phrase 'can comply'. This is particularly significant in the light of the purpose of the concept of indirect discrimination: namely, to capture those many situations where, for a great variety of reasons, women are less well-placed to compete than their male rivals. In *Price* v. *Civil Service Commission*[85] it was construed as meaning 'can in practice comply'.[86] Ms Price complained that a qualifying age range of between 17½ and 28 years for entry to the Executive Grade of the Civil Service was discriminatory against women, since many women within that age range would in practice be unable to apply because they were having children at the time. Phillips J in the Employment Appeal Tribunal said:

> In one sense it can be said that any female applicant can comply with the condition. She is not obliged to marry, or to have children, or to mind children; she may find somebody to look after them, and as a last resort she may put them into care. In this sense no doubt counsel for the Civil Service Commission is right in saying that any female applicant can comply with the condition. Such a construction appears to us to be wholly out of sympathy with the spirit and intent of the Act. . . . [Can] is a word with many shades of meaning, and we are satisfied that it should not be too narrowly – nor too broadly – construed in its context in s.1(1)(b)(i). It should not be said that a person 'can' do something merely because it is theoretically possible for him to do so: it is necessary to see whether he can do so in practice. Applying this approach to the circumstances of this case, it is relevant in determining whether women can comply with the condition to take into account the current usual social behaviour of women in this respect, as observed in practice, putting on one side behaviour and responses which are unusual or extreme.[87]

This ruling was later expressly approved by the House of Lords in *Mandla* v. *Lee*.[88]

The time at which it must be asked whether the woman 'can comply' is the time at which a detriment to her occurs.[89]

*The requirement or condition cannot be shown to be 'justifiable irrespective of the sex of the person to whom it is applied'*

The meaning of 'justifiable' is clearly vital to the effectiveness of the concept of indirect discrimination since, if established, it provides the alleged discriminator with a complete defence. It has, however, been interpreted in several significantly different ways by the courts.

In the first sex discrimination case to raise the issue directly, *Steel* v. *Union of Post Office Workers*,[90] the Employment Appeal Tribunal took a firm line. It held that a requirement could not be justified unless it was 'necessary' for some purpose of the employer. Citing the ruling of the US Supreme Court in *Griggs* v. *Duke Power Co.*[91]

that 'the touchstone is business necessity', the Employment Appeal Tribunal ruled that it is insufficient for an employer merely to demonstrate that the requirement is 'convenient' and it must be asked whether the employer can find some other and non-discriminatory method of achieving his object.[92] However, a gradual process of attrition began with *Singh* v. *Rowntree Mackintosh Ltd*,[93] a race relations case, where Lord McDonald held that although the test was 'necessity', that test must be applied 'reasonably and with common sense' and commercial factors were relevant. Then, in *Panesar* v. *Nestlé Co.*,[94] again under the Race Relations Act, Slynn J in the Employment Appeal Tribunal rejected 'necessity' and ruled instead that tribunals must look at all the circumstances of a case and then decide whether the requirement is 'right and proper' in those circumstances. This general approach was confirmed by the Court of Appeal in *Ojutiku* v. *MSC*,[95] although the *Panesar* case itself does not appear to have been cited there. The issue in *Ojutiku* was whether the Manpower Services Commission could justify a requirement that those they accepted for management courses should have previous managerial experience. It was accepted that such a requirement indirectly discriminated against coloured immigrants. The Court of Appeal held the requirement to be justifiable, unanimously rejecting the test of necessity. Kerr LJ said that 'justifiable' clearly applied a lower standard than 'necessary', and Eveleigh LJ held that 'if a person produces reasons for doing something which would be acceptable to right-thinking people as sound and tolerable reasons for so doing, then he has justified his conduct'.[96] Stephenson LJ, adopting perhaps the strictest approach, agreed with the *Singh* decision and said that in *Steel* v. *Union of Post Office Workers* Phillips J's words had been

> valuable as rejecting justification by convenience and requiring the party applying the discriminatory condition to prove it to be justifiable in all the circumstances on balancing its discriminatory effect against the discriminator's need for it. But that need is what is reasonably needed by the party who applies the condition.[97]

This formulation by the Court of Appeal left it unclear whether the test for justifiability was subjective or objective: was it sufficient to show merely that the employer considered the requirement justifiable, or would it be necessary to prove that it did actually achieve some legitimate object?

Some doubt was subsequently expressed by the Employment Appeal Tribunal as to the correctness of the Court of Appeal's view, albeit that it was accepted that that view was binding for the time being at least. The case was *Clarke and Powell* v. *Eley*[98] and, like *Kidd*

v. *DRG (UK) Ltd*,[99] it was concerned with the legality of a redundancy agreement which provided that part-time workers should be chosen for redundancy before full-time workers. All the company's part-time employees were women and it was alleged that the agreement was indirectly discriminatory on the ground of sex. Holding that it was, and that it was not justifiable, Browne-Wilkinson J expressed

> some apprehension as to the direction in which the decisions of the courts are going on this issue. To decide whether some action is 'justifiable' requires a value judgment to be made. On emotive matters such as racial or sex discrimination there is no generally accepted view as to the comparative importance of eliminating discriminatory practices on the one hand as against, for example, the profitability of a business on the other. In these circumstances, to leave the matter effectively within the unfettered decision of the many industrial tribunals throughout the country, each reflecting their own approach to the relative importance of these matters, seems to us likely to lead to widely differing decisions being reached. In our view, the law should lay down the degree of importance to be attached to eliminating indirect discrimination (which will very often be unintentional) so that industrial tribunals will know how to strike the balance between the discriminatory effect of a requirement on the one hand and the reasons urged as justification for imposing it on the other.[100]

On the facts, the industrial tribunal had taken into account that there was a need for a clearly defined redundancy selection policy, that the agreement was supported by the majority of the workers, that – since women full-time workers out-numbered the men full-time workers – the discrimination, in fact, was to the advantage of women rather than of men, that it was convenient to get rid of the part-time workers since that facilitated the closing of the evening shift, and that for part-timers to go first made it easier to arrange hours of availability for machines. Yet the tribunal nevertheless came to the conclusion that the agreement was not justifiable, and the Employment Appeal Tribunal endorsed this.[101]

Fortunately for the health of the concept of indirect discrimination, the most recent cases in this area have reverted to a more robust definition of justifiability. As in so many aspects of sex discrimination law, the lead has come from the European Court of Justice. In *Bilka-Kaufhaus* v. *Weber von Hartz*[102] that court ruled that sex discrimination over pay could only be excused by 'objectively justified factors unrelated to any discrimination on grounds of sex'. Such objective justification would only be established where the measures chosen by the employer correspond to a real need of his, are appropriate with a view to achieving this need and are 'necessary' to achieve it. An objective criterion of necessity is thus an inherent part of this test. It was seen in Chapter 2 that the House of Lords in effect adopted this ruling in the context of the Equal Pay Act in *Rainey* v. *Greater Glasgow Health Board*.[103] Lord Keith also held in that case that

> there would not appear to be any material distinction in principle between the need to demonstrate objectively justified grounds of difference for purposes of s.1(3) [of the Equal Pay Act] and the need to justify a requirement or condition under s.1(1)(b)(ii) of the Act of 1975.[104]

In other words, it appears that, in order to establish justifiability today, it must be shown to the satisfaction of the tribunal that the requirement is 'necessary' to achieve a legitimate demand of the employer. There can be no doubt that many of the old indirect discrimination cases, were they to be reheard today, would reach a different conclusion on the basis of this test.[105]

In the past, both the EOC and the CRE have argued for an amendment to the legislation, so as to substitute the word 'necessary' for 'justifiable'.[106] In the light of the recent case law, this would appear, strictly speaking, to be unnecessary but, for safety's sake and from the point of view of the clarity of the law, it would still be advisable for such an amendment to be made and for the legislation to make it clear that the test is an objective one, not satisfied merely by evidence as to the subjective intentions of the employer.

The statute requires that the discriminatory requirement or condition be justifiable irrespective of the sex of the person to whom it is applied. In the case of the Race Relations Act 1976, it must be justifiable 'irrespective of the colour, race, nationality or ethnic or national origins of the person to whom it is applied'.[107] In *Mandla* v. *Lee*,[108] the House of Lords held that this prevented the headmaster of a Christian school from objecting to the wearing of a turban by a Sikh pupil on the ground that it was an outward manifestation of a non-Christian faith. In the words of Lord Fraser of Tullybelton, 'the principal objection on which the respondent relies is that the turban is objectionable just because it is a manifestastion of the . . . appellant's ethnic origins. That is not, in my view, a justification which is admissible under paragraph (ii)'.[109] It would have been otherwise, had it been relevant and provable, if the headmaster's objection had been grounded on, for example, public health or the prohibitive cost of alternative action.

It is clear that the burden of proving justifiability lies on the respondent in the discrimination claim. This emerges from the wording of the subsection itself, which states that it is up to the respondent to 'show' that the requirement or condition can be justified. In *Home Office* v. *Holmes*[110] it was argued for the Home Office that it was self-evidently justifiable for an employer to demand full-time work rather than part-time service from his employees, since the bulk of industry in this country and most of the government service is organised on the basis of full-time work. The Employment Appeal Tribunal rejected this approach, saying:

> It seems to us that the issue whether in a particular case a requirement as to length of service was justified or not is precisely the line of inquiry that Parliament intended to entrust to the industrial tribunals by the scheme and language of the Sex Discrimination Act 1975.[111]

*The requirement or condition is 'to her detriment because she cannot comply with it'*

This part of the definition of indirect discrimination ensures that there is an actual victim of the discrimination and that the case is not a hypothetical one.[112] It has already been observed that the legislation defines discrimination in terms of adverse treatment, rather than simply differential treatment, and in the context of indirect discrimination, the element of adversity is supplied by the part of the definition which states that the requirement or condition must be to the woman's 'detriment because she cannot comply with it'. There has been little analytical case law on this part of the section but it is arguable that it is ambivalent. It might mean that the woman has to establish that her inability to comply with the requirement or condition is detrimental to her; in other words, she has to show not merely that she cannot comply with the requirement or condition, but also that this is in some way disadvantageous to her. Alternatively, and perhaps this is the more natural meaning of the words used, the statute may mean that the mere fact of her inability to comply with the requirement or condition is sufficient proof of detriment.

## Discrimination against a sub-class of women, sexual harassment and discrimination on the ground of pregnancy

An issue which presents problems is whether or not the Sex Discrimination Act applies where there is discrimination against women who possess a certain characteristic or can be said to form a sub-class: for example, women over a particular age or living in a particular area. The American courts call this the application of 'gender-plus' criteria and the problem is essentially one of causation. It has been pointed out that if gender-plus criteria are not held to be directly discriminatory, then vast gaps appear in the Sex Discrimination Act where, for instance, an employer says that he will employ any man with particular skills but only those women who have those skills and are over six feet tall; this will not constitute indirect discrimination since the criteria are not applied equally to men and women.[113] The British statute appears on its face to cover such a situation, since direct discrimination is defined as unfavourable treatment 'on the ground' of a woman's sex; this formulation would seem to extend not only to cases where the sole reason for the unfavourable treatment was the woman's sex, but also to those cases where sex formed a part of the basis for the unfavourable treatment.[114]

The problem of 'gender-plus' criteria is clearly presented in cases of sexual harassment, which is not a technical term defined by the legislation but has acquired a popular meaning and covers situations, for example, where an employer refuses to promote a particular woman unless she complies with his sexual demands. Here, the woman is being discriminated against on the ground not simply of her sex but also because she is attractive to the employer. American courts have accepted for some time that such a situation constitutes direct discrimination. For example, in 1977 the Court of Appeals for the District of Columbia Circuit applied the 'but-for' test of causation and ruled that a female employee had been unlawfully discriminated against when she was dismissed after refusing to have sexual intercourse with her supervisor. The Court of Appeals held that:

> But for her womanhood, her participation in sexual activity would never have been solicited. To say, then, that she was victimised in her employment simply because she declined the invitation is to ignore the asserted fact that she was invited only because she was a woman subordinate to the inviter in the hierarchy of agency personnel. Put another way, she became the target of her superior's sexual desires because she was a woman, and was asked to bow to his demands as the price for holding her job.[115]

Since she was harassed because she was a woman, and since a male employee would not have been harassed, the discrimination was held to be on the ground of sex.

British courts have also come to accept this analysis in gender-plus cases. For example, in *Hurley* v. *Mustoe*[116] it was accepted without argument that it was direct discrimination on the ground of sex to refuse to employ women with small children. In *Horsey* v. *Dyfed County Council*,[117] the matter was examined in rather more detail. Ms Horsey, a woman employee of the Council was refused a secondment in the London area because the Council believed that, at the end of the secondment, she would not return to work for the Council outside London. The reason for this belief was that her husband had a permanent job in London and it was assumed that Ms Horsey would remain with him. The alleged discrimination was, therefore, not on the ground of sex alone, but against women married to men with employment outside Dyfed. It was argued for the Council that the cause of the Council's decision was not sex or marital status, but doubt as to whether Ms Horsey would return. However, the Employment Appeal Tribunal rejected this line and said that there had been direct discrimination against Ms Horsey on the ground of her sex. Browne-Wilkinson J said that the expression 'discrimination on the ground of sex' does not 'only cover cases where the sole factor influencing the decision of the alleged discriminator is the sex . . . of the complainant'.[118] The strongest case to date on this issue has been *Porcelli* v. *Strathclyde Regional Council*,[119] in which the Court of Session ruled that where unfavourable conduct towards an employee (of the opposite sex) includes any significant element of a sexual nature then that constitutes direct discrimination on the ground of sex, albeit there were reasons other than the sex of the employee which precipitated the unfavourable conduct.

The problem of sexual harassment and whether or not it constitutes unlawful discrimination has been complicated for the British courts by s.5(3) of the Sex Discrimination Act. This provides that:

A comparison of the cases of persons of different sex or marital status under s.1(1) or 3(1) must be such that the relevant circumstances in the one case are the same, or not materially different in the other.

This provision led some to argue that sexual harassment cases would normally fall outside the Sex Discrimination Act: the necessary comparison could never be made because the relevant (sexual) circumstances would inevitably not be the same as between a male and female employee. The crucial question, of course, is which circumstances are 'relevant' for the purposes of a sex discrimination claim, and what is the meaning of 'materially different' in the subsection. A dangerously narrow view was taken of the type of comparison that can be made in *Turley* v. *Allders Department Stores Ltd*.[120] This concerned a woman who was dismissed from her job on account of pregnancy and who was unable to rely on the maternity provisions contained in the Employment Protection (Consolidation) Act 1978 because she had not been employed for the statutory qualifying period. She complained that the dismissal constituted unlawful discrimination under the Sex Discrimination Act. The majority of the Employment Appeal Tribunal held that it did not. Bristow J said:

> You are to look at men and women, and see that they are not treated unequally simply because they are men and women. You have to compare like with like. So, in the case of the pregnant woman there is an added difficulty. . . . Suppose that to dismiss her for pregnancy is to dismiss her on the ground of her sex. In order to see if she has been treated less favourably than a man the sense of [s.1] is that you must compare like with like, and you cannot. When she is pregnant a woman is no longer just a woman. She is a woman, as the Authorised Version accurately puts it, with child, and there is no masculine equivalent.[121]

The only woman sitting in the Tribunal, Ms P Smith, dissented and said:

> Pregnancy is a medical condition. It is a condition which applies only to women. It is a condition which will lead to a request for time off from work for the confinement. A man is in similar circumstances who is employed by the same employer and who in the course of the year will require time off for a hernia operation; to have his tonsils removed; or for some other medical reasons. The employer must not discriminate by applying different and less favourable criteria to the pregnant woman than to the man requiring time off. That is the 'like for like' comparison, not one between women who are pregnant and men who cannot become pregnant. . . . If the employer shows that the man would not be treated more favourably, then the Sex Discrimination Act would not give the women protection.[122]

The majority view in *Turley*'s case was, however, in effect rejected by the Employment Appeal Tribunal in *Hayes* v. *Malleable Working Mens' Club*.[123] Considerable sympathy was expressed there for Ms Smith's view, and the *Turley* decision was held to extend only to cases where the reason for dismissal was the actual pregnancy itself, and not a factor connected with pregnancy. Waite J stated that:

> Like Ms Smith, we have not found any difficulty in visualizing cases – for example, that of a sick male employee and a pregnant woman employee – where the circumstances, although they could never in strictness be called the same, could nevertheless be properly regarded as lacking any material difference.[124]

A major obstacle to the success of sexual harassment claims under the Sex Discrimination Act therefore seems, for the present at least, to have been removed.[125]

The *Hayes* case also represents a major breakthrough as far as pregnancy discrimination is concerned. As will be seen in Chapter 6, the Employment Protection (Consolidation) Act 1978 only protects employees against *dismissal* on the ground of pregnancy, and does not cover discrimination in relation to such matters as appointment and promotion; furthermore, it only applies where the complainant can prove a two-year qualifying period of service. Nevertheless, there would still seem to be a good case for amending the Sex Discrimination Act in this area, so as to eliminate any remaining doubt about this matter: discrimination on the ground of pregnancy should be outlawed explicitly and it should be provided that the necessary comparison should be with a member of the opposite sex placed in not materially different circumstances.

## DISCRIMINATION BY EMPLOYERS

Discrimination in the employment field is governed by Part II of the Act. Two subsections define the circumstances in which discrimination by employers is illegal. S.6(1) provides:

> It is unlawful for a person, in relation to employment[126] by him at an establishment in Great Britain,[127] to discriminate against a woman –
> (a)  in the arrangements he makes for the purpose of determining who should be offered that employment, or
> (b)  in the terms on which he offers her that employment, or
> (c)  by refusing or deliberately omitting to offer her that employment.

S.6(2) makes it unlawful

> for a person, in the case of a woman employed by him at an establishment in Great Britain, to discriminate against her –
> (a)  in the way he affords her access to opportunities for promotion, transfer or training, or to any other benefits, facilities or services, or by refusing or deliberately omitting to afford her access to them, or
> (c)  by dismissing her, or subjecting her to any other detriment.

This broad drafting would seem to cover the spectrum of relations between employer and employee or potential employee, from the moment at which candidates are sought for a post to the ending of employment. In practice, the EOC in general receives fewer inquiries in relation to promotion and training than in relation to recruitment or dismissal, but this is not surprising since in the former cases the applicant is still employed and may be concerned about possibly prejudicing future promotion prospects.

Included in the arrangements which the employer makes for the purpose of determining who should be offered a job are advertisements,[128] of both the public and the internal kind; the EOC is aware, in particular, of considerable discrimination in internal advertising. However, s.38 creates a separate head of liability in respect of discriminatory advertisements and only the EOC is enabled to bring proceedings for a breach of this section.[129] 'Advertisement' is defined broadly by s.82(1),[130] so that the relationship between s.38 and s.6(1)(a) is unclear, particularly as to when an individual complaint is permissible. Also included in the arrangements made for determining who should be offered a job are selection procedures, so that it would clearly be unlawful, for example, to set one entry examination for male candidates and a more difficult one for female candidates for the same post. In *Brennan* v. *Dewhurst Ltd*[131] the Employment Appeal Tribunal held that all that the legislation requires is that the arrangements made for the purpose of determining who should be offered a job in fact operate so as to discriminate against women; it is not necessary to show discrimination in the making of the arrangements, or that they were intended to be discriminatory.

A common area of complaint from women is questions asked at interview[132] and this was the issue in *Gates* v. *Wirral Borough Council*.[133] Ms Gates had applied for a post with the respondents as headteacher of a school for the handicapped. Among the five persons shortlisted she was the only headteacher and the only woman. At her interview she was asked a number of personal questions, which it was admitted were not asked of the male candidates. The job was given to another candidate who was less well qualified than Ms Gates and the other three applicants. The industrial tribunal held that the questions asked of Ms Gates amounted to discriminatory arrangements within the meaning of s.6(1)(a) and awarded her £200 damages.[134]

The word 'detriment', of vital significance since it is used as the residual category in s.6(2) for defining unlawful acts towards existing employees, is clearly susceptible of a range of meanings. Another value-laden term, no objective yardstick is provided by the legislation for the assessment of its content and again it is left to the judiciary to define its parameters. In *Ministry of Defence* v. *Jeremiah*,[135] Brandon LJ said: 'I do not regard the expression "subjecting to any other detriment" . . . as meaning anything more than "putting under a disadvantage" '.[136] Brightman LJ, however, demonstrated how subjective such a test can be; he said:

I do not say that the mere deprivation of choice for one sex, or
some other differentiation in their treatment, is necessarily unlawful
discrimination. The deprivation of choice, or differentiation, in the
sort of case we are considering, must be associated with a detriment.
It is possible to imagine a case where one sex has a choice but the
other does not, yet there is nevertheless no detriment to the latter
sex, that is to say, no unlawful discrimination. Railway carriages
used to have compartments marked 'Ladies only'. A lady had a
choice of travelling in an ordinary compartment or in a 'Ladies only'
compartment. A man had no such choice. In such a case a court
would conclude that there was no sensible detriment to the men
flowing from the absence of choice. A similar case might arise on
factory premises where there might be two canteens with equal
amenities, one canteen for men and women and the other for women
only. A court would conclude, other things being equal, that there
was no unlawful discrimination, though the ladies had a choice
where they ate and the men did not. . . . I think that a detriment
exists if a reasonable worker would or might take the view that the
duty was in all the circumstances to his detriment.[137]

It hardly needs to be pointed out that a more neutral connotation
of 'detriment' would encompass a restriction of choice for one sex,
since otherwise the judge has to make unwarranted assumptions,
as Brightman LJ did, about the precise wishes of all the members
of each group. In *Gill and Coote* v. *El Vinos Co. Ltd*,[138] in which it
was not necessary for the victims to prove detriment,[139] Sir Roger
Ormrod said that if Brightman LJ

had been asking himself the question whether the ladies were being
treated more favourably than the men in that situation he could only
have given one answer. If the men were standing in the corridor
when there were no seats in the rest of the train and the women
were sitting in half empty compartments, then the men were obviously being treated less favourably than the women.[140]

Clearly there is considerable scope for differences of judicial opinion
as to the meaning of detriment, and yet further scope for differences
of opinion as between male judges and female victims.

However, one potentially narrowing development as regards the
meaning of detriment was stopped by the Employment Appeal
Tribunal in *Home Office* v. *Holmes*.[141] It had been argued there that
since the Sex Discrimination Act uses the word 'detriment' in two
separate places, s.1(1)(b)(iii)[142] and s.6(2)(b), it must intend two
meanings for it; it was submitted that s.1(1)(b)(iii) employs a narrow
meaning, but that s.6(2)(b) intends a much wider construction. One
cannot, it was argued, have a double detriment composed of one

and the same disadvantage. The Tribunal rejected this approach, saying:

> We regard it as entirely consistent with the scheme and language of the Act that the same disadvantage to a woman employee may be relied on to found the detriment of incapacity under s.1 as to qualify under the broader head of detriment under s.6. That is not to say that there may not be cases in which, upon the facts, the head of detriment may turn out to be different in the one case from the other. We say only that there appears to us to be no basis for criticising a tribunal which has decided that the detriment is the same in both cases.[143]

One context in which the meaning of detriment is especially relevant is sexual harassment. Where an employer, or fellow-employee, makes compliance with sexual demands a condition for being taken into the employment in question or for being promoted or not dismissed, there is clearly a breach of s.6.[144] But what of the situation where no specific consequences in employment terms follow from the harassment but the fact of its occurrence makes the work situation unpleasant for the victim?[145] Is this a detriment within the meaning of the statute? In America, the Court of Appeals for the District of Columbia held in *Bundy* v. *Jackson* that such conduct 'illegally poisons the working environment'[146] and this principle was confirmed by the Supreme Court in *Meritor Savings Bank* v. *Vinson;*[147] the British Court of Appeal followed this lead in *De Souza* v. *Automobile Association*.[148] Rejecting the argument that a detriment would only be established where the employee was dismissed, was transferred to different employment or suffered some other tangible consequence in the employment situation, May LJ (with whom the other members of the Court of Appeal agreed) held that if the discrimination is 'such that the putative reasonable employee could justifiably complain about his or her working conditions or environment, then whether or not these were so bad as to be able to amount to constructive dismissal, or even if the employee was prepared to work on and put up with the harassment, I think this too could' amount to a detriment.[149]

Another context in which the concept of detriment could prove very important is that of job evaluation schemes. It was seen in Chapter 2, p. 41 *et seq.*, that an employee whose work is evaluated under a discriminatory scheme is enabled, notwithstanding the scheme, to claim that her work is of equal value to that of a more highly-rated male colleague. In the event that this claim fails however, she has no further redress under the equal pay legislation, even if she has established the discriminatory nature of the evaluation scheme. Rubenstein has argued that discrimination in the way the evaluation is carried out could constitute a detriment falling within the scope of the Sex Discrimination Act and thus be actionable *per se*.[150]

In 1980, the EOC drew attention to the growing problem of sex discrimination in relation to redundancy, another form which detriment may of course take.[151] In that year, approximately 18.8 per cent of the complaints referred to the Commission's Employment Section under the Sex Discrimination Act concerned redundancy. In later years, the Commission has continued to receive such complaints in abundance. In practice, in recessionary times, discrimination in respect of redundancy, of course, presents a very real threat to the female labour force; where one partner in a marriage is to be made unemployed, there is probably still considerable social pressure on employers to ensure that that one is the wife, and not the stereotypical 'male breadwinner'.

## POSITIVE ACTION

### The present situation

The term 'positive action', for which there is no statutory definition, covers a range of widely varying situations, from the redressing of discrimination and the encouragement of under-represented groups through outreach programmes, to reverse discrimination and the use of quotas.[152] Many writers and practitioners, however, draw a distinction between 'positive action' and 'positive' or 'reverse discrimination'. Rubenstein, for example, defines positive action to mean a 'measure taken to increase the likelihood that members of disadvantaged groups will have a fair chance of securing employment, training and promotion'; this he contrasts with reverse discrimination 'involving quotas, preferential hiring and standards'.[153] This convenient dichotomy will be used for the purpose of the following discussion.

The case for and against positive action and reverse discrimination is inevitably a complex one. In examining the pros and cons, it nevertheless emerges quite clearly that most of the disadvantages of such a system relate specifically to reverse discrimination, while most of the advantages are to be derived from the more neutral device of positive action.

A major strength of all forms of positive action is, as touched upon in Chapter 1, that they represent an attempt to address the problem that rivals for employment, education, housing, goods and services do not compete from an identical initial basis. Cultural background and economic and other circumstances render it very

much easier for certain groups to take advantage of the opportunities offered than for others. Hence, equality of treatment is
often far from being the equivalent of the desired aim of identicality
of opportunity. Against this it may be said that action to advantage
the disadvantaged may be contrary to the principle of achievement
by virtue of individual merit which is at the heart of the anti-
discrimination legislation. It is at this point that it becomes
important to deal with specifics and to depart from generalities.
Action taken simply to encourage the disadvantaged to take advantage of opportunities is not contrary to the merit principle, whereas
preferential selection (reverse discrimination) may indeed be so.
Even special preparation or training for disadvantaged groups
cannot truly be seen as objectionable, if it is realised that advantaged
groups are not in similar need. The difficulty for the legislature and
the legal system is to recognise and to articulate precisely what
actions fall each side of the line.

In favour of positive action it is also said that it often represents
the only effective remedy for the victims of discrimination: compensation is not what such victims are seeking but rather the benefit
which they have been denied on discriminatory grounds. This argument is frequently voiced in favour of quotas and preferential selection. However, it is unconvincing when taken to this extreme, since
it provides too crude a remedy from the individual's point of view.
It produces statistical redress for the disadvantaged group as a
whole, but it may well do little for the plight of the individual
victim and, furthermore, it may be carried out at the expense of
the advantaged, but in no way blameworthy, group. It can also be
argued that positive action schemes have the effect of widening the
pool of potential employees and so can result in a better-chosen and
more effective workforce. As against this are ranged the undoubted
obstacles that any such scheme necessarily relies on group categ-
orisation and that this heightens the population's awareness of
such divisions and even provides support for those minded to
argue that members of the disadvantaged group would be unable,
without extra help, to reach the required level of attainment. Again,
such arguments apply with much greater force to measures of
reverse discrimination than to positive action schemes falling short
of such discrimination.

The most compelling argument of all in favour of positive action
is that it enables the disadvantaged to penetrate into the establishment more quickly than would otherwise be the case, with the
result that, once in positions of status and influence, they are far
better able to alter practices, expectations and attitudes, and also
they provide role models for other members of the disadvantaged
group to emulate. Positive action, in other words, is the law's most

powerful antidote to gender stereotyping. As before, this argument is far more persuasive when not taken to the extreme of reverse discrimination. If quotas and preferential selection are used, the results are likely to be counter-productive, since the achievements of those selected will be down-graded. This is much less likely to be the case where measures, such as the encouragement of applications from the disadvantaged and the use of monitoring and targets, are relied upon to produce the desired changes.

The present legislation permits a small measure of positive action, but disallows most forms of reverse discrimination.[154] In particular, s.48 of the Sex Discrimination Act provides that the Act is not to render unlawful

> any act done by an employer in relation to particular work in his employment, being an act done in, or in connection with – (a) affording his female employees only, or his male employees only, access to facilities for training which would help to fit them for that work, or (b) encouraging women only, or men only, to take advantage of opportunities for doing that work, – where at any time within the twelve months immediately preceding the doing of the act there were no persons of the sex in question among those doing that work or the number of persons of that sex doing the work was comparatively small.

The narrowness of many aspects of this section should be highlighted. In particular, an employer may only provide special training facilities under it for women if those women are already his existing employees. In addition, he can only 'encourage' women to take advantage of opportunities to do a particular type of work and may not lawfully operate any preference system at the point of selection. It is not enough for the employer to show that there are very few women in his enterprise taken overall; he must show that there are very few women employed in relation to 'particular work', in other words, in specific jobs. And there is, of course, no indication in the statute of what is meant by 'comparatively small'. The EOC, in its *Code of Practice*[155] gives examples of the limited forms that positive action schemes can take under s.48:

> Employers may wish to consider positive measure such as: (a) training their own employees (male or female) for work which is traditionally the preserve of the other sex, for example, training women for skilled manual or technical work: (b) positive encouragement to women to apply for management posts – special courses may be needed; (c) advertisements which encourage applications from the minority sex, but make it clear that selection will be on merit without reference to sex; (d) notifying job agencies, as part of

a Positive Action Programme that they wish to encourage members of one sex to apply for vacancies, where few or no members of that sex are doing the work in question. In these circumstances, job agencies should tell both men and women about the posts and, in addition, let the under-represented sex know that applications from them are particularly welcome. Withholding information from one sex in an attempt to encourage applications from the opposite sex would be unlawful.

S.47 of the Sex Discrimination Act[156] also allows certain forms of positive action; it provides that the Act does not render unlawful

any act done in relation to particular work by any person in, or in connection with, (a) affording women only, or men only, access to facilities for training which would help to fit them for that work, or (b) encouraging women only, or men only, to take advantage of opportunities for doing that work, – where it reasonably appears to that person that at any time within the twelve months immediately preceding the doing of the act there were no persons of the sex in question doing that work in Great Britain, or the number of persons of that sex doing the work in Great Britain was comparatively small.[157]

However, this section does not apply in relation to any discrimination which is unlawful under s.6[158] so that, for example, employers cannot use it to provide single-sex training for their existing employees.

Sections 47 and 48 have to be read in conjunction with one another if they are to provide any meaningful possibilities from the point of view of employers. Provided that the statutorily defined imbalance in the workforce can be established, these provisions enable an employer to provide single-sex training for existing employees (s.48), or for non-employees (s.47); thereafter, the employer appears to be able to rely on s.48 to encourage applications from those whom he has trained, an essential feature if such a scheme is to hold any economic attraction for the employer. One important situation which remains unclear, however, is where the employer wishes to provide training and employment simultaneously in particular apprenticeships. This is an important area because the exclusion of women from apprenticeships in many industries is a major cause of job segregation.[159] However, it appears to fall foul of the wording of both sections; s.48 cannot apply because the applicant is not yet an employee, and s.47 is excluded since the arrangement would constitute a breach by the employer of s.6.

Provision is also made with respect to trades unions, employers' organisations and other trade and professional organisations. They may lawfully afford female members of the organisation only access to facilities for training which would help to fit them for holding a post in the organisation, or encourage female members only to take advantage of opportunities for holding such posts, provided that during the preceding 12 months there were no, or a comparatively small number of, women holding such posts in the organisation.[160] They may also encourage women to become members of the organisation[161] and reserve a minimum number of seats for women on elective bodies of the organisation.[162]

Positive action schemes have been utilised far more widely in the USA than in this country; there have been three ways in which they have been introduced there. First, a series of Executive Orders were issued by the President during the late 1960s and early 1970s; these now forbid all government departments and all employers with contracts with the government worth more than $50,000 from discriminating against women and ethnic minorities, and they spell out in detail what is required of employers. In particular, employers with more than 50 employees are required by the Orders to analyse their workforce according to race and sex, analyse major job classifications within their organisation and compare the numbers of women and minorities employed in them with the local labour pool, and if the figures compare unfavourably then the employer has to draw up an affirmative action plan to correct the deficiencies. The plan has to include goals for numbers of women and minorities to be brought into the organisation, and timetables for the attainment of those goals. The Equal Employment Opportunities Commission (EEOC) in turn produced guidelines for the achievement of goals and timetables, and the employer has either to show that he has achieved his goals and timetables or else that he has made a 'good faith effort' to do so, by which is meant that he must be able to show that he has adhered to the EEOC guidelines. If he fails to show either of these things then his contract may be withdrawn. The Office of Federal Contract Compliance Programs reviews about 5000 companies a year. A review takes place pre-contractually if the contract is worth more than $1 million, and a review may also take place if complaints have been received about the company or if analysis of the returns made by the company shows a significant imbalance in the workforce.

The second way in which positive action programmes have come into being in the USA is under the Civil Rights Act of 1964, which provides that the courts can impose such programmes as a requirement to remedy sex and race discrimination. Thirdly, the Equal Employment Act 1972 empowers the EEOC to include a positive action programme as part of a negotiated settlement agreed before the trial of a discrimination case. This last method is attractive to respondents in that it involves no finding of unlawful discrimination by them and in fact has been the source of most positive action schemes in the States.[163]

The permissible scope in law of positive action programmes has been questioned on several important occasions before the American courts,[164] but it now seems to be established that positive discrimination, even in the form of quotas, is permissible provided that it is embarked on in order to remedy the effects of past discrimination and that it ceases as soon as those effects have been remedied.

A number of local authorities in Great Britain in recent years have set up positive action programmes, based to a large extent upon the American system of contract compliance.[165] In doing so, the authorities have relied upon s.71 of the Race Relations Act 1976, which provides that

> it shall be the duty of every local authority to make appropriate arrangements with a view to securing that their various functions are carried out with due regard to the need (a) to eliminate unlawful discrimination; and (b) to promote equality of opportunity, and good relations, between persons of different racial groups.

Foremost among the local authority schemes was that begun by the Greater London Council (GLC), and later taken over by the Inner London Education Authority (ILEA), itself now under threat of abolition. The policy came into being through the GLC revising the equal opportunities clause in its Code of Practice on Tenders and Contracts so as to require all suppliers and contractors on the Council's 'approved list'[166] to agree to comply with the Sex Discrimination and Race Relations Acts, as well as the Disabled Persons (Employment) Act 1944, and also to provide such information as might be demanded so as to enable the Council to satisfy itself of the firm's compliance with those Acts. All organisations providing goods and services are required to promise to take all reasonable practical steps to ensure that there is the widest possible response from all sections of the community to employment opportunities within the company, that no job applicant or employee receives less favourable treatment than others on grounds which are not job-related, that all employees are treated fairly and equally with respect to employment opportunities, that there is progress towards a fair representation of women and ethnic minorities at all levels throughout the workforce, and that appropriate arrangements are made to review regularly and evaluate the company's progress in achieving equal opportunities. Unlike the American system, organisations are usually reviewed when they seek to be placed on the approved list, which has the practical advantage of not presenting an obstacle in terms of timing at the point when the contract is being agreed. If an organisation is found not to be in compliance, the ultimate sanction is for it not to be placed on the approved list or, if the contract is already on foot, for the Authority to treat it as terminated through breach.

The legality of such schemes has not been ruled on directly in the British courts. However, *Wheeler* v. *Leicester City Council*[167] provided indirect support for measures of positive action falling short of reverse discrimination in the field of race relations pursuant to s.71 of the Race Relations Act. Three members of Leicester Football Club accepted an invitation to play rugby in South Africa. Leicester City Council asked the Club a series of questions about this situation, in particular, whether they would press their players to withdraw from the tour. The Club replied by saying that it condemned apartheid but recognised that there were legitimate differences of opinion as to how it might be eradicated. The Club also pointed out that it had sent the players involved a memorandum from opponents of the tour and asked them to give it serious consideration. Leicester City Council decided that this response was insufficient and suspended the Club from using a Council-owned playing ground for training for 12 months. The Club sought judicial review of this decision and the House of Lords granted it *certiorari*. The House accepted that s.71 of the Race Relations Act was not restricted to the internal workings of local authorities and that it did empower them to use any of their statutory powers to punish those breaching the Race Relations Act. However, there was no such breach here and, in the words of Lord Templeman,

> a private individual or a private organisation cannot be obliged to display zeal in the pursuit of an object sought by a public authority and cannot be obliged to publish views dictated by a public authority. The club having committed no wrong, the Council could not use their statutory powers in the management of their property or any other statutory powers in order to punish the club.[168]

It follows that the Council's position would have been otherwise if the Club had been in breach of the Race Relations Act and that local authorities are acting *intra vires* in refusing to enter into contracts where the other party to the contract is guilty of such a breach. This reasoning would not, however, apply in the context of a breach of the Sex Discrimination Act, since this casts no duty on local authorities which is equivalent to s.71 of the Race Relations Act, so that similar action in relation to sex discrimination might be the subject of judicial review.

*Hughes* v. *London Borough of Hackney*[169] made it clear that local authority positive action schemes must stop short of reverse discrimination. The local authority in that case had tried to operate a policy of appointing gardening apprentices only from ethnic minorities, since members of ethnic minorities were very scarce in the parks department. The industrial tribunal held however that, whilst the authority could lawfully encourage applications from members of under-represented ethnic minorities, they could not prefer such candidates on grounds of their race at the point of selection.

However, local authority contract compliance schemes now appear to provide a particularly unpromising basis for positive action schemes, especially in the field of sex discrimination. The Local Government Bill, before Parliament at the time of writing, will prevent local authorities from considering 'non-commercial' matters in relation to their contracts. The only relic of their old powers will be that they will be permitted to take account of unlawful racial discrimination, though not the need to promote equality of opportunity, pursuant to s.71 of the Race Relations Act. The Bill makes no corresponding mention of unlawful sex discrimination, so that any attempt to scrutinise a contractor's behaviour in this respect will henceforth certainly be ultra vires.

## The possibilities for future development

It has been seen that there are strong arguments for the legislation to endorse a variety of forms of positive action, but in general to reject the use of reverse discrimination. It seems clear that the present statutory framework could, by means of relatively small amendments, be modified so as to encourage, and even in some circumstances mandate, far greater use of positive action schemes. First, sections 47 and 48 should be re-drafted, with the use of examples, so as to illustrate far more clearly than at present what forms of action they authorise. Statutory guidance is necessary in particular as to the meaning of 'comparatively small' and 'particular work'. Since the amendment of s.47[170] the two sections taken together hold quite a bit of potential, but this is far from apparent on a first reading of them and their relationship requires statutory clarification. In particular, the position with respect to apprenticeships needs elucidation. The statute should specifically permit the discriminatory offer of apprenticeships where a serious historical imbalance can be demonstrated. In addition, the EOC's *Code of Practice* urgently requires updating, so as to provide a colloquial explanation of the legislative provisions.

The question also arises as to whether sections 47 and 48 need further extension, so as to allow for other forms of positive action, in particular, the preferential selection of employees. The CRE has argued that an employer should be entitled, where there is under-representation of a particular racial group in the workforce, to carry out a policy of preferring a member of that group for employment in the narrowly confined situation where competing applicants are equally well qualified.[171] The EOC disagrees in the context of sex discrimination[172] and, on balance, the EOC's view is preferable. Preferential selection under these circumstances is likely to be coun-ter-productive. In addition, the chief value to be derived from these sections is really that they provide legislative approval for the *moni-toring* of workforces. It is unrealistic to believe that such voluntary measures are going to be relied on in large number of cases. The real potential of positive action schemes is to be found where they are backed by an effective sanction.

A second essential amendment is, therefore, to allow the courts and tribunals to order the implementation of a positive action programme, which could be monitored by the EOC, where they had found evidence of past discrimination within an organisation during the course of hearing an individual complaint. The legis-lation should indicate the essential elements of such a programme, in particular goals, timetables and monitoring facilities within the organisation itself. The organisation should be required to prove that it had achieved its goals within the prescribed time, or else that it had made a good faith effort to do so. If unable to show either, the EOC should be empowered to bring it back before the court or tribunal, which would be able to impose substantial fines. Were such a remedy specifically included in the Act, such programmes might also be expected to emerge in pre-trial settlements.[173]

A third device which would be extremely effective would be the adoption by central government of a system of contract compliance.[174] Such a programme should be extended from simply contracts to all forms of governmental grants and loans since the logic behind the programme is that no public money should be used to support inequality of opportunity. The great advantage of such a scheme lies, of course, in its coercive nature. It would also have a substantial public 'consciousness-raising' effect and would make more sense in practice than a wide variety of local schemes, all imposing somewhat different requirements. The legislation should expressly impose an obligation on central governmental depart-ments to exercise their powers with due regard to the necessity to eliminate sex discrimination and to provide equality of opportunity to all persons irrespective of sex. For the avoidance of doubt, the details of the system should be set out expressly in the legislation; in particular, all central government departments and all persons and bodies contracting with them or receiving grants or loans from them should be required to analyse their workforces and their major job categories according to sex, and compare these figures with the local labour pool. If the comparison were to prove unfavourable, then the body concerned should be required to draw up an affirmative action plan containing goals and timetables. Again, the organisation concerned should be required to show either that it had achieved its goals and timetables, or else that it had made a good faith effort to do so.

The EOC has also suggested[175] that a section equivalent to s.71 of the Race Relations Act 1976 should be imported into the Sex Discrimination Act. This would require all local authorities, in the performance of their functions, to pay due regard to the need to eliminate unlawful sex discrimination and to promote equality of opportunity irrespective of sex. Such a reform would represent a welcome legislative statement of respect for the principle of non-discrimination on the ground of sex but would, if the Local Government Bill is enacted in its present form, not provide a sufficient basis for local authority contract compliance schemes to include sex discrimination as a ground for refusal to contract with a particular organisation; still less would it enable a local authority to take the promotion of equality of opportunity irrespective of sex into account in deciding on its contractual relationships.

## DEFENCES AVAILABLE TO EMPLOYERS

That certain defences must be available to the respondent to a claim of sex discrimination is undeniable. His prime argument by way of defence will be that the conduct complained of was not grounded on sex, but on some other and innocent explanation. However, in addition to this essentially causation-type defence, the legislation also recognises a band of situations in which the sex of the employee can be relevant. As was indicated in Chapter 1, the only completely unobjectionable such situation is where the biology of a woman genuinely renders her unable to do the job in question or necessitates that she be treated in some way different from her male colleagues. The Sex Discrimination Act, however, also includes many more controversial cases in which social or cultural values are called into play. In many of these instances, it will be seen that the Act appears to create a wider defence than is really necessary and thus to undermine the principle of equality.

### Provision in relation to death or retirement

Until recently, the anti-discrimination legislation contained an extremely broad exception in relation to death or retirement. The rationale for this exception would appear to be two-fold: first, on average, women seem to live longer than men and therefore represent a different actuarial value *vis-à-vis* pension schemes; and, secondly, the state pensionable age is (unfortunately) different for men and women and this has a knock-on effect into other forms of retirement provision. S.6(1A)(b) of the Equal Pay Act provided that an equality clause was not to operate 'in relation to terms related to death or retirement, or to any provision made in connection with death or retirement'. Similarly, s.6(4) of the Sex Discrimination Act stated that ss.6(1)(b) and 6(2)[176] did not apply to 'provision in relation to death or retirement'. The only concession made to the principle of non-discrimination in this area was that there had to be 'equal access' to occupational pension schemes:[177] membership of such schemes was to be open to men and women on the same terms as to qualifying age and length of service and also as to whether membership was voluntary or obligatory.[178]

It was not long, however, before allegations began to be made that the wide exceptions for death or retirement were contrary to EEC law. In two cases in particular the EEC provisions were invoked successfully, in situations which would have appeared to be exempt under domestic law alone. The first, *Worringham* v. *Lloyds Bank*, concerned the Bank's separate pension arrangements for male and female employees. Under each scheme, the employee had to have worked for five years to qualify and the benefits were largely identical. Both schemes required that employees contribute 5 per cent of their salary but, whereas this applied to men as soon as they joined the scheme, it only applied to women from the age of 25.[179] Essentially, two forms of discrimination resulted. The first was related to the means the Bank adopted to ensure that its employees enjoyed parity in take-home pay with the employees of the other clearing banks; the pension schemes of these other banks were non-contributory, so Lloyds added 5 per cent to the national pay scales in respect of its employees who were required to contribute. In other words, for employees under 25, the gross pay of the men was 5 per cent higher than that of the women. Although net pay was not affected, the men gained an indirect advantage when applying for mortgages or other credit facilities which depended on gross pay. The second difference between the treatment of the two sexes occurred in the case of employees who left the Bank after less than five years' service. Not qualifying for any benefits under the Lloyds scheme, such employees might have their accrued pension rights transferred to the scheme of a new employer but more usually opted for a refund of their contributions. But where the employee's service comprised service under the age of 25 then only the men received anything: they were entitled to the value of the contributions paid in their name out of the extra 5 per cent salary. When Ms Worringham left the Bank under the age of 25, she received nothing since, of course, no contribution had been paid in her name. She complained of unlawful discrimination to an industrial tribunal.[180] She argued that she was engaged on 'like work' with her male colleagues and claimed equal pay in relation to the 5 per cent addition to the men's wages. The tribunal dismissed the claim on the basis of the pensions exclusion in the Equal Pay Act, saying that there was a direct and inter-related causal connection between the salary scales and the pension scheme and, therefore, that the additional salary payable to the men was made by way of provision in connection with death or retirement.

The Employment Appeal Tribunal disagreed.[181] They held that terms in a woman's contract must, under the Equal Pay Act, be compared with terms of the same kind in a man's contract. Terms relating to pay are distinct from terms relating to pensions, and the pensions exclusion covers only terms which relate to pensions. So, if the Bank had introduced a separate term into the contract of employment dealing with pensions, and that term had produced inequality but not a differential in gross pay, an equality clause would not have applied. However, as it was, there was inequality in the terms as to gross pay and so the equality clause was not excluded.

The Appeal Tribunal's decision was, however, soon undermined. In a trio of cases heard together, *Roberts* v. *Cleveland Area Health Authority*, *Garland* v. *British Rail Engineering Ltd* and *Turton* v. *MacGregor Wallcoverings Ltd*,[182] the Court of Appeal ruled that the parallel exclusion in the Sex Discrimination Act was to be given a broad construction: the words 'provision in relation to death or retirement' should be taken to mean simply provision 'about' death or retirement. Counsel for Ms Woringham then conceded that the pensions exclusion in the Equal Pay Act must be given the same construction and it thus extended to the arrangements made by Lloyds. So, in the Court of Appeal, the focus of the case switched to EEC law and, after a preliminary ruling from the European Court of Justice, Ms Worringham went on to win her case on this basis: the European Court ruled that the extra 5 per cent paid by Lloyds to contributing employees fell within the meaning of 'pay' in Article 119 of the EEC Treaty,[183] since it was included in the employee's gross salary.[184]

The issue next arose after *Garland* v. *British Rail Engineering Ltd* had been referred by the House of Lords to the European Court. A woman employee of British Rail complained that the practice of extending concessionary travel facilities (which had been enjoyed during employment) to the families of retired male employees but not retired female employees was unlawfully discriminatory. The facilities were not governed by the contract of employment but it was found as a fact that employees could legitimately expect them and it would have been difficult in practice for British Rail to withdraw them unilaterally without the agreement of the relevant unions. The question was, of course, whether the situation fell within the exemption conferred by s.6(4) of the Sex Discrimination Act. It was only when the case reached the House of Lords that the possible relevance of EEC law was suggested. The European Court ruled that this situation fell within the principle of equal pay for equal work, as laid down by Article 119 of the Treaty, and the House of Lords was then constrained to interpret the domestic legislation so as to make it conform with this result. The Employment Appeal Tribunal had held[185] that the words of s.6(4) ought not to be construed so widely as to include a privilege that had existed during employment and was allowed by the employer to continue after retirement, and with this conclusion the House of Lords in the end unanimously concurred.[186]

The Appeal Tribunal's view that the exemption ought to be given a restrictive construction thus received the blessing of the highest judicial authority, but the saga then took a curious twist. *Barber* v. *Guardian Royal Exchange Assurance Group* and *Roberts* v. *Tate and Lyle Ltd*[187] both concerned early retirement under company pension schemes. In *Roberts*, early retirement was offered alike to men and women of 55 and over; 55 was ten years before the normal retiring age in the case of a man, but only five years in the case of a woman. Ms Roberts was 53 and claimed that she ought to have been offered early retirement since she was within ten years of her normal age of retirement and this is how a comparable man would have been treated. *Barber* represented the converse situation; male employees were offered early retirement at 55 and female employees at 50, that is, in each case ten years before the normal date of retirement. Mr Barber was 52 and claimed to have been unlawfully discriminated against because a woman of his age would have been able to take early retirement. Ms Roberts of course argued that the relevant circumstance[188] to take into account for the purpose of seeing whether there was discrimination was age off retirement, and Mr Barber argued that it was actual age. The Employment Appeal Tribunal found that it was impossible to choose between these two tests but anyway held that both situations were excluded from the operation of the Act by s.6(4). Commenting on the state of the authorities in this area, Browne-Wilkinson J said that he was in some doubt as to the impact of the House of Lords' decision in *Garland* v. *British Rail Engineering Ltd* on the earlier cases in which the Court of Appeal had ruled that a broad view must be taken of s.6(4). In particular, although the Court of Appeal's decision in *Garland* itself was clearly over-ruled, the House of Lords did not even comment on the Court of Appeal's words in relation to *Roberts* v. *Cleveland Area Health Authority* nor *Turton* v. *MacGregor Wallcoverings Ltd*. He went on:

> There is nothing in the speeches in the House of Lords disapproving the general approach by the Court of Appeal. . . . However, we do not find it necessary to reach any concluded view on this point since on any view the decision of this Appeal Tribunal in the *Garland* case was approved by the House of Lords. Phillips J had said this: 'What, as it seems to us, has to be looked for is to see whether what is being done is part and parcel of the employer's system of catering for retirement, or whether, as here, the case is merely one where a privilege has existed during employment and has been allowed to continue after retirement.'[189]

Applying that test, the severance terms were part and parcel of the employers' system of catering for retirement and were therefore within s.6(4). In reaching this conclusion, the Employment Appeal Tribunal argued that the whole rationale of s.6(4) was such that it must be given a broad construction.

> Parliament, in enacting the 1975 Act, was seeking to eliminate all discrimination between men and women. However, it was faced by a widespread and inherently discriminatory practice deeply embedded in the social organisation of the country, namely the differential in retirement ages between men and women. This differential treatment was blatantly discriminatory. However, the effect of such discriminatory practice percolated throughout society. State pensions reflected the differential; the vast majority of occupational pension schemes reflected the differential; normal ages of retirement maintained the differential. Accordingly, unless all this was to be swept away, the Act had to exclude claims arising out of this inherently discriminatory practice. For this reason s.6(4) appeared in the Act. It was not sufficient for Parliament simply to legislate that benefits payable 'on or because of' retirement should be excluded. It was necessary to exclude any complaint based on the existence of contractual terms dealing with retirement since such terms would necessarily be linked to the differential in retirement ages. Thus, under s.6(1)(b) of the Act, an employee can complain of discrimination in the terms of his employment. A term that a woman employee should retire at 60 or that the rights under the pension scheme should differentiate

as between men and women would, in the absence of s.6(4), be discriminatory and actionable. Accordingly, it seems to us inescapable that the words 'provision relating to' apply not only to the benefits receivable on retirement but to the terms of access to such benefits and the circumstances under which the benefit is payable. Moreover, the mischief aimed at by s.6(4) requires that consequential provisions (linked directly or indirectly to the differential retirement age) have also to be excluded. Therefore, even if we are not bound by the decision, we agree with the basic approach reflected in the Court of Appeal decisions that the words have to be widely construed.[190]

The same reasoning would of course seem to apply to the exception contained in the Equal Pay Act.

The relationship between EEC law and the exception for death and retirement was thus extremely unclear. In particular, the extent to which pension provision was covered by the EEC provisions was highly speculative.[191] The situation was further complicated by the European Court's decision in *Burton* v. *British Railways Board*,[192] to the effect that different qualifying ages for men and women for access to a voluntary redundancy scheme were permissible, since the ages were linked to those stipulated in the state pension scheme, as to which discrimination continues to be permitted under EEC law.[193] The matter came to a head in *Marshall* v. *Southampton and SW Hants Area Health Authority*.[194] Ms Marshall was an employee of the Health Authority. It was the Authority's policy, and an implied term of Ms Marshall's contract of employment, that employees would retire at the age when they became entitled to draw the state retirement pension, in other words 65 in the case of a man and 60 in the case of a woman. Ms Marshall did not want to retire at 60 and she was allowed to continue working until she was 62, at which point she was dismissed. She complained of unlawful sex discrimination, but the industrial tribunal rejected her case on the basis of s.6(4). She appealed and, when the case reached the Court of Appeal, a ruling was sought from the European Court. That Court held that the matter was governed by Article 5 of the Equal Treatment Directive.[195] This applies the principle of equal treatment to working conditions, including dismissal, which the Court said must be interpreted widely. The present situation was not excused on account of the link with the state pensionable age, according to the Court, because that exception 'applies only to the determination of pensionable age for the purposes of granting old age and retirement pensions and the possible consequences thereof for other benefits'. The Court therefore concluded that Article 5 of the Directive must be interpreted as meaning that a general policy concerning dismissal involving the dismissal of a woman solely because she has attained the qualifying age for a state pension, which age is different under national legislation for men and for women, constitutes descrimination on grounds of sex, contrary to that Directive'.[196]

The effect of the *Marshall* decision was, therefore, to make it clear once and for all that discrimination over retirement provision can constitute a breach of EEC law and that the exceptions contained in the Sex Discrimination and Equal Pay Acts were far too wide-ranging. S.2 of the Sex Discrimination Act 1986 seeks to implement this ruling with respect to retirement provision (although it does not refer to pensionable age, since discrimination appears still to be permissible in this context.)[197] S.6(4) of the 1975 Act is now amended, so as to provide as follows:

> Subsections (1)(b) and (2) do not apply to provision in relation to death or retirement except in so far as, in their application to provision in relation to retirement, they render it unlawful for a person to discriminate against a woman –
> (a)  in such of the terms on which he offers her employment as make provision in relation to the way in which he will afford her access to opportunities for promotion, transfer or training or as provide for her dismissal or demotion; or
> (b)  in the way he affords her access to opportunities for promotion, transfer or training or by refusing or deliberately omitting to afford her access to any such opportunities; or
> (c)  by dismissing her or subjecting her to any detriment which results in her dismissal or consists in or involves her demotion.

Categories (a), (b) and (c) correspond roughly to the categories of employment discrimination forbidden by s.6(1) and s.6(2).[198] So, for example, category (a) makes it unlawful to offer someone a job on terms which discriminate with respect to retirement. Category (b), for example, forbids defining eligibility for promotion in terms of different ages for the two sexes; and category (c) covers the kind of situation which arose in *Marshall* itself. S.6(1A)(b) of the Equal Pay Act has been similarly amended so as to bring contractual discrimination over retirement within the Act; it now provides that an equality clause 'shall not operate in relation to terms related to death or retirement, or to any provision made in connection with death or retirement other than a term or provision which, in relation to retirement, affords access to opportunities for promotion, transfer or training or provides for a woman's dismissal or demotion'.[199]

S.3 of the Sex Discrimination Act 1986 equalises the upper age limit for bringing unfair dismissal complaints; hitherto, if there was a normal retiring age for an employee holding the relevant position, a female employee could complain of unfair dismissal if she had not reached that normal retiring age even if that age was over 60; however, in the absence of a normal retiring age, women could not claim unfair dismissal after the age of 60, whereas men could claim up to the age of 65. The effect of the new Act is to equalise the upper age limit at 65 for both sexes; this upper age limit applies if there is no normal retiring age for the relevant position or if the normal retirement age is different for men and women. (The latter provision covers cases of differential retirement ages for men and women, *both* of which were below 65: in such a case, *both* can now claim unfair dismissal up to 65.) One apparent anomaly continues to exist: no change has been made to the differing age limits for statutory redundancy payments, so that men are still entitled to redundancy payments up to the age of 65 whilst women lose their entitlement at 60.[200] The government explained this anomaly on the basis that it would be unfair if a woman aged between 60 and 65 was eligible for redundancy payments; she gets a state retirement pension at this age, whereas a man does not. The two 'benefits', in the government's view, 'cancel each other out'.[201]

### Benefits, facilities or services provided to the public

S.6(2), prohibiting discrimination by an employer against his existing employees, does not apply to the provision of benefits, facilities or services to a woman employee if the employer is concerned with the provision (for payment or not) of benefits, facilities or services of that description to the public, or to a section of the public comprising the woman in question. To this principle there are three exceptions: first, where the provision made for the public differs in a material respect from the provision made by the employer for his employees; secondly, where the provision of the benefits, facilities or services to the woman in question is regulated by her contract of employment; and thirdly, where the benefits, facilities or services relate to training.[202]

This exception is, however, by no means as extensive as it appears at first sight since, even if an act by an employer is exempted by this provision, it may well nevertheless be unlawfully discriminatory by virtue of ss.29 and 35.[203] The scheme of the legislation is to divide jurisdiction between industrial tribunals (employment cases) and county courts (discrimination over the provision of goods, facilities or services). So, for example, if a local authority provides housing to the public in general and also to its own employees in particular, a complaint of discrimination by an employee would have to go the county court. However, if another employer (not in the housing business) provided his employee with a house that went with the job, a complaint of discrimination would go to an industrial tribunal because the provision of housing would not be something given by the employer to the public at large.

## Genuine occupational qualification

S.7 contains the very important exception for cases in which sex is a genuine occupational qualification. It attempts to define the occasions on which biology or social or cultural values demand that a job be performed by one sex rather than the other. As was discussed in Chapter 1, the excuses, other than biology, which have been advanced over the ages for granting women different legal rights and opportunities from men are highly suspect, and so this section deserves special scrutiny. At various points, as will be seen, the section adopts undesirable formulations and has been the subject matter of considerable criticism.[204]

It permits discrimination on the ground of sex at the point of selection for, or promotion to,[205] a job for which being a man is a genuine occupational qualification. It does not exonerate discrimination against married persons or victimisation. Subsection (2) contains an exhaustive list[206] of cases in which being a man can be claimed to be a genuine occupational qualification.[207] The list is a long one, considerably longer in fact than ss.6(1) and (2) which define unlawful discrimination by employers. Fortunately, an amendment to the draft legislation which would have added the vague category of cases in which the tribunal was satisfied, having regard to equity and the substantial merits of the case, that the job should be held by a man, was rejected by Parliament. Nevertheless, it is arguable that the basic design of the section is wrong. First, since it contains such a lengthy list and is consequently so voluminous, it represents a virtual invitation to employers to make some use of it. Secondly, and more significantly, there is a real risk of its falling foul of EEC law; the parallel exception to the principle of equal treatment in EEC law extends only to 'those occupational activities and, where appropriate, the training leading thereto, for which, by reason of their nature or the context in which they are carried out, the sex of the worker constitutes a determining factor'.[208] It would be safer from the point of view of compliance with EEC law, and probably also from the applicant's point of view, if the section were redrafted very much more shortly and in accordance with the EEC wording, with perhaps a small number of examples drawn from the existing section.

At present, being a man is a genuine occupational qualification in nine cases, namely where:

(a)  the essential nature of the job calls for a man for reasons of physiology (excluding physical strength or stamina) or, in dramatic performances or other entertainment, for reasons of authenticity, so that the essential nature of the job would be materially different if carried out by a woman.

This is probably the least controversial category, covering cases where biological sex is essential to the job to be performed (such as where a biological male is needed for experimental purposes.)[209] Reasons of authenticity in dramatic performances are rather more nebulous, being subject to cultural and traditional influences.[210]

(b)  the job needs to be held by a man to preserve decency or privacy because – (i) it is likely to involve physical contact with men in circumstances where they might reasonably object to its being carried out by a woman, or
(ii)  the holder of the job is likely to do his work in circumstances where men might reasonably object to the presence of a woman because they are in a state of undress or are using sanitary facilities.

This, the decency exception, is the first of several to include the apparently objective test of reasonableness. Thus, a man can be required where the job involves physical contact with men[211] or where the job is likely to be done where men are in a state of undress[212] or using sanitary facilities, provided only that the men involved might reasonably object to the presence of a woman. Two points require to be made about such a test of reasonableness. First, the exception would make more sense if, in general, our society adopted a consistent rule forbidding the employment of one sex to perform acts involving physical contact with the opposite sex. However, we make no such rule and, if fact, find it perfectly acceptable, for example, for female nurses and physiotherapists to look after male patients, for male doctors to conduct even the most intimate examinations of female patients, and for swimming-pool lifeguards to be of either sex. Why then should it necessarily be reasonable for instance to demand a male attendant in a men's changing room? Secondly, even if a majority of the population would today agree that it would be unreasonable to employ a woman in a particular job, attitudes can change and are indeed likely to do so with a greater emancipation of women, so that judicial decisions in this area ought not to be seen as creating binding precedents.

(ba)   the job is likely to involve the holder of the job doing his work, or living, in a private home and needs to be held by a man because objection might reasonably be taken to allowing to a woman –
(i)   the degree of physical or social contact with a person living in the home, or
(ii)   the knowledge of intimate details of such a person's life, which is likely, because of the nature or circumstances of the job or of the home, to be allowed to, or available to, the holder of the job.

This exception was added to the list by the Sex Discrimination Act 1986,[213] following infringement proceedings brought against the UK by the EEC Commission.[214] The Sex Discrimination Act had hitherto contained a much broader exception in respect of all employment for the purposes of a private household, and also for small businesses with five or fewer employees. The European Court of Justice held that there could be no excuse for the latter exception and that the private household exception, although validly based on the principle of respect for privacy, was too broadly drafted. Accordingly, the small business exception has been repealed[215] and the private household exception made considerably narrower.

Once again, this exception touches the difficult ground of social mores. The reference to physical contact is probably justifiable, given that the context in which the job is performed is a private one. However, the expression 'social contact' is more obscure. The government explained, during the passage of the legislation through Parliament, that it refers to the fact that people frequently prefer companions of their own sex because they are more likely to share common interests. The part of the section referring to 'knowledge of intimate details' of a person's life seems most obscure of all. The government's explanation of this wording was that it is designed to cover the cases of the elderly who might need an employee to do washing or other personal domestic services and who might find it distasteful to think of a person of the opposite sex performing these tasks. If this is the only situation aimed at by this part of the section, the wording seems inapt since 'intimate details' are not restricted to physically intimate details and could cover such matters as financial or other behavioural details.

(c)   the nature or location of the establishment makes it impracticable for the holder of the job to live elsewhere than in premises provided by the employer, and –
(i)   the only such premises which are available for persons holding that kind of job are lived in, or normally lived in, by men and are not equipped with separate sleeping accommodation for women and sanitary facilities which could be used by women in privacy from men, and

(ii)   it is not reasonable to expect the employer either to equip those
       premises with such accommodation and facilities or to provide
       other premises for women.

Usually referred to as the 'oil rig exception', this appears to be a
special example of (b) but has been drafted in especially detailed
terms. As well as applying to oil rigs, it might apply for instance
to jobs on ships, lighthouses or very remote worksites.[216] Again,
the subsection uses the word 'reasonable' but contains no guidance
for its assessment. Is it inevitably reasonable for an employer to
refuse to hire a woman because it would involve him in additional
expense to provide sleeping accommodation for her, even if it
would only be a very small extra expense? The legislature's resolve
to keep (at least some) men's jobs exclusively male was demonstrated when, at the Committee Stage of the Sex Discrimination
Bill, the words 'normally lived in' were added after it had been
pointed out that, without them, the exception would not have
covered ships or rigs taking on crew for the first time, since it could
not be said in such cases that the premises were lived in by men.
In practice, the EOC has found that this exception constitutes a
serious obstacle to the careers of women engineers who may,
because of it, be denied practical experience, for example, on oil
rigs, which is necessary for promotion; it will probably become a
more popular defence now that employment on the continental
shelf has been brought within the ambit of the anti-discrimination
legislation[217] and tribunals should be urged to scrutinise the defence
strictly if the recent territorial extension of the statutes is not to be
undermined.

(d)   the nature of the establishment, or of the part of it within which
the work is done, requires the job to be held by a man because –
 (i)   it is, or is part of, a hospital, prison or other establishment for
       persons requiring special care, supervision or attention, and
(ii)   those persons are all men (disregarding any woman whose
       presence is exceptional), and
(iii)  it is reasonable, having regard to the essential character of the
       establishment or that part, that the job should not be held by
       a woman.

Presumably not all jobs in male prisons or hospitals are covered
since it will not be 'reasonable' in the case of employees not closely
connected with the inmates (such as kitchen staff) for the job not
be be held by a woman. This exception presents a barrier to the
career progression of women in the prison service, since it serves
to exclude them from the more numerous men's prisons in which
they would otherwise be able to gain experience. The EOC has

recommended the abolition of this part of s.7, on the grounds that the situations it caters for are covered by other parts of the section (in particular, (b), (c) and (e)), that it has proved to be of little practical use and that the Commission considers it to be in breach of EEC law.[218]

(e)   the holder of the job provides individuals with personal services promoting their welfare or education, or similar personal services, and those services can most effectively be provided by a man.

This would appear to cover a very narrow situation, since there can surely be very few cases indeed in which the efficacy of welfare services is related to the sex of the provider. However, it might on rare occasions cover such jobs as those of probation officer or social worker, and might be useful in relation to ethnic minorities for some of whom a male worker would not be acceptable in relation to a female client.

(f)   the job needs to be held by a man because of restrictions imposed by the laws regulating the employment of women.

This used to be a more important category than it is now. It preserved a body of 'protective legislation' which prohibited women from working in certain industries and regulated their hours of work. However, s.7 of the Sex Discrimination Act 1986 removed the major legislative restrictions contained in the Factories Act 1961, the Hours of Employment (Conventions) Act 1936 and the Mines and Quarries Act 1954. This repeal followed a survey conducted by the EOC,[219] which found that the protective legislation contributed significantly to the less favourable treatment of women in industry, in particular because employers could rely on it to argue that women made less flexible employees than men. Although there is scope for differences of opinion on the point,[220] in the view of the present writer the repeal of the protective legislation is to be welcomed. Not only was the legislation paternalistic in its origin, but it reinforced gender stereotyping without remedying any generalised disadvantages from which women today could be said to suffer.[221]

The EOC in fact believes that category (f) should be removed as a whole from the legislation, because it duplicates s.51 of the Sex Discrimination Act[222] which provides a defence for acts done under prior legislation.[223]

(g)   the job needs to be held by a man because it is likely to involve the performance of duties outside the UK in a country whose laws

or customs are such that the duties could not, or could not effectively,
be performed by a woman.

This category was included to allow discrimination in the recruitment of persons who will have to work in countries, in particular
in the Middle East, where a woman employee would be unacceptable. In realistic terms, it seems that this exception, though unwelcome, is necessary. However, it is by no means as far-reaching as
some employers appear to believe and scrutiny of the situation by
the tribunal may well demonstrate that it is inapplicable in particular
circumstances; for example, it could not be relied on by the Foreign
and Commonwealth Office to justify a decision not to promote a
woman diplomat to the post of Deputy High Commissioner in
Zambia. It was unsuccessfully argued that, as the Second Secretary
already in post was also a woman, an all-female political section
would be operationally ineffective in the conditions of a male-
dominated society such as Zambia.[224]

(h)   the job is one of two to be held by a married couple.

This category was not included in the original Sex Discrimination
Bill and its intention remains unclear, particularly since there have
been no cases in relation to it. Its effect runs counter to the anti-
discrimination legislation since it enables employers who employ
married couples to stipulate that the husband shall do one job (for
example, gardening or maintenance) and the wife another (say,
housework or cooking); if the two were employed as separate individuals no such stipulation based on sex stereotyping would be
permitted. For this reason, the EOC has recommended the repeal
of this category.[225]

The statutory exceptions apply where some only of the duties of
the job fall within paragraphs (a) to (g), as well as where all of them
do so.[226] However, these paragraphs do not apply in relation to the
filling of a vacancy if the employer already has male employees
who are capable of carrying out the duties in question, whom it
would be reasonable to employ on those duties, and whose
numbers are sufficient to meet the employer's likely requirements
without causing him undue inconvenience.[227] So, for example, a
bank recruiting staff, some of whom would have to travel for the
purposes of their employment to the Middle East, would not be
permitted to recruit solely male employees. The only situation
where this would be permissible would be where it would cause
undue inconvenience to send male employees on every occasion
where somebody had to travel to a country where a female
employee would be ineffective in the performance of her duties.[228]

## Special cases

The Act makes provision for several limited exceptions, most of which are explicable on unobjectionable biological grounds. Police constables may not be treated differently on the ground of sex, except in relation to the requirements relating to height, uniform or equipment,[229] or allowances in lieu of uniform or equipment, or so far as special treatment is accorded to women in connection with pregnancy or child-birth, or in relation to pensions to or in respect of special constables or police cadets.[230] Discrimination is allowed between male and female prison officers as to height requirements[231] and the Act does not apply to employment for the purposes of 'an organised religion where the employment is limited to one sex so as to comply with the doctrines of the religion or avoid offending the religious suceptibilities of a significant number of its followers'.[232]

Less easily justified is the existing exception in relation to miners. Before 1975 women were forbidden to work underground in mines. It is now provided that they may not be employed in a job the duties of which ordinarily require the employee to spend a significant proportion of time below ground in an active mine,[233] although there is no physical reason why such a job should be any more harmful to women than to men.

Also controversial is the rule that the employment provisions of the Act do not apply to service in the army, navy or air force or in any women's service administered by the Defence Council.[234] As discussed in Chapter 2, p. 20 et seq., this may well constitute a breach of EEC law.

There used to be an exception for midwives, and men could only train in this field in certain institutions approved by the Department of Health.[235] An action was brought before the European Court of Justice by the European Commission contesting the legality of this position under EEC law; although the Court upheld its legality,[236] the exception has since been repealed.[237]

## GENERAL DEFENCES AVAILABLE UNDER THE ACT[238]

### Pregnancy and childbirth

As discussed in Chapter 1, this is the one clearcut biological case in which an exception has to be made to the principle of the equal treatment of the sexes. Accordingly, the legislation permits specially favourable treatment for women, in circumstances where this would otherwise amount to unlawful discrimination, in connection with pregnancy and childbirth.[239]

## Charities

For no clear reason, discrimination is excepted from the Sex Discrimination Act where it occurs pursuant to a charitable instrument by which benefits are conferred 'on persons of one sex only (disregarding any benefits to persons of the opposite sex which are exceptional or are relatively insignificant.)'.[240] There is no equivalent (although there ought to be) in this context to s.34(1) of the Race Relations Act 1976, which provides:

> A provision which is contained in a charitable instrument (whenever that instrument took or takes effect) and which provides for conferring benefits on persons of a class defined by reference to colour shall have effect for all purposes as if it provided for conferring the like benefits –
> (a)   on persons of the class which results if the restriction by reference to colour is disregarded; or
> (b)   where the original class is defined by reference to colour only, on persons generally. . . .

In *Hugh-Jones* v. *St John's College, Cambridge*,[241] the Employment Appeal Tribunal held that the Sex Discrimination Act exception covered the statutes of the College, which were charitable since they were for the advancement of learning and research, and which could therefore lawfully restrict admission to college research fellowships to males.[242]

## Sport

In relation to any sport, game or other activity of a competitive nature, 'where the physical strength, stamina or physique of the average woman puts her at a disadvantage to the average man', s.44 provides that the legislation does not 'render unlawful any act related to the participation of a person as a competitor in events involving that activity which are confined to competitors of one sex'. The scope of this section is uncertain.[243] *Bennett* v. *FA Ltd*[244] concerned a 12-year-old girl who wanted to play football either in a mixed team or in teams which would be playing against boys. The Court of Appeal rejected her claim and Lord Denning MR remarked: 'Just reading [s.44] it seems to me that football is a game which is excepted from this statute. It is a game in which on all the evidence here the average woman is at a disadvantage to the average man because she has not got the stamina or physique to stand up to men in regard to it.' In *GLC* v. *Farrar*,[245] Slynn J in the

Employment Appeal Tribunal concluded that the *Bennett* decision established that 'in a case where it is desired to exclude, for example, a girl from a mixed team, or to exclude girls from playing in teams against other boys or men, such exclusion would not be unlawful'. However, he went on to hold that s.44 'is dealing with a situation in which men and women might both be playing in the same game or taking part in the same event. It is in that situation that the disadvantage of the woman because of physical strength, stamina or physique would become a relevant matter. It does not seem to us that this section is dealing with the situation where it is desired that a girl should play a game against a girl, or where teams of girls are to play teams of girls.'[246] Neither is s.44 relevant to the case of a woman acting as a referee in a sport, as distinct from where she participates as a competitor.[247]

It was argued in the *Bennett* case, on medical evidence, that boys and girls of twelve are equal in stamina and that only older women are at a disadvantage; therefore s.44 should be divided into games for under-twelves and those for over-twelves. However, the Court of Appeal rejected this approach and held that 'average' woman meant average woman not of any specific age, thus giving s.44 a very broad construction. The EOC is highly critical of this decision; it points out[248] that children of primary school age frequently play sports together both in school and outside and that it would therefore be sensible to make it possible for children of primary school age to have mixed teams for sporting competitions. It rightly considers that it is very much contrary to the promotion of equality of opportunity that primary-school-age girls should be debarred from taking part in team sports, which seem to them both enjoyable and prestigious, and it has therefore recommended that s.44 should be amended so as to exclude from its scope participation in sporting competitions by children of primary school age.

## Insurance policies

In relation to insurance and similar policies, women may be treated differently from men on the basis of reasonable actuarial or other data.[249]

In *Pinder* v. *The Friends Provident Life Office*,[250] the ambit of this exception was tested and found to be extremely broad. The plaintiff, who was a self-employed dentist, took out several health insurance policies with the defendants. For each she was required to pay a premium which was 50 per cent higher than that which would have been payable by a man. She claimed that this was unlawful discrimination[251] and the insurers claimed that it was covered by this exception. The county court held that it was so excepted; the court found, on the basis of the statistical data before it, that there was 'overwhelming' evidence that a substantial loading was justified. 'The decision as to the actual amount of the "loading" is ultimately a matter of commercial judgment', which had been exercised reasonably on these facts. Apart from the very wide discretion that this decision clearly leaves in the hands of the insurers, it is also unsatisfactory in relation to the key question of the composition of the groups to be compared actuarially. The groups compared here were single women and employed men, despite Ms Pinder's argument that her position should be compared with that of men engaged in a similar type of occupation to her own. The point is that such a crude comparison ignores the fact that the lack of equality of opportunity for women has probably led to higher overall sickness rates for them: it is well known that absentee rates vary with job level, so that one consequence of women's relegation to the lower echelons of employment is very likely to be their higher overall absentee rate. But it by no means follows that women engaged in more rewarding and stimulating occupations are also absent more frequently than their male colleagues. The court ought to have demanded evidence that women engaged in similar occupations to Ms Pinder's were absent for sickness more often than men in equivalent occupations, and should certainly not simply have assumed this on the basis of the overall figures.

The EOC is severely critical of the insurance exception, saying:

> Equality of treatment is, in law, a question of individual rights, unqualified by generalities related to sex. Arguably, the continued sanctioning of generalised differential treatment according to sex, uniquely in matters of insurance, lends support to modes of thinking and practice which the Sex Discrimination Act was intended to proscribe. Further, while the pooling of risks for the purpose of providing cross-subsidy between more and less fortunate insured persons is the essence of all insurance, the practice of segregating male and female risks results in two uniquely large and indiscriminate classes of insured persons. The effect of this practice, as it relates to individuals, is that it penalises all individuals of one sex, while awarding an unearned bonus to exceptional individuals of the other. The social undesirability of such a practice is particularly obvious when livelihoods are in question, as is the case in annuities and permanent health insurance.

For these compelling reasons, the EOC has proposed the repeal of the exception 'with the shortest practicable period for implementation'.[252]

## Acts done under statutory authority

S.51 provides that it is not unlawful for a person to do an act which is necessary in order to comply with a requirement of a pre–1975 Act. The exemption also extends to acts necessary to comply with an instrument made or approved under such an Act, even if the instrument is made or approved after 1975. This provision is potentially extremely far-reaching, as was demonstrated in *Hugh-Jones* v. *St John's College, Cambridge*,[253] where the Employment Appeal Tribunal held that it was lawful to exclude women from College research fellowships, in part because restriction to the male sex was necessary in order to comply with the College statutes which were made under the Universities of Oxford and Cambridge Act 1923. In *Page* v. *Freight Hire (Tank Haulage) Ltd*,[254] the Employment Appeal Tribunal ruled that an employer was entitled to rely, as a result of this exception, on the defence of attempting to preserve the health and safety of his employees, since an obligation to this effect was cast on him by the Health and Safety at Work Act 1974.[255]

The exception was given an extraordinarily generous interpretation by the Employment Appeal Tribunal in *GLC* v. *Farrar*,[256] in which it was held that it exonerated a licence granted by the GLC, pursuant to the London Government Act 1963, which discriminated against women wrestlers. Slynn J said:

> There is no doubt here that this licence was granted, and thereby made or approved, under an Act of Parliament on the face of it clearly giving powers to the local authority to include such terms as they thought right for the granting of the licence. Parliament, by s.51, has excluded from the ambit of Parts II to IV of the Act of 1975 acts necessary to comply with a requirement of a statute passed before the Act of 1975 or an instrument made or approved under it. It does not seem to us that the Act under which the instrument in made must itself specifically require that the act of the kind which is complained about shall be done. But for the provisions of the Act of 1975 it is not suggested that the licence was other than *intra vires*. The question is whether the Act of 1975 requires as a matter of law that this condition shall be removed. It does not seem to us that the Act of 1975 does require the condition to be removed. On the contrary, as long as it is valid within the Act of 1963, it seems to us that Parliament has expressly validated or excluded from the area of illegality anything which is done as a result of a requirement in that Act or an instrument made under it.[257]

This decision, on its particular facts, has now been reversed by s.5 of the Sex Discrimination Act 1986, which provides that if a public entertainment licence, or a regulation under which such a licence

is granted, requires discrimination which would be unlawful under
the employment provisions of the 1975 Act, the requirement is
invalid. However, this amendment does not alter the principle
underlying the *Farrar* decision, namely that, so long as the 'instrument' is *intra vires* the enabling Act, that enabling Act itself need
not require discrimination in order for the exception to apply. This
is quite unsatisfactory; if Parliament is to admit exceptions to the
principle of equal treatment, it should only be taken to do so by
very clear, express words.

The possibility is a live one that this exception will also, perhaps
inadvertently, lead to contraventions by the UK of its obligations
under EEC law. The EOC has recommended its repeal and
suggested that each Department of State should instead be required
to provide, and subsequently regularly to review, a schedule of any
remaining statutory provisions where it is considered necessary to
allow discrimination to continue.[258]

### Acts Safeguarding National Security

The Act provides that discrimination is lawful if done for the
purpose of safeguarding national security; and a certificate, signed
by a Minister of the Crown, which certifies that an act was done
for this purpose, is stated by the Act to be 'conclusive evidence' as
far as a court is concerned.[259] However, in *Johnston* v. *RUC*[260] the
European Court of Justice ruled that there is no general exception
to the principle of equal treatment in EEC law for national security;
if an act is to be justified, it must be brought within one of the
specific exceptions listed in the Equal Treatment Directive, none
of which expressly mentions national security.[261] Furthermore, the
Court ruled that the attempt to exclude judical review in this situation was contrary to EEC law and thus 'inapplicable'. It follows
that this exception must be removed *in toto* from the statute. In any
case, it is very hard to see what useful purpose it can serve, since
it is impossible to imagine a situation in which national security
alone genuinely renders it necessary to discriminate on the grounds
of sex.[262]

## DISCRIMINATION WITH RESPECT TO EMPLOYMENT BY PERSONS OTHER THAN EMPLOYERS

### Contract Workers

The Act extends the concept of unlawful discrimination to conduct
in relation to workers who are supplied to someone ('the principal')

under a contract.[263] An example occurs where temporary staff are supplied by an employment agency. The rationale of the provision is to guard against discrimination by anyone who is in a position to control another person's work prospects. The principal is forbidden to discriminate against a contract worker with respect to the work under the contract:

(a)   in the terms on which he allows her to do that work or
(b)   by not allowing her to do it or continue to do it, or
(c)   in the way he affords her access to any benefits, facilities or services or by refusing or deliberately omitting to afford her access to them, or
(d)   by subjecting her to any other detriment.[264]

There are exceptions where being a man is a genuine occupational qualification[265] for the work in question,[266] and where the alleged discrimination relates to benefits, facilities or services and the principal is concerned with the provision of these to the public.[267]


## Partnerships

It is unlawful for a partnership, in relation to a position as a partner in the firm, to discriminate against a woman in the arrangements made for determining who should be offered the position, in the terms on which the position is offered, by refusing to offer her the position, or, if the position is offered to her, in the way she is or is not afforded access to benefits, facilities or services or by expelling her or subjecting her to any other detriment.[268]

There is an exception where being a man is a genuine occupational qualification.[269] There is also a limited exception for death and retirement. S.11(4) provides:

Subsection (1)(b) and (d) [discrimination in relation to terms and in relation to existing partners] do not apply to provision made in relation to death or retirement except insofar as, in their application to provision made in relation to retirement, they render it unlawful for a firm to discriminate against a woman –
(a)   in such of the terms on which they offer her a position as partner as provide for her expulsion from that position; or
(b)   by expelling her from a position as partner, or subjecting her to any detriment which results in her expulsion from such a position.

This broadly mirrors the general exception for death and retirement in employment, and was amended in response to the European

Court's ruling in *Marshall* v. *Southampton and SW Hants Health Authority*.[270]

## Trade Unions and other Trade or Professional Organisations

Unlawful discrimination may also be committed by organisations of workers, by organisations of employers and by any other organisation whose members carry on a particular trade or profession for the purposes of which the organisation exists.[271] Such an organisation must not discriminate against a woman who is not a member in the terms on which it is prepared to admit her to membership.[272] This is a broadly drafted provision and means that, even where no woman has actually applied to become a member, the rulebook of the organisation must not discriminate against her sex. Neither must the organisation refuse on the grounds of sex to accept a woman who has applied for membership.[273] In the case of a woman who is already a member, the organisation must not discriminate against her in affording her access to benefits, facilities or services, by depriving her of membership or varying the terms of her membership, or by subjecting her to any other detriment.[274]

There are exceptions with respect to provisions made in relation to death or retirement from work of a member[275] and with respect to positive action.[276]

## Qualifying Bodies

It is unlawful for an authority or body which can confer an authorisation or qualification which is needed for, or facilitates, engagement in a particular profession or trade[277] to discriminate in specified ways against a woman.[278] The bodies covered include, for example, the General Council of the Stock Exchange, the Law Society and, as regards the Bar, the Common Professional Examination Board and the Council of Legal Education.[279] In particular, such a body must not discriminate against a woman in the terms on which it is prepared to confer the authorisation or qualification on her, by refusing her application, or by withdrawing her authorisation or qualification or varying its terms.[280]

Where such a body is required by law to satisfy itself as to a person's good character before conferring on him an authorisation or qualification, then the body must have regard to any evidence tending to show that either that person or any of his employees or agents has practised unlawful discrimination in any trade or professional context.[281]

This provision applies only to qualifications and not to prior acts of discrimination by professional or similar bodies. However, such acts might well be caught by the provisions outlawing discrimination in education and in the provision of goods, facilities and services.[282]

## Vocational Training Bodies

A vocational training body[283] is forbidden to discriminate against a woman seeking or undergoing training for employment in the terms on which she is offered access to courses, by refusal of such access to her or by the termination of her training.[284]

## Employment Agencies

An employment agency is defined, for the purpose of the Sex Discrimination Act, as 'a person who, for profit or not, provides services for the purpose of finding employment for workers or supplying employers with workers'.[285] The expression includes those giving guidance on careers and any other services related to employment.[286] It is unlawful for such an agency to discriminate against a woman:

(a) in the terms on which the agency offers to provide any of its services, or
(b) by refusing or deliberately omitting to provide any of its services, or
(c) in the way it provides any of its services.[287]

This is strategically a key provison. Employment agencies, handling numerous cases as they do, are in a factually extremely influential position. It is even more important that they be prohibited from discriminating at the point of selection for employment than that individual employers be so prevented.

The section does not apply if the discrimination only concerns employment which the employer could lawfully refuse to offer to the woman[288] (because one of the exceptions applies). The agency is not liable if it proves (the burden being on it) that it acted in reliance on a statement made to it by the employer to the effect that an exception did apply and it was reasonable to rely on that statement.[289]

## DISCRIMINATION IN EDUCATION

### Section 22

Part II of the Act begins by dealing with discrimination in education. Schools, universities and other educational establishments are forbidden to discriminate on grounds of sex. In particular, s.22 provides that such a body must not discriminate against a woman:

(a)   in the terms on which it offers to admit her to the establishment as a pupil, or

(b)   by refusing or deliberately omitting to accept an application for her admission to the establishment as a pupil, or

(c)   where she is a pupil of the establishment – (i) in the way it affords her access to any benefits, facilities or services, or by refusing or deliberately omitting to afford her access to them, or (ii) by excluding her from the establishment or subjecting her to any other detriment.[290]

As pointed out earlier, it is only discrimination on the ground of sex, and not on the ground of marital status, that is covered.

It is not, of course, unlawful to discriminate on the ground of sex as regards admission to single-sex schools, whose legality is preserved by the Act.[291] In the case of a co-educational establishment, it would, however, be unlawful to operate a quota for the number of girls to be admitted.[292] Once in a co-educational school, the statutory provision means that a girl is entitled to receive exactly the same benefits, facilities and services as she would receive if she were a boy; for example, she is entitled to attend courses and classes (even ones which are non-traditional for girls, such as woodwork), on equal terms with the boys. The EOC regularly receives complaints from parents and pupils on this score, particularly in relation to Craft, Design and Technology (CDT) and home economics.[293]

One limitation of s.22 is, however, that it applies only in relation to a particular educational establishment; thus, it is not possible for a girl to use it to complain that she has been treated less favourably on the ground of her sex than boys in another school (even if that other school is under the control of the same education authority). In addition, this provision does not prevent the continuation of separate facilities for boys and girls within a co-educational school, provided that the facilities given to each sex are equal. Nor does it place a school under an obligation to provide a new course, not already on the curriculum.

There is a significant lack of case-law on s.22 and the EOC has been criticised on this account. The Commission's response to such criticism is two-fold: first, it has found that LEAs are more than ready to co-operate with the Commission in amending unlawful practices when these are drawn to their attention, so that litigation often becomes unnecessary in practice. Secondly, however, it points out that the prospect of taking a complaint to the county court on a child's behalf is often a crucial factor which deters parents from pursuing cases;[294] for this reason, the Commission would prefer the legislation to be amended so as to enable it, rather than individual pupils, to initiate cases;[295] this would certainly seem a necessary and sensible reform in an area of critical importance to real equality of opportunity. One case heard in the county court was *Debell, Sevket and Teh* v. *London Borough of Bromley and Smith;*[296] this involved a claim on behalf of three 10-year-old girls who, together with five other girls, were kept in the third year junior class of their school for a second year because the top class was full. The headteacher had decided, not to keep down the eight youngest pupils, but the eight youngest girls. Some two years later, unlawful sex discrimination was admitted and each girl received 'a small sum' in damages for hurt feelings. The case illustrates the inability of the slow county court system to provide the kind of quick relief needed in these cases, but it is to be hoped that the deterrent value of this litigation, which received extensive publicity, was considerable.[297]

An establishment which provides education or training but is not included in the list set out in s.22 may nevertheless be caught by Part II of the Act, dealing with discrimination in employment,[298] or s.29 on the discriminatory provision of goods, facilities and services.[299]

## Section 23

S.23(1) renders it unlawful for an LEA, in carrying out such of its functions under the Education Acts 1944 to 1975 as do not fall under s.22, to do any act which constitutes sex discrimination.[300] Obvious examples of functions covered by s.23 are the award of discretionary grants under s.2 of the Education Act 1962 (as amended) and the provision of facilities for social and physical recreation under s.53 of the Education Act 1944 (as amended). However, the EOC maintains[301] that s.23(1) also covers more significant and wider-ranging functions. The government proposals for equal opportunities legislation stated in 1973:

Of the duties and powers assigned to LEAs under the Education Act, the most relevant to the possibility of sex discrimination are the following:

(a)  S.8 of the Education Act 1944 (as amended) places on LEAs in England and Wales the duty of ensuring that primary and secondary schools in their area are 'sufficient in number, character and equipment to afford for all pupils opportunities for education offering such variety of instruction and training as may be desirable in view of their different ages, abilities and aptitudes, and of the different periods for which they may be expected to remain at school, including practical instruction and training appropriate to their respective needs'.

(b)  S.41 of the Education Act 1944 (as amended) places on LEAs the duty of ensuring that the facilities for further education in their area are adequate for the part-time and full-time education of persons over compulsory school age, and also for leisure time occupation for such persons who are able and willing to profit by the facilities provided for that purpose.

(c)  S.76 of the Education Act 1944 (as amended) is to the effect that 'in the exercise and performance of all powers and duties conferred and imposed on them by this Act, the Secretary of State and LEAs shall have regard to the general principle that, so far as is compatible with the provision of efficient instruction and training and the avoidance of unreasonable public expenditure, pupils are to be educated in accordance with the wishes of their parents.'[302]

The EOC concludes that:

these statutory functions of Education Authorities are much wider than those falling within s.22 of the Act which is concerned with discrimination in relation to the admission of pupils to, the treatment of pupils within, or the exclusion of pupils from, a particular establishment. It would seem that in carrying out these wider functions, an LEA is therefore required by s.23 not to do any act which constitutes sex discrimination. For example, it would be unlawful for an Authority to treat girls less favourably than boys, on the ground of sex, in securing the provision of secondary schools or of facilities for further education in its area. The exception for single-sex establishments does not apply to s.23 because s.23 is not concerned with discrimination by a *particular establishment* but rather with discrimination by an LEA in carrying out its *general statutory functions*. For example, it would seem that an Authority, which in carrying out its functions under s.8 of the Education Act 1944, provided less favourable opportunities in its area for girls than for boys to learn advanced physics, and consequently treated a particular girl or girls less favourably on the ground of sex than it treated boys, would be acting contrary to s.23 read together with s.1(1)(a). This would be so, even though the better opportunities for boys arose from the existence of exempt single-sex boy's schools with more places for students of advanced physics.[303]

**Section 25**

This imposes a general duty on responsible bodies for educational establishments in the public sector to secure that their facilities are provided without sex discrimination; an act which contravenes s.25 may also be unlawful under s.22 or s.23.[304] The Secretary of State has the exclusive power to enforce the s.25 duty[305], but if the EOC becomes aware of any acts in respect of which the Secretary of State could exercise the enforcement powers under s.25, it must give notice of such acts to the Secretary of State.[306] In the absence of guidance from the Secretary of State as regards the proper performance of the s.25 duty by an LEA, the EOC thought it desirable to place on record its interpretation of s.25. This it did as follows in the Report of the formal investigation 'Tameside':[307]

Since an LEA is under a general duty to *secure* that its facilities are provided *without sex discrimination*, it is obliged by s.25 to take reasonable and sufficient steps to ensure that such provision does not, and is not likely to, result in acts of unlawful sex discrimination (whether direct or indirect). If an Authority has no regard to its s.25 duty in planning educational provision, this could well suggest that the actual provision results, or is likely to result, in unlawful sex discrimination. In the opinion of the Commission, in order to assess whether there has been a breach of the s.25 duty it is necessary to consider (a) whether educational provision has been planned on the principle of equality of opportunity for pupils of both sexes; (b) whether the actual provision made is in accordance with that principle; and (c) whether the actual provision made results or is likely to result in any act of unlawful sex discrimination. The s.25 duty is not performed merely by ensuring proportional equality between the sexes in access to particular provision (*e.g.* equal number of boys and girls in every class of every school.) Provision according to the abilities, aptitudes and needs of the individual pupils may result in there being a greater proportion of pupils of one sex within a school or part of a school. What matters therefore is not that there is a balance between the sexes but that pupils and applicants for admission have access to education provision irrespective of sex. An LEA must obviously have some regard to the demand, both demographic and parental, for the educational facilities in question. If there is a substantial disparity in the number of boys and girls in a given area, this may justify a corresponding disparity in the number of boys and girls receiving educational provision, provided that there is not actual or apprehended sex discrimination in any individual case (for example, because of the operation of a quota system). If however, the demand is unequal because of traditional conventions of thought among parents and their children, it cannot lawfully be made more equal by positive or reverse discrimination, but by emphasising that educational provision is made on the basis of equal opportunities for boys and girls. Such an emphasis is not required by the Act but it is desirable as a matter of good educational policy and practice. However, an Authority is not in breach of its s.25 duty if fewer girls apply for educational facilities than are qualified to enjoy them, unless the Authority's policy or practices are themselves responsible for the shortfall in demand. The nature and extent of the s.25 duty is complicated by the fact that s.25 does not apply to the admission to education of pupils at an exempt single-sex establishment (s.26(1) and (3).) However, the exemption for single-sex schools does not relieve an LEA from its general duty under s.25 to secure that education provision is made without sex discrimination. For example, in an area where there are several single-sex boy's schools maintained by an LEA, it must secure that girl pupils of equivalent age, ability and aptitude are afforded no less favourable provision than their counterparts in the exempt boy's schools. Planning is a continuous process. Provision which at one time ensures equality of opportunity may have to be altered to take account of changes in the numbers of pupils of each sex and in their abilities, aptitudes and needs. This necessitates a continuous process of monitoring by an LEA of its performance of the s.25 duty.

## The Exception for Physical Training

Sections 22, 23 and 25 do not apply to further education courses in physical training or designed for teachers of physical training.[308]

## DISCRIMINATION IN THE PROVISION OF GOODS, FACILITIES AND SERVICES AND IN THE DISPOSAL OR MANAGEMENT OF PREMISES

This matter is dealt with by Part III of the Act. S.29 makes it unlawful for any person concerned with the provision, for payment or not, of goods, facilities or services to the public, or a section of the public, to discriminate either directly or indirectly on the ground of sex (but not marital status); in particular, the supplier must not refuse or deliberately omit to provide a woman with goods, facilities or services, and he must not refuse or deliberately omit to provide them of the same quality, in the same manner or on the same terms as he would do in the case of a man. The section gives examples, though not an exhaustive list, of the facilities[309] and services covered: access to and use of any place to which the public or a section of the public are permitted to enter,[310] accommodation in a hotel or boarding house, facilities by way of banking or insurance or for grants, loans, credit or finance,[311] educational facilities,[312] facilities for entertainment, recreation[313] or refreshment,[314] facilities for transport or travel, and the services of any profession or trade or any local or other public authority.[315]

In *R* v. *Entry Clearance Officer, Ex p. Amin*[316] the practically very important question arose as to whether the Secretary of State had breached the Sex Discrimination Act in discriminating on the ground of sex in operating the 'special voucher' system, by which the holders of UK passports who would not otherwise be entitled to do so were permitted to enter this country. The majority in the House of Lords held that this situation was not governed by s.29(1) and followed the earlier ruling of the Court of Appeal in *R* v. *Immigration Appeal Tribunal, Ex p. Kassam*,[317] to the effect that the Secretary of State giving leave to enter or remain in the UK under the Immigration Act 1971 was not within s.29(1). Lord Fraser, in the majority, said that the examples in s.29(2) are useful pointers to the construction of subsection (1) and they reinforced his view that s.29 applies to the direct provision of facilities or services, but not to the mere grant or permission to use facilities. He also held that s.85(1), which states that the Sex Discrimination Act generally applies to Crown acts, refers only to acts done on behalf of the crown which are of a kind similar to acts that might be done by a private person; what the Secretary of State does in relation to immigration is not analogous to the act of a private person.[318] Lord Scarman, with whom Lord Brandon agreed, dissented strongly and held that s.29(1) did govern the situation and that s.85(1) was not to be confined in the way suggested. The EOC has pointed out that the effect of the majority decision in *Amin* is that a whole range of state activities are outside the ambit of the legislation and it wishes to see a statutory amendment reversing the decision.[319]

Another very significant limitation on the usefulness of s.29 arises from the fact that it only applies where the goods, facilities or services are provided 'to the public or a section of the public'. This wording covers wholesaler as well as retailer, but does not, unfortunately, extend to wholly private transactions such as the provision of refreshment or sports facilities to members of private clubs. This follows from the decisions of the House of Lords and Court of Appeal in *Charter* v. *Race Relations Board*[320] and *Race Relations Board* v. *Dockers' Labour Club and Institute*[321] to the effect that the words 'section of the public' in s.2 of the old Race Relations Act 1968 did not apply to members or associate members of many social clubs. Lord Simon of Glaisdale explained the test for what constitutes a 'section of the public' in the *Charter* case as follows:

> it is open to show that some so-called clubs – even some which purport to be private members' clubs – do in reality constitute merely

a section of the public. The dividing line, in my view, lies in the personal selection of members with a view to their common acceptability. No doubt a club may be less or more selective according to whether its membership is under strength, on the one hand, or it has a long waiting list, on the other. No doubt some clubs will provide for election by all members, so many blackballs perhaps excluding; while others may vest election in a committee. Most will require a candidate in any event to be sponsored by one or more existing members; and no doubt the status, personality or popularity of the sponsor will be influential in forwarding the interest of his candidate. The essential feature is that there should be a genuine screening at some stage as a pledge of general acceptability to fellow members. It is this screening that determines that membership is a private role. Without it the association remains a section of the public.[322]

After considerable public criticism, the race relations legislation was amended in this respect and private clubs now fall within its ambit if they have 25 or more members.[323] The Sex Discrimination Act, however, does not contain an equivalent proviso and the EOC has repeatedly commented that the exclusion of private clubs from its sphere of operation gives rise to a great deal of complaint from the public.[324]

By 1986, the Commission had received nearly 2000 such complaints and it observed that this was in spite of wide general awareness that there is no legal redress in this situation. Most of the complaints come from women affected, but some have also been received from male sympathisers who would like the support of the Act in seeking to change the club rules. The Commisssion reports that the problems usually arise from the existence of two categories of membership in private clubs: 'full' membership for men, bringing with it the full range of privileges including voting rights, and 'associate' membership for women, conferring limited privileges and restricted or no voting rights (commonly, for example, involving prohibition on the use of sporting facilities at weekends and during the evenings). The Commission's only resort in these cases is to encourage the complainants themselves to seek constitutional changes to the club rules, which can, of course, only be achieved if there are sympathetic male members. However, the Commission commented gloomily in 1986 that it was 'aware of no significant progress towards equality of status for women members of mixed private clubs resulting from such attempts; on the contrary, there is much evidence of repeated failure.'[325] The Commission therefore recommends that mixed private clubs should be brought within the scope of the sex discrimination legislation and suggests also that a time-clause should be included within the new provision to prevent all-male club committees from reacting to the proposed change by voting to discontinue female membership altogether.[326]

The meaning to be attached to 'facilities' in the context of s.29 was raised in *Jones* v. *Royal Liver Friendly Society*.[327] Ms Jones claimed that she had been discriminated against because, as a female member of the Society, she was forbidden to stand for election as a delegate to the Society's meetings. Policy-holders of the Society were automatically members of the Society and, since there were some seven million members, representation of members at meetings was by delegates. However, the Society's rules provided that only males could be delegates. Ms Jones had been a member for thirty years and gave notice of her intention to stand as a delegate in 1980. Her application was refused on the ground of her sex and a recommendation, made to the annual meeting later that year that the rule be changed, was defeated. Ms Jones then began proceedings under s.29, saying that she received the facility of insurance on less favourable terms than male members of the Society. The county court held that although the right to be a delegate at meetings of the Society was not in itself a 'facility' within the meaning of s.29, insurance was offered by this Society on terms that included participation in the government of the Society; this 'participatory insurance' was not available to female members on the same terms as male members and therefore the statute had been breached. The Court of Appeal confirmed this conclusion, saying that membership of the Society, and with it the right to be a delegate, could not be separated from the terms of insurance offered by the Society and that therefore the insurance which was offered to women was discriminatory. It did not consider the question of whether membership itself could constitute a 'facility' within the meaning of s.29.

There is an exception to s.29 where a particular skill is commonly exercised in a different way for men and for women; in such a case, it is not unlawful for a person who does not normally exercise the skill for women to insist on exercising it for a woman only in accordance with his normal practice or, if he reasonably considers it impractical to do that in her case, to refuse or deliberately omit to exercise it.[328] This would seem to cover such skills as hairdressing and tailoring.

S.30 deals with discrimination in the disposal or management of premises. It is unlawful for a person, in relation to premises in Great Britain of which he has the power to dispose, to discriminate against a woman in the terms on which he offers her the premises, or by refusing her application for the premises, or in his treatment of her in relation to a housing list.[329] It is also unlawful for a person who manages premises to discriminate against a woman occupying the premises in the way he affords her access to any benefits or facilities, or by refusing or deliberately omitting to afford her access to them, or by evicting her or subjecting her to any other detriment. There is an exception in the case of a person who owns an estate or interest in the premises and wholly occupies them, unless he uses an estate agent to dispose of the premises or unless he advertises the disposal.[330] There is also an exception for small dwellings (as defined) where the person disposing of the premises or a near relative of his lives and intends to continue to live on the premises.[331]

Political parties are permitted to make special provision for persons of one sex only in their constitution, organisation or administration[332], so that women's sections and committees can lawfully be set up, and non-statutory voluntary bodies may restrict membership and benefits to one sex only.[333] The latter in particular confers an extremely wide-ranging exemption and it has been suggested that it would be preferable to restrict it to organisations whose functions relate to needs which are exclusive to one sex.[334]

Also wide-ranging, and to some extent matching the numerous exceptions to the employment provisions of the Sex Discrimination Act, is s.35. This lays down that a person who provides facilities or services restricted to men does not contravene s.29 in three situations:

(a)　is where the place where the facility or service is provided is part of a hospital or other establishment for persons in need of 'special care'; 'special care' is not defined and is clearly extremely vague in its ambit;

(b)　is where the place is, either permanently or just for the time being, used for the purposes of an organised religion and the facilities or services are restricted to men so as to comply with the doctrines of that religion or to avoid offending the religious susceptibilities of a significant number of its followers;

(c)　is where the facilities or services are provided for two or more persons simultaneously and they are such that male users are likely to suffer serious embarassment at the presence of a woman or are such that a user is likely to be in a state of undress and a male user might reasonably object[335] to the presence of a female user.[336]

In addition, the section goes on to say that a person who provides facilities or services restricted to men does not for that reason alone contravene s.29 if the services or facilities are such that physical contact between the user and any other person is likely and that other person might reasonably object if the user were a woman.[337]

Nor do s.29 or s.30 apply where the situation in question is governed by the employment provisions of the Act.[338]

The EOC commented in 1986[339] that many single sex activities have become popular since the Sex Discrimination Act was enacted, which brings into question whether the Act requires extending in this area. As examples, it cites 'special provision for women which has developed over the last decade' and which is

> intended to raise their self-confidence (assertiveness training, training for life skills, girls-only careers conventions etc.), or to enable them to gain experience in fields which are traditionally male or are dominated by men such as the youth movements' attempts to encourage the greater participation of girls by running 'girls day activity' events to give them exclusive access for a period to facilities usually taken over by boys, or local authorities running women's sports days to encourage their greater use of public facilities, or 'taster' courses run by colleges to encourage women to consider pursuing educational courses which are traditionally male.

Really this is an aspect of positive action.[340] Such activities may well fall foul of the anti-discrimination legislation, for example if they are provided by a voluntary body which exists to provide services for both sexes. The EOC favours the extension of the Act in this area, expressed in gender-neutral terms so as to be of potential benefit to both sexes, where facilities or services 'are provided for the purpose of training, informing, or encouraging participation by persons of one sex in activities in which they have been previously under-represented.[341] Such an extension would be vulnerable to the usual arguments directed against positive action, but seems on balance to be justifiable on the ground of public demand and because it seeks to rectify historical imbalance.

The geographical scope of the goods, facilities or services provisions is complicated. The basic rule is that the Act only applies if the goods, facilities or services are provided inside Great Britain.[342] However, it does not apply to facilities by way of banking or insurance or for grants, loans, credit or finance, even if provided inside this country, where the facilities are for a purpose to be carried out, or in connection with risks arising, outside Great Britain.[343] Discrimination in this country as regards the provision of facilities for travel abroad is unlawful, even though the facilities necessarily relate to travel outside Great Britain.[344] Where British ships or aircraft are involved, it is unlawful to discriminate in providing goods, facilities or services whether they are provided inside or outside territorial limits.[345] If the application of s.29 results in a conflict with the laws of another country, our legislature has provided, rather weakly, that the laws of that other country prevail.[346]

## OTHER UNLAWFUL ACTS

Part IV of the Act defines an important category of unlawful acts, other than those dealt with in Parts II and III. S.37 is concerned with 'discriminatory practices', and its object is to make unlawful conduct which, although not itself amounting to unlawful discrimination, is designed to produce or result in such discrimination. A discriminatory practice is defined as

> the application of a requirement or condition which results in an act of discrimination which is unlawful by virtue of any provision of Part II or III taken with s.1(1)(b) or 3(1)(b)[347] or which would be likely to result in such an act of discrimination if the persons to whom it is applied were not all of one sex.[348]

An example is provided by an employer who lets it be known that nobody under six feet in height will be considered for a particular job vacancy to which height is irrelevant; such a requirement is indirectly discriminatory against women and, even if its imposition results in no actual act of discrimination because no women apply, it is unlawful. However, this is an extremely narrowly drafted provision in that it deals only with practices resulting in indirect discrimination; in a Race Relations Act case, *Percy Ingle Bakeries Ltd* v. *CRE*,[349] an industrial tribunal held that it does not catch a directly discriminatory requirement, such as that applicants be not of Pakistani origin, which results in no Pakistanis applying.[350] The statute clearly needs amendment so as to make it clear that it covers such situations.

Discriminatory advertisements are dealt with by s.38. 'Advertisement' is defined for this purpose as including

> every form of advertisement, whether to the public or not, and whether in a newspaper or other publication, by television or radio, by display of notices, signs, labels, showcards or goods, by distribution of samples, circulars, catalogues, price lists or other material, by exhibition of pictures, models or films, or in any other way.[351]

Such an advertisement is unlawful if it indicates, or might reasonably be understood as indicating, an intention by a person to do any act which is or might be unlawful by virtue of Part II or III;[352] it is a defence to show that the intended act would not in fact be unlawful.[353] The width of this wording suggests that it covers both direct and indirect discrimination, although this has never actually been tested in the courts. The section goes on to provide that the use of a job description with a sexual connotation – it gives as examples 'waiter', 'salesgirl', 'postman' and 'stewardess' – is to be taken to indicate an intention to discriminate, unless the advertisement contains an indication to the contrary.[354] In practice, advertisers often play safe by including a statement to the effect that applications from either sex will be considered, but it is questionable whether such a statement wholly dispels the subconscious impact of a sexist job description. As the EOC has pointed out,[355] there is prima facie evidence of discrimination if recruitment advertising is placed in journals directed exclusively, or apparently exclusively, at one sex only.

Liability is imposed on both advertiser and publisher,[356] but it is a defence for the latter to show that the advertisement was published in reliance on a statement made to him by the advertiser to the effect that the publication would not be unlawful and it was reasonable for him to rely on that statement.[357] If an advertiser knowingly or recklessly makes such a statement which is false or misleading in a material respect then he is liable to a substantial fine.[358] The section affects only advertisements which indicate an intention to discriminate unlawfully; it is not concerned with that much more insidious category of advertisements which portray women in stereotyped or unflattering roles. However, the EOC funded a study of the relative marketing effectiveness of traditional and modern portrayals of women in mass-media advertisements; the report, *Adman and Eve*, was published in 1982 and showed that a more adventurous and less circumscribed presentation of women in advertisements can, in fact, sell more products than the old familiar female stereotypes.

S.39 makes it unlawful for a person who has authority over another person, or in accordance with whose wishes that other person is accustomed to act, to instruct him to do any act which is unlawful by virtue of Parts II or III of the statute. This may occur, for example, where an employer instructs an employee to perform an unlawful act of discrimination. The EOC's experience of s.39 is confined to situations referred to the Commission by employment agencies which are encountering difficulties with particular employers.[359] There has been one Employment Appeal Tribunal decision, *CRE v. Imperial Society of Teachers of Dancing*,[360] on the equivalent s.30 of the Race Relations Act 1976. This established that a course of prior dealing between the agency and the employer had to be shown, a decision of which the EOC is critical. They estimate that, during 1985, at least 10 out of the 17 cases deemed unsuitable for legal action were not brought because of lack of such prior contact. The Commission

> takes the view that since the sole purpose of recruitment agencies is to provide employers with suitable candidates for vacancies the obligations imposed by the Act should apply from the moment that the employer seeks to use the services on offer. Anything less represents a dilution of the principle of non-discriminatory recruitment. Additionally an insistence on evidence of a pre-existing relationship between the agency and the client has the unintended effect of transferring the responsibility for observing the requirements of the Act from the client to the agency. If the agency complies with the Act by refusing to service the vacancy the client will suffer the inconvenience of filling the vacancy by other means, but the agency will suffer a loss of business. If the agency accepts the vacancy with discriminatory requirements then the agency itself is in breach of the Act.

Accordingly, the EOC makes the sensible recommendation that the Act should be amended so as to include a provision 'that no client using a recruitment agency may express gender preferences (unless these are permitted by virtue of the lawful exceptions) in relation to the vacancies being placed.'[361]

In similar vein, s.40 forbids a person to induce another to do an act which contravenes Parts II or III, and s.42 provides that a person who knowingly aids another to perform an act of unlawful discrimination is to be treated as having performed that act himself.[362]

S.41 extends the principles of vicarious liability to acts of unlawful discrimination. Anything done by a person in the course of his employment[363] is treated as done by his employer as well as by him,[364] even if it was done without the employer's knowledge or approval.[365] This principle finds application, for example, in the context of sexual harassment, where the harassment may emanate from a colleague rather than from the employer. However, the employer has a defence where he can show that he took such steps as were reasonably practicable to prevent the employee from doing the act in question;[366] this can clearly pose difficult practical questions where, for example, the employer's stated policy is to forbid sexual harassment but he has not dismissed an employee whose conduct has been the subject of earlier complaint. It is to be hoped that the employer's steps will only be seen as constituting a defence where, at the least, he has reacted to such an earlier complaint by instituting adequate disciplinary proceedings and an effective complaints procedure.[367] However, the signs are not encouraging. In *Balgobin and Francis* v. *London Borough of Tower Hamlets*,[368] the

Employment Appeal tribunal concluded, very weakly, that the employers had made out the defence where they were able to show merely 'proper and adequate supervision of staff' and that they had made known their equal opportunities policy. The Tribunal commented that it was 'very difficult to see what steps in practical terms the employers could reasonably have taken to prevent that which occurred from occurring'.

## REMEDIES

Part VII of the Act deals with enforcement and makes different provision in respect of the various categories of unlawful act.

### Enforcement in the Employment Field

Industrial tribunals[369] have jurisdiction over all complaints of discrimination made unlawful by Part II of the Act, over complaints that employers are vicariously liable under s.41 for such acts, and over complaints against persons alleged to have knowingly aided others, within the meaning of s.42, to commit unlawful discriminatory acts in the employment field.[370]

The services of a conciliation officer are available in such cases.[371] Considerable criticism has been directed at the role played by conciliation officers in this context. In particular, it can be argued, first, that conciliation is a wholly inappropriate device in a situation such as sex discrimination where a person's basic and non-negotiable legal rights are at stake and, secondly, it has been alleged that the ACAS officers responsible for conciliation in practice often dissuade women complainants from proceeding with their cases.[372] The EOC commissioned research into the role of ACAS conciliation and a report was published in June 1985.[373] This found some merit in the argument that conciliation is inappropriate in sex discrimination cases and concluded that

> conciliation and out-of-court settlement means for most ACAS officers in very many circumstances compromise. It is of course theoretically possible to produce settlements which seek to replicate the rigorous requirements of the legislation. This, we feel certain, is not what ordinarily happens. The culture and habits of conciliation officers are such that they will seek primarily to communicate the common ground between the parties – that often being synonymous with the lowest common denominator. Settlements are usually produced on that basis *even if* the strict legal requirements of the legislation

are flouted. Equal pay means equal pay and not a bargained reduction in the current differential between men and women, yet the latter, if attainable will occasionally form the basis for a settlement. We think that there is a central contradiction within the discrimination legislation in this respect which arises when undilutable standards are demanded on the one hand and out-of-court settlements on the other, channelled through officers whose working habits are determined by other employment legislation of a very different colour. If this contradiction is thought to be undesirable then legislation will be required to produce whatever results are thought most attractive.

As to the particular part played by ACAS, the researchers concluded:

on perhaps four or five occasions errors of judgment may have been made.[374] In three or four cases officers may have acted improperly and may have caused applicants to discontinue. It is important, however, to set these figures against the context of pressures on officers caused by the staffing reductions and the tiny proportion of their caseload which equal pay and sex discrimination cases represent. In all we were impressed by the general performance of ACAS officers and firmly convinced that it was not a significant influence on the pattern of case outcomes.

In the present writer's view, there would seem to be a great deal to be said for a very specialised form of conciliation in equal pay and sex discrimination cases, which would be able to take into account the particular difficulties experienced by litigants in these fields, possibly under the supervision of the EOC.

Where a case proceeds to an industrial tribunal, the remedies at the disposal of the tribunal are sadly limited. Where it finds a complaint to be well-founded, a tribunal can make any out of a list of three orders as it considers 'just and equitable'. The three available are (a) a declaration, (b) an order for the payment of compensation, and (c) a 'recommendation that the respondent take within a specified period action appearing to the tribunal to be practicable for the purpose of obviating or reducing the adverse effect on the complainant of any act of discrimination to which the complaint relates.[375] The amount of compensation which can be awarded is subject to a statutory maximum limit.[376] It can, however, include compensation for injury to feelings[377] and for such speculative matters as loss of prospective earnings. In *Hurley* v. *Mustoe (No. 2),*[378] an industrial tribunal awarded derisory compensation for injury to feelings, on the ground that this was 'just and equitable' since the complainant (having been involved in demonstrations against the respondent) had not come to court 'with clean hands'.

The Employment Appeal Tribunal overruled this decision, holding that the 'just and equitable' element of s.65(1) extends only to the *selection* of the remedy to be applied. Browne-Wilkinson J went on:

> The words 'just and equitable' do not cover the order to be made under paragraph (b) if that is the remedy which the tribunal has selected. When one turns to the words of paragraph (b), the order that can be made in respect of compensation is an order to pay compensation of an amount corresponding to any damages which could have been ordered by a county court if the complaint had fallen under s.66. Therefore, the amount of compensation is quantified directly by reference to the claim which could be established in the county court. Under s.66 there is no reference to the amount being limited to what is 'just and equitable'. Under s.66(1) the ordinary measure of damages payable in respect of tort is the relevant measure. S.66(4) amplifies this to make it clear that the damages include damages for injury to feelings. Therefore, in our judgment, the industrial tribunal erred in holding that the compensation payable was something other than the full measure of damages recoverable in tort for the statutory tort of unlawful discrimination. Finally, we would add that the introduction of the equitable doctrine of 'clean hands' into the assessment of common law damages is, as far as we are aware, a novelty. The equitable doctrine of coming to equity with clean hands is dealing with the exercise by a court of equity of its powers to grant an equitable remedy; it does not apply to claims for damages at common law.[379]

In practice, the amount of compensation awarded in sex discrimination cases is pitifully low.[380] This provides further reinforcement for the argument that greater specialisation and training for tribunal personnel is urgently required.[381] In a research exercise undertaken for the EOC, Leonard found that, between 1980 and 1984, over half the awards made by industrial tribunals were for less than £300; most of the complainants with recruitment claims were awarded a token sum only (usually of £100), purely as compensation for injury to feelings; and few of the complainants surveyed felt that the awards made to them had fully compensated them for the treatment they had received, many even considering their awards derisory.[382] The Commission itself believes that 'the present levels of awards reflect unfavourably on the gravity with which acts of discrimination ought to be viewed' and it is considering whether there should be a statutory minimum award of compensation.[383]

The Commission has recommended that a minimum figure for compensation for injury to feelings should be set.[384] The CRE agrees and in 1985 suggested a figure of at least £750 with provision to increase it from time to time by order.[385] An alternative approach would be to stipulate a norm in the legislation, which could be departed from in individual cases. Perhaps the best compromise would be to state statutory minimum and maximum levels for such an award, leaving the tribunal with a discretion between these limits. Meanwhile, little or no judicial consensus has emerged as to the level of awards for injury to feelings. In *North West Thames Regional Health Authority* v. *Noone*[386] an industrial tribunal awarded £5,000 compensation for injury to feelings in a race discrimination claim. On appeal, the Employment Appeal Tribunal held that this was quite out of line with other similar cases; it said that the highest recorded figure for such an award was £750 which, allowing for inflation, might properly by updated to £1,000. However, this is certainly not the highest recorded award in a sex discrimination claim; in *Porcelli* v. *Strathclyde Regional Council*[387] the complainant was awarded £3000 under this general heading in a sexual harassment claim.

In *Snowball* v. *Gardner Merchant Ltd*,[388] the Employment Appeal Tribunal restricted the potential scope of awards for injury to feelings in sexual harassment cases by ruling that the woman's attitude to sex was relevant to determine the degree of injury she had sustained. This ruling is grossly unfair, since it equates the woman's attitude to consensual sex with her attitude towards unwelcome advances.

As well as often experiencing difficulties in obtaining adequate awards of damages from industrial tribunals, complainants also encounter serious problems in enforcing their awards. Leonard's survey of complainants who had won cases at industrial tribunals found that almost half reported difficulty or delay in getting the employer to pay the compensation awarded and there were instances in which individuals had had to abandon their attempts completely.[389] The problems are exacerbated by the fact that the EOC does not grant assistance after the hearing. The EOC therefore proposes that a mechanism should be introduced to enable courts and tribunals to recover awards of compensation, perhaps on the lines of the Scottish sheriff officer.[390] Leonard herself suggests that applicants should receive their awards directly from the tribunal, leaving the tribunal to collect from employers.

The amount of compensation may be increased if the respondent fails without reasonable justification to comply with a recommendation made by the industrial tribunal.[391] The EOC considers that this is insufficiently powerful and recommends instead that tribunals should be empowered to award continuing compensation which would accrue on a daily basis until the changes ordered have been achieved; this would necessitate increasing (or perhaps removing) the statutory maximum limit for an award.[392]

A major restriction on the award of compensation is that such an order cannot be made where the discrimination is indirect and the respondent has proved that 'the requirement or condition in question was not applied with the intention of treating the claimant unfavourably on the ground of his sex or marital status.'[393] One acute problem which results from this formulation is that the courts, at least in race cases where the statutory provision is identical, have begun to apply it very subjectively. The statute does not say that damages cannot be awarded unless it can be shown that the person applying the requirement or condition *knew that the likely consequence of his behaviour would be adverse impact on one sex, or on married people.* It provides a let-out if the respondent can show that he did not *intend* to treat such people unfavourably. This comes very close to denying the existence altogether of such a category as intentional indirect discrimination, for a situation in which a requirement or condition is deliberately applied so as to disfavour a particular group looks suspiciously like direct discrimination. Yet, in *Orphanos* v. *Queen Mary College*,[394] the House of Lords held that a Cypriot student who had been indirectly discriminated against on the ground of race was not entitled to damages; the College had required him to pay the higher fees applicable to 'overseas' students because they did not consider that he had been ordinarily resident in the UK for three years before beginning his course. In the words of Lord Fraser of Tullybelton,

> When the College applied the residence test to Mr Orphanos their intention was to discriminate against persons who did not reside in the EEC area but there is, in my opinion, no ground for suggesting that they were intending to discriminate against them on the ground of their nationality or on any other racial grounds. Unfortunately, the discrimination on the grounds of residence cannot be justified irrespective of nationality, and it is therefore unlawful under the Act of 1976, but its unlawfulness is unintentional and accidental.[395]

Such decisions are not the only undesirable consequence of this part of the legislation. There is no sound reason in logic to deny the claimant her only real remedy under the existing legislation, namely damages, where the discrimination has been both indirect and unintentional. Anti-discrimination laws are concerned essentially with eliminating inequality of opportunity and inequality of treatment in practice; people's intentions are irrelevant in such a context, except sometimes to render what is bad or worse, so that if the claimant would obtain damages where the conduct was intentional than so, similarly, should she obtain such damages where it was unintentional. The present law conveys the impression that, for some unexplained reason, the legislature condones unintentional indirect discrimination and it deprives the claimant of an essential remedy in a very significant class of cases. Accordingly, the subsection barring damages in cases of unintentional indirect discrimination requires to be removed from the legislation. The CRE has recommended this course;[396] the EOC does not go this far, although it considers that

> the time has now come when for purposes of the award of compensation there should be a presumption of intention to treat the claimant less favourably on the ground of sex or marital status, a presumption which would be rebuttable. The Commission has issued a Code of Practice which contains considerable guidance as to the circumstances in which indirect discrimination might arise, and it takes the view that the circumstances in which it can legitimately be claimed that a requirement or condition was applied without the intention to discriminate are diminishing and that the approach of tribunals should reflect this.[397]

It will be evident that something which is lacking from the statutory list of remedies is any kind of specific and fully enforceable order; a recommendation is, after all, not mandatory. It has been argued earlier in this chapter that there is a need for the courts and tribunals to be empowered to order the implementation of a positive action programme, where they had found evidence of discrimination by the respondent in the course of hearing an individual's action.[398]

In addition, it is strongly arguable that there is a need for specific injunctive-type relief at the suit of an individual for what is in reality a statutory tort.[399] The absence of such a remedy is especially regrettable in cases of a continuing nature, in particular those involving sexual harassment. To argue that such a remedy would constitute an attempt by the law to interfere with personal relationships[400] over which the courts cannot exercise effective supervision is not an adequate answer; if Parliament has seen fit to devise an elaborate corpus of rules outlawing discrimination, then it must do its best to ensure that those rules are observed. There is nothing, in the overwhelming majority of employment cases, to make the situation a particularly personal one and, in the exceptional cases where it is, the court would always be at liberty to refuse to grant an order in the exercise of its statutory discretion. In any event, to restrain an act which breaches the anti-discrimination legislation will not usually amount to the specific enforcement of the contract of employment. It must, however, be admitted that to give industrial tribunals the power to grant orders which in any way resemble injunctions would represent a major increase in their powers and would militate against their intended informality.[401]

The nearest that the claimant can get to specific relief in this field in through the law on unfair dismissal, where the discrimination against her has taken the particular form of dismissal. For an unfair dismissal, she can ask for the remedy of reinstatement[402] but the Employment Appeal tribunal has held[403] that an unlawfully discriminatory dismissal is not necessarily an unfair one for the purpose of the Employment Protection (Consolidation) Act 1978; in the words of Browne-Wilkinson J,

> we do not think it necessarily follows that an employer has acted unreasonably within the meaning of s.57(3) (a question which involves considering the employer's conduct on the basis of factors known to him at the time he takes his decision) just because he has dismissed an employee as a result of an indirectly discriminatory condition (which does not necessarily involve the employer even being aware of the possibility that the dismissal was unlawfully discriminatory at the time he dismissed the employee.) [However, he went on to add] it would in our view need very special circumstances to justify a holding that an unlawfully discriminatory dismissal was a fair dismissal.[404]

In order to receive any remedy from the industrial tribunal, the proceedings must be begun within the very short time limit of three months from when the act complained of was done.[405] An appeal lies on a point of law to the Employment Appeal Tribunal.

## Enforcement in the Field of Education and in the Provision of Goods, Facilities, Services and Premises

The county court has jurisdiction over all claims that a person has committed an act of discrimination made unlawful by Part III of the Act, and over all cases in which an employer is alleged to be vicariously liable for such an act and also where it is alleged that another person has knowingly aided the commission of such an act.[406]

The EOC has pointed out that, since the introduction of the Sex Discrimination Act, only a handful of the thousands of complaints in the fields of education and consumer services have actually reached the county court. It believes that most complaints are deterred from bringing cases by the formality, procedural complications and expense involved. In addition, there is the further problem of the time it takes for complaints to reach the county court, especially in the field of education where a delay of twelve months or more between the alleged discriminatory treatment and possible redress renders action pointless. County courts, as a result, have had no real opportunity to gain experience and hence expertise in the anti-discrimination legislation and the Commission recommends that jurisdiction over all individual claims should therefore be transferred to the industrial tribunals, with special provision to ensure that there is appropriate lay representation in education and consumer cases.[407]

The remedies at present obtainable from the county court are those which would be available in a tort action in the High Court;[408] this means that an injunction is available in these cases,[409] as is a declaration, and also that there is no statutory maximum limit to the amount of damages that may be awarded. As with discrimination in the employment field, damages may include compensation for injury to feelings,[410] but no damages may be awarded in respect of unintentional indirect discrimination.[411] Proceedings must be brought within six months of when the act complained of was done.[412]

In the case of discrimination in education, there are certain extra complications to note. The main responsibility for securing compliance with the legislation in the public sector lies with the Secretary of State for Education and Science. The sanctions for breach of the general duty contained in s.25 are imposed by the Secretary of State[413] and they are the only sanctions for such a breach.[414] Where an individual claims to have been discriminated against contrary to s.22, or by an LEA contrary to s.23, before going to court the complaint must first be notified to the Secretary of State.[415] It can then be brought before the courts in the normal way either two months after it has been notified to the Secretary of State or before the end of two months if the Secretary of State has informed the complainant that he does not need further time to consider it.[416] If the Secretary of State has not reached a conclusion in two months he may, without prejudice to the complainant's right to bring proceedings, continue to consider the complaint. Such proceedings must be begun within eight months from the date when the act complained of was done.[417]

There is considerable overlap between these various provisions because discrimination contrary to s.22 or s.23 may also constitute a breach of s.25. It has just been seen that the individual has a right of action before the courts in respect of the s.22 and s.23 claim, but only the Secretary of State can bring s.25 proceedings. However, where the claim falls into both categories, the individual is still permitted to proceed with her claim under s.22 or s.23.[418]

As will be discussed in Chapter 5, the EOC is authorised to conduct formal investigations for any purpose connected with the carrying out of its duties.[419] If in the course of a formal investigation it becomes satisfied that a person is committing, or has committed, an unlawful discriminatory act, then it may issue a non-discrimination notice.[420] This means that in the field of education, if, for example, it suspects that unlawful discrimination is occurring, it may conduct a formal investigation;[421] at its termination, it must prepare a report of its findings[422] and, if it appears necessary or expedient, it may make recommendations with a view to promoting equality of opportunity between men and women.[423] However, in the last resort, the EOC's powers in this area lack real teeth because it may not issue a non-discrimination notice about a discriminatory act relating to a public sector educational institution; all it can do in the situation where it becomes aware of such an act is notify the Secretary of State.[424]

## Enforcement in other Cases

S.71 confers powers on the EOC to deal with cases of 'persistent discrimination'. These powers come into play where a non-discrimination notice[425] has become final or where a county court or industrial tribunal has found the respondent to have committed an act of unlawful discrimination or a breach of s.1 of the Equal Pay Act 1970. If within five years of any of these events it appears to the Commission that, unless restrained, the respondent is likely to commit another unlawful act, the Commission can apply to a county court for an injunction to restrain him from doing so.[426] This provision is interesting in that it indicates that the legislature is prepared, at least in the last resort, to countenance relief by injunction in employment cases. However, the procedure in such cases is extraordinarily convoluted, since it is provided that the Commission may not allege that the respondent has done an act which is within the jurisdiction of an industrial tribunal[427] unless a finding by an industrial tribunal to that effect has become final.[428] What this means in practice is that, where an employer has been held to have committed an act of unlawful discrimination in the employment field, even if the EOC is satisfied that he has offended against the same legislation again, it cannot proceed straight to the county court; it must first go to the industrial tribunal, establish the second act of unlawful discrimination, and wait until the time allowed to the respondent for an appeal has elapsed. Only then can the EOC go on to seek its injunction. As will be seen in Chapter 5, the EOC has made little or no use of this ultimate legal sanction.

S.72 deals with the enforcement of sections 38. 39 and 40 (on discriminatory advertising, instructions to discriminate and pressure to discriminate).[429] Proceedings for contravention of these sections can only be brought by the EOC and they are before an industrial tribunal in a case which is based on a provision of Part II of the Act, and before the county court in any other case.[430] The EOC can either ask for a decision that the alleged contravention has occurred,[431] or else it can seek an injunction from the county court if it considers that there is a likelihood of the commission of further offences;[432] however, the proviso again applies that the Commission may not allege that the respondent has committed an unlawful act which is within the jurisdiction of an industrial tribunal unless a finding by an industrial tribunal to that effect has become final.[433] The same problem of circuity of proceedings thus applies as in relation to s.71. Furthermore, there are two very important defects in the procedures provided for the enforcement of sections 38, 39 and 40. The first is the absence of a power in the court to impose a fine or to require the payment of compensation. A fine would appear to be the obvious way in which to deter discriminatory advertising, and an order for compensation would seem appropriate where a person has been injured by an act of unlawful discrimination instigated by another. However, the absence of the remedy of compensation is attributable to the second major limitation inherent in these procedures, namely, the fact that an individual, is not given a remedy. Whilst this may be acceptable in most advertising cases, where no particular individual can be shown to have been injured, this is not the case where an act of discrimination has taken place under pressure or instructions from a third party; there seems no logical reason why that third party should not be joined as a defendant in a complaint brought before an industrial tribunal or county court. The practical enforcement of sections 38, 39 and 40 will be discussed in Chapter 5.

The law relating to discriminatory practices under s.37 is also enforceable only by the EOC, and in this case only via the complicated procedures of formal investigation and non-discrimination notice[434] or else under s.71 where the particular circumstances set out in that section have occurred.[435]


## THE INDIVIDUAL'S CLAIM

In those situations in which the individual is enabled to bring a claim under the anti-discrimination legislation, the published statistics show a generally poor success rate,[436] although a significant upturn is evident in recent years. Until 1982, the success rate for sex discrimination claims before industrial tribunals was always under 10 per cent; in 1982, it jumped to 16 per cent, reached a record 23 per cent in 1983, but has fallen back to between 15 and

20 per cent since then. By comparison, the success rate in unfair dismissal cases actually heard by industrial tribunals in 1984 was 28.7 per cent.

The reasons why only a relatively small number of anti-discrimination cases are successful are probably many and varied. Reference has been made elsewhere in the present work to the predominantly male composition of industrial tribunals, to the background of tribunal members which encourages them to uphold the legality of practices with which they may well be personally familiar, to the scope offered by the legislation for subjective assessments of what it is 'reasonable' for a woman to expect, to the complexity and, in places, the extreme narrowness of the statutes, and to the lack of legal aid before tribunals. In addition, the procedure before industrial tribunals is defective in that it does not guarantee a pre-hearing review, in which the issues are clarified and the evidence which will be necessary at the hearing identified.

The EOC has also pointed out that industrial tribunals not infrequently make basic mistakes in applying the anti-discrimination laws. This emerges from two research exercises; Leonard studied cases heard by industrial tribunals between 1980 and 1982, and found serious deficiencies and considerable unevenness in the way cases were decided. A number of tribunals had misapplied the legislation, in particular, by relying on standards of 'reasonableness' and 'fairness' which are relevant in unfair dismissal claims, but have no place in this context.[437] A survey by Earnshaw arrived at similar conclusions.[438] It was seen in Chapter 2 that the EOC considers that the solution to these kinds of problem lies in better training for the personnel of industrial tribunals in the provisions of the legislation, and in a greater degree of specialisation in the future for both chairs and wing members, so as to provide for the most economic use of such training.[439] These are welcome proposals. There can be little doubt that systematic training in this complex area of law is necessary in order to avoid legal errors, nor that experience of actual cases is essential in order to raise the consciousness of tribunal members and make them sensitive and sympathetic to the problems experienced by the victims of discrimination.

In addition, there are also two essentially procedural matters which place unnecessary obstacles in the complainant's path and which could be remedied by means of relatively small amendments to the legislation. These are the burden of proof in anti-discrimination claims and the rules relating to the discovery of documents.

## The Burden of Proof

In *Oxford* v. *DHSS*,[440] Phillips J said that the Employment Appeal Tribunal recognised the difficulties but that there was 'no doubt that, although the Act of 1975 is silent upon the burden of proof, the formal burden of proof lies on the applicant'.[441] In other words, the legal burden of providing unlawful discrimination is on the applicant and she will lose her action if at the end of the day she has not established her case on the balance of probabilities.[442]

In practice, the first obstacle that the applicant will encounter is the absence of clear evidence, since it will only be in the rarest of cases that she will be able to point to a statement from the respondent to the effect that he intended to discriminate on the ground of sex. In the words of Lord Lowry C J in *Wallace* v. *South Eastern Education and Library Board*.[443]

> only rarely . . . will direct evidence be available of discrimination on the grounds of sex; one is more often left to infer discrimination from the circumstances. If this could not be done, the object of the legislation would be largely defeated, so long as the authority alleged to be guilty of discrimination made no expressly discriminatory statements and did not attempt to justify its actions by evidence.[444]

If the applicant is able to produce evidence from which discrimination is inferred by tribunal, then the evidential burden of proof will shift to the respondent; in other words, the applicant will then be entitled to succeed, unless the respondent can produce a similar weight of contrary evidence. As Phillips J explained in *Humphreys* v. *St George's School*,[445] although the burden of proof is formally on the applicant, 'it is a burden which may move very easily to the respondent, as a result of the evidence of the applicant.[446] Browne-Wilkinson J went into greater detail in *Chattopadhyay* v. *Headmaster of Holloway School*,[447] a case involving racial discrimination but in which the main issues were identical to a case on the ground of sex:

> a person complaining that he has been unlawfully discriminated against faces great difficulties. There is normally not available to him any evidence of overtly racial discriminatory words or actions used by the respondent. All that the applicant can do is to point to certain facts which, if unexplained, are consistent with his having been treated less favourably than others on racial grounds. In the majority of cases it is only the respondents and their witnesses who are able to say whether in fact the allegedly discriminatory act was motivated by racial discrimination or by other, perfectly innocent, motivations. It is for this reason that the law has been established that if an

applicant shows that he has been treated less favourably than others in circumstances which are consistent with that treatment being based on racial grounds, the industrial tribunal should draw an inference that such treatment was on racial grounds, unless the respondent can satisfy the industrial tribunal that there is an innocent explanation.[448]

Although these evidential rules appear neutral enough on their face, in practice they give rise to three related problems from the applicant's point of view. The first and most obvious is that she, without legal aid and perhaps single-handed, faces the entire burden of proving the case; as Jo Richardson MP pointed out in Parilamentary debate of the Bill,[449] one must accept the practicalities of the situation, which are that the woman will often be facing a large organisation with access to money, information, legal resources and expertise. The burden of proof, she concluded, ought to be 'on the side of the big battalions'.

Much more subtle is the question of what kind and weight of evidence the applicant needs to adduce in order to raise the inference which shifts the evidential burden of proof. The English courts have, unlike their American counterparts,[450] unfortunately not analysed this matter in any great detail.[451] They appear to accept that an inference of discrimination will be made where the applicant shows that her qualifications for the job in question are superior to those of the successful candidate; and in *Conway* v. *Queen's University of Belfast*[452] Lord Lowry CJ even indicated that a prima facie case of sex discrimination could be made out where the applicant was equally as well qualified as the successful candidate. In practice, however, it is difficult to show that two candidates are identically qualified for a post and it will often be necessary for the tribunal to have regard to other evidence as well, such as the employer's overall past record with respect to the employment of women. This the UK courts and tribunals have been noticeably unwilling in the past to do; for example in the race relations case, *Owens and Briggs* v. *James*,[453] the Court of Appeal ruled that a question as to whether the firm involved had any coloured employees was only permissible since 'if answered yes, it would have been helpful to Mr Briggs' firm. The negative answer was not relied on by the tribunal as part of their reasons for their decision, and there was certainly no need for the tribunal to pursue it further.' And yet it can be argued that a negative answer was highly relevant in these circumstances, since it would provide evidence to support the claim that the firm practised racial discrimination and from which such discrimination could be inferred.[454] In the more recent *West Midlands Passenger Transport Executive* v. *Singh*,[455] the Employment Appeal Tribunal showed itself to be aware of this point of view and held that a complainant was entitled to discovery of the total number of applicants, both successful and unsuccessful, classified by race, for similar posts in the two years prior to his own unsuccessful application for promotion. The Tribunal held that these statistics were relevant as evidence from which an inference might be drawn that the employers had adopted a racially discriminatory policy which manifested itself on other occasions as well as the present one.[456] In particular, the Tribunal noted that the CRE's Code of Practice advocates the monitoring of employees and job applicants, as does the EOC's also. This shows that Parliament intended that the results of such monitoring should be to indicate to employers whether or not in practice, as opposed to theory, they were providing equal employment opportunities. 'Unless the monitoring were to be merely an academic exercise', held the Tribunal, 'there could be no purpose in the Code of Practice encouraging the production of statistics save to use them as some indication of whether racial discrimination was being practised or not.[457] It is certainly to be hoped that this decision marks a new and more sensitive approach on the part of our courts and tribunals to the proof of discrimination.

The third serious problem from the applicant's point of view is that, even where the evidential burden has shifted to the respondent, all that he has to do to shift it back to her again is to adduce evidence of similar weight to her own; if that happens, since the applicant continues throughout to bear the legal burden of proof, she will lose her action.[458] This is in contrast to the American position where, once the evidential burden of proof has shifted to the respondent he has to prove that he acted for a legitimate and non-discriminatory reason.[459] In this country, it can even be sufficient from the respondent's point of view for him merely to articulate the reasons for his decision, without going so far as to try to prove them. It is at this stage that many claims, in fact, probably fail, since the respondent rarely encounters difficulty in producing a plausible-sounding explanation for the events in question.

In the somewhat similar area of unfair dismissal, the legislation places a very much more positive onus of proof on the employer.[460] Griffiths L J in *Maund* v. *Penrith District Council*[461] described the position thus:

> The law that has to be applied by an industrial tribunal in a situation such as this is clear enough. S.57 subsections (1) and (2) of the Employment Protection (Consolidation) Act of 1978 places the onus on the employer to show the reason, and if more than one reason

the principal reason, for the dismissal; and to show that the dismissal was for one of the reasons set out in subsection (2) of s.57 or for some other, substantial reason of a kind such as to justify the dismissal. If the employer is unable to show any such reason, the decision must be deemed to be unfair. Furthermore, s.58 provides that if the dismissal is because of trade union activity it is deemed to be unfair. The legal burden of proving the reason for the dismissal is, by the wording of the Act, placed on the shoulders of the employer. This is obviously sensible; the employer knows why he dismissed the employee, but the employee may not.[462]

Considerations such as all these have led to considerable pressure for a reversal of the legal burden of proof in sex discrimination cases.[463] In particular the EOC has recommended that, once the applicant proves less favourable treatment in circumstances consistent with grounds of sex, a presumption of discrimination should arise requiring the respondent to prove non-sexual grounds for that treatment.[464] Such an amendment of the legislation would undoubtedly go a long way towards improving the applicant's chances of success in an anti-discrimination claim, but it would also be necessary for the statute to stipulate in what circumstances precisely the presumption would arise and, in particular, make it clear that in employment cases this would not be restricted to situations in which the applicant was better qualified than the successful candidate.

## Discovery of Documents

The second major procedural obstacle encountered by claimants springs from the rules adopted by the courts with respect to the disclosure of documents, especially confidential ones. In sex discrimination cases, perhaps more than in almost any other class of case, the evidence required by the claimant will be in the control of the respondent; in order to make out her claim, it is vital that the woman have access to documents such as those which evidence the respondent's decision-making process. Without such information, she will often have little or no idea of whether she has even the beginnings of a ground of complaint.

The legislation itself provides the claimant with some help in the early stages of the action through the questionnaire procedure. S.74 is stated to exist in order to help a person who considers that she may have been the victim of unlawful discrimination to decide whether or not to begin proceedings and, if she does so, to formulate and present the case in the most effective manner.[465] Any person who thinks she may have been discriminated against may question a potential respondent about his reasons for doing any relevant act or on any other relevant matter. The questions and any replies to them are admissible in evidence in any subsequent proceedings[466] and if it appears to the court or tribunal that the respondent has deliberately, and without reasonable excuse, omitted to reply within a resonable period, or that the respondent's reply is evasive or equivocal, then it may draw any inferences that it considers just and equitable, including the inference that the respondent discriminated unlawfully against the complainant.[467] The Act gives the Home Secretary power to prescribe the form of questionnaire and to lay down time-limits within which the questionnaire must be served. He has prescribed forms[468] but it is not essential to use the official forms. In proceedings before industrial tribunals, the questionnaire may be served at any time before an originating application is issued or within 21 days of proceedings being begun; questionnaires served outside these time-limits cannot be admitted in evidence without the leave of the court.

In practice, the questionnaire procedure is useful in a variety of ways. As well as sometimes directly providing the basis for the inference that there has been unlawful discrimination, it can also be used to obtain information about such matters as the other candidates for a job, the respondent's business practices and the general statistical situation within an enterprise.[469] Its use in no way precludes the normal process of discovery of documents and it is governed by the same rules as to what information can be demanded.[470]

It is in this latter respect that the law is unnecessarily restrictive from the claimant's point of view. Both the industrial tribunal and the county court may grant discovery of documents on the application of a party to the proceedings, but no order is to be made if the tribunal 'is of the opinion that it is not necessary either for disposing fairly of the proceedings or for saving costs'.[471] In *Nassé* v. *Science Research Council*,[472] the Court of Appeal took a very narrow view of this discretion and ruled that confidential documents should only be ordered to be disclosed in very rare cases where, after inspection of a particular document, the judge or tribunal chair had decided that it was essential in the interests of justice that the confidence should be overriden, and then only subject to such conditions as to divulging as he thought fit to impose. Fortunately, the House of Lords took a broader view but even it ruled that relevance was not the only criterion.[473] In the words of Lord Wilberforce,

There is no principle in English law by which documents are protected from discovery by reason of confidentiality alone. But there is no reason why, in the exercise of its discretion to order discovery, the tribunal should not have regard to the fact that documents are confidential, and that to order disclosure would involve a breach of confidence. In the employment field, the tribunal may have regard to the sensitivity of particular types of confidential information, to the extent to which the interests of third parties (including their employees on whom confidential reports have been made, as well as persons reporting) may be affected by disclosure, to the interest which both employees and employers may have in preserving the confidentiality of personal reports, and to any wider interest which may be seen to exist in preserving the confidentiality of systems of personal assessment. . . . it should be added that relevance alone, though a necessary ingredient, does not provide an automatic sufficient test for ordering discovery. The tribunal always has a discretion . . . The ultimate test in discrimination (as in other) proceedings is whether discovery is necessary for fairly disposing of the proceedings. If it is, then discovery must be ordered notwithstanding confidentiality. But where the court is impressed with the need to preserve confidentiality in a particular case, it will consider carefully whether the necessary information has been or can be obtained by other means, not involving a breach of confidence. In order to reach a conclusion whether discovery is necessary notwithstanding confidentiality the Tribunal should inspect the documents. It will naturally consider whether justice can be done by special measures such as 'covering up', substituting anonymous reference for specific names, or, in rare cases, hearing in camera.[474]

Lord Salmon, although agreeing with the rest of the House's ultimate conclusion, expressed himself somewhat more broadly, saying that tribunals should not approach cases involving confidentiality 'with any preconceived notion that discovery should not be ordered "except in very rare cases" and in the last resort.' He considered that 'these cases should be approached with a completely open mind, the question being "is discovery necessary for fairly disposing of these proceedings?".' He concluded that, if the answer to that question was in the affirmative, and he thought that it often would be, discovery should be ordered.[475]

Unfortunately, the House of Lords' decision has subsequently been given a restrictive interpretation by the lower courts. For example, in *Williams* v. *Thomas and Dyfed County Council*[476] the Employment Appeal Tribunal held that an industrial tribunal had been wrong to order the disclosure of photocopies of all applications for a post in respect of which Mr Williams claimed to have been discriminated against on the ground of his sex. Wood J said that:

where discrimination is involved, then very often the person who is making the complaint will quite naturally want to know where the comparison lay and how he or she may have compared with others who were in the field for a particular post, and it seems to us that there are certain basic pieces of information, which may vary from case to case, which the claimant should be entitled to know: for instance, the sex of the person, the approximate age of the person, the qualifications of the person (provided that identity is not disclosed through qualification) and the work experience in general terms (provided that again identification is not possible through the work experience details). It would, however, be quite wrong and, indeed, destructive of the confidential relationship that some of the information which is given under that relationship between an applicant for a post and the proposed employer should be made public. It seems quite unnecessary for us to expand on the perils that could flow from a breach of confidence, and in this field, as in so many others, our community bases itself (and rightly) on trust and confidence. It seems to this Tribunal, therefore, that the balance must be maintained between the essential maintenance of confidence and trust, and the necessary information to be supplied to the claimant so as to ensure that he has a fair hearing.[477]

The Tribunal went on to rule that the correct procedure would be for the employer, after receiving a request for particulars, to prepare a document in respect of each applicant who could be called A, B, C and D, disclosing the essential information ordered by the tribunal. The Regional Chairman could then appoint someone to verify the essential facts by checking against the original document, but the original should not be disclosed to anyone apart from this checker. The trouble with this procedure is that it places the burden of arguing for the disclosure of particular pieces of information squarely on the shoulders of the claimant.

The real difficulty inherent in these judicial decisions is that they vest a crucial discretion in the tribunal, and there is a strong chance of that discretion being exercised in widely varying ways by different chairs. A case may be won or lost, depending on the attitude in this respect of a particular tribunal. There remains a good argument for general orders for discovery in discrimination claims (with the identity of individuals being disguised). simply on the ground that confidential information will almost invariably be essential to prove the case. It seems likely that undue weight is attributed by the courts to the 'candour' argument; it is doubtful whether the revelation of a small number of confidential references in judicial proceedings is really sufficient to deter the vast majority of referees from presenting their candid opinion.

# NOTES

1. The EOC's power to take widescale enforcement action is discussed in Chapter 5, p. 246 *et seq.*
2. The judges frequently refer to the two Acts together as a 'code'. See for example Browne-Wilkinson J in *Jenkins* v. *Kingsgate (Clothing Productions) Ltd (No. 2)* [1981] IRLR 388, 394, and Orr and Bridge LJJ in *Shields* v. *Coomes (Holdings) Ltd* [1978] ICR 1159, 1174, 1178. See also the remarks of Lord Denning MR in the last-mentioned case, discussed also in Chapter 2, p. 36.
3. For example, Atkins, 'Equal Pay for Work of Equal Value' (1983) 8 *ELR* 48; and the EOC in *Legislating for Change? Review of the Sex Discrimination Legislation* (1986). The Race Relations Act 1976 outlaws both contractual and extra-contractual discrimination on the ground of race.
4. Sex Discrimination Act 1975, s.6(5) and s.8(3). See also s.8(4). Hereafter, unless otherwise stated, the notes in this chapter making reference to statutory sections refer to the Sex Discrimination Act 1975.
5. *Meeks* v. *NUAAW* [1976] IRLR 198. See also Chapter 2, p. 36 *et seq.*
6. The industrial tribunal commented: 'Presumably the reason why a provision for the payment of money under a contract of employment was excluded from the scope of the Sex Discrimination Act was that it was envisaged by Parliament that such matters should be dealt with exclusively under the Equal Pay Act . . . however, there is a resultant gap in the case of indirect discrimination where there is no comparable employee in employment with the same or an associated employer. This gap is closed to some extent by s.37 of the Sex Discrimination Act which provides that it is a "discriminatory practice" to apply a requirement or condition which would be likely to result in an act of discrimination contrary to s.1(1)(b) or 3(1)(b) if the persons to whom it applied were not all of one sex.' Ibid., at p. 202. See 'Other unlawful acts' section *infra*, particularly p. 140, for further discussion of discriminatory practices.
7. S.8(5). *Oliver* v. *Malnick and Co. (No. 2)* [1984] ICR 458.
8. S.6(6).
9. It does not, however, deal with such vital areas as taxation, social security, or nationality and immigration. As to the last, see section on 'Discrimination in the provision of goods . . .' *infra*, particularly p. 135 *et seq.*
10. Its main provisions are drafted in terms of discrimination against women but they also apply *mutatis mutandis* to discrimination against men: s.2(1). This same terminology will be used for the purposes of the present chapter.
11. S.3.
12. *Hurley* v. *Mustoe* [1981] IRLR 208. See also *Thorndyke* v. *Bell Fruit Ltd* [1979] IRLR 1. See section on 'The meaning of discrimination' *infra*, particularly p. 80 *et seq.*, for discussion of the concept of indirect discrimination.
13. The EOC encounters a considerable amount of discrimination against single persons, in particular, on the part of institutions such as banks, insurance companies and building societies. The Act does not extend either to discrimination against single persons on the ground of their intended marriage: *Bick* v. *Royal West of England Residential School for the Deaf* [1979] IRLR 326; this seems quite illogical in the light of the fact that discrimination against such persons immediately after their marriage and on the ground of that marriage *is* prohibited.
14. In EOC, *Legislating for Change? Review of the Sex Discrimination Legislation* (1986).
15. EEC Directive 76/207, 1976 OJ No. L39/40. See also Chapter 4, p. 202 *et seq.*

16. The same form of words also appears in the Occupational Social Security Directive, Directive 86/378, OJ No. L225/40, discussed in Chapter 4, p. 194 *et seq*.

17. In its *Fifth Annual Report* (1980), the EOC recommended that the Sex Discrimination Act be amended to include discrimination on the grounds of either marital or family status. However, by 1986 it had drawn back and stated, in *Legislating for Change? Review of the Sex Discrimination Legislation*, that 'decisions made by the Employment Appeal Tribunal in *Hurley* v. *Mustoe* and *Skyrail Oceanic Ltd* v. *Coleman* [1981] ICR 864 [also discussed later in the present chapter, p. 79] marked important advances in the identification and outlawing of discrimatory assumptions related to marital or family status, and the Commission has modified its recommendation to a call for these decisions to be codified in statute. Such a position would not however deal, for example, with the situation mentioned in the text of discrimination against unmarried parents.

18. Ss.4(1) and (2).

19. CRE, *The Race Relations Act 1976 – Time for a Change?* (1983); and CRE, *Review of the Race Relations Act 1976: Proposals for Change* (1985).

20. See also *British Airways Engine Overhaul Ltd* v. *Francis* [1981] IRLR 9. For further discussion of what circumstances are relevant for the purposes of the Sex Discrimination Act, see sections on 'Discrimination by employers', 'Discrimination . . . by persons other than employers', 'Discrimination in education', 'Discrimination in the provision of goods', and 'Other unlawful acts', *infra*, pp. 94, 126, 130, 134 and 140.

21. *Kirby* v. *MSC* [1980] 3 A11 ER 334.

22. *Aziz* v. *Trinity Street Taxis Ltd* [1986] IRLR 435.

23. Ibid., at p. 439.

24. *Cornelius* v. *University College of Swansea* [1987] IRLR 141.

25. See EOC, *Legislating for Change? Review of the Sex Discrimination Legislation* (1986).

26. Graham and Lewis, *The role of ACAS conciliation in equal pay and sex discrimination cases* (1985, EOC), Leonard, *Pyrrhic victories* (1987, HMSO), and an unpublished internal study of complaints to the EOC.

27. The reversal of the burden of proof would occur where the applicant had proved a detriment in circumstances consistent with victimisation.

28. *Amies* v. *Inner London Education Authority* [1977] ICR 308.

29. *Steel* v. *Union of Post Office Workers* [1978] ICR 181.

30. Ibid., at p. 185.

31. *R.* v. *Immigration Appeal Tribunal, Ex p. Kassam* [1980] 1 WLR 1037 and *R.* v. *Entry Clearance Officer, Ex p. Amin* [1983] 3 WLR 258.

32. As has the race relations legislation.

33. See Chapter 2 for the respective numbers of men and women who sit on industrial tribunals.

34. For discussion of these situations, see *infra* in the present chapter.

35. The EOC considered this suggestion in *Legislating for Change? Review of the Sex Discrimination Legislation* (1986), but rejected it on the ground that it would place too great an investigative burden on the tribunal.

36. S.1(1)(a). Notice also that s.1(2) provides that if a person treats or would treat a man differently according to the man's marital status, his treatment of a woman is for the purposes of s.1(1)(a) to be compared to his treatment of a man having the like marital status.

37. *Peake* v. *Automotive Products* [1977] ICR 968.

38. Paradoxically, or perhaps not, several important early cases under the Sex Discrimination Act were brought by men.

39. *Peake* v. *Automotive Products* [1977] ICR 968, at p. 973.
40. It is reminiscent of the reasoning of the nineteenth-century judges in the 'Persons Cases', described by Sachs and Wilson in *Sexism and the Law* (1978, Martin Robertson).
41. *Peake* v. *Automotive Products* [1977] ICR 968, at p. 974.
42. Ibid., at p. 975.
43. For discussion of this approach by the Employment Appeal Tribunal, see *Grieg* v. *Community Industry* [1979] ICR 356.
44. *Ministry of Defence* v. *Jeremiah* [1979] 3 A11 ER 833.
45. Brightman LJ appeared to agree with Lord Denning MR about the inapplicability of these defences: see Slynn J's remarks in the Employment Appeal Tribunal in *Page* v. *Freight Hire (Tank Haulage) Ltd* [1981] ICR 299, 303. But note that the latter case preserves, on other grounds, the defence of safety: see *infra*, p. 125.
46. *Gill and Coote* v. *El Vinos Co. Ltd* [1983] IRLR 206.
47. In the provision of goods, facilities and services under s.29. See also section on 'Discrimination in provison of goods . . .' *infra*, p. 134.
48. *Gill and Coote* v. *El Vinos Co. Ltd* [1983] IRLR 206, at p. 207.
49. Ibid., at p. 208.
50. *Jackson* v. *Bridgford and Sons* (1983) unreported.
51. *Hurley* v. *Mustoe* [1981] IRLR 208. At p. 210, Browne-Wilkinson J said: 'We do suggest that industrial tribunals should look with care at the unsupported evidence of a respondent that a particular class of person lacks desirable features that others possess, especially when such evidence leads to discriminatory practices.'
52. *Horsey* v. *Dyfed County Council* [1982] ICR 755.
53. *Skyrail Oceanic Ltd* v. *Coleman* [1981] ICR 864. See also *Noble* v. *David Gold and Son (Holdings) Ltd* [1980] ICR 543; and *McClean* v. *Paris Travel Service Ltd* [1976] IRLR 202.
54. *R.* v. *CRE, Ex p. Westminster City Council* [1985] ICR 827. See also *R.* v. *Birmingham City Council, Ex p. EOC* (1988) 18 EOR 45.
55. Discussed in Chapter 5, particularly at p. 253 *et seq.*
56. *R.* v. *CRE, Ex p. Westminster City Council* [1984] ICR 770.
57. Cf. *Balgobin and Francis* v. *London Borough of Tower Hamlets* (1987) 15 *EOR* 37, where the Employment Appeal Tribunal appeared to misapprehend this distinction.
58. CRE, *Review of the Race Relations Act 1976: Proposals for Change* (1985).
59. *White* v. *British Sugar Corporation* [1977] IRLR 121: dismissal of a female transvestite in circumstances in which a male transvestite would also have been dismissed.
60. The Race Relations Act 1976 is more broadly drafted and states in s.1(1): 'A person discriminates against another in any circumstances relevant for the purposes of any provision of this Act if (a) on racial grounds he treats that other less favourably than he treats or would treat other persons.' This enabled the Employment Appeal Tribunal in *Showboats Entertainment Centre Ltd* v. *Owens* [1984] 1 WLR 384 to hold that it amounted to unlawful discrimination on racial grounds against Mr Owens, who was white, to dismiss him for refusing to carry out his employer's instructions to discriminate against black persons.
61. For a useful survey of the law and practice in this field, see Byre, *Indirect Discrimination* (1987, EOC).
62. S.1(1)(b).
63. The White Paper, 'Equality for Women', Cmnd. 5724 (1974) intended the legislation to extend only to intentional direct discrimination. For an account

of the events leading to the broadening of the scope of the Sex Discrimination Bill, see McCrudden, 'Institutional Discrimination' (1982) 2 *OJLS* 303, 336–8.

64. The leading American case in this field is *Griggs* v. *Duke Power Co.* 401 US 424 (1971). On the wisdom of this legal transplant, see Hepple, 'Judging Equal Rights' (1983) *Current Legal Problems*, 71.

65. S.66(3) is discussed further in section on 'Remedies' *infra*, p. 146 *et seq.*

66. *Perera* v. *Civil Service Commission* [1983] IRLR 166. See also *Meer* v. *London Borough of Tower Hamlets* (1987) 16 *EOR* 43.

67. Ibid., at p. 169 (Stephenson LJ).

68. CRE, *Review of the Race Relations Act 1976: Proposals for Change* (1985).

69. EOC, *Legislating for Change? Review of the Sex Discrimination Legislation* (1986).

70. *Home Office* v. *Holmes* [1985] 1 WLR 71. See also *Clarke and Powell* v. *Eley* [1982] IRLR 482, where Browne-Wilkinson J held in the Employment Appeal Tribunal that the spirit of the legislation requires that the term 'requirement or condition' be given as wide a construction as possible without distorting the wording of the statute; and *Watches of Switzerland Ltd* v. *Savell* [1983] IRLR 141, where secretive promotional procedures were held by the Employment Appeal Tribunal to be capable of being indirectly discriminatory requirements or conditions.

71. *Home Office* v. *Holmes* [1985] 1 WLR 71, at p. 75.

72. *Wong* v. *GLC*, unreported decision of 15 October 1980, EAT 524/79.

73. *Greencroft Social Club and Institute* v. *Mullen* [1985] ICR 796.

74. Ibid., at p. 802.

75. See *infra*.

76. *Kidd* v. *DRG (UK) Ltd* [1985] ICR 405.

77. Ibid., at p. 409.

78. CRE, *Review of the Race Relations Act 1976: Proposals for Change* (1985).

79. EOC, *Legislating for Change? Review of the Sex Discrimination Legislation* (1986).

80. However, in some cases they will provide the vital backbone to the woman's claim. See, for example *Huppert* v. *UGC* (1986) 8 *EOR* 38. Byre, in *Indirect Discrimination* (1987, EOC), makes the sensible suggestion that the EOC should provide for interested members of the public the basic statistics which they have collected in relation to each of the main types of situation where indirect discrimination occurs (for example, age bars, mobility, family responsibilities and part-time work).

81. S.5(3), see further *infra*, p. 92 *et seq.*

82. *Kidd* v. *DRG (UK) Ltd* [1985] ICR 405.

83. *R* v. *Secretary of State for Education, Ex p. Schaffter* [1987] IRLR 53, a case concerning discrimination over the provision of vocational training contrary to the Equal Treatment Directive, Directive 76/207, OJ 1976 No. L39/40, as to which see Chapter 4, p. 202 *et seq.*

84. Ibid., at p. 56.

85. *Price* v. *Civil Service Commission* [1977] IRLR 291.

86. This ruling was followed in *Bohon-Mitchell* v. *Common Professional Examination Board* [1978] IRLR 325.

87. *Price* v. *Civil Service Commission* [1977] IRLR 291, at p. 293. See also *Huppert* v. *UGC* and *Leavers* v. *Civil Service Commission* both reported in (1986) 8 *EOR* 38.

88. *Mandla* v. *Lee* [1983] IRLR 209; cf. the somewhat idiosyncratic decision of the Court of Appeal in *Turner* v. *Labour Party* [1987] IRLR 101.

89. *Clarke and Powell* v. *Eley* [1982] IRLR 482. See also *Steel* v. *Union of Post Office Workers* [1978] ICR 181.

90. *Steel* v. *Union of Post Office Workers* [1978] ICR 181. See also *Bohon-Mitchell* v. *Common Professional Examination Board* [1978] IRLR 325.

91. *Griggs* v. *Duke Power Co.* (1971) 401 US 424, at p. 431.
92. For criticism of this approach, see Thomson (1980) 96 *LQR* 329.
93. *Singh* v. *Rowntree Mackintosh Ltd* [1978] IRLR 199.
94. *Panesar* v. *Nestlé Co.* [1980] IRLR 60.
95. *Ojutiku* v. *MSC* [1980] IRLR 418. The House of Lords in *Mandla* v. *Lee* [1983] IRLR 209 apparently endorsed *Panesar* but without any real discussion of the issues.
96. Ibid., at p. 421.
97. Ibid., at p. 423.
98. *Clarke and Powell* v. *Eley* [1982] IRLR 482.
99. *Kidd* v. *DRG (UK) Ltd* [1985] ICR 405.
100. [1982] IRLR 482, at p. 487.
101. In *Kidd* v. *DRG (UK) Ltd* [1985] ICR 405, Waite J distinguished the *Clarke and Powell* decision in the following terms: 'The present case . . . illustrates the flexibility of the concept of indirect discrimination, and shows how the maintenance of flexibility may lead to different results in cases of superficial similarity. That should not necessarily be seen as a disadvantage. When the authors of the anti-discrimination legislation framed the concept of indirect discrimination they clearly attributed a high priority to flexibility – even if that meant leaving the concept exposed to criticism by the orderly minded as lacking form or precision. It would be unwise and unsafe, therefore, for anyone with a taste for drawing generalised conclusions to set the decision in the present case beside, for example, the recent decision of the Appeal Tribunal in *Home Office* v. *Holmes* [1984] ICR 678, or the earlier decision of the Appeal Tribunal in *Clarke and Powell* v. *Eley*, for the sake of deriving supposed differences of principle from the fact that in apparently similar contexts they have arrived at different results' (at p. 417).
102. *Billka-Kaufhaus* v. *Weber von Hartz;* Case 170/84 [1986] IRLR 317, also discussed in Chapters 2 and 4, p. 48 *et seq.* and p. 193 *et seq.*,
103. *Rainey* v. *Greater Glasgow Health Board* [1986] 3 WLR 1017.
104. Ibid., at p. 1028. Cf. *Hampson* v. *Department of Education and Science* (1988) 18 *EOR* 41.
105. Note in particular that a discriminatory term in the rules of the Community Programme for the long-term unemployed was upheld as 'justifiable' by a UK industrial tribunal under the old law: see *Chandler* v. *Secretary of State for Employment* (only Employment Appeal Tribunal decision reported, [1986] ICR 436.) Employment via the Programme is only available to those in receipt of 'appropriate benefit' either directly or through their partners, a provision which was admitted to operate in a discriminatory fashion as regards married women. The EEC Commission has begun proceedings against the UK as a consequence of this case: see CREW Reports (1988) Vol. 8, No. 1.
106. See in particular EOC, *Legislating for Change? Review of the Sex Discrimination Legislation* (1986), and CRE *Review of the Race Relations Act 1976: Proposals for change* (1985).
107. Race Relations Act 1976, s.1(1)(b).
108. *Mandla* v. *Lee* [1983] IRLR 209.
109. Ibid., at p. 213. See also *Orphanos* v. *Queen Mary College* [1985] AC 761.
110. *Home Office* v. *Holmes* [1984] ICR 678.
111. Ibid., at p. 684.
112. See section on 'Other unlawful acts', *infra*, p. 140, for discussion of 'discriminatory practices', where there need be no actual victim.
113. Pannick, 'Sexual Harassment and the Sex Discrimination Act' (1982) *Public Law*, 42.

114. See *Owen and Briggs* v. *James* [1982] IRLR 502.
115. *Barnes* v. *Costle* CA DC (1977) 15 FEP Cases 345. See also 'Sexual Harassment Law in the United States' (1987) 12 *EOR* 18.
116. *Hurley* v. *Mustoe* [1981] IRLR 208.
117. *Horsey* v. *Dyfed District Council* [1982] IRLR 395.
118. Ibid., at p. 397.
119. *Porcelli* v. *Strathclyde Regional Council* [1986] ICR 564.
120. *Turley* v. *Allders Department Stores Ltd* [1980] IRLR 4. Likewise, the industrial tribunal decision *Reaney* v. *Kanda Jean Products Ltd* [1978] IRLR 427. See also Pannick, 'Sex Discrimination and Pregnancy: Anatomy is not Destiny' (1983) 3 *OJLS* 1.
121. Ibid., at p. 5. As Rubenstein points out in 'The Law of Sexual Harassment at Work' (1983) 12 *ILJ* 1, taking this argument to its logical extreme it would mean that, as men are not biologically identical to women, all discrimination against women would be permissible.
122. Ibid., at p. 6.
123. *Hayes* v. *Malleable Working Men's Club* [1985] ICR 703.
124. Ibid., at p. 709. This decision opens up the possibility of challenge to the many non-contractual sick pay schemes which exclude or restrict benefits when the cause of absence is pregnancy-related.
125. After a year long survey of the law in all 12 Member States of the EEC, Rubenstein concluded that no EEC country provided adequate legal protection against sexual harassment and recommended that a new directive outlawing sexual harassment be drafted: Rubenstein 'The Dignity of Women at Work: A Report on the Problem of Sexual Harassment in the Member States of the European Community', COM V/412/87.
126. The definition of 'employment' in s.82(1) is the same as under the Equal Pay Act. For its interpretation by the courts, see Chapter 2, p. 19.
127. See Chapter 2, p. 20, for the meaning of 'establishment in Great Britain'.
128. *Brindley* v. *Tayside Health Board* [1976] IRLR 364.
129. S.72(1). See section on 'Remedies' *infra*, and Chapter 5.
130. See section on 'Other unlawful acts' *infra*, p. 140.
131. *Brennan* v. *Dewhurst Ltd* [1983] IRLR 357.
132. These were assumed to be capable of being 'arrangements' within s.6(1)(a) in *Saunders* v. *Richmond upon Thames Borough Council* [1977] IRLR 362. See also *Knight* v. *Attorney General* [1979] ICR 194 and the EOC's *Sixth Annual Report* (1981).
133. *Gates* v. *Wirral Borough Council*, unreported, but described in the EOC's *Seventh Annual Report* (1982). The EOC has produced an information leaflet on this case, which recommends that questions at interview about marriage plans or family intentions should not be asked.
134. See aso *McKenzie* v. *West Lambeth Health Authority* and *Smith* v. *North Western Regional Health Authority*, both reported in (1987) 15 *EOR* 42.
135. *Ministry of Defence* v. *Jeremiah* [1979] 3 A11 ER 833.
136. Ibid., at p. 837. Cf. *Peake* v. *Automotive Products Ltd* [1977] IRLR 365 (CA) and *Schmidt* v. *Austicks Bookshops Ltd* [1977] IRLR 360 (Employment Appeal Tribunal), in which it was said that a detriment must be 'serious' or 'important'.
137. Ibid., at pp. 843–4.
138. *Gill and Coote* v. *El Vinos Co. Ltd* [1983] IRLR 206.
139. Because the action was under s.29 not under s.6, see section on 'Discrimination in the provision of goods . . .' *infra*, p. 134 *et seq.*.
140. *Gill and Coote* v. *El Vinos Co. Ltd* [1983] IRLR 206, at p. 208. See also *R* v. *Birmingham City Council, Ex p. EOC* (1988) 18 EOR 45.

141. *Home Office* v. *Holmes* [1984] ICR 678.
142. See *supra*, p. 90.
143. *Home Office* v. *Holmes* [1984] ICR 678, at p. 683. In effect, the Tribunal has here supported a neutral definition of 'discrimination', see section on 'Indirect discrimination' *supra*. In similar vein were the remarks of Lord Emslie in the Court of Session in *Porcelli* v. *Strathclyde Regional Council* [1986] ICR 564: 'Although it is necessary for a woman seeking to found a claim upon s.6(2)(b) of the Act to establish that her employer had discriminated against her by dismissing her or subjecting her to some other detriment it is accepted by the employers for the purposes of this appeal that, if the applicant who was not dismissed, was discriminated against within the meaning of s.1(1)(a) she was subjected to a detriment within the meaning of s.6(2)(b). The employers in my opinion were well advised to make that concession on the facts of this case for, as was pointed out by Brandon LJ in *Ministry of Defence* v. *Jeremiah* [1980] ICR 13, 26, "detriment" simply means "disadvantage" in its statutory context' (at p. 568).
144. For example, in *Walsh* v. *William Rutter Ltd* and *Horton* v. *Pointon* (both 1983 and both unreported), industrial tribunals held that dismissal following a complaint of sexual harassment was unlawful sex discrimination. However, in each case the defence was struck out because of the respondent's failure to comply with a tribunal order, so that the argument did not range fully.
145. See Mackinnon, *Sexual Harassment of Working Women* (1979, Yale University Press).
146. *Bundy* v. *Jackson* (1981) 24 FEP Cases 1155.
147. *Meritor Savings Bank* v. *Vinson* (1986) 40 FEP Cases 1822.
148. *De Souza* v. *Automobile Association* [1986] ICR 514.
149. Ibid., at p. 524. Notice the objective nature of this test: the individual susceptibilities of the victim are not relevant.
150. Rubenstein, *Equal Pay for Work of Equal Value: the New Regulations and their Implications* (1984, Macmillan).
151. EOC, *Fifth Annual Report* (1980).
152. For detailed discussion of the many forms of 'positive action', see McCrudden, 'Rethinking Positive Action' (1986) 15 *ILJ* 219.
153. Rubenstein, 'Positive Action and Positive Discrimination' (1986) 10 *EOR* 40.
154. See 'Achieving Equal Opportunity Through Postive Action' (1987) 14 *EOR* 13.
155. EOC, *Code of Practice: Equal Opportunity Policies, Procedures and Practices in Employment* (1985). See also Chapter 5, p. 274 *et. seq.*
156. As amended by the Sex Discrimination Act 1986, s.4. The section used to apply only to 'training bodies' as therein defined.
157. And see s.47(3), which permits special training for those who have been discharging domestic or family responsibilities. See also *Hughes* v. *London Borough of Hackney* (1986) 7 *EOR* 27.
158. S.47(4), as amended by the Sex Discrimination Act 1986 s.4(4).
159. See EOC, *Legislating for Change? Review of the Sex Discrimination Legislation* (1986).
160. S.48(2).
161. S.48(3); provided that during the preceding twelve months there were no, or a comparatively small number of, women members.
162. S.49(1) and (2).
163. See further Robarts, Coote and Ball, *Positive Action for Women – the Next Step* (1981, NCCL).
164. In particular, *Bakke* v. *Regents of the University of California* (1978) 438 US 265; *Kaiser Aluminium* v. *Weber* (1979) 443 US 193; *Fullilove* v. *Klutznick* (1980) 448

US 448; and *Johnson* v. *Transportation Agency* (1987) 43 FEP Cases 411. See also 'US Supreme Court Endorses Sex – Conscious Postive Action Plan' (1987) 14 *EOR* 18.

165.   See 'Equal Opportunities and Contract Compliance' (1986) 8 *EOR* 9. See also 'Contract Compliance: the UK Experience' (Institute of Personnel Management, 1987).

166.   This is a list of persons and organisations meeting the Council's general requirements as to such matters as creditworthiness, efficiency and safety of their products and past record.

167.   *Wheeler* v. *Leicester City Council* [1985] 3 WLR 335.

168.   Ibid., at p. 343. See also *R* v. *London Borough of Lewisham, Ex p. Shell UK Ltd* (1988) 18 *EOR* 43.

169.   *Hughes* v. *London Borough of Hackney* (1986) 7 *EOR* 27.

170.   By the Sex Discrimination Act 1986, s.4.

171.   See CRE, *Review of the Race Relations Act 1976: Proposals for change* (1985).

172.   EOC, *Legislating for Change? Review of the Sex Discrimination Legislation* (1986).

173.   See also Chapter 5, particularly p. 259, for discussion of possible reform of the present statutory scheme relating to formal investigations so as to provide for positive action programmes.

174.   See 'A Review of the Effects of Executive Order 11246 and the Federal Contract Compliance Programme on Employment Opportunities of Minorities and Women' (1983, Office of Federal Contract Compliance Programs, US Department of Labour); Jonathan Leonard, 'The Impact of Affirmative Action on Minority and Female Employment' (1983, National Bureau of Economic Research and the University of Berkeley); and Herbert Hammerman, 'A Decade of New Opportunity: Affirmative Action in the 1970s' (1984, Potomac Institute).

175.   In EOC, *Legislating for Change? Review of the Sex Discrimination Legislation* (1986).

176.   Discussed in section on 'Discrimination by employers' *supra*, p. 94.

177.   Social Security Pensions Act 1975 s.54(2) and Equal Pay Act 1970 s.6(1A)(a).

178.   Social Security Pensions Act 1975 s.53(2). For criticism of the narrowness of the equal access requirements, see the Report of the Occupational Pensions Board, 'Equal Status for Men and Women in Occupational Pension Schemes', Cmnd. 6599 (1976).

179.   The reason the Bank gave for this difference was that 70–80% of their female employees left their employment under the age of 25, and it had been decided to reduce administrative costs by not requiring contributions from them and thus not having to refund any money on the ending of their employment.

180.   *Worringham* v. *Lloyds Bank* [1979] IRLR 26.

181.   *Worringham* v. *Lloyds Bank* [1979] ICR 174.

182.   *Roberts* v. *Cleveland Area Health Authority, Garland* v. *British Rail Engineering Ltd, Turton* v. *MacGregor Wallcoverings Ltd* [1979] ICR 558.

183.   As to which, see Chapter 4.

184.   *Worringham* v. *Lloyds Bank* Case 69/80 [1981] ECR 767.

185.   *Garland* v. *British Rail Engineeering Ltd* [1978] ICR 495.

186.   *Garland* v. *British Rail Engineering Ltd* [1982] 2 WLR 918. The European Court's judgement in the case (Case 12/81) is also reported here.

187.   *Barber* v. *Guardian Royal Exchange Assurance Group* [1983] IRLR 240. *Roberts* v. *Tate & Lyle Ltd* was sent on a preliminary reference to the European Court of Justice and reported in [1986] 2 A11 ER 602 (Case 151/84).

188.   Under s.5(3), see *supra*, p. 92.

189.   *Barber* v. *Guardian Royal Exchange Assurance Group* [1983] IRLR 240, 243.

190. Ibid., at p. 243.
191. See further Chapter 4, p. 190 *et seq.*
192. *Burton* v. *British Railways Board:* Case 19/81 [1982] 3 A11 ER 537.
193. See Chapter 4, particularly p. 216.
194. *Marshall* v. *Southampton and SW Hants Health Authority:* Case 152/84 [1986] 2 WLR 780.
195. EEC Directive 76/207, OJ 1976 No. L 39/40, as to which see Chapter 4, p. 202 *et seq.*
196. *Marshall* v. *Southampton and SW Hants Area Health Authority:* Case 152/84 [1986] 2 WLR 780, at p. 797. The European Court apparently sought to distinguish this situation from that in *Burton* v. *British Railways Board*, although on what basis is uncertain. It seems most likely that the latter case is distinguishable because there was a *pensions* element in it: as well as taking voluntary redundancy, employees under that scheme also took an early retirement pension. This also appears to be inherent in the reasoning of the European Court in *Roberts* v. *Tate & Lyle Ltd:* Case 151/84 [1986] 2 All ER 602.
197. See also Chapter 4. In *Duke* v. *Reliance Systems Ltd* [1988] 2 WLR 359, Lord Templeman commented that the respondent in that case 'could not reasonably be expected to appreciate the logic of community legislators in permitting differential retirement pension ages but prohibiting differential retirement ages' (at p. 373).
198. See section on 'Discrimination by employers' *supra*, p. 94.
199. As amended by the Sex Discrimination Act 1986, s.2(4). How this provision will actually work in practice is debatable. For example, where contractual terms provide that men are to retire at 65 and women at 60, who is being treated less favourably, the men because they have to carry on work for longer or the women because they are denied that opportunity?
200. Query whether this situation accords with EEC law. The Employment Appeal Tribunal held in *Hammersmith & Queen Charlotte's Special Health Authority* v. *Cato* (1988) 17 *EOR* 38 that a contractual redundancy scheme which discriminated against women contravened Article 119 of the EEC Treaty; the industrial tribunal had already held that the situation conflicted with Article 5 of the Equal Treatment Directive.
201. However the EOC reported in May 1987 that it had negotiated a substantial settlement on behalf of a woman employee aged 63 who was made redundant by a regional health authority: see EOC News Release 29 May 1987. The Government has subsequently announced that it plans to introduce new legislation to equalise statutory redundancy payments as between women and men: see (1988) 17 *EOR* 2.
202. S.6(7).
203. See section on 'Discrimination in the provision of goods . . .' *infra*, p. 134.
204. For detailed discussion of his section, see Pannick, 'When is Sex a Genuine Occupational Qualification?' (1984) 4 *OJLS* 198 and 'Genuine Occupational Qualification' (1988) 18 *EOR* 24.
205. But not at the point of dismissal; this is inherent in the wording of s.7 and was confirmed by the Employment Appeal Tribunal in *Timex Corporation* v. *Hodgson* [1982] ICR 63.
206. See *Page* v. *Freight Hire (Tank Haulage) Ltd* [1981] ICR 299.
207. It does not include, for example, the situation where an employer is recruiting a member of a team in which there is currently an imbalance between the sexes: *Roadburg* v. *Lothian Regional Council* [1976] IRLR 283.
208. EEC Equal Treatment Directive, Directive 76/207 OJ 1976 No. L 39/40, Article 2(2). See further Chapter 4, particularly p. 209 *et seq.*

209.   Even this category is not without its difficult cases. Is it permissible, for example, for a store to employ only female floor detectives, on the ground that most shoplifters are women and detectives need to be able to mix unnoticed among them?

210.   There is, for example, the thorny problem of the legality of demanding a female principal boy and a male pantomime dame!

211.   *Wylie* v. *Dee Ltd* [1978] IRLR 103.

212.   Applied so as to permit discrimination against a man in *Sisley* v. *Britannia Security Systems* [1983] ICR 628. The Employment Appeal Tribunal also held in that case that (b) can be invoked, not only where being in a state of undress is a necessary part of the employee's work, but also where it is reasonably incidental to it.

213.   S.1(2).

214.   *Commission* v. *UK* Case 165/82 [1984] 1 CMLR 44. See Chapter 4.

215.   By the Sex Discrimination Act 1986, s.1(1).

216.   In *Sisley* v. *Britannia Security Systems* [1983] ICR 628, the Employment Appeal Tribunal held that the words 'live in' involve the concept of residence, either temporary or permanent, and do not cover cases where the employee stays on the premises for only a limited time (even though he is literally 'alive in' the premises during such a temporary time). Lighthouse keepers and persons working on oil rigs were said to be 'obviously' covered.

217.   See Chapter 2, n. 24.

218.   EOC, *Legislating for Change? Review of the Sex Discrimination Legislation* (1986).

219.   The report was entitled *Health and Safety Legislation: Should We Distinguish Between Men and Women?* (1979 EOC).

220.   See for example Gregory, *Sex, Race and the Law* (1987, Sage).

221.   The EEC Commission considers that the UK is still in breach of EEC law as a result of discriminatory legislation relating to employment on board ships and manual earthwork. See also Chapter 4.

222.   Discussed *infra*, p. 125 *et seq*.

223.   EOC, *Legislating for Change? Review of the Sex Discrimination Legislation* (1986). The Government has stated that it intends to obtain the repeal of s.7(2)(f): see *Consultative Document on the Restrictions on the Employment of Young People and the Removal of Sex Discrimination in Legislation* (1988, Department of Employment).

224.   See *EOC News Release*, 24 November 1986.

225.   EOC, *Legislating for Change? Review of the Sex Discrimination Legislation* (1986).

226.   S.7(3).

227.   S.7(4).

228.   See also *Wylie* v. *Dee Ltd* [1978] IRLR 103.

229.   The word 'equipment' in this context is undesirably broad.

230.   S.17. See also *Wilts Police Authority* v. *Wynn* [1980] ICR 649.

231.   S.18(1). S.18(2) for the first time allowed male governors of female prisons.

232.   S.19(1).

233.   S.21.

234.   S.85(4).

235.   S.20 and Schedule 4 paragraph 3.

236.   *Commission* v. *UK:* Case 165/82 [1984] 1 CMLR 44.

237.   By the Sex Discrimination Act 1975 (Amendment of section 20) Order, SI 1983 No. 1202, Article 2. Note, however, that patients can still choose to be cared for by a female midwife if they prefer, and, if a male midwife is provided, he must be subject to appropriate supervision.

238.   The defences outlined in this section apply to all unlawful discrimination

under the Act and are not confined to discrimination in the field of employment.

239. S.2(2). See also Chapter 2 and note expecially *Coyne* v. *Export Credits Guarantee Department* [1981] IRLR 51.
240. S.43.
241. *Hugh-Jones* v. *St John's College, Cambridge* [1979] ICR 848.
242. The EEC Commission is believed to be contemplating bringing an infringement action against the UK for allowing the remaining single-sex colleges at Oxford and Cambridge to continue to recruit as fellows members of their own sex only.
243. Its underlying rationale is also opposed to that of the Sex Discrimination Act, which is that individual attainment is to form the basis for a person's assessment, rather than generalised notions of the average capacity of the sex in question. For further discussion of the appropriateness and fairness of the exception, see Pannick, 'Sex Discrimination in Sport' (1983, EOC).
244. *Bennett* v. *FA Ltd* unreported, 28 July 1978.
245. *GLC* v. *Farrar* [1980] ICR 266.
246. Ibid., at p. 272.
247. *British Judo Association* v. *Petty* [1981] ICR 660.
248. In EOC *Legislating for Change? Review of the Sex Discrimination Legislation* (1986).
249. S.45. As early as the date of its Second Annual Report (1977) the EOC expressed concern that insurance companies were treating s.45 as a general sanction to discriminate; it commented that even new schemes still offered differing premia according to sex, when it would presumably have been possible to assess the total risks and charge accordingly. The EOC has continued to reiterate this complaint in subsequent years, although no specific enforcement action has been taken by it. In *Turner* v. *Prudential Assurance Company*, Ms Turner alleged that the personal protection policy which she had taken out discrimated against her in that it offered her only £6 per week benefit for each £1000 of income, while a man paying the same premium would get £10 per week. Proceedings were begun but, before the case came to court the Prudential agreed to pay £500 damages and gave an assurance that in future benefits under this policy for women would be brought up to the same level as for men (see EOC's *Seventh Annual Report* (1982)).
250. *Pinder* v. *The Friends Provident Life Office* (1986) 5 EOR 31.
251. Under s.29, as to which see section on 'Discrimination in the provision of goods . . .' *infra*, p. 134.
252. EOC, *Legislating for Change? Review of the Sex Discrimination Legislation* (1986).
253. *Hugh-Jones* v. *St John's College, Cambridge* [1979] ICR 848.
254. *Page* v. *Freight Hire (Tank Haulage) Ltd* [1981] ICR 299.
255. The overlap between this exception and s.7(2)(f) has been noted *supra*, p. 119.
256. *GLC* v. *Farrar* [1980] ICR 266.
257. Ibid., at p. 270.
258. EOC, *Legislating for Change? Review of Sex Discrimination Legislation* (1986). See also Chapter 4, particularly p. 212. The Government is understood to be planning to introduce new legislation to amend s.51 so as to bring it into compliance with EEC law: see (1988) 17 *EOR* 2 and *Consultative Document on the Restrictions on the Employment of Young People and the Removal of Sex Discrimination in Legislation* (1988, Department of Employment).
259. S.52.
260. *Johnston* v. *RUC*: Case 222/84 [1986] 3 WLR 1038.
261. See Chapter 4, p. 209 *et seq*.

262. The Government has produced a draft Order in response to *Johnson* v. *RUC*; this preserves the defence of national security but requires it to be proved by means of evidence and disapplies those parts of s.52 giving conclusive weight to the Ministerial certificate: see (1988) 17 *EOR* 2.

263. S.9(1). In *Rice* v. *Phon-A-Car* [1980] ICR 133, Slynn J held in the Employment Appeal Tribunal: 'The proper construction of s.9(1) is that the work referred to is work which is done by someone who is employed by another person who supplies the work "under a contract made with the principal" to supply the worker. It is not sufficient, in a case to which s.9(1) applies, merely that work shall be done by one person for the benefit of someone else unless there is an undertaking under the contract to supply the worker' (at p. 136).

264. S.9(2).

265. See section on 'Defences available to employers' *supra*, particularly p. 115 *et seq.*

266. S.9(3).

267. S.9(4).

268. S.11(1), as amended by the Sex Discrimination Act 1986. The section used to contain an exemption for small partnerships, along the same lines as that in respect of small businesses, see section on 'Defences available to employers' *supra*, particularly p. 117.

269. S.11(3).

270. *Marshall* v. *Southampton and SW Hants Health Authority*: Case 152/84 [1986] 2 WLR 780, discussed in section on 'Defences available to employers' *supra*, p. 112 *et seq.*

271. S.12(1).

272. S.12(2)(a).

273. S.12(2)(b).

274. S.12(3).

275. S.12(4). This provision did not require amendment in response to the European Court's decision in *Marshall* v. *Southampton and SW Hants Health Authority*: Case 152/84 [1986] 2 WLR 780, since the relevant EEC law is concerned only with employment conditions.

276. See section on 'Positive action' *supra*, particularly p. 101.

277. The Employment Appeal Tribunal held in *British Judo Association* v. *Petty* [1981] ICR 660, that this provision covers all cases where the qualification *in fact* facilitates the woman's employment, whether or not it is *intended* by the authority or body which confers the qualifications so to do.

278. S.13(1).

279. *Bohon-Mitchell* v. *Common Professional Examination Board* [1978] IRLR 325.

280. S.13(1).

281. S.13(2).

282. See section on 'Discrimination in education' and 'Discrimination in the provision of goods . . .' *infra*, pp. 130 and 134.

283. As defined by s.14(2).

284. S.14(1). See also section on 'Positive action' *supra*, particularly p. 100 *et seq.*, in relation to positive action in training.

285. S.82(1).

286. S.15(3).

287. S.15(1).

288. S.15(4).

289. S.15(5). A person who knowingly or recklessly makes such a statement which is false or misleading in a material respect is guilty of a criminal offence under s.15(6).

290. In its *Second Annual Report* (1977) the EOC said it was of the opinion that rules

about school uniform which might be said to subject a pupil to detriment on the ground of her sex, 'for example, in refusing to allow girls to wear trousers', are questionable under the Act, although no case has directly raised the issue. Threatened proceedings on the point have been settled out of court: see EOC, *Seventh Annual Report* (1982).

291.  S.26(1). See also s.27, which deals with single-sex establishments becoming co-educational.

292.  See the report of the EOC's formal investigation 'Tameside' (1977).

293.  See for example the EOC's comments in its *Ninth Annual Report* (1984).

294.  EOC's *Seventh Annual Report* (1982).

295.  EOC, *Tenth Annual Report* (1985).

296.  *Debell, Sevket and Teh* v. *London Borough of Bromley and Smith* unreported, but described in the EOC's *Ninth Annual Report* (1984).

297.  In the parallel field of race relations, see *Orphanos* v. *Queen Mary College* [1985] 2 WLR 703.

298.  See section on 'Discrimination by employers' *supra*, p. 94.

299.  See section on 'Discrimination in the provision of goods . . .' *infra*, p. 134.

300.  S.23(2) makes similar provision in respect of education authorities in Scotland.

301.  In the EOC Report of its formal investigation 'Tameside' (1977).

302.  'Equal Opportunities for Men and Women' (Government Proposals for Legislation, September 1973) Department of Employment, Department of Education and Science, Home Office, HMSO, Appendix 2, paragraph 3.

303.  Report of the EOC's formal investigation 'Tameside' (1977). In 1987, the EOC obtained a declaration from the High Court in judicial review proceedings that the imbalance in the numbers of boys and girls given grammar school places in Birmingham constituted a breach of the City Council's statutory duty under s.23: see *R* v. *Birmingham City Council, Ex p. EOC* (1988) 18 EOR 45 and see also Chapter 5, p. 265.

304.  S.25(1).

305.  Sections 25(2), (3) and (4). For discussion of the enforcement of the education provisions in general, see section on 'Remedies' *infra*, particularly p. 149 *et seq.*

306.  S.67(6).

307.  EOC, *Report of Formal Investigation 'Tameside'* (1977).

308.  S.28.

309.  In *Alexander* v. *Home Office* (1987) 15 EOR 36, a county court held that the opportunity of being considered for a particular job in a prison was a 'facility' within the meaning of the equivalently worded s.20(1) of the Race Relations Act 1976. The significance of this ruling lies in the fact that the work of prisoners has not in the past been considered as work under a contract of employment or a contract for services so as to bring it within the employment provisions of the legislation. The decision was later upheld by the Court of Appeal and the plaintiff's damages increased although this particular point was not then in issue: *The Independent* 17 February 1988.

310.  See for example *Gill and Coote* v. *El Vino's Ltd* [1983] IRLR 206 and *Twambly* v. *Jamals Wine Bar* (unreported but described in the EOC's *Seventh Annual Report* (1982)).

311.  For example, hire purchase facilities: *Quinn* v. *Williams Furniture Ltd* [1981] ICR 328. Mortgages are another example and the EOC has repeatedly pressed the building societies to adopt procedures in the case of married couples which direct consideration first to the higher of the spouse's incomes (irrespective of whether that is husband's or wife's), and which allow in all cases for the expressed intentions and preferences of couples themselves to

be taken into account. In 1978, it published a Report, *It's Not Your Business, It's How the Society Works . . .* , which showed that more than one in three building society branch offices then discriminated against couples in which the wife was the higher earner. No litigation or enforcement action by the EOC ever got off the ground but, in 1980, the EOC felt able to report that the number of complaints it was receiving in this area had shown a sharp decline (*Fifth Annual Report* (1980)). See also *Seventh Annual Report* (1982). There was an upturn again in the number of complaints in 1983 (*Eighth Annual Report* (1983)). In its *Tenth Annual Report* (1985), the Commission reported a recent sharp increase in the number of complaints about retail credit, especially where complex and unexplained credit-scoring systems were in use. Some credit companies operate openly discriminatory policies. The EOC has requested the Office of Fair Trading to endeavour to identify such policies when looking into the overall qualifications of credit companies seeking licences; this is provided for by the Consumer Credit Act 1976, s.25(2)(c).

312.    S.35(3) provides, however, that discrimination which is unlawful under the educational provisions (see section on 'Discrimination in Education' *supra*, p. 130) is not also unlawful under this Part of the Act.

313.    In practice, the EOC has found the discriminatory provision of sports facilities to present a particular problem.

314.    See, for example, *Gill and Coote* v. *El Vino's Ltd* [1983] IRLR 206 and *Twambly* v. *Jamals Wine Bar* (unreported but described in the EOC's *Seventh Annual Report* (1982)).

315.    The services of a public authority include the Inland Revenue, since they provide a service to the public by collecting taxes and by giving relief from taxes and advice about taxes: *Savjani* v. *IRC* [1981] QB 458. Other examples might include medical services or library facilities: per Lord Fraser in *R.* v. *Entry Clearance Officer, Ex p. Amin* [1983] 3 WLR 258, at p. 268.

316.    *R.* v. *Entry Clearance Officer, Ex p. Amin*[1983] 3 WLR 258.

317.    *R.* v. *Immigration Appeal Tribunal, Ex p. Kassam* [1980] 1 WLR 1037.

318.    Following Woolf J in *Home Office* v. *CRE* [1982] QB 385.

319.    EOC, *Legislating for Change? Review of the Sex Discrimination Legislation* (1986).

320.    *Charter* v. *Race Relations Board* [1973] AC 868.

321.    *Race Relations Board* v. *Dockers' Labour Club and Institute* [1974] 1 All ER 713.

322.    [1973] AC 868, at p. 903.

323.    Race Relations Act 1976. s.25.

324.    See, for example, EOC's *Fourth Annual Report* (1979) and its *Eighth Annual Report* (1983). In its *Eleventh Annual Report* (1986) it commented that, over the years, no other single issue has produced so many consumer-related complaints to the Commission.

325.    EOC, *Legislating for Change? Review of the Sex Discrimination Legislation* (1986).

326.    Ibid.

327.    *Jones* v.*Royal Liver Friendly Society, The Times*, 2 December 1982. See also EOC's *Sixth Annual Report* (1981) and *Seventh Annual Report* (1982).

328.    S.29(3).

329.    The first successful application under this section came in *Taylor* v. *Burnett and Hilltree Park Ltd* (unreported but discussed briefly in the EOC's *Eighth Annual Report* (1983)).

330.    S.30(3). S.31 prohibits sex discrimination by landlords as regards the disposal of premises where their consent is needed for the disposal.

331.    S.32. This exception also applies to the provision of accommodation under s.29(1). Note also that under the Estate Agents Act 1979 the EOC is under a duty to inform the Office of Fair Trading of any finding of unlawful

discrimination by an estate agent. The Director General of Fair Trading may prohibit such a person from employment as an estate agent.

332. S.33.
333. S.34. For example, the Boy Scouts.
334. See Coote and Gill, *Women's Rights* (3rd edn. 1981, Penguin).
335. As with s.7, an apparently objective standard is being used here but perceptions of what is reasonable in such a context are likely to be subject to great variation.
336. S.35(1).
337. S.35(2).
338. S.35(3).
339. In EOC, *Legislating for Change? Review of the Sex Discrimination Legislation*.
340. Discussed in section on 'Positive action' *supra*, p. 98.
341. EOC, *Legislating for Change? Review of the Sex Discrimination Legislation* (1986).
342. S.36(1)(a). See *R* v. *Entry Clearance Officer, Ex p. Amin* [1983] 3 WLR 258.
343. S.36(1)(b).
344. S.36(2).
345. S.36(3).
346. S.36(4).
347. These sections deal with indirect discrimination, see the section on 'The meaning of discrimination' *supra*, particularly p. 80 *et seq.*
348. S.37(1).
349. *Percy Ingle Bakeries Ltd* v. *CRE* unreported, July 1982.
350. However, in arriving at this conclusion, the tribunal followed the decision of the Employment Appeal Tribunal in *Wong* v. *GLC* (unreported decision of 15 October 1980, EAT 524/79), which was discussed in the section on 'The meaning of discrimination' *supra*. It has been seen that the Appeal Tribunal declined to follow this ruling in *Greencroft Social Club and Institute* v. *Mullen* [1985] ICR 796, in the context of the Sex Discrimination Act.
351. S.82(1). The relationship between s.38 and s.6 has been discussed in the section on 'Discrimination by employers' *supra*, particularly p. 95.
352. An industrial tribunal in *EOC* v. *Robertson* [1980] IRLR 44 commented that the words 'or might be unlawful' are meaningless.
353. Sections 38(1) and (2). Not that the definition is not confined to advertisements for jobs, but also extends to advertisements for goods, facilities, services and premises.
354. S.38(3).
355. See EOC, *Fourth Annual Report* (1979).
356. S,38(1).
357. S.38(4).
358. S.38(5).
359. EOC, *Legislating for Change? Review of the Sex Discrimination Legislation* (1986).
360. *CRE* v. *Imperial Society of Teachers of Dancing* [1983] ICR 473.
361. EOC, *Legislating for Change? Review of the Sex Discrimination Legislation* (1986).
362. In *GLC* v. *Farrar* [1980] ICR 266, the Employment Appeal Tribunal commented that it would be reluctant to construe 'aids' in this context as meaning 'aiding and abetting' in the technical sense of the criminal law; instead, it was accepted, but without detailed consideration, that it means 'assisting or supporting'.
363. The employee need not be of managerial status and the meaning of 'course of employment' is the ordinary meaning in the law of tort: per May LJ in *De Souza* v. *Automobile Association* [1986] ICR 514, at p. 521.
364. See *Read* v. *Tiverton District Council* [1977] IRLR 202.
365. S.41(1). The same is true for agents, as well as employees, by virtue of

s.41(2). However, although the employer is liable for an act by an employee which is an unauthorised or prohibited way of doing an authorised act, he is not vicariously liable for an unauthorised act which is outside the sphere of the employment and for which the employment provided only the opportunity: *Irving* v. *Post Office* [1987] IRLR 289.

366.  S.41(3). The CRE objects to this provision, arguing that there is no reason why discrimination should be treated differently from any other civil wrong by the addition of a separate and special defence. See CRE, *Review of the Race Relations Act 1976: Proposals for change* (1985).

367.  For discussion of union and employer approaches to sexual harassment, see 'Harassment at work' (1985) 4 *EOR* 8.

368.  *Balgobin and Francis* v. *London Borough of Tower Hamlets* (1987) 15 *EOR* 37.

369.  For comments as to the appropriateness, in particular in terms of skill and composition, of industrial tribunals in cases involving discrimination, see Chapter 2, p. 38 *et seq.*

370.  S.63(1). The only exception is for a complaint under s.13(1) (as to which see section on 'Discrimination . . . by persons other than employers' *supra*) about an act in respect of which there is a statutory right of appeal: s.63(2).

371.  S.64. Similarly, in individual complaints under the Equal Pay Act 1970.

372.  Gregory, 'Equal Pay and Sex Discrimination: Why Women are Giving Up the Fight', *Feminist Review*, no. 10 (February 1982) p. 75; and Gregory, 'The Great Conciliation Fraud', *New Statesman*, 3 July 1981, p. 6.

373.  Graham and Lewis, *The Role of ACAS Conciliation in Equal Pay and Sex Discrimination Cases* (1985, EOC).

374.  95 applicants were surveyed.

375.  S.65(1)(c). In *Prestcold Ltd* v. *Irvine* [1981] ICR 777, the Court of Appeal held that a recommendation under (c) may not relate to the payment of compensation, since this matter is fully dealt with by paragraph (b).

376.  At the time of writing, this statutory maximum limit was £8500: see the Unfair Dismissal (Increase of Compensation Limit) Order 1986 (SI 1986/2284).

377.  S.66(4).

378.  *Hurley* v. *Mustoe (No. 2)* [1983] ICR 422.

379.  Ibid., at pp. 425–6.

380.  *The Times* for 14 May 1987 reported an award of £8000 in a sexual harassment case, commenting that this sum, the then statutory maximum, was double the previous highest award. The editors of the *Equal Opportunities Review* observe that compensation awards, both those made by tribunals and those agreed by the parties, tend to be substantially higher in sexual harassment cases than in any other type of sex discrimination claim: see (1987) 14 EOR 2. See also *The Independent*, 16 October 1987, for discussion of a case in which a settlement was reached by which the victim of sexual harassment received £7000 damages and a public apology.

381.  See Chapter 2, p. 38 *et seq.*

382.  Leonard, *Pyrrhic Victories* (1987, HMSO).

383.  EOC, *Legislating for Change? Review of the Sex Discrimination Legislation* (1986).

384.  Ibid.

385.  CRE, *Review of the Race Relations Act 1976: Proposals for change* (1985).

386.  *North West Thames Regional Health Authority* v. *Noone* (1987) 12 *EOR* 39.

387.  *Porcelli* v. *Strathclyde Regional Council* (1986) 9 *EOR* 2.

388.  *Snowball* v. *Gardner Merchant Ltd* [1987] ICR 719.

389.  Leonard, *Pyrrhic Victories* (1987, HMSO).

390.  EOC, *Legislating for Change? Review of the Sex Discrimination Legislation* (1986).

391.  S.65(3). See *Nelson* v. *Tyne and Wear Transport* [1978] ICR 1183, where Phillips J said: 'The whole of s.65 makes it quite clear that it was contemplated that

it may take a little while by order to eliminate established acts of discrimination; and it seems to us that the very terms of s.65(3) imply as much. The situation, in a way, is not unlike that where a court grants an injunction to prohibit the continuation of a nuisance . . . but suspends its operation for a period of twelve months to give a reasonable opportunity for remedial steps to be taken' (at p. 1189).

392. EOC, *Legislating for Change? Review of the Sex Discrimination Legislation* (1986). To the same effect, see also the proposals of the CRE in *Review of the Race Relations Act 1976: Proposals for Change* (1985).

393. S.66(3).

394. *Orphanos* v. *Queen Mary College* [1985] 2 WLR 703. Although not concerned with employment, the principles involved in this case were identical to those relating to employment.

395. Ibid., at p. 714.

396. CRE, *Review of the Race Relations Act 1976: Proposals for Change* (1985).

397. EOC, *Legislating for Change? Review of the Sex Discrimination Legislation* (1986).

398. See section on 'Positive action' *supra*, particularly p. 106.

399. If such a remedy were introduced, it should also be possible to obtain interim relief; at present, the absence of such relief is another serious lacuna in the legislation.

400. In any event, there is now a long list of other exceptions to the old equitable principle that a contract of personal service would not be specifically enforced. See Treitel, *Law of Contract* (7th edn, 1987, Stevens & Sons) pp. 792–4, and the references therein.

401. But note the power of magistrates' courts to grant exclusion orders under the Domestic Proceedings and Magistrates Courts Act 1978, s.16, which is in essence little different from a power to injunct. If the legislature believed the sanction of committal too drastic to entrust to industrial tribunals, it might consider a monetary sanction or provide that the new order could only be obtained from the Employment Appeal Tribunal.

402. Employment Protection (Consolidation) Act 1978, s.69. Note that the principle of no specific enforcement of contracts of personal service is still evident in the rule that, if the employer does not comply with the order for reinstatement, in the last resort he can only be made to pay compensation.

403. In *Clarke and Powell* v. *Eley* [1982] IRLR 482.

404. Ibid., at p. 488. See also *Timex Corporation* v. *Hodgson* [1982] ICR 63.

405. S.76. This is the same limitation period as for unfair dismissal claims, but the parallel is not really a very close one in this context since the termination of employment will almost always make itself obvious immediately whereas a complaint of sex discrimination will not. Contrast the usual three- and six-year limitation periods in respect of other torts. See also *Hutchinson* v. *Westward Television Ltd* [1977] ICR 279.

406. Ss.66(1) and (2). In Scotland, the sheriff court has jurisdiction.

407. EOC, *Legislating for Change? Review of the Sex Discrimination Legislation* (1986).

408. S.66(2).

409. Cf. 'Enforcement in the employment field' *supra*, p. 148 *et seq*.

410. S.66(4).

411. S.66(3).

412. S.76(2)(a).

413. Ss.25(2) and (3).

414. S.25(4).

415. S.66(5).

416. S.66(5).

417. S.76(2)(b).

# SEX DISCRIMINATION LAW

418. S.25(4).
419. S.57(1).
420. S.67(2).
421. As it did in the Tameside case in 1977.
422. S.60(2).
423, S.60(1).
424. S.67(6).
425. As to which, see Chapter 5, p. 253 *et seq.*
426. S.71(1).
427. That is, an act of unlawful discrimination in the field of employment (Part II of the Act).
428. S.71(2). The procedure whereby the Commission may obtain a finding by an industrial tribunal is set out in s.73.
429. See section on 'Other unlawful acts' *supra*, particularly p. 140 *et seq.*.
430. S.72(3). The sheriff court again takes the place of the county court in Scotland.
431. S.72(2)(a).
432. Ss.72(2)(b) and 72(4).
433. S.72(5).
434. S.37(3). See Chapter 5 for discussion of the use made by the EOC of its power to conduct formal investigations and issue non-discrimination notices.
435. See *supra* in the present section.
436. See Bindman, 'Proving Discrimination: Is the Burden Too Heavy?' (1980) *Law Soc. Gaz.* 1270.
437. Leonard, *Judging Inequality* (1987, Cobden Trust).
438. Earnshaw, *Sex Discrimination and Dismissal: A Review of Recent Case Law*, University of Manchester Institute of Science and Technology, Department of Management Sciences, Occasional Paper no. 8505 (1985).
439. EOC *Legislating for Change? Review of the Sex Discrimination Legislation* (1986).
440. *Oxford* v. *DHSS* [1977] ICR 884.
441. Ibid., at p. 886.
442. The only exception is where there is evidence of indirect discrimination: this will be assumed to be unjustified unless the respondent proves the contrary. See the section on 'The meaning of discrimination' *supra*, particularly p. 86 *et seq.*
443. *Wallace* v. *South Eastern Education and Library Board* [1980] IRLR 193.
444. Ibid., at p. 195.
445. *Humphreys* v. *St George's School* [1978] ICR 546.
446. Ibid., at p. 549.
447. *Chattopadhyay* v. *Headmaster of Holloway School* [1982] ICR 132.
448. Ibid., at p. 137. See also *Khanna* v. *Ministry of Defence* [1981] ICR 653; and *Moberly* v. *Commonwealth Hall* [1977] ICR 791. Cf. *Conway* v. *Queen's University* [1981] IRLR 137. Evidence of events subsequent to the alleged discriminatory act will not usually be relevant but, if exceptionally it is, then it can be admitted: *Chattapadhyay* v. *Headmaster of Holloway School* [1982] ICR 132.
449. Parliamentary Debates (Hansard) HC, 18 June 1975, vol. 893, col. 1468.
450. See in particular *McDonnell Douglas Corporation* v. *Green* US Sup. Ct. (1973) 5 FEP Cases 965.
451. See Pannick, 'The Burden of Proof in Discrimination Cases' (1981) 131 *NLJ* 895.
452. *Conway* v. *Queen's University of Belfast* [1981] IRLR 137.
453. *Owen and Briggs* v. *James* [1982] IRLR 502.
454. See also Hepple 'Judging Equal Rights' 1983 *Current Legal Problems* 71.
455. *West Midlands Passenger Transport Executive* v. *Singh* (1987) 15 *EOR* 35.

456. The Employment Appeal Tribunal expressly disagreed with its own earlier decision in *Jolota* v. *Imperial Metal Industries (Kynoch) Ltd* [1979] IRLR 313 on this point.
457. *West Midlands Passenger Transport Executive* v. *Singh* (1987) 15 *EOR* at p. 36.
458. See, for example, *Saunders* v. *Richmond upon Thames Borough Council* [1977] IRLR 362.
459. *Texas Department of Community Affairs* v. *Burdine* 450 US 248 (1981).
460. Under the Employment Protection (Consolidation) Act 1978, s.57(3), as amended by the Employment Act 1980.
461. *Maund* v. *Penrith District Council* [1984] IRLR 24.
462. Ibid., at p. 25.
463. See, for example, Pannick, 'The Burden of Proof in Discrimination Cases' (1981) 131 *NLJ* 895. As early as its *Fifth Annual Report* (1980) the EOC said that it was concerned that unwillingness by the lower courts to draw inferences of discrimination 'may have already snapped the resolve of many would-be complainants, which the Commission believes may have contributed substantially to the reduction in the number of individual cases under the Sex Discrimination Act. . . . As the number reduces so the level of practical awareness of the scope of the legislation is also likely to reduce, resulting in a vicious circle of decline in confidence in the effectiveness of the legislation. The Commission has reached the conclusion therefore that there should be a more equitable distribution of the burden of proof in sex discrimination cases'.
464. EOC, *Legislating for Change? Review of the Sex Discrimination Legislation* (1986). The CRE made a similar recommendation in *Review of the Race Relations Act 1976: Proposals for change* (1985). The EEC Commission is also preparing a draft directive which will relieve the complainant of at least some of the burden of proving sex discrimination.
465. The questionnaire procedure applies only to claims under the Sex Discrimination Act and not to those under the Equal Pay Act, although similar difficulties of knowing whether or not there is any prima facie case arise also under the Act.
466. S.74(2)(a).
467. S.74(2)(b).
468. The Sex Discrimination (Questions and Replies) Order 1975, SI 75/2048.
469. The EOC has pointed out that it is also useful sometimes to show up more widespread and varied manifestations of discrimination than those initially revealed by the original complaint: *Fourth Annual Report* (1979). See further Donnelly, 'Discrimination Claims – the Questionnaire Procedure' (1983) *Law Soc. Gaz.* 2340. It is not ordinarily to be used to find out the names and addresses of successful candidates for jobs because that is likely to cause trouble: *Oxford* v. *DHSS* [1977] IRLR 225.
470. S.74(5). See also Lord Salmon in *Nassé* v. *Science Research Council* [1979] IRLR 465, at p. 469.
471. Industrial Tribunal (Labour Relations) Regulations 1974 (SI 1974 No. 1368) and County Court Rules 014, r.2(2).
472. *Nassé* v. *Science Research Council* [1978] IRLR 352.
473. *Nassé* v. *Science Research Council* [1979] IRLR 465.
474. Ibid., at pp. 467–8. The procedure in such cases was to be worked out by the industrial tribunals and the Employment Appeal Tribunal in the light of experience; it should be flexible and have regard to such matters as the nature of the case and the volume of documents involved; the judgment of Arnold J in *BRB* v. *Natarajan* [1979] IRLR 45 was approved: per Lord Fraser of Tullybelton at p. 476.

475.	Ibid., at p. 470.
476.	*Williams* v. *Thomas and Dyfed County Council* (1986) 8 *EOR* 29.
477.	Ibid., at p. 30.

# 4 The EEC law on sex discrimination

## THE STATUS AND EFFECT OF EEC LAW IN THIS COUNTRY

A member of the European Economic Communities since 1973,[1] the UK is obliged, by Article 5 of the EEC Treaty,[2] to 'take all appropriate measures . . . to ensure fulfilment of the obligations arising out of this Treaty or resulting from action taken by the institutions of the Community'.[3] The 'action' which can be taken by the institutions is outlined in Article 189 and includes three types of secondary legislation, namely, regulations, directives and decisions.[4]

Regulations are 'of general application', are binding in their entirety and 'directly applicable in all Member States'.[5] This means that as soon as they are made they automatically penetrate into the legal systems of the Member States and need no municipal act of implementation before they take legal effect. Provision was made for them in this country by s.2(1) of the European Communities Act 1972.[6] A directive, on the other hand, is declared to be 'binding as to the result to be achieved, upon each Member State to which it is addressed, but shall leave to the national authorities the choice of form and methods'.[7] Intended to be an instrument for achieving harmonisation rather than uniformity, the directive thus requires transformation into municipal law[8] and s.2(2) of the European Communities Act enables this to be done here by Order in Council or ministerial regulation.[9] Decisions are merely binding on those to whom they are addressed,[10] so that they too do not automatically become law in the Member States.

Early in the life of the Communities, the European Court of Justice made two important pronouncements with respect to the characteristics of EEC law.[11] The first was that some provisions of the Treaty are 'directly effective', that is to say, enforceable in their own right by individuals in domestic courts, provided only that they satisfy certain criteria of precision so as to ensure that they are susceptible of judicial application. The reason given for this by the

European Court in *Van Gend en Loos* v. *Nederlandse Tariefcommissie*[12] was that 'the purpose of the EEC Treaty – to create a Common Market, the functioning of which directly affects the citizens of the Community – implies that this Treaty is more than an agreement creating only mutual obligations between the contracting parties. This interpretation is confirmed by the Preamble to the Treaty which, in addition to mentioning governments, affects individuals.' This notion of direct effect was soon extended to regulations.[13] Directives and decisions, however, presented more of a problem: not being 'directly applicable', that is to say, not being automatically law in the Member States, it was hard to see how the concept of direct effect could extend to them. How can an individual rely in court on an instrument which is not yet the law of the land? Despite this difficulty, the European Court decided in a series of cases[14] that individuals did derive rights from certain provisions contained in directives and decisions. The most convincing reasoning presented by the Court to support this was given in the *Ratti* case,[15] to the effect that a state which has not complied with a directive[16] within the time-period specified in the instrument is in breach of its own obligations and must not be permitted to rely on its own wrong-doing as against the individual litigant; in other words, the state will be taken to have done that which it ought to have done and to have conferred on the individual those rights which the directive intends to be conferred on him. The 'direct effect' of a directive is thus in essence a reflex of the obligation cast on the state and is, therefore, perhaps better described as being an effect 'similar' to direct effect.[17]

The second important characteristic of EEC law which has been consistently upheld by the European Court is its supremacy over conflicting domestic law. This principle applies whether the conflicting domestic law ante-dates or post-dates the EEC law[18] and irrespective of whether the EEC law is contained in the Treaty itself or in secondary legislation.[19]

The notion of supremacy of EEC law is given effect in the UK by s.2(4) and s.3(1) of the European Communities Act.[20] S.2(4) provides that any enactment 'passed or to be passed . . . shall be construed and have effect subject to the foregoing provisions of this section'; since one of the foregoing provisions is s.2(1),[21] granting legal effect in this country to all Community rights, and since the right to have EEC law treated as supreme is clearly a Community right, the subsection appears to protect EEC law against conflicting British law, whether the latter is earlier or later in date than the EEC law. This conclusion is reinforced by s.3(1), which raises decisions of the European Court to binding precedents for British courts; since the supremacy of EEC law has been reaffirmed on many occasions by the European Court, British courts are obliged by this subsection also to respect the principle.

Despite apprehension in some quarters that these statutory provisions would be insufficient to protect the supremacy of EEC law,[22] the courts of this country have in the main proved obedient to the principle.[23] Indeed, in *Macarthys Ltd* v. *Smith*[24] Lord Denning MR proclaimed that

> Community law is now part of our law: and, whenever there is any inconsistency, Community law has priority. It is not supplanting English law. It is part of our law which overrides any other part which is inconsistent with it.[25]

In the light of these principles, the potential significance of the EEC law on sex discrimination is obvious. Not only does such law bind the UK on the international plane, but the possibility presents itself of the direct enforcement by individuals of those aspects of EEC law which have not been complied with by the Member State. Added to this is the notion of supremacy which means that no Member State may use its own legislation to derogate from the terms of EEC law and which, therefore, places the latter above national law; it is tempting to draw a parallel between the EEC law on sex discrimination and a constitutional-type protection for women's rights.[26] The profound repercussions of such a parallel in turn make necessary a thorough examination of the terms and ambit of the EEC provisions on the matter.[27]

## ARTICLE 119

The only article in the EEC Treaty to make explicit reference to non-discrimination on the ground of sex is Article 119.[28] It provides:

> Each Member State shall during the first stage ensure and subsequently maintain the application of the principle that men and women should receive equal pay for equal work.[29]

Unlike the domestic Equal Pay Act, the Article refers only to pay and not to other contractual terms. It was included in the Treaty by way of a compromise between the original six Member States. Their respective employment laws were at considerably different stages of development. France considered that her legislation was especially favourable to workers and, therefore, correspondingly expensive for employers; in particular, French legislation of 1957 had provided for equal pay for men and women. The French were keen to ensure that the price of their goods would not be undercut, especially in the textile industry, once the Common Market was established, by goods manufactured in countries where wage costs were lower.[30] Accordingly, the French delegation insisted that equal pay must be mandatory throughout the Community. The European Court, reviewing the origins of Article 119 in the *Second Defrenne* case,[31] commented:

> Article 119 pursues a double aim. First in the light of the different stages of development of social legislation in the various Member States, the aim of Article 119 is to avoid a situation in which undertakings established in states which have actually implemented the principle of equal pay suffer a competitive disadvantage in intra-Community competition as compared with undertakings established in states which have not yet eliminated discrimination against women workers as regards pay. Secondly, this provision forms part of the social objectives of the Community, which is not merely an economic union, but is at the same time intended, by common action, to ensure social progress and seek the constant improvement of the living and working conditions of their people. . . . This double aim, which is at once economic and social, shows that the principle of equal pay forms part of the foundations of the Community.[32]

This emphasis on the function and consequent importance of Article 119 has enabled the European Court on several later occasions to give the Article an extensive interpretation.

### Implementation of Article 119

The end of the first stage was 31 December 1961. As this date approached, the Member States became aware that they were not all going to be able to comply in time with Article 119. A conference of Member States, therefore, resolved on 30 December 1960 to institute a new deadline, 31 December 1964, for the ending of all discrimination both direct and indirect.[33]

However, even this second deadline was not complied with and the Commission threatened proceedings against those States still in breach of Article 119. No such action was, in fact, taken at that time, perhaps because there seemed to be an increased political will on the part of the Member States to implement the principle of equal pay; as a result of the October 1972 Summit, the Commission proposed to the Council a 'Social Action Programme' aimed at bringing about a 'situation in which equality between men and women obtains in the labour market throughout the Community, through the improvement of economic and psychological conditions, and of the social and educational infrastructure', and in January 1974 the Member States resolved to adopt the necessary measures.[34] In February of the following year, the Commission sent a memorandum to the Member States which it called a 'Community Programme' for women workers.[35]

In addition to this heightened interest in the subject, the European Court began around this time to deliver judgments in several sex discrimination cases which gave cause to believe that the EEC law in this area was a very helpful weapon in the hands of women.

## The effects of Article 119

The first really important decision on the effect of Article 119 was the *Second Defrenne* case.[36] Ms Defrenne was an air hostess employed by Sabena Airlines. She claimed compensation in the Belgian courts in respect of past losses she had sustained through not having been paid equally with her male colleagues, known as 'cabin stewards', who performed work identical to her's. The Brussels Cour du Travail requested a preliminary ruling from the European Court[37] as to whether Article 119 was directly effective and, if so, from what date. The European Court held that it was directly effective, notwithstanding that the Commission and some Member States had sometimes taken the contrary view.[38] The words of the Article had been relied on to support this contrary view, particularly in that they refer to the 'principle' of equal pay and also because the Article is addressed to the Member States, which could be taken to suggest that legislative action is necessary by them. The Court rejected both arguments. The word 'principle', it held, is specifically used in the Treaty to indicate the fundamental nature of certain provisions;[39] and the fact that certain provisions of the Treaty are formally addressed to the Member States does not prevent rights from being conferred at the same time on any individual who has an interest in the performance of the duties so laid down. Article 119, the Court said, imposes a duty on the Member States to bring about a specific result within a fixed period and is sufficiently clear to satisfy the criteria of precision for direct effect. Moreover, the effectiveness of the Article could not be undermined by the non-compliance of some Member States with it, nor by the failure of the Commission to react energetically to this breach, since 'to accept the contrary view would be to risk raising the violation of the right to the status of a principle of interpretation, a position the adoption of which would not be consistent with the task assigned to the Court by Article 164.[40]

However, the Court admitted that Article 119 is not directly effective over the whole area of its application. It drew a distinction between what it then called 'direct and overt discrimination which may be identified solely with the aid of the criteria based on equal work and equal pay' and 'indirect and disguised discrimination which can only be identified by reference to more explicit implementing provisions of a Community or national character'.[41] The complete ending of all sex discrimination, it held, will require measures on a massive scale, but it went on:

> Among the forms of direct discrimination which may be identified solely by reference to the criteria laid down in Article 119 must be included in particular those which have their origin in legislative provisions or in collective labour agreements and which may be detected on the basis of a purely legal analysis of the situation. This applies even more in cases where men and women receive unequal pay for equal work carried out in the same establishment or service, whether public or private. As is shown by the very findings of the judgment making the reference, in such a situation the court is in a position to establish all the facts which enable it to decide whether a woman worker is receiving lower pay than a male worker performing the same tasks. In such a situation, at least, Article 119 . . . may thus give rise to individual rights which the courts must protect.[42]

It seemed to follow that direct effect should be attributed to the Article from 1 January 1962 for the original Member States.[43] However, the UK and Irish governments argued that such a holding, if it resulted in claims for back-pay by large numbers of people, would produce disastrous financial consequences for many undertakings. The Commission, by not bringing proceedings against the Member States in breach, had consolidated the general wrong impression as to the effect of the Article. The Court heeded these arguments[44] and produced a compromise formula which finds no obvious basis in the Treaty and is an unashamed example of judicial legislation;[45] it held that:

> as the general level at which pay would have been fixed cannot be known, important considerations of legal certainty affecting all the interests involved, both public and private, make it impossible in principle to reopen the question as regards the past. Therefore the direct effect of Article 119 cannot be relied on in order to support claims concerning pay periods prior to the date of this judgment,[46] except as regards those workers who have already brought legal proceedings or made an equivalent claim.[47]

Two further points were clarified in the course of the *Second Defrenne* case. The first was as to the operation in practice of Article

119. Trabucchi AG explained that where a pay rate for women is invalidated because it contravenes Article 119, it is automatically replaced by the higher rate payable to men performing equal work.[48] If a female air hostess is paid £80 a week, therefore, and male cabin stewards receive £100 for identical work, then the pay clause in the woman's contract is automatically invalidated by Article 119 and replaced by the promise to pay £100 a week. This is clearly a very useful sanction for the enforcement of equal pay and, according to the Advocate General, it can be reinforced by national measures imposing penal sanctions on those who disobey the principle.[49]

The full extent to which a Treaty article can have direct effect was also revealed.[50] Article 119 was held to impose obligations on all employers, and not just on the Member States to whom it is addressed. Trabucchi AG explained that

the decisive factor in determining what the effects of a Community provision are in national law is not the identity of those to whom it is addressed but its nature, which the Court defines on the basis of 'the spirit, the general scheme and the wording' of the provision itself.[51]

The significance of this is that the principle of equal pay binds not only states when they produce national legislation and employ government servants, but also public and private employers making both individual contracts of employment and collective agreements. Where a Treaty provision not only creates rights for individuals but also produces obligations for them in this way, it is usually described as being 'horizontally directly effective'.[52]

Decisions of the European Court since the *Second Defrenne* case have made it clear that the direct effects of Article 119 extend beyond obvious cases of direct discrimination. *Jenkins* v. *Kingsgate Clothing Productions) Ltd* concerned a complaint by a woman part-time employee that she received some 10 per cent less pay per hour than a male colleague employed full-time on the same work.[53] The British industrial tribunal held that this variation in pay was genuinely due to a material difference other than sex within the meaning of s.1(3) of the Equal Pay Act 1970, namely that Ms Jenkins worked for fewer hours than the full-timer.[54] When Ms Jenkins appealed to the Employment Appeal Tribunal, that Tribunal sought a preliminary ruling from the European Court, asking essentially whether Article 119 forbids paying part-time workers less than full-timers when the category of part-time workers is exclusively or predominantly made up of women.[55] At the time of the proceedings, the part-timers employed by Kingsgate were all female, with the exception of one male part-timer who had just retired and who had, exceptionally and for short periods, been allowed to go on working. Such a situation reflected the general picture in the UK, where the great majority of part-time workers are women.[56]

The European Court ruled that Article 119 is concerned only with equal pay for men and women doing the same work. Therefore, the fact that part-time work is paid at an hourly rate lower than pay for full-time work does not amount *per se* to discrimination prohibited by the Article, provided that the hourly rates are applied to workers belonging to either category without distinction based on sex. However, if it can be shown that far fewer women than men are able to work full-time for an employer, any inequality of pay will be contrary to Article 119 if 'the pay policy of the undertaking in question cannot be explained by factors other than discrimination based on sex'.[57] The Court went on to explain that

> where the hourly rate of pay differs according to whether the work is part-time or full-time it is for the national courts to decide in each individual case whether, regard being had to the facts of the case, its history and the employer's intention, a pay policy such as that which is at issue in the main proceedings although represented as a difference based on weekly working hours is or is not in reality discrimination based on the sex of the worker.[58]

The ruling finally given by the Court was that

> a difference in pay between full-time workers and part-time workers does not amount to discrimination prohibited by Article 119 of the Treaty unless it is in reality merely an indirect way of reducing the level of pay of part-time workers on the ground that that group of workers is composed exclusively or predominantly of women.[59]

Finally, the Court held that Article 119 is directly effective in this situation, a conclusion which it later reiterated in *Bilka-Kaufhaus GmbH* v. *Weber Von Hartz;*[60] in other words (confusing though they may be), this means that Article 119 is directly effective even with respect to indirect discrimination.[61]

Unfortunately, as discussed in Chapter 2, the European Court's judgment left unclear the question of whether Article 119 prohibited all indirect discrimination over pay, or only that which was intentional. On the case's return to the Employment Appeal Tribunal, the domestic provisions were held to extend to both intentional and unintentional discrimination, and the ambiguity in the EEC provisions appears to have been similarly resolved by the European court's statement in *Bilka-Kaufhaus* that indirect discrimination is only excusable where it can be explained by 'objectively justified factors unrelated to grounds of sex'.[62]

As is the case with the UK's domestic laws on equal pay, it would appear from the wording of Article 119 that its ambit does not extend to the adjustment of unjustified or unfair differentials, where the two jobs being compared are not identical in nature or at least of equal value. The Article, in other words, does not outlaw all discrimination in respect of pay.[63]

## The meaning of 'equal pay'

The meaning to be attached to 'pay' in Article 119 is crucial, especially since it is the only term of a contract of employment covered by the Article. Some elucidation is provided by the second paragraph of the Article, which provides:

> 'Pay' means the ordinary basic or minimum wage or salary or any other consideration, whether in cash or in kind, which the worker receives, directly or indirectly, in respect of his employment from his employer.

This lays down two criteria in particular, namely, that the payment must come from the employer (whether directly or indirectly) and that the payment must arise out of the worker's employment.[64] The second of these criteria received the attention of Roemer AG in *Sabbatini* v. *European Parliament*.[65] Proceedings were brought by two Community officials to overturn decisions of the relevant institutions denying them expatriation allowances;[66] such allowances were payable to people having to live in a foreign country in order to work for the EEC. One of the applicants' contentions was that the refusal of these allowances constituted a breach of Article 119 and a preliminary issue arose as to whether such an allowance was 'pay'. The Commission pointed out[67] that the allowance represented, not payment for work done, but compensation for having to work away from home; it was payable quite independently of the work done and could not therefore be considered 'pay'. The European Court dealt with the case on a different footing[68] but the Advocate General submitted that acccount should be taken not just of wages *stricto sensu* but also of all other payments made by reason of the links binding workers to their employers. Expatriation allowances fell within the concept of 'pay' because they were so closely connected with the official's work. In effect, the Advocate General was making the point that Article 119 uses the words 'consideration . . . which the worker receives . . . in respect of his employment', rather than 'consideration for the job done'. If the Advocate General is correct, then it follows that Article

119 covers other compensatory payments made by an employer, such as the refund of business, travelling or removal expenses. It would also appear to cover redundancy payments.[69] Article 119 expressly mentions consideration in kind, so that EEC law extends to perks such as concessionary railway fares.[70]

The extent, if any, to which Article 119 covers pension schemes has presented considerable difficulty for the European Court; in particular, does the principle of equality apply to the contributions payable to pension schemes and to the benefits received from them? In the UK, as was seen in Chapter 3, there have been, and continue to be, restrictions on the principle of equality in relation to the treatment of employees in the context of death and retirement, so that the EEC provisions assume a special importance. It is clear from *Garland* v. *British Rail Engineering Ltd*[71] that Article 119 certainly does extend to certain benefits conferred after a contract of employment has come to an end. During their employment, all employees of BREL enjoyed concessionary travel facilities, as did their families. However, a female employee complained that, on retirement, whilst male employees continued to receive the facilities for themselves and their wives and dependent children, female employees received them only on their own behalf and not for their families as well. The European Court held that the facilities did constitute 'pay' for the purpose of Article 119; it was not important that they were received after the employment had come to an end, nor that there was no contractual obligation binding BREL to provide them. The essential point, said the Court, was that they were granted 'in respect of employment'. Any discrimination in the provision of the facilities was therefore a breach of Article 119, which was directly effective in such a case.

The pensions issue was first directly raised before the European Court in the *First Defrenne* case.[72] Ms Defrenne, like all Sabena's air hostesses, was forced to retire at the age of 40. She was then faced with the fact that a Belgian Royal Decree established a pension scheme for 'all members of air crews with the exception of air hostesses', this special scheme being much more lucrative than the general state pension and available when the ex-employee was 55; under the general scheme, women could not claim their pension until the age of 60. Ms Defrenne objected on two scores: first, her years of service with the airline before the age of 40 were only taken into consideration under the less favourable general scheme; and secondly, she could not claim any pension at all until she was 60. She brought an action in the Belgian courts, which resulted in a reference to the European Court; in particular, the national court asked whether a pension granted under a social security scheme financed by workers' and employers' contributions, as well as by state grants, fell within Article 119. The European Court held that a retirement pension 'instituted within the framework of a statutory social security scheme' does not fall within the Article, partly because the employer's contribution in such a case is not paid directly or indirectly to the worker and partly because the payment does not arise out of the worker's employment: he is entitled to benefit provided only that he complies with the statutory conditions, irrespective of whether the employer in fact pays his contribution. The Court thus held that both general state pension schemes and special state schemes, such as the one in question, are not within Article 119.[73]

However, doubts remained after the *First Defrenne* case because Dutheillet de Lamothe AG indicated that he considered that certain pension schemes are covered by Article 119, in particular those which he described as 'supplementary' schemes: providing workers in some occupations and in some undertakings with a pension which is added to that paid by the general social security system. One difficulty here is that the pension is not paid by the employer, but instead by the administrators of the fund. None the less the Advocate General believed that Article 119 extends to such a situation for two reasons:

> 1. The fact that the pension is partly financed by wage and salary-earners who have not yet reached retirement age cannot set aside by itself application of Article 119, as it does not stipulate that it only applies to emoluments borne *solely* by the employer. . . .
> 2. The link, which Article 119 implies must necessarily exist between the emolument, the employer, the wage or salary-earner and the employment, appears to me to be sufficiently established in the case of supplementary pensions, as there is no doubt that these arise only out of certain kinds of employment. . . . [74]

The situation became even more complicated after the decision in the *First Defrenne* case. In particular, legislation in this country governing occupational pension schemes had the effect of blurring the distinction between 'state schemes' and 'supplementary schemes', and this for two reasons: first of all, the UK's state retirement pension scheme has for some years consisted of a basic component and an earnings-related component;[75] provided that a given occupational scheme fulfilled the requirements laid down in the Social Security Pensions Act 1975,[76] its members could be 'contracted-out' of the earnings-related component. The occupational pension was thus a substitute for part of the state pension. Secondly, if a scheme was approved under the Finance Act 1970, certain fiscal advantages would follow for both employer and employee, so that the scheme was in a sense subsidised by the state.

It was hoped by many that *Worthingham* v. *Lloyds Bank*[77] would clarify whether or not Article 119 covers such an occupational scheme. The Bank had separate pension schemes for male and female employees. The schemes were contributory for all male employees and for females over 25. In order to maintain pay parity with the other clearing banks, Lloyds added an extra 5 per cent, the cost of the contribution, to the salaries of all contributing employees. This money went straight to the pension fund and was therefore a 'notional' payment to the employee. *Inter alia,*the arrangement meant that if a man left the Bank before qualifying for any benefits, he received a refund of the contributions paid on his behalf; on the other hand, if a woman under 25 left in parallel circumstances, she received nothing. Two women under 25 leaving the Bank's employment complained to the courts of sex discrimination. The 'pensions exclusion'[78] exempted the situation from the principle of equal pay from the viewpoint of domestic law, but the Court of Appeal sought a preliminary ruling from the European Court as to the effect of EEC law on this situation. They asked whether the contributions paid by an employer to a retirement benefits scheme and the rights and benefits of a worker under such a scheme constitute 'pay' within the meaning of Article 119. In the light of the view taken by the Court, only Warner AG really dealt with these questions.

His opinion was that the Lloyds pension scheme would fall within Article 119 were it not for its link with the state scheme through the contracting-out system. If Article 119 applied to such schemes, a Member State would[79] have had to ensure that a contracted-out scheme afforded equal rights to men and women, but it would not have been under any such obligation with respect to its state scheme. That would, according to the Advocate General, be 'an unbalanced result to achieve, as well as one calculated to deter contracting-out'.[80] He concluded, therefore, that 'where a privately established pension is designed, not as a supplement to the state social security scheme . . . but as a substitute for it or for part of it, it must be regarded as outside the scope of Article 119'.[81] If he was wrong about this, he went on to submit that Article 119 would not anyway be directly effective in relation to such a pension scheme because the conferment of equal rights on men and women in this situation would give rise to problems which could only be solved by legislation, so that the criteria of precision for direct effect would not be fulfilled; as an example, the Advocate General took the case of maternity leave and said that a court could not decide simply on the basis of Article 119 whether that should be treated as a period of pensionable service.

As it turned out, the case was ill-chosen as a testing-ground for the applicability of Article 119 to private pension schemes. The European Court, after examining the facts,[82] concluded that the 5 per cent extra paid by Lloyds to contributing employees fell within the notion of 'pay', since it was included in the employee's gross salary. It was therefore unnecessary to answer the broader question of whether the pension scheme itself was covered by Article 119. In addition, the Court held that the Article was directly effective in this situation since the national court could identify the discrimination solely with the aid of the criteria of equal work and equal pay referred to in the Article itself.

Later cases however contained a clearer indication that at least certain types of pension might fall within the scope of Article 119. In the Employment Appeal Tribunal in *Barber* v. *Guardian Royal Exchange Assurance Group*[83] Browne-Wilkinson J commented: 'As we read the decision of the ECJ in *Burton* v. *British Rail*[84] . . . the quantum of benefit payable under a retirement scheme may be "pay" within the meaning of Article 119.'[85] The European Court itself ruled in *Razzouk* v. *Beydoun*[86] that the Community's own Staff Regulations could not permit discrimination between male and female employees as regards the provision of survivors' benefits. Slynn AG submitted that a retirement pension received by a Community employee, as well as a survivor's pension received by such a person's widow or widower, was 'pay' and subject to a principle analogous to Article 119, since it is 'part of the consideration (albeit deferred) which he receives in respect of his employment'.[87] The Court itself did not go so far and indeed rather hinted at the inapplicability of Article 119, as distinct from the general principle of equality of treatment in EEC law, in this situation; it stated that 'in relations between the Community institutions, on the one hand, and their employees and the dependants of employees, on the other, the requirements imposed by the principle of equal treatment are in no way limited to those resulting from Article 119'.[88]

At last, however, in *Bilka-Kaufhaus GmbH* v. *Weber Von Hartz*[89] the European Court finally came down off the fence and held that at least one type of pension scheme fell within Article 119. Bilka belonged to a West German chain of department stores which had a supplementary pension scheme for its employees, which formed a part of the contract of employment for each employee. Under the scheme, part-time employees could obtain pensions only if they had worked full-time for at least 15 years over a total period of 20 years. Ms Weber Von Hartz, who had worked part-time for Bilka for a number of years, could not satisfy this requirement and Bilka refused to pay her an occupational pension under its scheme. She brought proceedings before the German labour courts challenging the legality of this refusal and arguing that the 15 year rule discriminated against women employees in a manner contrary to Article 119. On a reference to the European Court, that Court agreed that this situation could constitute a breach of Article 119. The Court first reminded itself of its own decision in the *First Defrenne* case that 'although pay within the meaning of Article 119 could in principle include social security benefits, it did not include social security schemes or benefits, in particular retirement pensions, directly governed by legislation which do not involve any element of agreement within the undertaking or trade concerned and are compulsory for general categories of workers'.[90] It went on to stress the importance of a relationship between the employer's contribution to the funding of the scheme and the individual contract of employment. It concluded that this occupational pension scheme.

> although adopted in accordance with the provisions laid down by German legislation for such schemes, is based on an agreement between Bilka and the staff committee representing its employees and has the effect of supplementing the social benefits paid under national legislation of general application with benefits financed entirely by the employer. The contractual rather than the statutory nature of the scheme in question is confirmed by the fact that . . . the scheme and the rules governing it are regarded as an integral part of the contracts of employment between Bilka and its employees. It must therefore be concluded that the scheme does not constitute a social security scheme governed directly by statute and thus outside the scope of Article 119. Benefits paid to employees under the scheme therefore constitute consideration received by the worker from the employer in respect of his employment, as referred to in the second paragraph of Article 119.[91]

This judgment finally, it would seem, enables one to conclude that a pension scheme and the benefits receivable under it fall within Article 119 provided that three conditions are satisfied: the scheme must be funded at least in part by the employer (otherwise it does not constitute consideration received from the employer within the wording of Article 119); it must be supplementary to, rather than substitutive of, the relevant state pension scheme;[92] and it must be contractual in nature rather than set up by statute.[93]

Occupational pension schemes, although as has just been seen, at least sometimes potentially within the scope of Article 119, are now governed specifically by a Directive adopted on 24 July 1986.[94] The Directive applies the principle of equal treatment to occupational schemes providing protection against sickness, invalidity, old age (including early retirement), industrial accidents, occupational diseases and unemployment.[95] It does not apply to individual contracts or schemes having only one member.[96] It provides that the principle of equal treatment in this context means that there must be 'no discrimination on the basis of sex, either directly or indirectly, by reference in particular to marital or family status', especially as regards the scope of the scheme or conditions of access to it, the obligation to contribute and the calculation of contributions, and the calculation of benefits and the conditions governing the duration and retention of entitlement to benefits.[97]

There are, however, three very important exceptions to the principle of equality contained in the Directive. Member States are permitted to defer compliance with the Directive, firstly, in relation to the determination of pensionable age for the purposes of granting old-age or retirement pensions (and the possible implications for other benefits) either until the date on which such equality is achieved in statutory schemes or, at the latest, until such equality is required by a directive; secondly, in relation to survivors' pensions until a directive requires the principle of equal treatment in statutory social security schemes in that regard; and, thirdly, where actuarial calculations indicate different levels of benefit for the two sexes.[98] The undesirability of allowing such actuarial calculations to influence any insurance benefit, on account of their arbitrary effects and because the practice reinforces sex stereotyping, was discussed in Chapter 3 (see pp. 124–5).

Despite the existence of the new Directive, it seems likely that the possible application of Article 119 to pension schemes will remain of some practical importance. The Court might be prepared to hold that Article 119 applies in areas excepted from the Directive.[99] For example, even though a temporary exception is created for survivors' benefits by the Directive, it is possible that Article 119 might remain of use to a litigant complaining of sex discrimination as regards the quantum of a survivor's benefit provided under an occupational scheme complying with *Bilka-Kaufhaus* conditions.[100] Furthermore, the Directive does not become fully operational until the beginning of 1993.[101] And, even after this date, if a Member State has not translated the Directive into domestic law or has done so defectively, any possible direct effect of the instrument will be limited to enforcement against organs of the Member State and will not be available against private legal persons. This is the consequence of *Marshall* v. *Southampton and SW Hants Area Health Authority*[102] in which the European Court held that a directive is incapable of 'horizontal direct effect'.[103] Where it is sought to enforce the principle of equality against, for example, the trustees of a pension fund and the Directive has not been properly acted on by the relevant Member State, the complainant will therefore be thrown back on to Article 119 of the Treaty. Indeed, the inability of directives generally to produce horizontal direct effects is likely to lead (and perhaps already to have led) the European Court to widen still further the scope of Article 119.


## The meaning of 'equal work'

It has been quite clear since the *Second Defrenne* case[104] that the expression 'equal work' contained in Article 119 covers the situation where two people perform identical jobs in the same establishment, and moreover that the Article is directly effective here. The Court has never given a clear ruling on whether it also extends (and, if so, whether there is direct effect here) to cases in which the two employees work in different establishments.[105]

It has been established that, where identical jobs have been performed for the same employer, they need not have been held simultaneously in order to attract the direct effect of Article 119. In *Macarthys Ltd* v. *Smith*,[106] Macarthys employed a Mr McCullough until 1975 and paid him £60 a week. After he left, the post remained vacant for four months and then Ms Smith was appointed to it. However, she was paid only £50 a week. When she complained to the courts, it was held that the domestic equal pay legislation extended only to comparisons between the pay of employees working contemporaneously with one another; the Court of Appeal, therefore, referred the case to the European Court, asking whether Article 119 extended to the situation of successive employment. The answer was that it did, the European Court holding that

> the decisive test lies in establishing whether there is a difference in treatment between a man and a woman performing 'equal work' within the meaning of Article 119. The scope of that concept, which is entirely qualitative in character in that it is exclusively concerned with the nature of the services in question, may not be restricted by the introduction of a requirement of contemporaneity.[107]

The ruling of the Court was to the effect that Article 119 applies where a woman receives less pay 'than a man who was employed prior to the woman's period of employment'. One matter which remains unclear is how long ago the man's employment can have been: would it, for example, have been possible to compare Ms Smith's pay with Mr McCullough's if there had been a five-year break between his employment and hers? It would seem that the answer to this is 'yes', but presumably a domestic court applying EEC law would have to take account of the effect of inflation between the two periods of employment. It would be of little value to establish a right to a wage equal to one paid five years ago.

Although the Court in *Macarthys Ltd* v. *Smith* was prepared to allow wage comparison with a man previously employed, there were some limits beyond which it would not go. Ms Smith wanted to establish that EEC law also extends its protection to workers who cannot directly compare their work with persons of the opposite sex because the employer has divided the jobs into 'women's work' and 'men's work'; she therefore urged the Court to adopt an interpretation of Article 119 which would cover comparison with a hypothetical, as well as an actual, male worker doing the same job.[108] However, the European Court held that such a comparison could not be made on the basis of Article 119 alone; it would require further implementing legislation so that the national courts would know what criteria of assessment to adopt.

Welcome though it was to women employees, the European Court's decision in *Macarthys Ltd* v. *Smith* revealed serious difficulties for the UK's industrial tribunals when they came to applying the law to actual cases. This was demonstrated in *Albion Shipping Agency* v. *Arnold*,[109] where again a woman employee was claiming pay parity with a male predecessor. Browne-Wilkinson J in the Employment Appeal Tribunal pointed out that, since the Court of Appeal had held in *Macarthys Ltd* v. *Smith* that the Equal Pay Act did not extend to cases of successive employment, such a claim technically arises by virtue of Article 119.[110] However, does Article 119 operate by impliedly amending the Equal Pay Act, or does it confer a separate 'free-standing' right which is independent of that Act? The question was important for two reasons. First, it seemed at the time of the case that different defences might be open to the employer under EEC law from under domestic law.[111] Secondly, it was important because it had been doubted judicially and at high levels[112] whether industrial tribunals had jurisdiction to hear cases other than those in which they have been expressly clothed with jurisdiction by statute, since they themselves are exclusively creatures of statute. Browne-Wilkinson J commented that whether or not the industrial tribunals have jurisdiction over these cases 'may ultimately depend on whether [the] claim is properly to be treated as a right under the Act of 1970 amended by Article 119 (in which case there is jurisdiction) or under Article 119 alone'.[113] However, he concluded that he need not answer this question himself, since he was bound by the Court of Appeal's decision in *Macarthys Ltd* v. *Smith* to hold that the tribunal had jurisdiction:

In that case, the Court of Appeal, having held that the claimant had no right under the Act of 1970, on receiving the ruling of the ECJ that she had a claim under Article 119, dismissed the appeal against the decision of this Tribunal holding in favour of the claimant. Although the jurisdiction point was neither argued nor expressly dealt with in the judgment of the Court of Appeal, it is a decision which can only have been made on the basis that the industrial tribunal and the Employment Appeal Tribunal had jurisdiction to hear and determine the case . . . a conclusion which we reach with relief since to hold otherwise would produce a chaotic result in which cases under the Act of 1970 where Article 119 might be in point would have to be conducted partly before the industrial tribunal (which has exclusive jurisdiction under the Act of 1970) and partly in the ordinary courts.[114]

The Employment Appeal Tribunal thus avoided dealing on this occasion with the exact juridical basis in the UK of successive employment claims, but it did express the hope that Parliament would as soon as possible amend the Equal Pay Act so as to give full effect to Article 119 and obviate the sort of confusion which had arisen in this case.

It is not entirely clear from decisions of the European Court whether that Court regards Article 119 as also taking direct effect where the two jobs being compared are not identical, but are alleged to be of equal value. To begin with, it denied that the principle of Article 119 even applied in such cases; for example, it stated in the *Second Defrenne* case[115] that the Equal Pay Directive[116] 'extended' the coverage of Article 119 to include equal pay for work of equal value. However, it later changed its mind on this score and commented in *Jenkins* v. *Kingsgate (Clothing Productions) Ltd*[117] that the Equal Pay Directive was 'principally designed to facilitate the practical application of the principle of equal pay outlined in Article 119 of the Treaty' and 'in no way alters the content or scope of that principle as defined in the Treaty'.[118] Similarly, in *Worringham* v. *Lloyds Bank Ltd*[119] it said that 'Article 1 of the Directive explains that the concept of "same work" contained in the first paragraph of Article 119 of the Treaty includes cases of "work to which equal value is attributed" '.[120] It has sometimes also included the equal value situation in its formulation of the extent of the direct effect of Article 119, most notably in the *Worringham* decision where it said that Article 119 applied directly

to all forms of discrimination which may be identified solely with the aid of the criteria of equal work and equal pay referred to by the Article in question, without national or Community measures being required to define them with greater precision in order to permit of their application. Among the forms of discrimination which may thus be judicially identified, the Court mentioned in particular cases where men and women receive unequal pay for equal work carried out in the same establishment or service, public or private. In such a situation the court is in a position to establish all the facts enabling it to decide whether a woman receives less pay than a man engaged in the same work *or work of equal value*.[121]

Such statements, coupled with the Court's willingness to apply the principle of direct effect even in cases of indirect discrimination[122] have led some academic writers to argue that Article 119 is directly effective in equal value situations.[123] The English Court of Appeal confirmed this conclusion in *Pickstone and others* v. *Freemans plc*,[124] where it held that women applicants, precluded from an equal value claim under UK law because of the existence of men paid the same as themselves and engaged on like work with them in the same employment,[125] could rely on the direct effect of Article 119 to prove that their work was of equal value to that of other male colleagues engaged on different work and paid at a higher rate.

## THE EQUAL PAY DIRECTIVE

As has been seen, the implementation of the principle of equal pay in all the Member States proved to be slow. In an effort to facilitate progress, the Council produced Directive 75/117,[126] on the approximation of the laws of the Member States relating to the application of the principle of equal pay for men and women.[127]

Since Article 119 itself does not bestow any secondary legislative power on the Community institutions, authority to legislate in order to clarify it had to be sought elsewhere in the Treaty. The Council relied on Article 100 to pass the Equal Pay Directive.[128]

### The possible direct effect of the equal pay directive

The possible direct effect of this Directive has been in issue, but not resolved, in several cases before the European Court.[129] It has been seen above that the European Court has consistently maintained that directives can be capable of direct effect; the principle was extended in the *Verbond* case[130] to a directive based, as is the Equal Pay Directive, on Article 100.[131] However, there remains the difficulty that, as seen above, the European Court has ruled out any possibility of directives taking horizontal direct effect. This of course is especially significant in an area such as equal pay where the litigant seeks to enforce her rights against her employer, who may well be a private person and not an organ of the state. The denial to directives generally of horizontal direct effect has robbed this particular Directive of much of its former practical significance.

## Content of the Equal Pay Directive

Article 1(1) of the Directive states:

> The principle of equal pay for men and women outlined in Article 119 of the Treaty, hereinafter called 'principle of equal pay', means, for the same work or for work to which equal value is attributed, the elimination of all discrimination on grounds of sex with regard to all aspects and conditions of remuneration.

It has been seen that it was originally thought that this provision expanded the scope of Article 119 because of its reference to work of equal value,[132] but that the European Court has more recently taken the view that all the Directive in fact achieves is greater articulation of the principle of pay equality. In one respect, however, it is still unclear whether or not the Directive seeks to enlarge on Article 119, and that is in relation to its spatial application. When infringement proceedings were brought against the UK for failure to implement this Directive adequately,[133] the European Court's remarks about the spatial scope of the Directive were unfortunately ambiguous. It ruled that 'a worker must be entitled to claim before an appropriate authority that his work has the same value as *other work*'[134] but it did not explain whether that other work was confined to the same establishment or employment, or whether comparisons might be made with other organisations. However, in *Commission* v. *Denmark*,[135] although the Court itself did not deal with the point, Ver Loren Van Themaat AG expressed his opinion quite strongly, saying:

> As appears from the second sentence of Article 1 of the Directive . . . a comparison of duties within the same fixed establishment of an undertaking or even within a single undertaking will not always be sufficient. In certain circumstances comparison with work of equal value in other undertakings covered by the collective agreement may be necessary. . . . In sectors with a traditionally female workforce comparison with other sectors may even be necessary.[136]

Article 1(2) of the Directive provides:

> In particular, where a job classification system is used for determining pay, it must be based on the same criteria for both men and women

and so drawn up as to exclude any discrimination on grounds of sex.

In *Rummler* v. *Dato-Druck*,[137] a German Labour Court asked the European Court whether this provision was to be interpreted as meaning that a job classification system could not take account of the extent to which a job required physical effort; if physical effort was a permissible factor, could the scheme take into account the extent to which particular work is especially heavy for women? The European Court ruled that the Directive does not prohibit the use in a job classification system

> of the criterion of muscle demand or muscular effort or that of the heaviness of the work if, in view of the nature of the tasks involved, the work to be performed does require the use of a certain degree of physical strength, so long as the system as a whole, by taking into account other criteria, precludes any discrimination on grounds of sex. [However,] . . . the use of values reflecting the average performance of workers of one sex as a basis for determining the extent to which work makes demands or requires effort or whether it is heavy constitutes a form of discrimination on grounds of sex, contrary to the Directive. [It went on to hold that] in order for a job classification system not to be discriminatory as a whole, it must, insofar as the nature of the tasks carried out in the undertaking permits, take into account criteria for which workers of each sex may show particular aptitude.[138]

Given the conceptual basis of job evaluation (discussed in Chapter 2), this is a logical conclusion and is particularly to be welcomed in its refusal to entertain any notions of the abilities of 'average women'.

The law of the UK before the Equal Pay (Amendment) Regulations 1983 allowed only a very limited possibility of attack by an employee on a concluded job evaluation study.[139] In response to the allegation that such a position might well be in breach of Article 1(2) of the Directive, it is now provided that an existing evaluation study is not to constitute a barrier to the making of an equal value claim where the employee can show that the scheme is discriminatory.[140] Many difficulties, however, both substantive and procedural, face an employee who seeks to prove that an existing scheme is discriminatory, and these have been discussed in Chapter 2 (see p. 41 *et seq.*).

Article 2 of the Directive obliges the Member States to introduce into their national legal systems such measures as are necessary to enable all employees who consider themselves wronged by failure to apply the principle of equal pay to pursue their claims by judicial process after possible recourse to other competent authorities; and Article 3 obliges the States to abolish all pay discrimination between the sexes arising from laws, regulations or administrative provisions. Article 4 provides that the Member States must take the necessary measures to ensure that provisions appearing in collective agreements, wage scales, wage agreements or individual contracts of employment which are contrary to the principle of equal pay shall be, or may be declared, null and void or may be amended; s.6 of the Sex Discrimination Act 1986 now provides for the automatic invalidity of such provisions in Great Britain.[141]

Article 5 prohibits the victimisation (through dismissal) of any employee who has complained of a pay inequality. It was seen in Chapter 3 (at p. 72 *et seq.*) that the provisions of the Sex Discrimination Act 1975 forbidding victimisation are cast in unnecessarily restrictive terms and have received a narrow interpretation by the courts. It might, therefore, be argued that they represent an unsatisfactory fulfilment on the part of the UK of its obligations under this part of the Directive.[142]

Article 7 obliges Member States to give publicity to the right to equal pay, for example at places of employment.


## THE EQUAL TREATMENT DIRECTIVE

Although Article 119 mentions only equal pay, the Member States have for some time expressed respect for a wider notion of equal treatment between men and women as regards all aspects of employment law and related areas.[143] The Equal Treatment Directive[144] gives tangible form to this aspiration. Its aim is expressed in Article 1(1) to be

> to put into effect in the Member States the principle of equal treatment for men and women as regards access to employment, including promotion, and to vocational training and as regards working conditions. . . .

It is based on Article 235, which gives power to the EEC institutions to take 'appropriate measures' where action by the Community is necessary to attain one of the objectives of the Community but the Treaty does not specifically confer the necessary authority.[145] It is unfortunate that the institutions chose a directive as the appropriate measure in this instance, since the adoption of a regulation would have obviated the difficulties relating to horizontal direct effect which have already been referred to.

## Substantive rights conferred by the Equal Treatment Directive

The principle of equal treatment is defined by Article 2(1) as forbidding all employment discrimination 'whatsoever' on grounds of sex both direct and indirect 'by reference in particular to marital or family status'. The ambivalence of these closing words was discussed in Chapter 3 (p. 72); it is unclear whether all discrimination on account of marital or family status is banned, or whether such discrimination is only caught by the Directive where it also constitutes sex discrimination. If the former is the correct interpretation, the British sex discrimination legislation fails to implement this part of the Directive properly; an individual's rights in this situation would therefore depend, first, on whether the European Court was prepared to declare the paragraph directly effective (a distinct possibility, since the scope of its meaning would appear to be reasonably clear) and, secondly, whether the employer was an 'organ of the state' against whom a directive can be enforced.[146]

It is also to be observed that paragraph 1 is phrased extremely broadly. Its full scope remains to be explored by the European Court but it is at least arguable that, unlike the UK's anti-discrimination laws and also unlike Article 119 of the EEC Treaty, it extends to proscribing unjustifiable pay *differentials* between men and women not engaged in comparable work, since it requires 'no discrimination *whatsoever*'.

The Directive goes on to define its sphere of application, which roughly mirrors the employment provisions of the Sex Discrimination Act 1975; Article 3 states:

1. Application of the principle of equal treatment means that there shall be no discrimination whatsoever on grounds of sex in the conditions, including selection criteria, for access to all jobs or posts, whatever the sector or branch of activity, and to all levels of the occupational hierarchy.
2. To this end, Member States shall take the measures necessary to ensure that:
   (a) any laws, regulations and administrative provisions contrary to the principle of equal treatment shall be abolished;
   (b) any provisions contrary to the principle of equal treatment which are included in collective agreements, individual contracts of employment, internal rules of undertakings or in rules governing the independent occupations and professions shall be, or may be declared, null and void or may be amended;
   (c) those laws, regulations and administrative provisions contrary to the principle of equal treatment when the concern for protection which originally inspired them is no

longer well founded shall be revised; and that where similar provisions are included in collective agreements labour and management shall be requested to undertake the desired revision.

The Commission brought successful infringement proceedings against the UK under this Article, arguing in particular that, at the date of the action (1982), neither the Sex Discrimination Act 1975 nor any other legislative instrument in force in the UK provided that discriminatory provisions contained in collective agreements, rules of undertakings or rules governing independent occupations and professions were, or could be declared, void, or could be amended. The UK government's answer to this was that the complaint was unfounded since s.18 of the Trade Union and Labour Relations Act 1974 provided that collective agreements were presumed not to have been intended by the parties to be legally enforceable unless they were in writing and contained a provision in which the parties expressed their intention that the agreements were to be legally enforceable. In fact, the government pointed out that collective agreements were not usually legally binding in this country and indeed it asserted that it was not aware of the existence at the time of the action of any binding collective agreements at all. Anyway, it argued that, even if collective agreements containing provisions contrary to the principle of equal treatment did exist, those provisions would be rendered void by s.77 of the Sex Discrimination Act.[147] Similarly, any discriminatory provisions contained in the internal rules of an undertaking, or of an occupational body, would be void if they were incorporated into an individual's contract of employment; and if any discrimination in employment were to result from the existence of such a discriminatory provision in the internal rules of an undertaking or of an occupational or professional body, that discrimination would be caught by s.6 of the Sex Discrimination Act.[148] Finally, the government drew to the attention of the European Court s.13(1) of the Sex Discrimination Act, [149] which makes it unlawful for a body which can confer an authorisation or qualification to discriminate on the ground of sex.

However, these arguments were insufficient to satisfy either Rozès AG or the Court. The Advocate General pointed out that workers were more likely to have access to collective agreements and company rule books than to the Equal Treatment Directive or the Sex Discrimination Act, so they might well believe that the discriminatory provisions did have legal force.[150] The Court agreed and held that the Directive covers all collective agreements without distinction as to the nature of the legal effects which they do or do not produce. The reason for that generality lies in the fact that, even if they are not legally binding as between the parties who sign them or with regard to the employment relationships which they govern, collective agreements nevertheless have important *de facto* consequences for the employment relationships to which they refer, particularly insofar as they determine the rights of the workers and, in the interests of industrial harmony, give undertakings some indication of the conditions which employment relationships must satisfy or need not satisfy. The need to ensure that the Directive is completely effective therefore requires that any clauses in such agreements which are incompatible with the obligations imposed by the Directive upon the Member States may be rendered inoperative, eliminated or amended by appropriate means.[151]

This ruling was given effect to by means of s.6 of the Sex Discrimination Act 1986, which now provides for the automatic invalidity of discriminatory provisions contained in collective agreements, employers' rules and the rules of trade unions, employers' associations, professional organisations and qualifying bodies.[152]

Article 4 is cast in similar terms to Article 3, but applies to 'access to all types and to all levels of vocational guidance, vocational training, advanced vocational training and retraining'. Both have been held by the European Court to be directly effective parts of the Directive.[153]

Article 5 applies to working conditions and provides:

1. Application of the principle of equal treatment with regard to working conditions, including the conditions governing dismissal, means that men and women shall be guaranteed the same conditions without discrimination on grounds of sex.
2. To this end, Member States shall take the measures necessary to ensure that:
   (a) any laws, regulations and administrative provisions contrary to the principle of equal treatment shall be abolished;
   (b) any provisions contrary to the principle of equal treatment which are included in collective agreements, individual contracts of employment, internal rules of undertakings or in rules governing the independent occupations and professions shall be, or may be declared, null and void or may be amended;
   (c) those laws, regulations and administrative provisions contrary to the principle of equal treatment when the concern for protection which originally inspired them is no longer well founded shall be revised; and that where similar provisions are included in collective agreements labour and

management shall be requested to undertake the desired revision.

The meaning of 'dismissal' in Article 5(1) has been raised in at least two important cases before the European Court. In *Burton* v. *British Railways Board*[154] British Rail decided to pay voluntary redundancy benefits to certain of its employees, provided that they were aged 55 or over in the case of women and 60 or over in the case of men. Mr Burton, who wanted to take advantage of this scheme, was 58 and claimed that he was being discriminated against by comparison with a female colleague. Being exempted from the domestic anti-discrimination legislation,[155] the issue became whether the situation was covered by the Equal Treatment Directive. The European Court, to which the matter was referred for a preliminary ruling, said that 'dismissal' must be 'widely construed so as to include termination of the employment relationship between a worker and his employer, even as part of a voluntary redundancy scheme'.[156] Access to voluntary redundancy is therefore within the scope of Article 5. However, in the end the Court was not prepared to condemn this situation as an infringement of the Directive since the qualifying ages for access to this redundancy scheme were linked to the differential state retirement pension ages for men and women; both men and women became eligible for the voluntary scheme five years before they reached the state retirement pension age. The Social Security Directive[157] permits the continuation of such differential state retirement pension ages, and so the Court held that no breach of EEC law had occurred.

As was seen in Chapter 3 (especially at pp. 112–3) compulsory retirement is also covered by Article 5(1). In *Marshall* v. *Southampton and SW Hants Health Authority*[158] the European Court reiterated the need for 'dismissal' to receive a broad construction and ruled that 'a general policy concerning dismissal involving the dismissal of a woman solely because she has attained the qualifying age for a state pension, which age is different under national legislation for men and for women, constitutes discrimination on grounds of sex, contrary to the Equal Treatment Directive'.[159] The Court added further importance to this ruling by also holding that Article 5(1) is directly effective and thus enforceable by the individual against Member States.

It will be observed that both Article 3(2)(c) and Article 5(2)(c) require out-dated protective provisions to be revised.[160] The Directive does not on its face offer any explanation of what are meant by such protective provisions, but it does provide in Article 2(3)[161] that it is 'without prejudice to provisions concerning the protection of women, particularly as regards pregnancy and maternity'. In

*Johnston* v. *RUC*[162] the European Court explained that Article 2(3) determines the scope of Article 3(2)(c)[163] and must be interpreted strictly. 'It is clear', said the Court, 'from the express reference to pregnancy and maternity that the Directive is intended to protect a woman's biological condition and the special relationship which exists between a woman and her child.'[164] The EEC Commission published a report in March 1987 on the existing protective laws in the Member States (apart from Spain and Portugal).[165] It found that 'a mosaic of extremely varied and highly specific regulations exists, the reasons for which are not clearly defined'. The Commission's view is that protective legislation which does not relate to pregnancy or maternity should apply equally to both sexes and it recommends that certain protective measures should either be extended to both sexes or repealed. It plans to bring infringement proceedings against any Member States which maintain in force unjustifiable protective provisions. Despite the repeal of much British protective legislation by the Sex Discrimination Act 1986,[166] the Commission still includes the UK amongst Member States which continue to retain in force unjustifiable measures.

Article 6 lays down that:

> Member States shall introduce into their national legal systems such measures as are necessary to enable all persons who consider themselves wronged by failure to apply to them the principle of equal treatment within the meaning of Articles 3, 4 and 5 to pursue their claims by judicial process after possible recourse to other competent authorities.

The meaning and effect of this provision were in dispute in *Von Colson and Kamann* v. *Land of North Rhine-Westphalia*.[167] The plaintiffs were women social workers, who had applied for posts in a male prison but had been rejected. It was established that discrimination on the ground of sex had occurred but the national court came to the conclusion that, under German law, the only available remedy was an award of damages of an amount equal to the expenses incurred by the plaintiffs in making their applications. The plaintiffs considered this quite unsatisfactory and argued that, as a result of Article 6 of the Equal Treatment Directive, they had the right to be offered the posts for which they had applied or, alternatively, damages amounting to six months' salary. The national court referred the case to the European Court, asking essentially what sanctions were required in such a case by the Directive. The Court began by pointing out that, although Article 189 of the EEC Treaty left to the Member States the choice of form and methods of translating a Directive into national law, those States were nevertheless obliged to take all the steps necessary to give full effect to it. The aim of the Equal Treatment Directive was the implementation of the principle of equal treatment between men and women, and Article 6 required the Member States to adopt measures which were sufficiently effective to achieve that aim and to ensure that those measures could be invoked before national courts. Such measures might, for example, the Court held, include provisions requiring an employer to take on an applicant for a job against whom he was found to have discriminated unlawfully, or offering such an applicant the possibility of adequate financial compensation, possibly backed up by a system of fines. The Court emphasised, however, that the Directive did not require Member States to make available any particular type of sanction but left them to choose from amongst all those sanctions which would satisfy the aim of the Directive. None the less, whatever sanction was chosen had to be sufficient to ensure effective legal protection for the rights of litigants and to exercise a real deterrent effect on employers. If a Member State therefore chose to penalise breaches of the principle of equal treatment by an award of compensation, any such award had to represent adequate recompense for the injury suffered; and national legislation which limited such compensation to a purely nominal amount, such as reimbursement of expenses incurred in applying for a job, did not therefore conform with the requirement that the Directive be implemented in an effective manner.

The significance of this ruling in the UK is considerable. It was pointed out in Chapter 3 (see p. 143 *et seq*.) that the remedies provided for a breach of the Sex Discrimination Act are extremely limited; in particular, no damages can be claimed for unintentional indirect discrimination and the remedies of recommendation and declaration are not specifically enforceable. No injunction is obtainable at the suit of an individual litigant. It is certainly arguable that this situation falls short of 'effective' implementation of the Directive, so that the UK might be liable to prosecution under Article 169 of the EEC Treaty on this score,[168] and individual actions testing the compatibility of British law with the Directive in this area are to be anticipated.

Further light was shed on the direct effectiveness of Article 6 in *Johnston* v. *RUC*.[169] It was held by the European Court in that case to be contrary to the Directive for Article 53 of the Sex Discrimination (Northern Ireland) Order 1976 to attempt to exclude judicial review of a ministerial certificate which states that a discriminatory act is necessary to safeguard national security.[170] In the words of the Court,

The requirement of judicial control stipulated by [Article 6] reflects a general principle of law which underlies the constitutional traditions common to the Member States. That principle is also laid down in Articles 6 and 13 of the European Convention for the Protection of Human Rights and Fundamental Freedoms of 4 November 1950 (1953 Cmnd. 8969). . . . By virtue of Article 6 . . . interpreted in the light of the general principle stated above, all persons have the right to obtain an effective remedy in a competent court against measures which they consider to be contrary to the principle of equal treatment. . . . A provision which . . . requires a certificate such as the one in question in the present case to be treated as conclusive evidence that the conditions for derogating from the principle of equal treatment are fulfilled allows the competent authority to deprive an individual of the possibility of asserting by judicial process the rights conferred by the Directive. Such a provision is therefore contrary to the principle of effective judicial control laid down in Article 6.[171]

Furthermore, the Court went on to explain that, although Article 6 is not precise enough with respect to the types of sanction which must be available to an individual for it to be directly effective in this respect, this does not mean that the Article is of no direct use to the individual at all. Although it does not enable the individual to demand *specific* remedies, it nevertheless does enable the individual to insist on *some* judicial remedies and is thus directly effective where, as here, the Member State seeks to block all judicial redress in a particular situation.

The Equal Treatment Directive also contains similar provisions to the Equal Pay Directive with respect to the victimisation of employees and with respect to publicity for the rights which it confers.[172]

## Exceptions to the principle of equal treatment

According to the European Court in *Johnston* v. *RUC*,[173] the only permissible exceptions to the principle of equal treatment are those contained in the Directive itself. In particular, Article 2 mentions three excepted situations, the first of which is contained in paragraph 2, which states:

This Directive shall be without prejudice to the right of Member States to exclude from its field of application those occupational activities and, where appropriate, the training leading thereto, for which, by reason of their nature or the context in which they are carried out, the sex of the worker constitutes a determining factor.

This provision, roughly the EEC equivalent of the UK's genuine occupational qualification exception,[174] was in issue in the Commission's second prosecution of the UK for defective implementation of the EEC's sex equality laws.[175] The Commission alleged that three of the exceptions contained in the Sex Discrimination Act 1975 were in conflict with Article 2(2) of the Directive. The first two were the exceptions then conferred by s.6(3) of the Act, namely for employment in a private household and where the number of persons employed by the employer did not exceed five. The UK government argued that these exceptions were permissible in EEC law because they involve close personal relationships between employer and employee. The Commission argued, and Rozès AG agreed, that the exception created by Article 2(2) of the Directive must be strictly construed, and also that it only permits Member States to exempt *certain* occupational activities because of the context in which they are carried out; the UK had, in fact, exempted *all* occupational activities carried out in the two particular contexts of private households and small businesses. Rozès AG also commented that no other Member States possessed exceptions similar to s.6(3) of the Sex Discrimination Act and that 'it would be quite astonishing if it were only in the UK that the present stage of social development prevented the application of the Directive to employment for the purposes of a private household or in very small undertakings'.[176]

The European Court, whilst expressing some sympathy with the UK government's submissions, also ultimately rejected them. It held:

> It must be recognised that the provision of the 1975 Act in question is intended, insofar as it refers to employment in a private household, to reconcile the principle of equality of treatment with the principle of respect for private life, which is also fundamental. Reconciliation of that kind is one of the factors which must be taken into consideration in determining the scope of the exception provided for in Article 2(2) of the Directive. Whilst it is undeniable that, for certain kinds of employment in private households, that consideration may be decisive, that is not the case for all the kinds of employment in question. As regards small undertakings with not more than five employees, the UK has not put forward any argument to show that in any undertaking of that size the sex of the worker would be a determining factor by reason of the nature of his activities or the context in which they are carried out. Consequently, by reason of its generality, the exclusion provided for in the contested provision of the 1975 Act goes beyond the objective which may be lawfully pursued within the framework of Article 2(2) of the Directive.[177]

As seen in Chapter 3 (see p. 117) legislation was subsequently passed in the UK to remove the small business exception and to narrow down the private household exception.

The third exception in the UK's legislation contested by the Commission was s.20 of the Sex Discrimination Act 1975, which excluded midwives from the operation of the statute. The government argued that this exception was justified by Article 2(2) of the Directive because of the nature of the occupation of midwife and the conditions in which midwives work and it emphasised that, in the UK, midwives usually play a unique role in the pre-natal and post-natal periods (for example, visiting patients at home). Furthermore, the government pointed out that the legislation in issue had been reviewed in the light of Article 9(2) of the Directive, which states that there must be periodical assessment of 'the occupational activities referred to in Article 2(2) in order to decide, in the light of social developments, whether there is justification for maintaining the exclusions concerned'; such review had led the government, before the oral hearing of the case, to announce changes in the legislation so as to remove the restrictions on the training and employment of men as midwives.[178] All this was insufficient to persuade Rozès AG of the legality of the UK's position, but the Court itself was prepared to accede to the government's arguments.[179] It held that it must be recognised that 'at the present time personal sensitivities may play an important role in the relation between midwife and patient. . . . [B]y failing to apply the principle laid down in the Directive, the UK has not exceeded the limits of the power granted to the Member States by Article 9(2) and 2(2) of the Directive'.[180]

Some further guidance about the ambit of the exception created by Article 2(2) was provided by the European Court in *Johnston* v. *RUC*.[181] The Court pointed out that the Chief Constable could not justify his refusal to provide female police reservists with firearms training by relying on the part of Article 2(2) which refers to the exclusion of those occupational activities whose nature requires male workers, because the Sex Discrimination (Northern Ireland) Order 1976 expressly applies to employment in the police. However, the part referring to the context in which the job has to be carried out was potentially more helpful. The Chief Constable had argued that if women police were armed they might become a more frequent target for assassination and their firearms might fall into the hands of their assailants, that the public would not welcome the carrying of firearms by women and that armed policewomen would be less effective in police work of a social nature. The Court commented that the reasons which the Chief Constable thus gave for his policy were related to the special conditions in which the police must work in the situation existing in Northern Ireland, having regard to the requirements of the protection of public safety in a context of serious internal disturbances.[182] [It went on to hold that] the possibility cannot be excluded that in a situation characterised by serious internal disturbances the carrying of firearms by policewomen might create additional risks of their being assassinated and might therefore be contrary to the requirements of public safety. In such circumstances, the context of certain policing activities may be such that the sex of police officers constitutes a determining factor for carrying them out. . . . It must also be borne in mind that, in determining the scope of any derogation from an individual right such as the equal treatment of men and women provided for by the Directive, the principle of proportionality, one of the general principles of law underlying the Community legal order, must be observed. That principle requires that derogations remain within the limits of what is appropriate and necessary for achieving the aim in view and requires the principle of equal treatment to be reconciled as far as possible with the requirements of public safety which constitute the decisive factor as regards the context of the activity in question.[183]

This part of the European Court's judgment is open to criticism in that no explanation at all was provided by it as to why policewomen might be more likely to be assassinated than policemen; it is possible that the Court's reasoning became confused at this point and that, instead of comparing the risk to a police*woman* carrying out general police duties with the risk to a police*man* carrying out the same duties, it in fact compared the risk to a policewoman between general police duties and those on which women were currently being employed.[184]

It was pointed out in Chapter 3 that several of the existing defences provided by the Sex Discrimination Act 1975 in UK law are of wider scope than Article 2(2) of the Directive permits, in particular the genuine occupational qualification exception provided in s.7, the exception for charities in s.43 and the exception for acts performed in compliance with pre–1975 statutes under s.51.[185] It is clear from *Johnston* v. *RUC*[186] that the direct effect of the Directive can be of use to the litigant (against the Member State) in a case where an exception is pleaded which is not permitted by EEC law. A derogation from the principle of equal treatment provided for by national law may be 'set aside in so far as it exceeds the limits of the exceptions permitted by Article 2(2)'.[187]

The second major exception to the Directive is in Article 2(3), which states:

This Directive shall be without prejudice to provisions concerning the protection of women, particularly as regards pregnancy and maternity.

The use of the word 'particularly' here suggests that there are other grounds upon which women may lawfully be 'protected' apart from pregnancy and maternity. The European Court made a somewhat delphic pronouncement on this point in *Johnston* v. *RUC*.[188] The UK argued in that case that the RUC's discriminatory policy with respect to firearms training could be excused because its aim was the protection of women from becoming targets for assassination. The Court ruled that Article 2(3), like Article 2(2), must be interpreted strictly. It went on to say that

it is clear from the express reference to pregnancy and maternity that the Directive is intended to protect a woman's biological condition and the special relationship that exists between a woman and her child. That provision of the Directive does not therefore allow women to be excluded from a certain type of employment on the ground that public opinion demands that women be given greater protection than men against risks which affect men and women in the same way and which are distinct from women's specific needs of protection, such as those expressly mentioned. It does not appear that the risks and dangers to which women are exposed when performing their duties in the police force in a situation such as exists in Northern Ireland are different from those to which any man is also exposed when performing the same duties.[189]

It would seem from these remarks that the Court's view is that Article 2(3) is directed specifically towards the protection of women with respect to reproduction, that it does not permit them to be afforded greater protection than men where the hazards to both are the same, but that there may be certain other unspecified hazards to which women but not men may be exposed. This last category is somewhat perplexing: if it refers to biological vulnerability, it is unclear what biological difference between the sexes the Court could have had in mind. If it refers to some other type of vulnerability, it is a dangerous erosion of the principle of equality since it might enable the judiciary to perpetuate a cultural stereotype of the role which is properly to be played by women in our society.[190]

Article 2(4) states, by way of a third exception to the principle of equal treatment, that it is:

Without prejudice to measures to promote equal opportunity for men and women, in particular by removing existing inequalities which affect women's opportunities in the areas referred to in Article 1(1).

This is an obscure provision, whose meaning has never been elucidated by the European Court. In particular, it is unclear whether
it can be used to justify measures in favour of women which would
otherwise be illegal under the Directive, or whether it simply
provides legislative encouragement for those measures of positive
action which fall short of reverse discrimination.[191]

## THE SOCIAL SECURITY DIRECTIVE

Unlike the UK's anti-discrimination laws, which do not extend to
the field of social security,[192] the EEC has made special provision
in the matter by means of the Social Security Directive.[193] Like the
Equal Treatment Directive,[194] it was adopted under the enabling
authority of Article 235.

The group of persons covered by the Directive is broad. Article
2 provides that it applies to 'the working population'. This is not
confined to those presently in work, because the Article goes on to
say that the category includes 'self-employed persons, workers and
self-employed persons whose activity is interrupted by illness, accident or involuntary unemployment and persons seeking employment'. The Directive also extends to 'retired or invalided workers
and self-employed persons'. However, certain notable groups
within the population are omitted from this definition, in particular
those persons who because of some disability have never been able
to work and those, mainly women, of course, who are not seeking
employment because they are engaged in domestic work caring for
spouses and families.

Article 1 explains that the purpose of the Directive is the
'progressive implementation' of the principle of equal treatment in
the field of social security and other elements of social protection.
Article 3 defines the forms of social security with which the Directive is concerned, namely:

  (a)  statutory schemes which provide protection against the
       following risks:
       – sickness,
       – invalidity,
       – old age,
       – accidents at work and occupational diseases,
       – unemployment;
  (b)  social assistance, insofar as it is intended to supplement or
       replace the schemes referred to in (a).

The Directive does not apply to survivors' benefits, nor to family
benefits except those granted by way of increases in benefits receiv-

able in category (a).[195] By implication, it also does not cover occupational schemes, since in Article 3(3) it provides for a further instrument to deal with these; as seen earlier in the present chapter (see pp. 194–5) a Directive on Occupational Social Security Schemes was passed in 1986. The type of protection afforded by the scheme in issue was at the heart of the *Drake* case.[196] Ms Drake was a married woman who had given up paid employment in 1984 to care for her disabled mother, who had come to live with her and her husband. Two months after the Directive had come into force,[197] she made a claim for invalid care allowance but was met with a statutory rule which excluded married and cohabiting women from this benefit.[198] She argued that this was incompatible with the principle of equal treatment enshrined in the Directive. The social security commissioner referred the case to the European Court, asking whether a benefit payable to someone caring for a disabled person constituted part of a statutory scheme providing protection against invalidity, within the meaning of Article 3(1)(a) of the Directive. There was some reason to suspect that such a benefit, in fact, fell outside the purview of the Directive, since traditionally such schemes have not been regarded as employment-related. If the objective of the Directive was restricted to equality in the context of employment, such a benefit might, therefore, well be excluded from it. The extent to which the EEC protection of sex equality has moved away from its original economic basis and towards a social or humanitarian goal is demonstrated by the Court's decision that this benefit was within the scope of the Directive. It held that the fact of payment of benefit to third parties rather than to the disabled person did not matter. Article 3(1) must be given a broad interpretation so as to include any benefit which forms part of one of the statutory schemes, in order to ensure that the progressive implementation of the principle of equal treatment 'is carried out in a harmonious manner throughout the Community'.[199] This purposive approach is especially significant given the complexity and the diversity of the benefits available in all the Member States.

The most important part of the Directive is Article 4 which defines the principle of equal treatment in the same way as the Equal Treatment Directive (that is to say, so as to mean that there must be 'no discrimination whatsoever on the ground of sex either directly, or indirectly by reference in particular to marital or family status') and applies the principle in particular as regards:

- – the scope of the schemes and the conditions of access thereto,
- – the obligation to contribute and the calculation of contributions,
- – the calculation of benefits including increases due in respect of a

spouse and for dependants and the conditions governing the
duration and retention of entitlement to benefits.

It is now clear from two cases that this Article is directly effective.[200] In the *FNV* case[201] the European Court held that Article 4(1)
was sufficiently precise and unconditional to be relied upon (from
the date when it came into force) by individuals before the national
courts; it added that a Member State may not rely on its discretion
in the choice of means for the implementation of the equal treatment
principle in order to deny direct effect to the Article. Similarly, in
*McDermott and Cotter* v. *Minister for Social Welfare and Attorney
General*[202] it held that the women claimants could base their actions
directly on the Article, in the absence of national implementing
measures; furthermore, in the absence of such measures, the Article
entitled the women to have the same rules applied to them as are
applied to men who are in the same situation, since those rules
remain the only valid point of reference.

The meaning which the European Court ascribes to indirect
discrimination in this context is especially significant in the light of
the fact that many Member States, including the UK, have social
security systems which on their face are gender-neutral, but which
are based upon the continued model of a breadwinner and a
dependant. In order to provide anything like true equality in this
context, it is necessary for the Court to examine the reality of the
situation and not just its superficial appearance.[203]

There are a number of important exceptions contained in the
Social Security Directive. The principle of equality is to be applied
'without prejudice to the provisions relating to the protection of
women on the grounds of maternity'.[204] In addition, Article 7
entitles the Member States to exclude from the principle of equality:

(a)  the determination of pensionable age for the purposes of
     granting old-age and retirement pensions and the possible
     consequences thereof for other benefits;
(b)  advantages in respect of old-age pension schemes granted to
     persons who have brought up children; the acquisition of benefit
     entitlements following periods of interruption of employment
     due to the bringing up of children;
(c)  the granting of old-age or invalidity benefit entitlements by
     virtue of the derived entitlements of a wife;
(d)  the granting of increases of long-term invalidity, old-age, acci-
     dents at work and occupational disease benefits for a dependent
     wife;
(e)  the consequences of the exercise, before the adoption of this
     Directive, of a right of option not to acquire rights or incur
     obligations under a statutory scheme.

However, the Member States are obliged to examine periodically the exceptions contained in their own law, in the light of social developments, in order to ascertain whether they are still justified.[205] It has been noted earlier that the exception in respect of pensionable age has had a particularly substantial and undesirable knock-on effect in other areas of law.

The Directive requires the Member States to abolish all laws, regulations or administrative provisions in conflict with it[206] and to introduce adequate remedies for persons complaining of breaches of the Directive.[207]

## THE GENERAL PRINCIPLE OF EQUAL TREATMENT

As has been well documented elsewhere,[208] the European Court has often had recourse to 'general principles of law', not precisely set out in the Treaty but none the less supplementing it. That one such general principle is the equal treatment of the sexes is evidenced by various decisions of the Court.[209] One reason for invoking a general principle is in order to contest the validity of secondary legislation made by the institutions under Article 189. The standing of an individual to seek the annulment of a Community measure is limited[210] but, provided that standing can be established, it can be successfully argued that a measure is void if it contravenes the general principle of equal treatment. Alternatively, use can be made of Article 184, in order to contest the validity of an underlying regulation, where a decision is sought to be enforced against an individual. A plea of this kind was sustained in *Sabbatini* v. *European Parliament*.[211]

Ms Sabbatini was a Community employee who had received an expatriation allowance before her marriage. Once married, however, she became subject to the Civil Service Regulations which provided: 'An official loses entitlement to the allowance, if, marrying a person who, at the time of marriage, does not fulfil the conditions required for the grant of that allowance, he (or she) does not become the head of the family.' Under the Regulations, the 'head of the family' was normally the husband, except in the event of his disability. Ms Sabbatini contested the decisions stopping her allowance, arguing that the decision was based on the Regulation which was itself invalid since it breached the 'higher' rule prohibiting any discrimination on grounds of sex. Roemer AG denied that such a higher rule existed, but the Court upheld the claim.[212]

Another application of the general principle of non-discrimination on the ground of sex came in *Razzouk and Beydoun* v. *Commission*.[213] The widower of a deceased employee of the Commission was denied a survivor's pension by the Commission in circumstances in which, according to the Staff Regulations, a surviving widow would have been entitled to a pension. He complained that this amounted either to the breach of a principle applicable to Community officials and analogous to Article 119, or else to the breach of a more general superior rule of EEC law that officials should be treated equally in like or comparable situations. Slynn AG commented that his claim was, in substance, for the annulment of the Commission decision refusing the survivor's pension. There was, he said, clearly discrimination between officials, and consequentially between their spouses, on the ground of sex, since both male and female officials made the same pension contributions during their employment but stood to receive different benefits in the event of their pre-deceasing their spouses. This discrimination, he held, had not been shown to be justified on any objective ground. It offended against both the general principle of non-discrimination and the narrower principle analogous to Article 119, so that the Commission decision must be annulled. The Court agreed that the decision must be annulled, but based its decision purely on the general principle of non-discrimination, saying that the Staff Regulations were 'contrary to a fundamental right and therefore inapplicable in so far as they treat surviving spouses of officials unequally according to the sex of the persons concerned.[214]

The occasions on which an individual is likely to want to challenge a Community measure on grounds of sex discrimination are necessarily fairly limited and it is not surprising that the cases so far have all involved employees of the Communities or their spouses contesting decisions about their own pay or pensions. The importance of the wholehearted acceptance by the European Court of the general principle of non-discrimination should not however be underestimated, for it demonstrates a serious regard on the part of at least one higher court for the notion of sex equality. Nevertheless, it will of course be far more common in practice for a woman to need to challenge a provision of domestic law, or otherwise to enforce her rights in a domestic court, so that the direct effect of the EEC legislation is of greater practical significance than the underlying 'general principle'.

## OTHER ACTION BEING TAKEN BY THE EEC TO COUNTER SEX DISCRIMINATION[215]

The EEC is attempting to challenge sex discrimination in a number of ways apart from those so far mentioned. The European Parliament has proportionately more women members than the national parliaments of the Member States[216] and it has been active in discussing matters of special importance to women. It has an influential Committee on Women's Rights. The Commission contains the 'Women's Information Service' which (as its name indicates) provides information relating to women and publishes a bi-monthly journal entitled *Women of Europe;* the Commission also houses the Equal Opportunities Office which deals with all aspects of policy relating to women's employment and equal treatment. There is, in addition, a considerable repository of knowledge of the law affecting women within the Legal Service of the Commission. The Commission has also recently set up a community-wide 'network' on the application of the equality directives, which is made up of independent specialists from the legal profession and the two sides of industry.

The European Social Fund (ESF), established by the EEC Treaty itself,[217] is designed to improve employment opportunities for workers in the Common Market and to contribute thereby to raising the standard of living. As far as women are concerned, the Fund has been used mainly to help them gain access to traditionally male jobs or to fields offering new employment opportunities; for example, in 1981 the East Leeds Women's Workshop set a precedent by receiving such aid towards the salary of a nursery nurse to care for the children of mothers on a training project; and the South Glamorgan Women's Workshop, which trains women who have missed out on education and training in their youth in computing and micro-electronics, has also received backing from the Fund. The ESF is administered by the Commission on the basis of Guidelines which used to name women as a specific category for consideration; despite this, on this basis only about 30 per cent of the Fund's total beneficiaries were women, although they formed over 50 per cent of the Community's population and unemployment was known at the time to be higher amongst women than men in the EEC.[218] The Council agreed to a general revision of the Fund's rules in June 1983;[219] this resulted in the removal of separate budget lines for particular types of beneficiaries and an agreement in principle that at least 75 per cent of the Fund would hitherto be devoted to youth projects. Yearly Guidelines now have to be drawn up by the Commission, after consultation with the European Parliament, setting out which projects are currently in favour. The first year of operation of the new system, 1983, was not encouraging from the point of view of women. Although the percentage of women beneficiaries from the Fund actually rose to 39 per cent, the amount of money given for women's training projects dropped dramatically to 15.8 million ecus, (European currency units), less than half of what had been paid out the previous year and less than 1 per cent of the total Fund budget.[220] In 1985, only 38 per cent of people receiving assistance from the Fund were women, despite the fact that at that date women constituted 43 per cent of the Community's unemployed; projects in that year specifically for women, 'to promote a more even mix of the sexes in jobs where women are underrepresented', accounted for only 1.35 per cent of the total Fund budget.[221] In 1986, women received only 36 per cent of the Fund .[222] In reply to a written question in the European Parliament, the Commission has stated that, on average, women have been receiving about a third of ESF grants annually since 1981, but that the figures could be no more than estimates because many of the applications for grants concern both men and women. The number of women beneficiaries rose from 393,000 in 1981 to just over one million in 1985.[223] The UK, not previously one of the major recipients of the Fund, received the biggest slice of it, 32.1 per cent in 1984,[224] 16.3 per cent in 1984 and 18.8 per cent in 1986.[225] In 1985, it received the largest share for women's projects, with more than 50 per cent of applications approved.[226] A number of serious criticism of the Fund and the way in which it operates have been voiced, in particular by the European Parliament. For example, although reasonably convenient from the viewpoint of governmental organisations, the Fund is ill-designed to cope with the cash-flow problems encountered by voluntary groups; this is because the groups have to begin running their activities before the decision on whether or not to grant funding is made by the ESF. In addition, they are required to raise half the capital needed beforehand from national authorities; the half of their funding which can then be provided by the ESF arrives in two equal tranches, the second of which is only receivable *after* the money has actually been spent. The Fund has also been criticised for having become too 'political', being in reality a means of reimbursing national contributions to the EEC budget, and for the slow processing of applications and general red-tape involved. The Parliament has, for some years, been demanding a more active role in the management and disbursement of the Fund.[227] Structural changes to the Fund seem likely in the intermediate future, if current Commission plans to reform all social, regional and agricultural funds by 1992 are accepted by the Council.

At the end of 1981, in response to a European Parliament Resolution of 10 February 1981 on the situation of women in the EEC, the then Social Affairs Commissioner, Sir Ivor Richard, unveiled a Community 'Action Programme' designed to promote equal opportunities for women and intended to last from 1982 until 1985.[228] The Council adopted the Programme in May 1982. The Programme was intended to operate against the background of economic difficulties, whose effect had been to slow down progress towards equality. It envisaged measures being taken in two general directions: the reinforcement of individual legal rights and the dismantling of barriers to equality of opportunity through positive action schemes (which would help women to take on non-traditional jobs). All this was to be accompanied by an information campaign, to make women more aware of their rights and to persuade the public to accept women as equals in all sectors of society and realise the benefits flowing from such a change. At the same time, an Advisory Committee on Equal Opportunities for Women and Men was set up; the reason for this was that the Commission felt that better results were likely to be obtained if there was a pooling of views and experience by agencies, such as the EOC, with specific responsibility for equal opportunities within the Member States. The Committee consists of representatives of the national equality bodies and the British EOC has played an important part. The Committee's formal mandate is to assist the Commission in formulating and implementing policy on the advancement of women's employment and equal opportunities, and also to arrange for a continuous exchange of information between the interested bodies.

A Second Action Programme for 1986 to 1990 has also been agreed, again in part as a result of pressure from the European Parliament.[229] This Programme is designed to:

- consolidate rights under Community Law, particularly by improving the application of existing provisions and adopting the proposals under examination;
- follow-up and develop action launched under the 1982–1985 Action Programme, in particular the networks for contacts and exchanges which represent a new form of social dialogue in this area and which have made a very positive contribution;
- intensify efforts to involve all those concerned through a broader dialogue and a consciousness-raising campaign aimed at the people involved and at a wider target public;
- develop and intensify support for specific actions, in particular those intended to develop women's employment;
- develop and adopt such action, in particular with regard to the most vulnerable and/or disadvantaged categories:
- examine the situation in the new Member States of the Community.[230]

In particular, by virtue of the Second Action Programme, grants are available from the Commission to help women to create their own businesses. Priority is given to projects which create jobs for categories of women with special problems (such as the unemployed) and or create non-traditional jobs for women. The grant is for the starting-up costs of the project in its first year and is non-renewable.

Several new sex equality Directives have been proposed in recent years, some as a direct consequence of the First Action Programme. The Commission produced a Draft Directive on part-time working in December 1981[231] and a Draft Directive on temporary work in April 1982.[232] The first (which was revised somewhat in 1983) would provide equal rights for part-timers (most of whom, of course, are female) with full-timers as regards working conditions, dismissal, entitlement to participate in workers' representative bodies, access to vocational training, promotion, social facilities and medical care; remuneration, holiday pay, redundancy and retirement payments would also have to be equal, although proportional to the hours worked.[233] The temporary work draft contains provisions designed to protect temporary workers (again, often female) supplied by agencies and those on fixed term contracts and to bring their rights more closely into line with those of permanent workers; it also covers the protection of permanent workers against the misuse of temporary staff and provides for the control of employment agencies. Both drafts, however, remain unadopted by the Council at the time of writing, largely because of opposition to them by the UK, whose government in recent years has been keen to deregulate employment.

A Directive on parental leave is also awaiting adoption.[234] The new Directive on Occupational Social Security Schemes has been mentioned earlier in the present chapter. A new Directive has also recently been adopted on the self-employed.[235] This covers all self-employed workers and 'their spouses, not being employees or partners, where they habitually, under the conditions laid down by national law, participate in the activities of the self-employed worker and perform the same tasks or ancillary tasks'.[236] It applies the principle of equal treatment to all such persons[237] and obliges the Member States to take the measures necessary to ensure the elimination of all provisions which are contrary to the principle of equal treatment, especially in respect of the establishment, equipment or extension of a business or the launching or extension of any other form of self-employed activity including financial facilities.[238] Member States are also required to ensure that the conditions for the formation of a company between spouses are not more restrictive than those that apply between the unmarried[239] and that spouses have voluntary access to contributory social security schemes.[240] The Directive makes very weak provision in respect of maternity rights for the self-employed, obliging Member States only to examine whether, and under what conditions, they should be available.[241] The Member States have until the end of June 1989 in which to comply with the Directive.[242] A Draft Directive is also expected to be proposed by the Commission to reverse the burden of proof in discrimination cases. This received the backing of the Advisory Committee on Equal Opportunities in May 1987.[243]

Mention should also be made of certain non-legislative measures taken recently in the area of sex equality, but with the caveat that such measures in the Community context often in practice represent an unwillingness on the part of the Member States to do more than pay lip-service to the issue in question. A Council Resolution was passed in June 1984 on action to combat unemployment amongst women and, in June 1985, the Education Council adopted a ten-point action programme on equal opportunities for girls and boys in schools; this pledges the Member States to eradicate sex-role stereotyping in teaching materials, to encourage both the sexes to make non-traditional career choices, to include equal opportunities as a component in teacher training courses and to ensure a balance of the sexes in postings, promotion and training of teachers. The Commission has also recently decided in principle to adopt a recommendation on vocational training for women.

The fate of positive action schemes within the EEC has been disappointing, despite the prominence accorded the matter in the First Action Programme. A study of positive action was conducted for the Commission by Professor Vogel-Polsky of the Brussels National Centre for the Sociology of Labour Law.[244] This suggested that a directive would be the best way of ensuring that positive action programmes were implemented throughout the EEC, since it would enable the national authorities to be flexible in introducing such schemes whilst at the same time forcing them into action. Community-wide legislation would also, it was pointed out, prevent firms from becoming less competitive because of the cost of such programmes. The directive would make positive action programmes obligatory in Community institutions and national public bodies. The EEC could also introduce an equality clause into all its contracts with outside firms, making the contracts conditional on the firms' use of positive action, on the same lines as in the USA.[245] EEC finance could also be given on such a condition, as could finance and contracts in the public sector in the Member States. However, only a few months after the report was presented, the Advisory Committee on Equal Opportunities for Women and Men rejected the idea of a directive in favour of a mere non-binding recommendation to the Member States; it seemed to be felt that a directive had no chance of approval by the Council and so was politically inadvisable. The Commission therefore opted for a recommendation only on the matter, in spite of the contrary views of both the European trades unions and the European Parliament.

The Recommendation was adopted by the Council in December 1984.[246] Certain of the Commission's more radical proposals were removed by the Council, such as the fixing of recruitment targets to ensure greater female representation in industry. However, the Council did approve the idea of a national positive action plan for both public and private sectors; the public sector was accepted as providing an important example for private industry, which should be encouraged to follow suit wherever possible. A code of good practice for employers, more flexible hours and conditions of work, and measures 'designed to foster greater sharing of occupational and social responsibilities' were approved. What possible incentives or sanctions should exist in this area is not dealt with in the Recommendation, but the Commission is required to report back in three years on the general progress achieved.[247] In its Second Action Programme, the Commission has promised to present to the Council, the Member States, the two sides of industry and potential promotors of positive action plans, a Code of Practice to assist and inform them on the implementation of such schemes.

## NOTES

1. Treaty of Accession of 22 January 1972.
2. References to Treaty articles hereafter in this chapter will be to the EEC Treaty, unless otherwise stated.
3. Failure to fulfil such an obligation may result in proceedings being brought against the Member State under Article 169 or 170.
4. For more detailed discussion of the characteristics of these instruments, see Hartley, *The Foundations of European Community Law* (1981, Clarendon Press) Chapter 4.
5. Article 189.
6. European Communities Act 1972, s.2(1) provides: 'All such rights, powers, liabilities, obligations and restrictions from time to time created or arising by or under the Treaties, and all such remedies and procedures from time to time provided for by or under the Treaties, as in accordance with the Treaties are without further enactment to be given legal effect or used in the UK shall be recognised and available in law, and be enforced, allowed and followed accordingly.'
7. Article 189.
8. Which may take the form of a constitutional guarantee, see *Commission* v. *Germany:* Case 248/83 [1986] 2 CMLR 588.
9. Subject to the limitations laid down in Schedule 2 of the Act. The Equal Pay (Amendment) Regulations 1983, discussed in Chapter 2, were made under the authority of this section.
10. Article 189.
11. See especially *Van Gend en Loos* v. *Nederlandse Tariefcommissie:* Case 26/62 [1963] ECR 1; and *Costa* v. *ENEL:* Case 6/64 [1964] ECR 585.
12. *Van Gend en Loos* v. *Nederlandse Tariefcommissie:* Case 26/62 [1963] ECR 1.
13. See, for example, *Leonesio* v. *Italian Ministry of Agriculture:* Case 93/71 [1972] ECR 287.

14. See especially *Grad* v. *Finanzamt Traunstein:* Case 9/70 [1970] ECR 825; *SACE* v. *Italian Ministry of Finance:* Case 33/70 [1970] ECR 1213; *Van Duyn* v. *Home Office:* Case 41/74 [1974] ECR 1337; *Verbond* v. *Inspecteur der Invoerrechten en Accijnzen:* Case 51/76 [1977] ECR 113; *Pubblico Ministero* v. *Ratti:* Case 148/78 [1980] 1 CMLR 96; *R* v. *Home Office, Ex p. Santillo:* Case 131/79 [1980] 2 CMLR 308.
15. *Pubblico Ministero* v. *Ratti:* Case 148/78 [1980] 1 CMLR 96.
16. Or, presumably, a decision.
17. For further discussion of direct effect, see Collins, *European Community Law in the UK* (3rd edn, 1984, Butterworths) Chapter 2; Wyatt and Dashwood, *The Substantive Law of the EEC* (1980, Sweet and Maxwell) Chapter 3; Usher, *European Community Law and National Law* (1981, George Allen & Unwin) Chapter 2; and Winter, 'Direct Application and Direct Effect: Two Distinct and Different Concepts in Community Law' (1972) 9 *CML Rev.* 425.
18. In *Costa* v. *ENEL:* Case 6/64 [1964] ECR 585, the conflicting domestic law post-dated the EEC law and the principle of supremacy was held to prevail over the assumption that *lex posterior derogat priori.*
19. For an example of the supremacy of a regulation, see *Politi Sas* v. *Minister of Finance:* Case 43/71 [1971] ECR 1039.
20. At least for the time being, though there seems no reason in legal theory why the European Communities Act could not be repealed.
21. Set out *supra*, n. 6.
22. For discussion of the problems involved, see Hood Phillips, 'Parliament and Self-Limitation' (1973) 4 *Cambrian Law Review* 71; 'Has the "Incoming Ride" Reached the Palace of Westminster?' (1979) 95 *LQR* 167; 'High Tide in the Strand? Post–1972 Acts and Community Law' (1980) 96 *LQR* 31; Winterton, 'The British Grundnorm: Parliamentary Supremacy Re-examined' (1976) 92 *LQR* 591; Thomson, 'The Supremacy of European Community Law' [1976] SLT 273; and Trinidade, 'Parliamentary Supremacy and the Primacy of European Community Law' (1972) 35 *MLR* 375.
23. See, for example, *Re Residence Conditions* [1978] 2 CMLR 287 and *Albion Shipping* v. *Arnold* [1981] IRLR 525.
24. *Macarthys Ltd* v. *Smith* [1980] IRLR 209.
25. Ibid, at p. 210. See also Ellis, 'Supremacy of Parliament and European Law' (1980) 96 *LQR* 511.
26. For the view that the European Court has over-involved itself in law-making, see Rasmussen, *On Law and Policy in the European Court of Justice* (1986, Nijhoff).
27. For general discussion of the EEC law on sex discrimination, see *Women's Rights and the EEC* (Rights of Women Europe, 1983); Landau, *The Rights of Working Women in the European Community* (1985, Commission of the European Communities, European Perspective Series); and Hoskyns, 'Women, European Law and Transnational Politics' (1986) 14 *International Journal of the Sociology of Law* 299.
28. To be found among the Social Provisions.
29. The Wording of the Article is derived from International Labour Organisation Convention No. 100 of 29 June 1951, 165 UNTS 303, 'concerning equal remuneration for men and women workers for work of equal value'. But note the distinction between 'equal work' and work of equal value' and see *infra*, p. 198 *et seq* for further discussion of this matter.
30. See Forman, 'The Equal Pay Principle under Community Law' (1982) *LIEI* 17.
31. *Defrenne* v. *Sabena:* Case 43/75 [1976] 2 CMLR 98.
32. Ibid., at p. 122.

33. This resolution was ineffective to modify the Treaty, since it did not comply with the amendment procedure laid down in Article 236; see the *Second Defrenne* case, Case 43/75 [1976] 2 CMLR 98, at p. 127.
34. See OJ 1974 No. C13/1.
35. See *European File*, April 1980.
36. *Defrenne* v. *Sabena:* Case 43/75 [1976] 2 CMLR 98.
37. Under Article 177.
38. See the opinion of Trabucchi AG: *Defrenne* v. *Sabena:* Case 43/75 [1976] 2 CMLR 98, at p. 112.
39. As examples, the Court took the heading of Part One of the Treaty which is simply 'Principles', and also Article 113 which provides that the commercial policy of the Community is 'based on uniform principles'.
40. *Defrenne* v. *Sabena:* Case 43/75 [1976] 2 CMLR 98, at p. 128.
41. Ibid., at p. 123.
42. Ibid., at pp. 123–4.
43. And from the date of their accession to the Communities for the new Member States.
44. An inconsistency in the Court's reasoning, since it had earlier rejected the notion that the effectiveness of Article 119 could be undermined by the dilatoriness of the Commission, see *supra*, p. 185. On this matter the Court differed from the Advocate General.
45. For discussion of the prospective effect of rulings of the European Court of Justice see Wyatt, 'Prospective Effect of a Holding of Direct Applicability' (1975–6) 1 *ELR* 399; for discussion of the matter in a somewhat different context, see L. Neville Brown, 'Agromonetary Byzantinism and Prospective Overruling' (1981) 18 *CML Rev*. 509 (and the references cited therein). A problem highlighted by this aspect of the decision in the *Second Defrenne* case is the lack of any real means of challenging pronouncements of this Court, from whose decisions there can be no appeal.
46. 8 April 1976.
47. *Defrenne* v. *Sabena:* Case 43/75 [1976] 2 CMLR 98, at p. 128.
48. Ibid., at p. 117. The Court's agreement can be inferred from its remarks on p. 123.
49. See also *Von Colson and Kamann* v. *Land of North Rhine-Westphalia:* Case 14/83 [1986] 2 CMLR 430, commented on by Arnull in (1984) 9 *ELR* 267. For further discussion of this case, see *infra*, p. 207 *et seq*.
50. On the same point but in a different context, see *Walrave and Koch* v. *Union Cycliste Internationale:* Case 36/74 [1975] 1 CMLR 320.
51. [1976] 2 CMLR 98, at p. 116. The Advocate General's remarks in this respect were accepted by the Court.
52. See, for example, Easson, 'Can Directives Impose Obligations on Individuals?' (1979) 4 *ELR* 67, and 'The Direct Effect of EEC Directives' (1979) 28 *ICLQ* 319.
53. The reason given by the employer for the disparity in pay was that he wanted to encourage productivity and the maximum use of his machinery.
54. See Chapter 2, p. 47.
55. The last paragraph of Article 119 provides: 'Equal pay without discrimination based on sex means: (a) that pay for the same work at piece rates shall be calculated on the basis of the same unit of measurement; (b) that pay for work at time rates shall be the same for the same job.'
56. The European Court proceeded from the premiss that 93% of all part-timers in the UK at the time of the case were women. See also Chapter 2, n. 189.
57. *Jenkins* v. *Kingsgate (Clothing Productions) Ltd* Case 96/80 [1981] IRLR 228, at p. 234.

58. Ibid., also at p. 234. The evidence showed that, before the British Equal Pay Act came into effect, Kingsate did not pay the same wages to male and female employees but the hourly rates of pay were identical whether the work was part-time or full-time. From November 1975, the pay for full-time work became the same for male and female employees but the rate for part-time work became lower.
59. Ibid., at p. 234.
60. *Bilka-Kaufhaus GmbH* v. *Weber Von Hartz*: Case 170/84 [1986] IRLR 317.
61. See also *Worringham* v. *Lloyds Bank*: Case 69/80 [1981] ECR 767; and *Sotgiu* v. *Deutsche Bundespost*: Case 152/73 [1974] ECR 153. The Commission is, at the time of writing, considering proposing legislation which would define indirect discrimination for the purposes of EEC law: see CREW Reports (1987) vol. 7, no. 8/9.
62. See Chapter 3, p. 88.
63. Whether or not the Article is directly effective in equal value cases will be discussed *infra*, p. 198 *et seq.*
64. See the remarks to this effect of Dutheillet de Lamothe AG in *Defrenne* v. *Belgium 'The First Defrenne case'*: Case 80/70 [1974] 1 CMLR 494, at p. 500.
65. *Sabbatini* v. *European Parliament*: Case 32/71 [1972] CMLR 945.
66. Article 179 confers jurisdiction on the European Court of Justice in disputes between the Community and its servants.
67. On this occasion, the Commission was a defendant and therefore wanted to restrict the meaning of Article 119, in contrast to its usual task, as watchdog of the Treaty under Article 155, of arguing for an extensive reading of the law in this area.
68. *Infra*, p. 217.
69. Redundancy payments were involved in *Burton* v. *British Railways Board*: Case 19/81 [1982] 3 All ER 537 but, since the issue was not discrimination as to the amount of the payments receivable, the European Court of Justice did not decide whether or not they constituted 'pay' within the meaning of Article 119. However, in *Hammersmith and Queen Charlotte's Special Health Authority* v. *Cato* (1988) 17 *EOR* 38, the Employment Appeal Tribunal ruled that a contractual redundancy payment was 'pay' for the purposes of Article 119.
70. *Garland* v. *British Rail Engineering Ltd*: Case 12/81 [1982] 2 WLR 918. The *Fourth Annual Report* of the EOC (1979) stated that discrimination in respect of the provision of fringe benefits prompted a significant number of complaints to them. In particular, women in management and senior grades frequently complained that they were denied perks offered to their male colleagues, such as company cars and free subscriptions to medical and life insurances. Such discrimination will, of course, often constitute a breach of domestic law as well as of EEC law.
71. *Garland* v. *British Rail Engineering Ltd*: Case 12/81 [1982] 2 WLR 918. Also discussed in Chapter 3, particularly p. 109 *et seq.*
72. *Defrenne* v. *Belgium*: Case 80/70 [1977] 1 CMLR 494.
73. State and occupational pension schemes are now regulated by two directives, as to which see *infra*, p. 194 *et seq.* and p. 214 *et seq.*
74. *First Defrenne* case: Case 80/70 [1974] 1 CMLR 494, at pp. 502–3.
75. Important changes to pension schemes in the UK were introduced by the Social Security Act 1986.
76. For example, as to the minimum annual rate of pension and as to benefits for widows.
77. Also discussed in Chapter 3, particularly p. 108 *et seq.*
78. See Chapter 3, p. 108 *et seq.*

79. Since the end of 1961 in the case of the original Member States and since accession in the case of the new Member States
80. *Worringham* v. *Lloyds Bank* Case 69/80 [1981] ECR 767, at p. 806.
81. Ibid., at p. 806.
82. In more detail than is usual in a ruling under Article 177, which is concerned only with the interpretation of the law and not the application of that law to the facts of a case.
83. *Barber* v. *Guardian Royal Exchange Assurance Group* [1983] IRLR 240.
84. *Burton* v. *British Rail* [1982] 3 All ER 537.
85. *Barber* v. *Guardian Royal Exchange Assurance Group* [1983] IRLR 240, at p. 243.
86. *Razzouk* v. *Beydoun* Cases 75 and 117/82 [1984] ECR 1509.
87. Ibid., at p. 1540.
88. Ibid., at p. 1530.
89. *Bilka-Kaufhaus GmbH* v. *Weber Von Hartz:* Case 170/84 [1986] IRLR 317.
90. Ibid., at p. 319.
91. Ibid., at p. 320.
92. This element was confirmed by the European Court in *Newstead* v. *Department of Transport* Case 192/85 [1988] 1 All ER 129, especially p. 150.
93. Query the status of the two types of pension introduced in the UK by the Social Security Act 1986, namely occupational and personal schemes. They are required to be funded in part by employers and will be a matter of contractual arrangement between employer and employee, but can they truly be said not to substitute for the state scheme?
94. Directive on the implementation of the principle of equal treatment for men and women in occupational social security schemes, Directive 86/378, OJ 1986 No. L 225/40. This Directive is foreshadowed in Article 3(3) of the Social Security Directive, Directive 79/7, OJ 1979 No. L 6/24.
95. Occupational Social Security Directive, Article 4.
96. Ibid., Article 2(2).
97. Ibid., Article 5(1).
98. Ibid., Articles 9 and 6(1). Note also however that, in October 1987, the EEC Comission adopted a new draft Directive, intended to provide equality in survivors' benefits and to standardize pensionable age: see CREW Reports (1988) vol. 8, no. 1.
99. See its remark in *Defrenne* v. *Sabena:* Case 43/75 [1976] 2 CMLR 98, at p. 127 to the effect that no implementing provision, whether adopted by the institutions of the Community or by the national authorities, could adversely affect the direct effect of Article 119'.
100. The European Court held in *Newstead* v. *Department of Transport* Case 192/85 [1988] 1 All ER 129 that an unmarried male worker, forced to contribute part of his gross salary to provide for a survivor's benefit, in circumstances where his unmarried female colleagues did not have to do the same, was not discriminated against contrary to either Article 119 or any of the equality directives. The latter excluded survivors' benefits from their scope and the former was irrelevant *on the facts* because the complaint was not about the *gross pay* received by Mr Newstead but about the fact of *being required* to make the contribution.
101. Occupational Social Security Directive, Article 8(1). Member States must bring into force such laws, regulations and administrative provisions as are necessary in order to comply with the Directive at the latest three years after its notification: Article 12(1).
102. *Marshall* v. *Southampton and SW Hants Area Health Authority:* Case 152/84 [1986] 2 WLR 780.
103. 'Horizontal direct effect' is discussed supra in relation to Treaty provisions.

See also *Johnston* v. *RUC:* Case 222/84 [1986] 3 WLR 1038. Difficult, and as yet largely unresolved, problems result as to who precisely is an 'organ of the State'. In the *Johnston* case, the Court stated that individuals may rely on a directive 'as against an organ of the State whether it acts "qua" employer or "qua" public authority. As regards an authority like the Chief Constable, he is an official responsible for the direction of the police service. Whatever its relations may be with other organs of the State, such a public authority, charged by the State with the maintenance of public order and safety, does not act as a private individual' (at pp. 1060–1). In *Rolls-Royce plc* v. *Doughty, The Times*, 10 March 1987, the Employment Appeal Tribunal held that Rolls-Royce, even though state-owned, was not an organ or agent of the state. To the same effect, see also *Foster* v. *British Gas plc* (1987) 16 *EOR* 43. The inability of directives to produce horizontal effects results from the reasoning adopted by the European Court in the *Ratti* case (Case 148/78 [1980] 1 CMLR 96), namely that the device enabling an individual to rely on a directive, which is by definition (in Article 189 of the EEC Treaty) not itself part of the national legal system, is the principle that the Member State is estopped from pleading its own wrongful non-implementation of the instrument. Such an argument clearly cannot apply where another private person or company, rather than a Member State, is the defendant. It should be remembered, however, that, even where it does not produce direct effects, a directive may still influence the construction placed on domestic legislation: see *Beets-Proper* v. *Van Lanschot Bankers NV:* Case 262/84 [1986] ICR 706; s.2(4) of the European Communities Act 1972; and *Garland* v. *British Rail Engineering Ltd* in the House of Lords [1982] 2 WLR 918. But note also the restrictive interpretation placed on the Equal Treatment Directive in *Duke* v. *Reliance Systems Ltd* [1988] 2 WLR 359. This case however concerned the interpretation of s.6(4) of the Sex Discrimination Act 1975 in the short period between the judgment in *Marshall* v. *Southampton and SW Hants Area Health Authority* Case 152/84 [1986] 2 WLR 780 and the entry into effect of the Sex Discrimination Act 1986 (see Chapter 3, p. 112 *et seq.*) It is to be hoped that the decision is confined to its own special facts and not intended to enunciate any general principle to the effect that domestic legislation which *pre-dates* a relevant EEC law may not be interpreted so as to comply with that EEC law. After all, it can be argued that Parliament, in leaving the original domestic law unchanged on the statute book, considered it a satisfactory formulation from the point of view of UK obligations under EEC law.

104.  *Defrenne* v. *Sabena* Case: 43/75 [1976] 2 CMLR 98.
105.  Conflicting dicta are to be found in the *Second Defrenne case; Worringham* v. *Lloyds Bank:* Case 69/80 [1981] ECR 767; *Jenkins* v. *Kingsgate (Clothing Productions) Ltd:* Case 96/80 [1981] IRLR 228; *Commission* v. *Denmark:* Case 143/83 [1986] 1 CMLR 44; and *Macarthys Ltd* v. *Smith:* Case 129/79 [1980] ICR 672.
106.  *Macarthys Ltd* v. *Smith* Case 129/79 [1980] ICR 672.
107.  Ibid., at p. 690.
108.  For more detailed discussion of this matter, see Chapter 2, p. 36 *et seq.*
109.  *Albion Shipping Agency* v. *Arnold* [1981] IRLR 525.
110.  As made operative by the European Communities Act 1972, ss.2(1) and 2(4).
111.  This difficulty was later resolved by the decision of the House of Lords in *Rainey* v. *Greater Glastow Health Board* [1986] 3 WLR 1017, discussed in Chapter 2, p. 48 *et seq.*
112.  See in particular *Amies* v. *ILEA* [1977] ICR 308; and *Snoxell* v. *Vauxhall Motors Ltd* [1977] IRLR 123; cf. *Shields* v. *Coomes (Holdings) Ltd* [1978] ICR 1159.
113.  *Albion Shipping Agency* v. *Arnold* [1981] IRLR 525, at p. 529.

114. Ibid., also at p. 529.
115. *Defrenne* v. *Sabena:* Case 43/75 [1976] 2 CMLR 98, at p. 199.
116. Discussed *infra*, p. 353 *et seq.*.
117. *Jenkins* v. *Kingsgate (Clothing Productions) Ltd:* Case 96/80 [1981] IRLR 228.
118. Ibid., at p. 234. This remark was repeated in *Newstead* v. *Department of Transport* Case 192/85 [1988] 1 All ER 129, at p. 151.
119. *Worringham* v. *Lloyds Bank Ltd:* Case 69/80 [1981] ECR 767.
120. Ibid., at p. 791. See also *Commission* v. *Denmark* Case 143/83 [1986] 1 CMLR 44.
121. *Worringham* v. *Lloyds Bank Ltd:* Case 69/80 [1981] ECR 767, at p. 792; emphasis added. See also *Murphy* v. *Bord Telecom Eireann* Case 157/86, Unreported at the time of writing.
122. Discussed *supra*, p. 187 *et seq.*
123. See, in particular, Arnull, 'Article 119 and Equal Pay for Work of Equal Value' [1986] *ELR* 200. Cf. Forman, 'The Equal Pay Principle Under Community Law' [1982] *LIEI* 17.
124. *Pickstone and others* v. *Freemans plc* [1987] IRLR 218. At the time of writing, an appeal to the House of Lords against this decision was pending.
125. See Chapter 2, p. 33 *et seq.*
126. OJ 1975 No. L 45/19, 19 February 1975.
127. The decision of the European Court about the direct effect of Article 119 in the *Second Defrenne* Case: Case 43/75 [1976] 2 CMLR 98, shortly after the issue of this Directive, robbed the latter of some of its purpose.
128. Article 100 provides: 'The Council shall, acting unanimously on a proposal from the Commission, issue directives for the approximation of such provisions laid down by law, regulation or administrative action in the Member States as directly affect the establishment or functioning of the Common Market.' Query whether this provision is sufficiently broad to authorise a directive *enlarging* on Article 119 of the Treaty.
129. *Macarthys Ltd* v. *Smith:* Case 129/79 [1980] ICR 672; *Worringham* v. *Lloyds Bank:* Case 69/80 [1981] ECR 767; *Jenkins* v. *Kingsgate Ltd:* Case 96/80 [1981] IRLR 228; *Garland* v. *British Rail Engineering Ltd:* Case 12/81 [1982] 2 WLR 918; and *Burton* v. *British Railways Board:* Case 19/81 [1982] 3 All ER 537. The point came before the English courts in *Sim-Chem Ltd* v. *O'Brien* [1980] 2 All ER 307 and [1980] 1 WLR 1011. The issue was, oddly, not raised in *Rummler* v. *Dato-Druck:* Case 237/85 (1987) 11 EOR 37, discussed *infra*, p. 201.
130. *Verbond* v. *Inspecteur der Invoerrechten en Accijnzen:* Case 51/76 [1977] ECR 113.
131. This demonstrates that the Directive itself creates the individual's right, rather than the underlying Treaty Article, since Article 100 is not concerned with substantive law at all.
132. Though its legal ability to do so has not been directly tested before the European Court.
133. *Commission* v. *UK:* Case 61/81 [1982] 3 CMLR 284, discussed in Chapter 2, p. 31 *et seq.*
134. Ibid., at p. 298; emphasis supplied.
135. *Commission* v. *Denmark:* Case 143/83 [1986] 1 CMLR 44.
136. Ibid., at p. 47. The Advocate General went on to explain that he is one of those who believes that Article 119 also requires comparisons to be made outside the employee's immediate establishment.
137. *Rummler* v. *Dato-Druck:* Case 237/85 (1987) 11 *EOR* 37.
138. From the transcript of the judgment.
139. See in particular the Equal Pay Act 1970, s.1(5); *Greene* v. *Broxtowe DC* [1977] IRLR 34; *Hebbes* v. *Rank Precision Ltd* [1978] ICR 489; *Eaton* v. *Nuttall* [1977]

ICR 272; and *Arnold* v. *Beecham Group Ltd* [1982] IRLR 397, discussed in Chapter 2, p. 42.

140. Equal Pay (Amendment) Regulations 1983 (SI 1983 No. 1794), ss.2A(2) and (3).

141. But, as discussed in Chapter 2, no statutory collective machinery is laid down for determining the possible invalidity of a discriminatory term and, furthermore, there is no satisfactory legal procedure provided for its amendment.

142. This point is discussed further *infra*, n. 168, in relation to the Equal Treatment Directive.

143. See for example the Council Resolution of January 1974, OJ 1974 No. C13/1.

144. Directive 76/207, OJ 1976 No. L 39/40, 14 February 1976.

145. *Verbond* v. *Inspecteur der Invoerrechten en Accijnzen:* Case 51/76 [1977] ECR 113 suggests that there is no legal obstacle to the possible direct effect of such a directive.

146. See the discussion of horizontal direct effect *supra*, p. 195 *et seq.*.

147. The Sex Discrimination Act 1975, s.77(1) states: 'A term of a contract is void where (a) its inclusion renders the making of the contract unlawful by virtue of this Act, or (b) it is included in furtherance of an act rendered unlawful by this Act, or (c) it provides for the doing of an act which would be rendered unlawful by this Act.'

148. See Chapter 3, particularly p. 94 *et seq.*

149. See Chapter 3, p. 128 *et seq.*

150. *Commission* v. *UK* Case 165/82 [1984] 1 CMLR 44, especially at p. 51.

151. Ibid., at p. 60.

152. See also Chapter 2, p. 17.

153. See *Johnston* v. *RUC:* Case 222/84 [1986] 3 WLR 1038.

154. *Burton* v. *British Railways Board:* Case 19/81 [1982] 3 All ER 537.

155. See Chapter 3, p. 108 *et seq.*

156. *Burton* v. *British Railways Board:* Case 19/81 [1982] 3 All ER 537, at p. 549. See also *Hammersmith and Queen Charlotte's Special Health Authority* v. *Cato* [1988] 17 *EOR* 38, where an industrial tribunal held that it followed from Article 5 of the Equal Treatment Directive that men and women were entitled to demand equal contractual redundancy payments.

157. Discussed *infra*, p. 214.

158. *Marshall* v. *Southampton and SW Hants Health Authority:* Case 152/84 [1986] 2 WLR 780.

159. Ibid., at p. 797. For discussion of the possible distinction between this case and the *Burton* decision, see Chapter 3, n. 196.

160. Article 9(1) obliged the Member States to carry out 'a first examination and if necessary a first revision' of such provisions within four years of the notification of the Directive, notwithstanding a general compliance period for the rest of the Directive of 30 months from notification.

161. As to which, see *infra*, p. 212 *et seq.*

162. *Johnston* v. *RUC:* Case 222/84 [1986] 3 WLR 1038.

163. And presumably also of Article 5(2)(c), since it is worded identically.

164. [1986] 3 WLR 1038, at p. 1059. Whether women have any other interests which can lawfully be protected under EEC law is discussed further *infra*, p. 213.

165. 'Communication on Protective Legislation for Women in the Member States of the European Community' COM (87) 105 final. See also CREW Reports (1987), vol. 7, no. 4.

166. See Chapter 3, p. 119.

167. *Von Colson and Kamann* v. *Land of North Rhine-Westphalia:* Case 14/83 [1986] 2 CMLR 430, commented on by Arnull in (1984) 9 ELR 267.
168. Similarly, the Commission has argued (COM (78) 711 final, at p. 136) that the remedies provided by the Sex Discrimination Act for victimisation (*i.e.* compensation, declaratory order and recommendation) are insufficient in EEC law; Article 5 of the Equal Pay Directive (and also Article 7 of the Equal Treatment Directive, *infra*) obliges Member States to 'take the necessary measures to protect employees against dismissal' in such a situation. The Commission contends that, in order to satisfy this provision, it must be possible for national courts to order reinstatement.
169. *Johnston* v. *RUC:* Case 222/84 [1986] 3 WLR 1038.
170. See also Chapter 3, p. 126.
171. *Johnston* v. *RUC:* Case 222/84 [1986] 3 WLR 1038, at pp. 1054–5.
172. See Articles 7 and 8 of the Directive.
173. *Johnston* v. *RUC* Case 222/84 [1986] 3 WLR 1038.
174. As to which, see Chapter 3, p. 115 *et seq.*
175. *Commission* v. *UK:* Case 165/82 [1984] 1 CMLR 44.
176. Ibid., at p. 54.
177. Ibid., at p. 61.
178. Put into effect by the Sex Discrimination Act 1975 (Amendment of Section 20) Order, SI 1983 No. 1202.
179. And, incidentally, because the Commission failed to convince the Court on this one aspect of the case, it ordered each party to pay its own costs. It is to be hoped that this magnanimity does not indicate a greater sympathy with the UK's case than the Court felt able to express in its judgment.
180. *Commission* v. *UK:* Case 165/82 [1984] 1 CMLR 44, at p. 62.
181. *Johnston* v. *RUC:* Case 222/84 [1986] 3 WLR 1038.
182. Ibid., at p. 1057.
183. Ibid., at p. 1058.
184. See also Ellis, 'Can Public Safety Provide an Excuse for Sex Discrimination?' (1986) 102 *LQR* 496.
185. The Commission has issued a reasoned opinion to the UK under Article 169, stating that s.51 is contrary to the Equal Treatment Directive.
186. *Johnston* v. *RUC:* Case 222/84 [1986] 3 WLR 1038.
187. Ibid., at p. 1061.
188. Ibid.
189. Ibid., at p. 1059.
190. For discussion of the biological, cultural and other reasons which have been advanced for granting differential legal rights to the two sexes, see Chapter 1, p. 4 *et seq.*.
191. See Chapter 3, p. 98 *et seq.* for discussion of positive action generally and see *infra*, p. 223 *et seq.*, for other moves being made in this field by the EEC.
192. See Chapter 3, particularly n. 9.
193. Directive 79/7, OJ 1979 No. L 6/24, 10 January 1979.
194. In Article 1(2) of which it is foreshadowed thus: 'With a view to ensuring the progressive implementation of the principle of equal treatment in matters of social security, the Council, acting on a proposal from the Commission, will adopt provisions defining its substance, its scope and the arrangements for its application.'
195. Article 3(2) of the Directive.
196. *Drake* v. *Chief Adjudication Officer:* Case 150/85 [1986] 3 WLR 1005.
197. It came into force on 23 December 1984; Article 8(1) provided for it to be implemented by the Member States within six years of its notification.
198. Under the Social Security Act 1975, s.37(3)(a)(i), since repealed.

199. *Drake* v. *Chief Adjudication Officer:* Case 150/85 [1986] 3 WLR 1005, at p. 1014.
200. The problem of the inability of directives to produce horizontal direct effects is not of practical importance in this context, since the Member State, as provider of social security, is inevitably the defendant to the action.
201. *Netherlands* v. *Federatie Nederlandse Vakbeweging:* Case 71/85, unreported at the time of writing.
202. *McDermott and Cotter* v. *Minister for Social Welfare and Attorney General* Case 286/85 [1987] 2 CMLR 607. See also *Borrie Clark* v. *Chief Adjudication Officer:* Case 384/85 *The Times*, 25 June 1987.
203. Great concern has been expressed by the European Network of Women (a pressure group formed in Brussels in 1983 to lobby the EEC on issues affecting women) at the ways in which all the Member States have implemented the Social Security Directive. In particular, it is argued that many national Social Security systems continue to be based on the outmoded stereotype of earning husband and dependent wife. The Network is pressing for the individualisation of social security rights in all Member States; it is argued that benefits should no longer be linked in any way to a person's living situation or marital status and that all forms of the cohabitation rule, means-testing based on household or family units, aggregation of incomes and concepts of adult dependency should be abolished: see CREW Reports (1984) vol. IV, no. 1; see also *Teuling* v. *Bedrijfsver eniging voor der Chemische Industrie* case: Case 30/85, unreported at the time of writing; and Luckhaus, 'Test Case Strategy and the *Drake* Case: a Feminist View', in University College, London, Faculty of Laws, Working Paper no. 5.
204. Article 4(2) of the Directive.
205. Article 7(2) of the Directive.
206. Article 5 of the Directive.
207. Article 6 of the Directive. The detail of the legislative amendments adopted by the UK is outside the scope of the present work, but for further discussion see Atkins and Hoggett, *Women and the Law* (1984, Blackwell) pp. 170–6; Atkins 'Social Security Act 1980 and the EEC Directive on Equal Treatment in Social Security Benefits' (1981) *JSWL* 16; and Luckhaus, 'Social Security: the Equal Treatment Reforms' (1983) *JSWL* 325.
208. See, for example, Brown and Jacobs, *The Court of Justice of the European Communities* (2nd edn,) (1983, Sweet and Maxwell) Chapter 14.
209. See, for example, the *Third Defrenne* case, *Defrenne* v. *Sabena:* Case 149/77 [1978] ECR 1365.
210. See Article 173(2).
211. *Sabbatini* v. *European Parliament:* Case 32/71 [1972] CMLR 945.
212. The same principle was also applied in *Airola* v. *Commission:* Case 21/74 [1975] ECR 221. Cf. *Van den Broeck* v. *Commission:* Case 37/74 [1975] ECR 235, in which there was an essential factual difference.
213. *Razzouk and Beydoun* v. *Commission:* Cases 75 and 117/82 [1984] ECR 1509.
214. Ibid., at p. 1530.
215. See 'Equal Opportunities for Women' *European File*, October 1987.
216. Women of Europe, Supplement no. 4 (1980) and no. 36 (1984).
217. Article 123.
218. See CREW Reports (1983) vol. 3, no. 1.
219. See CREW Reports (1983) vol. 3, no. 6.
220. CREW Reports (1984) vol. V, no. 10.
221. CREW Reports (1986) vol. 6, no. 12.
222. See Written Question no. 1570/86 of 17 October 1986, OJ No. C 117/23, 4 May 1987.
223. CREW Reports (1987) vol. 7, no. 5.

224. CREW Reports (1985) vol. V, no. 1.
225. CREW Reports (1987) vol. 7, no. 4.
226. CREW Reports (1986) vol. 6, no. 12.
227. See, for example, CREW Reports (1986) vol. 6, nos 2 and 4.
228. *Women of Europe*, November/December 1981, no. 23.
229. In particular, its Resolution of 17 January 1984 on the situation of women in Europe.
230. 'Medium Term Community Programme 1986–90' *Bull. Supp.* E.C. 3/86. See also *Women of Europe*, Supplement no. 23 (1985) and Second Council Resolution of 24 July 1986, 86/C 203/02, OJ No. C 203 of 12 August 1986.
231. 22 December 1981, COM (81) 775 final.
232. 30 April 1982, COM (82) 155 final.
233. See further, 'Part-time Workers' (1987) 16 EOR 6.
234. This is discussed in Chapter 6, p. 301 *et seq.*
235. 11 December 1986, Dir. 86/613, OJ 1986 No. L 359.
236. Directive on the Self-Employed, Article 2. Assisting spouses in this latter category mainly work in agriculture.
237. Ibid., Article 3.
238. Ibid., Article 4.
239. Ibid., Article 5.
240. Ibid., Article 6.
241. Ibid., Article 8.
242. Apart from Article 5, for which they have until the end of June 1991: Article 12.
243. See CREW Reports (1987) vol. 7, no. 6.
244. CREW Reports (1983) vol. 3, no. 3.
245. See Chapter 3, p. 102 *et seq.*
246. Recommendation 84/635, OJ 1984 No. L 331/34.
247. The Commission's report is expected to be published during 1988.

# 5 The Equal Opportunities Commission

The blueprint for the EOC is to be found in the White Paper 'Equality for Women',[1] which preceded the Sex Discrimination Act 1975. The government of the day found itself faced with an apparent choice between two models on which to base the new legislation. There was the model in which individual complainants would themselves bring legal proceedings in the industrial tribunals, with no public body responsible for enforcing the law on behalf of the community as a whole. Alternatively, there was the 'old Race Relations Act' model, in which a public body would possess the exclusive right to bring legal proceedings, having initially investigated every complaint and attempted to achieve compliance with the law through conciliation. This body would also have power to conduct investigations on its own initiative, where it was satisfied that to do so would promote the aims of the legislation, and to secure positive action to promote equal opportunity. In the end, the Government rejected both models, in favour of a combination of each. It concluded:

> By itself, the first model is inadequate because it would depend too heavily on the initiative of individuals in presenting and pursuing complaints, and would therefore tend to be random in its operation and impact. The second model is unsatisfactory because a requirement that the enforcement body should investigate all individual complaints would create a vast, costly and wasteful administrative burden. Such a requirement would be especially onerous in relation to sex discrimination, where the number of complaints is likely to be much greater than in the field of racial discrimination. It would cause unacceptable delay in the handling of cases and involve the creation of a very large administrative staff to process the complaints. The complainant would feel justifiably aggrieved at being denied the right to seek legal redress while his or her complaint was waiting to be processed. Above all, the enforcement agency would be distracted by an ever increasing backlog of individual complaints from playing

its crucial general role in changing discriminatory practices and encouraging positive action to secure equal opportunity.

For these reasons, the Government proposes to combine the right of individual access to legal redress with the strategic functions of a new public body. The name of the body – the Equal Opportunities Commission – will be the same as that suggested by the previous Government. But, unlike the body proposed by the previous Government, the new Commission will have a major role in enforcing the law in the public interest. Although it will be able to represent individuals in suitable and significant cases, its main task will be wider policy: to identify and deal with discriminatory practices by industries, firms or institutions. It will be empowered to issue 'non-discrimination notices' . . . which could, if breached, be enforced through the civil courts, and to follow up court and tribunal proceedings. It will also be able to conduct general inquiries and research, to advise Government, and to take action to educate and persuade public opinion. The Commission will have adequate powers to require the production of relevant information.[2]

It will be observed that the main function of the EOC was thus envisaged as the elimination of widescale, institutionalised discrimination; aid to individuals involved in bringing their own proceedings was to be a secondary function only. In practice, however, aid to individuals was bound to assume great importance, since only individual proceedings can yield compensation for the victims of discrimination and establish the law authoritatively. It is also noticeable that the White Paper made no attempt to explain how the Commission was to operate in practice to enforce the law in the public interest, in particular, how much of its time and attention was to be devoted to law enforcement *stricto sensu* and how much to promotional work.

## COMPOSITION OF THE EOC

The White Paper, 'Equality for Women' stated that the Commission was to consist of a chairman and not more than 14 other members, appointed by the Home Secretary after consultation with other Ministers. It was not considered appropriate for the legislation to specify fixed quotas of men and women members, but the government promised to ensure that both sexes were substantially represented; in practice, both sexes have always been represented on the Commission, although there have always been more female than male members. Commissioners were to be 'persons with a wide range of relevant knowledge and experience (e.g. from industry, commerce, the professions, education, women's organisations, and those with special knowledge and experience of the operation of anti-discrimination legislation)'.[3] The Commission was to include both full and part-time members (no doubt, so as to avoid any element of indirect discrimination), and to be able to appoint additional Commissioners to conduct special inquiries. It was to have 'a number of offices in different parts of the country' and to be 'adequately staffed in terms of numbers and appropriate specialist qualifications'.[4]

The Sex Discrimination Act 1975[5] established a body of Commissioners, consisting of between eight and 15 individuals,[6] appointed by the Secretary of State on a full or part-time basis.[7] In practice, there have to date usually been fourteen Commissioners. This seems an unnecessarily large and unmanageable number of persons, especially in view of the relatively small size of the staff of the Commission.[8] Assuming the Commission to continue to exist in its present form, it would be preferable for the Secretary of State to appoint fewer in future; ten would seem adequate for the purpose.

The method of appointment of Commissioners, though common to the membership of many other similar organisations, is open to serious criticism. Government, almost of its nature, is very unlikely to select persons other than those of a fairly non-controversial, 'establishment' nature. In an area such as the elimination of sex discrimination, particularly in the early days of new legislation, tougher individuals, really dedicated to this issue, are what is required, since their role will inevitably be to take on large and well-respected organisations and persons. Even given the large consistuency from whom the White Paper suggested that the Home Secretary should select, appointments do not in practice range very widely. By now well-established convention, three of the Commissioners are nominated by the CBI and three by the TUC. The remaining group always includes a representative from Scotland and one from Wales, a practising solicitor, an individual from the field of education and also someone from the media. No comparable system of nominations applies to this third group. It is noticeable that no representatives from the ethnic minorities are included, despite the obvious parallel between their situation and that of women. Even more serious is the absence of any truly grassroots representation; even the TUC nominees tend in practice to be senior union officials. The reality, therefore, is that there is not even one individual on the Commission who can really be said to represent victims of discrimination in general.

Furthermore, the variety of backgrounds from which Commissioners come, even though guaranteeing a wide measure of experience and ability on their parts, is not productive of a cohesive, strategy-forming body.[9] Although all are clearly interested in sex equality, their approaches to the issue are, of course, often divergent. It has also been suggested that the six Commissioners who come from the two sides of industry have, on some occasions in the past (though there is no evidence of this happening at present) united to oppose action which might further equality of opportunity but might at the same time threaten the conventional system of collective bargaining in industry.[10] These factors combine to yield a directionless body of Commissioners. As will be seen later in the present chapter, a recurrent criticism of the Commission has been that it has failed to formulate clear strategies for the use of its powers. This, to a large degree, is attributable to its design, which would be better suited to an organisation in which policy was formulated elsewhere and then scrutinised, and perhaps toned down, by the Commissioners.

In the present author's view, therefore, an alternative structure must be found in order to ensure an effective and consistent Commission. Probably the most acceptable solution would be to abolish the Commissioners altogether, leaving simply the Chair, along similar lines to the system operating at present in relation to the Directorate of Fair Trading. The effect of such a move would certainly be to reduce the Commission's role as an authorised public critic, but correspondingly to increase its decisiveness, especially in the field of law enforcement.

The Commission is explicitly distanced from central government by the provision that it is not a servant, agent or emanation of the Crown,[11] so that, for example, the Commissioners and members of staff of the EOC are not, as such, civil servants.[12]

Commissioners can be appointed for a maximum of five years for a single term. In practice, no appointments have been made for this period. The norm has been two-year terms with reappointment up to a total of six years. Commissioners may resign during their term of office and can be removed by the Secretary of State for non-attendance at Commission meetings, bankruptcy or incapacity.[13] The Commission is permitted, with the approval of the Secretary of State, to appoint one or more additional Commissioners for the purposes of a formal investigation.[14] The legislation also provides for the appointment and reappointment of a Chairman and Deputy Chairman by the Secretary of State.[15] It is a great pity that the legislature failed, on this significant occasion, to depart from the sexist title 'Chairman'.[16] Many persons, both inside and outside the EOC itself, consider that this word represents a most unfortunate acceptance by our lawmakers that, despite the Act, society will continue to be male-dominated. In practice, all the Chairmen of the EOC appointed to date have been women.[17] Nevertheless, it is important, albeit symbolically, that the Act be amended in this respect so that the title becomes gender-neutral; for this purpose, the term 'Chair' would seem the most appropriate.

The Commission is enabled to appoint such officers and staff as it thinks fit, but it is required to consult with the Secretary of State on this matter and must receive the approval of the Minister for the Civil Service as to numbers, remuneration and other terms and conditions of service,[18] despite the fact that the individuals involved are not actually civil servants. The history of the Commission's early staff appointments is curious; it seems that the Commission's initial needs turned out to be more modest than anticipated by the Home Office and Civil Service Department in 1975. It had been expected that at the end of 1976 there would be a staff of 166 at the Manchester headquarters, but the number actually appointed was only 101. However, the Commission did apparently believe that it needed more staff than originally envisaged at Chief Officer and other senior levels, so it decided to trade quantity for quality. In its First Annual Report (1976) it commented that most of its staffing requests were ultimately accepted by the Civil Service Department, with one serious exception and this concerned the level of Legal Adviser to be responsible for the Legal Section. As a result, the Commission was unfortunately forced throughout 1976 to rely on outside legal advice. At the end of the year, an appointment was finally made, but not at the level which the Commission considered necessary. The Legal Department has since been enabled to grow considerably, especially in recent years; at present it consists of four lawyers (the Legal Adviser, Deputy Legal Adviser and two Principal Legal Officers), together with five support staff and two secretaries. Although obviously an improvement on the earlier position, this staffing complement is in reality the bare minimum in the light of the Commission's present caseload.

As already noted, it was originally envisaged that the EOC, like the CRE, would develop a network of regional offices and would employ some 220 of its projected staff total of 400 in eight locations. The Commission decided early on, however, that its first priority must be to establish a soundly-based headquarters, so it concentrated on its Manchester office to begin with. In 1978, regional offices were set up in Glasgow and Cardiff, although these amount to little more in practice than Commission 'presences' in these regions and do not deal with casework beyond the preliminary stages.[19] The anticipated full countrywide network of EOC offices has never come about, although the Commission continues to argue for it and has asked the Government for a substantial extra sum of money for this purpose. There is also a Commission Press Office in London.

By 1986, the Commission's staffing complement had risen to 166½, but this is clearly inadequate to enable it to carry out many of the functions which it would like, and feels it ought, to undertake. The government is seriously to blame here, for reneging on its original staffing promises, which would have yielded a Commission over twice the present size.

The legislation, it will be observed, says nothing about the relations between and relative spheres of operation of Commissioners on the one hand and the staff of the Commission on the other, although in some instances it explicitly provides that the Commission itself must act. In practice, this area has caused real difficulties from the point of view of the efficient functioning of the Commission. When it first came into existence, there was no other comparable body for the Commission to model itself on, and it appears that for some time poor management led to the Commissioners themselves feeling constrained to take a hand in the detailed running of the organisation. This, of course, distracted their attention from the broader issues of policy which the legislation clearly intended them to consider. In addition, it seems to have contributed to a tension between staff and management.[20] A clearer definition of roles has emerged in recent times, which seems to be largely attributable to the attitude of individual Commissioners, as well as to the relative experience of senior staff and Commissioners. However, even today it appears that there are odd occasions on which Commissioners feel constrained to deal with details which staff consider to be their province.

## THE EOC'S BUDGET

The legislation provides for the Commission to be funded by central government,[21] and it is obliged to send annual statements of account to the Secretary of State.[22] The overall grant is divided by the government into staff costs and other costs, with 10 per cent virement permissible as between these heads. Otherwise, the government imposes no conditions on the way the grant is allocated and this becomes a matter for the Commission itself to decide according to its own priorities. Table 5.1 shows the annual grant made to the Commission since 1976.

Not only have these sums failed in several years to keep pace with inflation (despite government assurances to the contrary) but they have not risen anything like as fast as original government promises had indicated. For example, the budget was supposed to be £2.25 million a year (at 1974 prices) by 1978 – 9. At 1984 prices, the Commission calculated that this would have meant a grant of

**Table 5.1:   Annual grant to EOC from central government**

| Year | Grant £ | % increase on preceding year |
|------|---------|------------------------------|
| 1976–7 | 850,430 | |
| 1977–8 | 1,460,699 | 42 |
| 1978–9 | 1,644,650 | 11 |
| 1979–80 | 2,146,422 | 23 |
| 1980–1 | 2,520,270 | 15 |
| 1981–2 | 2,911,000 | 13 |
| 1982–3 | 3,046,000 | 4 |
| 1983–4 | 3,168,000 | 4 |
| 1984–5 | 3,387,000 | 6 |
| 1985–6 | 3,434,000 | 1 |

about £7.1 million, as against the actual £3.4 million it received in that year. These are pitiful sums by comparison with the budget of the CRE which, unlike the EOC, is not designed to cater primarily for the needs of anything like half the population.[23] It is impossible to resist the conclusion that the government does not view the problem of the inequality of the sexes with anything like the serious-ness that it views race relations, no doubt in part on account of the latter's connection with civil disorder.

## RELATIONS BETWEEN THE EOC AND THE GOVERNMENT

The EOC, as is the case with other regulatory agencies, such as the CRE in Britain and the Fair Employment Agency in Northern Ireland, is placed in an ambivalent position in relation to govern-ment. On the one hand, as has been seen, the legislation places a definite barrier between the two, providing that the Commission and its staff are in no way part of the government. Yet, on the other hand, individual Commissioners and even the Chairman and Deputy Chairman owe their appointments directly to the govern-ment, and the funding of the organisation is directly controlled by the government too. The cynic might be tempted to comment that, even though there is no evidence of a direct attempt by government to influence the Commission's actions, this design is perfect from the government's point of view, giving it considerable authority but the minimum of accountability.

The Commission is subject to periodic Home Office Reviews carried out in pursuance of a central government requirement to keep non-departmental public bodies under regular scrutiny. The last such review was in February 1986 and was moderately critical of the EOC. It concluded that the Commission was deficient in the formulation of strategies and priorities, and that there should be more delegation where permitted by the legislation.[24] One tangible result has been that the Commission has moved from annual planning to a planning cycle of three to five years, and its *Eleventh Annual Report* (1986) contains a considerably clearer statement of priorities than hitherto.

In practice, relations between the Commission and central government are fairly detached. There are no regular meetings between the Chairman or staff of the Commission and Ministers, although meetings take place quite frequently in relation to specific issues in which the government is involved and over which the Commission is concerned to make representations. Although the Commission's views, and especially those of the Chairman, are treated with increasing respect by Ministers, there can be little doubt that those views are often at odds with those of a government intent on deregulation. From an early stage of its operations, the Commission has therefore publicly voiced its dissatisfaction with the low priority attached by the government to sex equality. For example, in its *Fourth Annual Report* (1979), the Commission commented:

> The work of the Commission can only be effective in the context of national policies which, broadly speaking, work in the same direction. We are bound to draw [the Home Secretary's] attention in this context to the effect on the morale of men and women generally of various . . . aspects of government policy. The outcry occasioned by the Government's proposed new immigration rules has led many people, men and women, to call into question the viability and effectiveness of an Equal Opportunities Commission set up to promote the principle of non-discrimination when other government policies appear to run contrary to that principle.

## FUNCTIONS OF THE EOC

The White Paper 'Equality for Women'[25] listed the Commission's projected main functions thus:

(a)   to conduct investigations in areas covered by the Bill and to take action to eliminate unlawful practices;

(b)   to assist and represent individual complainants in appropriate cases;

(c)   to conduct inquiries into matters outside the scope of the legislation which may affect the relative positions and opportunities of the sexes, and to make recommendations;

(d)   to review the operation of the legislation and make recommendations;

(e)   to conduct research and to take action to educate and persuade public opinion.[26]

The Act now defines the Commission's duties exhaustively, though broadly, as being:

(a)   to work towards the elimination of discrimination,

(b)   to promote equality of opportunity between men and women generally, and

(c)   to keep under review the working of this Act and the Equal Pay Act 1970 and, when they are so required by the Secretary of State or otherwise think it necessary, draw up and submit to the Secretary of State proposals for amending them.[27]

The Commission engages in a considerable number of activities in relation to publicity and co-operative enterprises with commercial organisations, in the exercise of these general statutory duties. In addition, further perusal of the Act reveals that the Commission is also entrusted with seven specific legal functions, namely: research and education in the areas of discrimination and equality of opportunity; the review of discriminatory statutory provisions particularly in the field of health and safety at work; the conduct of formal investigations and issue of non-discrimination notices; the enforcement of the legislation in cases of persistent discrimination, discriminatory practices, discriminatory advertisements, and instructions and pressure to discriminate; the provision of assistance to complainants and prospective complainants; the production of a code of employment practice; and the review of the legislation.

In the succeeding sections it will be seen that the Commission has, in practice, preferred to exercise its strict legal powers sparingly and to proceed by encouraging and negotiating good equal opportunities practices wherever possible. This is a policy which is, of course, perfectly within the terms of its enabling legislation but it makes an assessment of the Commission's effectiveness extremely difficult since in many cases the outcome of negotiations is not revealed publicly in any detail.

## Research and Educational Activities

S.54(1) permits the Commission to 'undertake or assist (financially or otherwise) the undertaking by other persons of any research and any educational activities, which appear to the Commission necessary or expedient' for discharging its functions under the legislation.

It resolved early on to use this power to establish an Information Centre, incorporating a library and research register, primarily for its own internal needs but also as an aid to members of the public researching into the area of sex equality. It also decided to set up a statistical unit, although this did not actually come into being until 1980. A small research staff joined the Commission in 1977 and began work in two fields: preparatory and support work for formal investigations and the production of statistical data; and short-term projects arising directly out of the Commission's own policy priorities. Later it began to devote its attentions also to assembling a coherent body of research information for public use. Today, 23½ posts are devoted to research and policy co-ordination (including those in the Information Centre and some concerned with social policy issues).

In 1986, just under £120,000 was available for research and grants. This head of expenditure has been reduced recently, along with all other heads apart from legal expenditure, in order to absorb increased staffing costs. There is obviously keen competition from outside researchers for grants, especially since the availability of funding from other sources has diminished rapidly in recent years. Only a small proportion of applicants to the EOC are successful, therefore, although the Commission regularly comments that many of the unsuccessful projects are very worthwhile.

The Commission was keen to make public, at an early stage of its life, the conditions under which it was prepared to grant funding, stating in its *First Annual Report* (1976):

In settling upon a policy for research, the Commission has concluded that it would be undesirable for it to come to be regarded as a source of funding for research, which is properly the function of universities, polytechnics and research institutes. The Commission has decided, first, that it will place the main emphasis on research which it commissions itself rather than on spontaneous applications received by it; secondly, that it will concentrate mainly on short-term projects, arising directly out of the Commission's own policy priorities, so that the outcome of research can be seen to be visibly linked to decisions on policy options; and thirdly, that it should emphasise in the clearest possible way to all those bodies and foundations which have hitherto financed research on issues of sex discrimination or equality of opportunity for women that it expects them to consider future applications for funding on these issues on the same basis as they have done in the past. It would, in the Commission's view, be wholly undesirable for existing sources of support to dry up and for the Commission to come to be regarded as the exclusive agency for the support of the many long-term and fundamental research projects which will continue to have to be undertaken.

In practice, the kinds of outside projects usually supported by the Commission are those which complement research which the Commission has already engaged in or which fit in with the Commission's general plans but which, for resource or other reasons, the Commission cannot do itself. Projects are approved formally by the Commission's Development Committee, which considers the recommendations of the staff after extensive internal assessment has been carried out.

In its first ten years, the Commission supported 171 research or educational projects and 300 conferences. There can be no doubt that many of the resulting works have been of great value in furthering knowledge about discrimination and the promotion of equality of opportunity.[28] However, some commentators have criticised the Commission's use of its s.54 (1) power, arguing that research could have been used more vigorously as a means of underpinning the Commission's other activities.[29] This is a criticism which is easy to make and hard to refute. It should be borne in mind that empirical research does not always yield conclusive results and, even more importantly, that evidence acquired in the course of conducting research may be confidential and therefore not easily susceptible of use in the context of law enforcement.

## Review of Discriminatory Statutory Provisions

In consultation with the Health and Safety Commission, the EOC is required to keep under review those statutory provisions which require men and women to be treated differently and, if the Commission considers it necessary, to draw up and submit to the Secretary of State proposals for amending them.[30]

It was noted in Chapter 3 that the EOC published a report on the existing protective legislation in 1979.[31] concluding that it contributed significantly to the less favourable treatment of women in industry. The bulk of the legislation was subsequently removed by s.7 of the Sex Discrimination Act 1986. However, the EOC has pointed out that the 1986 Act did not, unfortunately, carry out its recommendations that there should be transitional protection for women currently employed and that a Code of Practice on hours of work should be introduced.[32]

Small pockets of discriminatory protective legislation still remain on the statute book, in particular, as regards the hours of work of young people under the Factories Act 1961 and the Shops Act 1950, as regards employment underground in mines under the Mines and Quarries Act 1954, and as regards the maximum weights to be handled in the pottery, jute and textile industries. The EEC Commission is threatening legal proceedings against those states which retain in force discriminatory protective legislation.[33] The EOC has played an important part in this area by advising the European Commission's Advisory Committee on Equal Opportunities in respect of its review of health and safety legislation.

## The Conduct of Formal Investigations and Issue of Non-Discrimination Notices[34]

### The Legislative Scheme

*The subject matter of formal investigations*   The Commission is empowered, either on its own initiative or if required by the Secretary of State, to 'conduct a formal investigation for any purpose connected with the carrying out of' its duties.[35] This means that the object of a formal investigation may be the elimination of discrimination, the promotion of equality of opportunity between men and women generally,[36] or the review of the anti-discrimination legislation.[37] Formal investigations are divisible into 'general' investigations, in which there is no allegation of unlawful discrimination, and 'belief' investigations into the conduct of named persons or organisations who are suspected by the Commission of unlawful discrimination.[38] Although this distinction seems sensible on a first reading of the legislation, in practice it has led to extreme complication.

*The preliminary stages*   The first stages of a formal investigation are governed by s.58.[39] Its first subsection provides that an investigation cannot be embarked upon until the rest of the section has been complied with. Subsections (2) and (3) deal with the drawing up of terms of reference for the investigation and the giving of notice; in particular, the Commission must give general notice of the holding of the investigation unless the terms of reference confine it to the activities of persons named, in which case the Commission must give those persons notice of the investigation.

The fourth subsection[40] then provides that where the terms of reference confine the investigation to activities of named persons and the Commission proposes to investigate an unlawful discriminatory act which they believe a named person may have done, they must inform that person of their belief and of their proposal to investigate the act, and also offer him an opportunity of making oral and or written representations, with legal or other help if the person concerned wishes. The correct interpretation of this provision has been disputed, in particular, because it refers to the named person having the right to make representations with regard to 'it'. In *R. v. CRE, Ex p. Hillingdon LBC* in the Court of Appeal,[41] the CRE argued that 'it' refers to the *proposal to investigate*, so that the effect of the provision is to require the Commission to give the named person the opportunity to persuade them that they should not embark on the investigation. The alternative view is to regard 'it' as referring to the *discriminatory act*; in this case, the obligation of the Commission before embarking on the investigation would be limited to offering an opportunity to make representations about the act in question *during the course of the investigation*, but not before the investigation begins.[42] The courts have now come down in favour of the first construction, but the result is that there has to be a preliminary inquiry before a full belief investigation can take place. Lord Diplock pointed out in delivering the judgment of the House of Lords in the *Hillingdon* case[43] that the purpose of representations at this stage is not explained by the legislation but he considered that they might be aimed at dissuading the Commission from proceeding with the full investigation, or persuading them to narrow the terms of reference, or towards influencing the manner in which the full investigation should be conducted.

The question of exactly when the fourth subsection applies arose in *R. v. CRE, Ex p. Prestige Group plc*.[44] The CRE had embarked on a general investigation but during its course had discovered matters which led it to suspect unlawful discrimination by the company. A preliminary inquiry had never been held and the company alleged that this was unlawful. The CRE argued that, besides general and belief investigations, there existed a third category: that into a named person but where no unlawful discrimination is suspected at the outset. In such a case, it was argued, the requirement of a preliminary investigation will always be excluded because the fourth subsection only applies at the beginning of an investigation. The CRE reasoned that this analysis was consistent with the wording of the fourth subsection, which refers to those investigations in which persons are named *and* in which the proposal is to investigate unlawful discrimination, suggesting that a named person investigation does not have to be so confined. In addition, the CRE pointed out that in a general named person investigation it would not have independent power to subpoena information[45] and this further supported the proposition that there was no need here for a preliminary inquiry, since the fourth subsection is intended, according to the CRE, to confer the right to a preliminary inquiry only on those exposed to the risk of an investigation in which the Commission would have such subpoena powers.

Lord Diplock again delivered the judgment of the House of Lords and, unfortunately, took a highly legalistic approach, paying little or no apparent attention to the social context or spirit of this legislation. The House held that the fourth subsection applies whenever its literal terms are fulfilled: in other words, *at any time* in a case in which the terms of reference confine the investigation to the activities of named persons, and the Commission in the course of it proposes to investigate any act made unlawful by the legislation. The CRE should, therefore, have held a preliminary inquiry when it began to suspect Prestige of unlawful conduct. There was, the House held, no third category of investigations, besides belief and general. This ruling has very serious consequences for the conduct of formal investigations, the most important being that it is not at all clear what the Commission is to do when minded to begin an investigation into a field of activity exclusively occupied by one individual or institution who, even if not actually named in the terms of reference, is identifiable. An instance would be provided by a government department (such as the Home Office), a local authority or a nationalised industry.[46] Furthermore, if a non-belief investigation cannot take place into the activities of one named person, neither presumably can such an investigation be concerned with the activities of any finite number of named persons. Assuming that the courts would not be satisfied by the mere subterfuge of not naming those involved, where is the line to be drawn between an investigation into a number of individuals and a general investigation? Such an argument eventually leads to the conclusion that there may never be able to be a valid general investigation, but this obviously flies in the face both of the legislation and of the avowed intent of the government which promoted the antidiscrimination legislation that formal investigations were to provide the major thrust in the effort to counter inequality of opportunity. It is highly regrettable, though understandable, if the EOC declines to mount general investigations in the future for fear of their breaching the legislation and resulting in successful judicial review proceedings.[47]

In general, there is no doubt that the necessity for a preliminary inquiry has caused great practical difficulties, in particular, for the CRE which has used its statutory powers in this area much more often than the EOC.[48] The House of Commons Home Affairs Committee recommended in 1981 that the fourth subsection be replaced[49] and this has been echoed both by the EOC and the CRE.[50] In the *Hillingdon* case, the preliminary inquiry lasted three days and produced extensive paperwork. Of course, it is scarcely surprising that a person named should put up a determined fight to prevent the holding of what to him may turn out to be a very damaging investigation, but the fact is that, if the named person fails to persuade the Commission to drop the investigation, he is perfectly at liberty to deploy the same arguments a second time during the full investigation.

*Terms of reference*  The major issue in the *Hillingdon* case was the permissible breadth of the terms of reference in a belief investigation. The House of Lords' ruling circumscribed the Commission's powers to an extent not at first obvious from the legislation. The practical limits of these powers are best exemplified by looking at the facts of the case. The CRE had begun an investigation into the policy of Hillingdon Council with respect to the housing of homeless families in general. The Commission's suspicions had been aroused that racial discrimination was being practised by the differential treatment accorded to a Kenyan Asian family, the Janmohameds, and a white Rhodesian family, the Turveys, both of whom had recently arrived at Heathrow Airport from abroad. The Council was under a statutory duty to provide housing for persons within their borough who were unintentionally homeless. The Janmohameds had had accommodation in Kenya but had deliberately left it to come to England, and the Council classed them as intentionally homeless. The Turveys had left Rhodesia during the war there, when the school at which Mr Turvey worked had been forced to close; the Council considered them to be unintentionally homeless and found them a temporary home while Mr Turvey looked for another job.

Meanwhile, the Chairman of the Hillingdon Housing Committee, Councillor Dicks, decided to take the opportunity to protest about the fact that the whole burden of supporting refugee families from abroad fell on Hillingdon Council, since the airport is located within that borough. Councillor Dicks believed that this responsibility should fall on central government and therefore arranged for the Janmohameds to be taken in a taxi and dumped outside the Foreign Office. The House of Lords ruled that 'the Commission's belief *as stated in the terms of reference* defines and limits the scope of the full investigation'.[51] The Commission had admitted that it had no real belief that the Council was discriminating over the housing of any persons other than those arriving at the airport; the terms of reference were therefore much wider than the Commission's belief and accordingly were invalid. That 'the belief as stated in the terms of reference defines and limits the scope of the full investigation' is remarkable, both from the point of view of statutory interpretation and bearing in mind the objects of the legislation. S.58(3) of the Sex

Discrimination Act[52] speaks simply of the possibility of confining an investigation to the activities of named persons; and, as seen earlier, the fourth subsection begins: 'Where the terms of reference of the investigation confine it to activities of persons named in them *and* the Commission in the course of it propose to investigate any act made unlawful by this Act which they believe that a person so named may have done,[53] which suggests that the Commission is not confined in the investigation to those unlawful acts but may investigate other of the person's activities.

In practice, of course, the effect of the ruling depends on what meaning the courts give to 'belief'. Discrimination of its nature does not usually occur by accident, but rather by design or, at least, habit. It is reasonable to suppose, therefore, that, where discrimination is disclosed in one sphere of a person's operations, it may well also exist in his other spheres of operation. Yet it would be straining the normal meaning of 'belief' to say that it is 'believed' that the person is discriminating in those other spheres. It is certainly arguable that the enforcement powers of the Commission should be broad enough to enable it to investigate those other spheres as well, but is this consistent with the meaning ascribed to 'belief' by the judges in *Hillingdon*? Unfortunately, no clear consensus appears from the case as to the meaning of 'belief'. It appears that all the judges involved considered there to be in essence two components of belief: actual evidence and inference drawn from that evidence. As to how much proof is needed before there can be said to be evidence, Lord Diplock said in the House of Lords that it is 'enough that there should be material before the Commission sufficient to raise in the minds of reasonable men, possessed of the experience of covert racial discrimination that has been acquired by the Commission, a suspicion that there may have been acts by the person named of racial discrimination'.[54] In the *Prestige* case,[55] the test was stated at an even lower level, Lord Diplock saying that all that was necessary was that the Commission should have formed a suspicion that the named persons 'may have committed some unlawful act of discrimination and had at any rate *some* grounds for so suspecting, albeit that the grounds upon which any such suspicion was based might, at that stage, be no more than tenuous because they had not yet been tested'.[56]

More problematic is the question of what the Commission can properly infer from the evidence they have, so as to formulate a 'belief' and thus delimit the scope of the terms of reference. The judges in the lower courts were divided on this issue, but Lord Diplock held in the House of Lords in *Hillingdon* that if the Commission is of opinion from individual acts which raise a supicion that they may have been influenced by racial discrimination an inference can be drawn that the persons doing those acts were also following a more general policy of racial discrimination, the Commission are entitled to draw up terms of reference wide enough to enable them to ascertain whether such inference is justified or not.[57]

Although this formulation appears to allow sufficient flexibility to the Commission over the extent of its belief, there will always be scope for different opinions as to what inferences can justifiably be drawn; for example, Woolf J thought that there was sufficient evidence in *Hillingdon* for the CRE to suspect racial discrimination against the Janmohamed family. In the Court of Appeal, Waterhouse J agreed, but Lord Denning MR and Griffiths LJ did not. The latter commented that the evidence before the Commission disclosed only one example of a coloured family being regarded by the Council as intentionally homeless and that he personally

would not have believed that the Council may have been acting on racial grounds in the treatment of the Janmohamed family; the circumstances . . . point far more strongly to the reason for the treatment being solely a desire to demonstrate how unfairly the Housing (Homeless Persons) Act 1977 operated against the Council.[58]

Conversely, some might feel that the inference could be drawn that the Council's entire housing policy was suspect. In these circumstances, the only prudent course for the Commission to take has to be a minimalist one, resulting in cautiously narrow terms of reference and putting a serious practical brake on the Commission's enforcement powers.

It is clear from the *Hillingdon* case that the terms of reference must inform a suspected person quite specifically what it is that he is suspected of, otherwise he cannot effectively exercise his statutory right to make representations against the holding of the investigation.

*The full investigation*  The legislation says remarkably little about the conduct of the full investigation. However, it is clear that, at least during a belief investigation, a person named by the Commission has the right to make representations, with the aid if he wishes of legal or other advisers. The Court of Appeal in the *Hillingdon* case expressly held that this must necessarily follow if the person has the right to make such representations even before the investigation begins.[59] It is not, however, apparent to what extent the rules of natural justice would demand a right to make representations in a general investigation, and clarification from the courts may be needed here.

S.59 allows the EOC to require people, for the purposes of a formal investigation, to produce written information and to appear in person to give oral evidence about, and produce, documents in their possession. However, no information or documents can be demanded which could not similarly be demanded in civil proceedings before the High Court.[60] Where a person fails to comply with the Commission's demand for information or documents, or the Commission has reasonable cause to believe that he intends not to comply, the Commission can apply to a county court for an order requiring him to comply. It is an offence, punishable by fine, wilfully to alter, suppress, conceal or destroy a document required to be produced, or knowingly or recklessly to make a statement which is false in a material particular.

However, there are two important restrictions on the EOC's subpoena powers. First, the prior authorisation of the Secretary of State is required unless 'the terms of reference of the investigation state that the Commission believe that a person named in them may have done or may be doing . . . [discriminatory acts made unlawful by the legislation] and confine the investigation to those acts'.[61] In other words, it is only in a belief investigation that the Commission automatically has the right to demand information and documents. The second restriction is that the Commission has no power to order the retention of evidence from the outset of an investigation; evidence may therefore be destroyed before being subpoenaed and under the present legislation such conduct is lawful. This is obviously unsatisfactory and, irrespective of more radical changes which need to be made,[62] the legislation requires amendment so as to ensure that the destruction of any evidence, after notice of the intention to embark on an investigation has been served, is an offence.

The Commission is empowered to make recommendations, both during the course of an investigation and after it has finished, including recommendations to the Secretary of State for changes in the law.[63] It must produce a report of its findings in a formal investigation.[64] The report must be published by the Secretary of State where the investigation was required by him, and by the Commission where it instigated it.[65] The legislation does not, however, lay down any timetable for the publication of the report and it need not be published or made available immediately that the investigation is concluded.[66] The exact status of the report is confused because there may, at a later stage of the procedure, be an appeal to a court against the facts found during an investigation.[67]

Restrictions are placed on the disclosure of information given to the Commission during a formal investigation, breach of the law being punishable by a substantial fine.[68] Such information may be disclosed only on a court order, in a summary or other general statement published by the Commission which does not identify the informant or any other person to whom the information relates, in the report of the investigation, to the Commission's employees or in court proceedings. Moreover, in preparing any report for publication or inspection, the Commission must, so far as possible, exclude any matter relating to the private affairs of an individual or a person's business interests, where the publication of the matter might prove prejudicial.

*The non-discrimination notice*   Like the legislation governing the early stages of a formal investigation, that dealing with non-discrimination notices is beset with complication, defects and uncertainties. If, in the course of a formal investigation, the Commission becomes convinced that a person is committing or has committed an unlawful discriminatory act or is guilty of a discriminatory practice,[69] or has been guilty of publishing a discriminatory advertisement, giving instructions to another to discriminate or putting pressure on another to discriminate, then it may issue a non-discrimination notice.[70] Since the *Hillingdon*[71] and *Prestige*[72] decisions, it is unlikely that the power exists in a general, as distinct from a belief, investigation. The Commission cannot unfortunately serve a non-discrimination notice on a body in the public sector of education but must instead give notice of its findings to the Secretary of State and leave it to him to decide whether to take further action under his statutory powers.[73] The Secretary of State's decision would seem to be open to challenge by way of judicial review. The purpose of the notice is not punishment for past discrimination, but the prevention of further unlawful acts. This means that the notice is directed against a particular person or organisation for the future, which offers scope to the unscrupulous, where the respondent is a company, to wind up the concern and set up a new company which is not then bound by the notice.

The permissible contents of a non-discrimination notice are so restricted by the legislation as to undermine the usefulness of the remedy. The notice must require the respondent not to commit any more unlawful acts and, where to achieve this will involve changes in his practices or other arrangements, it may require him to inform the Commission that he has made the changes and what they are and also oblige him to take such steps as may be reasonably required by the notice to afford that information to other persons concerned. He may also be obliged to give the Commission other information to enable it to check that the notice has been complied with,[74] at any time up to five years after the notice has become final.[75] As with the demand for information during the course of an investigation, the Commission can obtain a county court order compelling the furnishing of information required by a non-discrimination notice.[76] However, and this is a very serious defect in practice, the Commission has no power to force the respondent to take particular steps to remedy past discrimination and *a fortiori* has no power to require the respondent to adopt any sort of positive action programme; it must be content with merely recommending specific action[77] and with explaining informally to the respondent what course of action would be acceptable to the Commission.

A non-discrimination notice may not be served until three safeguards have been provided for the respondent.[78] The first is that the Commission must send him a 'minded letter', in other words, an indication that it is minded to issue a non-discrimination notice to him, specifying the ground. Secondly, it must offer him the opportunity of making oral and or written representations within a period of not less than 28 days; and thirdly, it must take account of any such representations. It has been held by the Divisional Court that the right to make representations does not extend to the right to cross-examine the witnesses on whose evidence the Commission relied in reaching their decision.[79] When this procedure has been complied with, the Commission can issue a non-discrimination notice if it is satisfied on the balance of probabilities that there has been an unlawful act of discrimination.[80]

The respondent has a right to appeal against 'any requirement' of a non-discrimination notice.[81] The appeal must be brought within six weeks of service of the notice and is to an industrial tribunal so far as the requirement relates to acts which are within the jurisdiction of such a tribunal, and to a county court so far as the requirement relates to acts within that jurisdiction. Where the appellate tribunal considers the requirement to be unreasonable because it is based on an incorrect finding of fact or for any other reason, it must quash the requirement and can replace it with another,[82] *CRE* v. *Amari Plastics Ltd*[83] involved the question of whether this appeal is against 'conviction' or merely 'sentence', an important issue in practice because at the time of the litigation every single non-discrimination notice issued against an employer by the CRE was being appealed. It was argued for the Commission that there was no right of appeal against the notice itself, but only against a requirement contained in it. The contention was that Parliament wanted the Commission to be the fact-finding body, that it did not intend the whole lengthy investigation to be reopened at this stage and that the accused person's position was adequately safeguarded by his right to make representations. The Court of Appeal rejected this argument. They held that the requirements in the notice not to commit discriminatory acts are based on the judgment that acts of discrimination have been committed, and that the reasonableness of these requirements can be ascertained only by inquiring into whether the facts on which they are based are correct. This means that, on appeal, all the facts found by the Commission in the course of its investigation can be disputed, with all the usual trappings of a judicial hearing such as the evidence of witnesses and cross-examination.[84] Not only may such a hearing overturn the Commission's findings, but it has the effect of enormously prolonging the proceedings which have to be gone through before the Commission's enforcement measures can bite. The practical outcome of the right of appeal is that, on occasion, the Commission will be better advised not to issue a non-discrimination notice at all, but instead to rely simply on the publication of the report and its attendant publicity, which may well cause embarrassment to those named in it, there being no right of appeal against the report alone.

The Commission must maintain a register of non-discrimination notices which have become final, and the register must be open to public inspection.[85]

*The injunction* The Commission has further enforcement powers in the event of persistent discrimination. These powers come into play at any time up to five years after an accused person has received a non-discrimination notice or been found guilty by a court or tribunal of an act of unlawful discrimination.[86] If it appears to the Commission that, unless restrained, the person concerned is likely to commit more acts of unlawful discrimination, the Commission can obtain from a county court an injunction restraining him from doing so.[87] Here again the procedure involved is extraordinarily complex. The Commission cannot allege that the accused has committed an unlawful act which is within the jurisdiction of an industrial tribunal unless there has been a finding to that effect by such a tribunal.[88] This means that in employment cases, because they fall within the jurisdiction of the industrial tribunals, the Commission cannot go straight to the county court as soon as it suspects breach of its non-discrimination notice; instead it must first apply to an industrial tribunal for a finding of unlawful discrimination. (The same procedure does not apply to non-employment cases, such as discrimination in the provision of goods, facilities or services; since these cases are within the county court's jurisdiction, the Commission can simply apply to that court for both the finding of unlawful discrimination and the injunction.) Even if the industrial tribunal finds such discrimination, the

Commission still has to wait until the time for appealing to the Employment Appeal Tribunal has expired or until an appeal has been dismissed, and only then may it seek its injunction.

According to Lord Denning MR in the *Hillingdon* case,[89] the injunction itself must be very carefully worded, so as to tell the accused exactly what he may or may not do; if it is too wide, it may be set aside by the court.

### Reform of the legislative scheme

It is clear from the foregoing account that the legislation in this area is of such unparalleled complexity as to undermine its usefulness very considerably.[90] Both the EOC and the CRE have made proposals for its reform.

The EOC, in its recent document *Legislating for Change? Review of the Sex Discrimination Legislation*,[91] comments:

> The procedures for an investigation should, in the Commission's view, ensure both that the Commission can carry out a speedy and effective investigation and that any individual being investigated has an adequate opportunity to defend himself and state his case. The present procedure, particularly the provision for representations by an individual investigatee in accordance with s.58(3A) of the Act fails to achieve either of these objectives.

It goes on to make four proposals for reform. First, as seen earlier, it proposes the repeal of the provision for pre-investigation representations, which it sees as unduly formal, time-consuming and restrictive of the Commission's powers. It also wishes the provision for representations against a non-discrimination notice to be repealed, since this merely duplicates the respondent's right of appeal against the notice. Thirdly, it recommends that there should be power to order changes to practice or procedure by means of a non-discrimination notice. Its fourth recommendation is that the Commission should be granted an additional power to issue a complaint in the appropriate court or tribunal, alleging unlawful discrimination by any person; it explains its reasoning in support of this as follows:

> Formal investigations should be reserved for complex situations and issues which actually require investigation, and more speedy and simple procedure made available where the object is simply the determination of whether a specific act, practice or procedure is contrary to the legislation and if so to ensure its termination. There is no machinery within a formal investigation to obtain an authoritative ruling on a relevant legal issue. This can only be done by a

subsequent challenge to a finding of the Commission. What is needed is an additional power for the Commission to commence legal proceedings against any person it suspects of unlawful discrimination.

The EOC also points out another problem in this area and invites observations on it. Formal investigations sometimes reveal that individuals have been subjected to unlawful discrimination and have consequently sustained damage. One possiblity here would be for the Commission to have power to include in its report recommendations for the payment of compensation to such individuals, but, of course, these recommendations would not be enforceable. An alternative would be to allow the people affected to apply to an industrial tribunal for compensation within a short period of publication of the recommendations, even though the normal time limits had passed.[92]

The CRE, perhaps not surprisingly in view of its history of skirmishes with the courts over formal investigations and non-discrimination notices, has suggested more far-reaching reforms. In its document, *Review of the Race Relations Act 1976: Proposals for Change*,[93] like the EOC, it seeks the removal of the right to make pre-investigation representations. As it points out, this would mean that the effect of the *Prestige* case would be reversed and the Commission's powers 'to conduct a formal investigation for any purpose connected with the carrying out of' its duties would thereby be clearly established.

However, more fundamentally, it proposes that the role of law enforcement following the carrying out of a formal investigation should be transferred from the Commission to the industrial tribunals. It points to three particular defects in the present procedures:

(i)   [Formal investigations] are ill-designed to resolve disputes of fact according to traditional notions of fairness appropriate to law enforcement;
(ii)  They place the decision on whether the remedy of non-discrimination notice is appropriate in the hands of the investigating Commission;
(iii) Remedies are aimed only at general practices and not also at reparation or satisfaction for individuals involved.

It goes on to criticise the present legislation as follows:

In the words of Lord Denning in the *Amari* case, the Commission 'have been caught up in a spider's web spun by Parliament from which there is little hope of their escaping.' It has become a spider's web because the protection appropriate to law enforcement powers has been added to the protection appropriate to a report-making process. This has led to long delays. Per Lord Denning again: 'The machinery is so elaborate and so cumbersome it is in danger of grinding to a halt.' Also, because that process is so complex, it has also offered opportunities for a series of judicial reviews. The effect of these is that investigations have been delayed by *procedural issues* instead of being able to concentrate, as was intended, on *substantive issues* concerning discrimination.

The Commission needs to keep an investigative fact-finding function and also an involvement in law enforcement. But the nature of its involvement with law enforcement should change. The system should permit the Commission, whenever it has unearthed it, to put evidence of discrimination before an *independent* tribunal of fact, for a decision (after full opportunities for cross-examination) as to whether discrimination has occurred and what remedies are appropriate.

Non-discrimination notices should accordingly, in the view of the CRE, be replaced by tribunal orders which could prescribe particular changes in practice. Furthermore, the tribunal should have the power to award compensation to any person whom it found to have suffered unlawful discrimination, provided only that the person joined the proceedings within a specified time and sought the compensation.

The present author would advocate reform of the legislation to a more radical extent even than the CRE. The EOC is perhaps inhibited in seeking widescale changes to this legislation because, as will be seen later in the present chapter, it has not found occasion to utilise its law enforcement powers nearly so frequently as the CRE. Nevertheless, the original intentions behind the legislation must not be forgotten: investigation by an independent agency is essential to the outlawing of unlawful discrimination and the promotion of equality of opportunity. Discriminatory or discouraging behaviour which is practised across a wide range of situations is unsuitable for redress through individual proceedings. Furthermore, there may be no single individual who experiences such behaviour and is willing to bring legal proceedings. Investigations are also necessary to unearth patterns and areas of discrimination and inequality within society. with a view to their eradication as well as to the compensation of individuals affected. The CRE's analysis of what is wrong with the legislation is accurate and to the point: the legislation is trying to force two incompatible roles on the Commissions, those of reporting agency and law enforcer. The Commissions are, rightly, perceived by many members of the public as both prosecutor and judge, and this carries the inevitable taint of possible bias in the enforcement process.

Specific amendments to the existing law, as the EOC suggests, would certainly be an improvement on the present position. However, if the enforcement of the anti-discrimination legislation is really to be effective, then there is no other solution than to remove the existing remedial jurisdiction from the Commissions and transfer it to the industrial tribunals, which would then be able directly to order changes in the respondent's practices and procedures. Certainly the right to a preliminary inquiry must be abolished but, as the CRE points out, this involves no damage to the respondent since he will be guaranteed a proper opportunity to present his version of events at the tribunal hearing. The proposal to allow an individual to join in such proceedings where he or she had been the victim of unlawful discrimination is also sensible and just. In one way, however, the CRE's proposals require strengthening, and that is with respect to the remedies at the disposal of the industrial tribunal after a finding of unlawful discrimination following a formal investigation. It was seen in Chapter 3 (see p.103) that the US courts have come to accept the validity of positive action schemes as a remedy which is entirely consistent with the underlying aims of the anti-discrimination legislation where unlawful practices have been in operation. This principle ought to be applied by the British legislation, so that the tribunals would be entitled to impose a positive action plan on any organisation found to be practising unlawful discrimination; the plan, which would incorporate goals and timetables though not quotas (since the latter would probably be counter-productive), would be binding on the organisation until such time as it had remedied its history of discrimination, and the EOC (and CRE) should be designated by the legislation to monitor implementation of the plan.

*The EOC's activities in the field of formal investigations and non-discrimination notices*[94]

Despite the fact that the EOC began life emphasising that promotional and educational work was as important to it strategically as law enforcement,[95] it in fact launched its first formal investigation in 1976. It had received complaints from parents and others that Tameside Education Authority had discriminated against girls in allocating places in its selective schools after May 1976. Until that date, the plan had been to introduce comprehensive education from September 1976, but then a new Council was elected with a clear mandate to reverse this policy in the very short period of four months. The EOC's report came only a year after the start of the investigation. Although it absolved the Authority from unlawful discrimination, it contained useful discussion of the scope of the (then quite new) legislative provisions on education. Nevertheless, it did represent a somewhat idiosyncratic first use by the EOC of its enforcement powers, since the factual issue was so specialised and unlikely to recur.

In 1977, again only one investigation was begun, this time into allegations of discrimination at Electrolux Ltd. The initiative for this investigation seemed to come, not from within the EOC, but from the then-President of the Employment Appeal Tribunal, Phillips J, who, when faced with the possibility of over 600 equal pay claims against the company going to industrial tribunals, suggested that the EOC intervene.[96] However, the Annual Report for 1977 indicated that the Commission itself planned to start making more vigorous use of the power to conduct formal investigations and stated that the Commission had been busy during the preceding months elaborating a long-range strategy to give greater emphasis to law enforcement.

Despite this, no new investigation at all was begun the following year, although the Commission resolved to embark on one into the Society of Graphical and Allied Trades (SOGAT). The 1977 Annual Report contained a defensive paragraph in which the Commission said that it had developed its strategies considerably with regard to formal investigations (though without saying how), and in which it commented that those who criticised the Commission for having undertaken few investigations had little appreciation of the legal complexities or the staff expertise and time involved. It was stressed that the Commission had a comprehensive programme for formal investigations in employment which took into account the repercussions of each investigation undertaken.

At the same time, what seemed a useful experiment in an alternative and more conciliatory approach was tried with Debenhams Stores. After receiving complaints of discrimination over credit facilities, the Commission warned Debenhams that it was considering starting a formal investigation. The company responded by offering to co-operate in a joint review with the EOC of their credit procedures and the Commission accepted because it thought that the necessary information would be more readily available in this way. The result was a report which made recommendations to the retail credit industry as a whole for the introduction of practical measures to eliminate discrimination. The company itself drew up a revised credit sanctioning system and introduced a new staff training programme, which satisfied the Commission. The Commission has subsequently commented[97] that enforcement action is rarely required in such cases, since the organisations concerned quickly come to realise that equality of opportunity means an increase in business.

1979 saw much more activity by the EOC than hitherto in the field of formal investigations. Four new investigations were begun and the Annual Report for the year explained that each dealt with an issue that the Commission had identified as a priority, although little guidance was given as to why. Two concerned the teaching profession. In both cases the Commission had received complaints from a sizeable number of staff of the institutions concerned, suggesting possible widespread discriminatory practices. The first concerned the appointment and promotion of female teaching staff to senior teaching posts at the Sidney Stringer School, Coventry. The second concerned the promotion of female staff in the Business Studies Department of the North Gwent College of Further Education. The third investigation begun was that into SOGAT mentioned in the previous Annual Report; the Commission suspected that the membership conditions of the two London branches of SOGAT restricted women to less favourable employment than that available to men, and that the industry's recruitment system pressurised employers to discriminate against women because they could only recruit from a single-sex labour pool. In 1976 an ACAS report on industrial relations in the newspaper industry pointed out that there were no women employed in the national newspaper houses in either the organisation, machining or publishing areas of production, and in 1977 the Royal Commission on the Press called on the EOC to consider investigating the newspaper industry.[98] The fourth investigation was into the Leeds Permanent Building Society and concerned the obstacles to women's opportunities in an industry traditionally employing very few women. The investigation arose from a complaint by a woman who claimed that she had been discriminated against when applying for a management traineeship. Three areas of the Society's employment practices were singled out: their recruitment of management trainees; the possibly indirectly discriminatory effect on women of the Society's requirement that all staff should be mobile; and the Society's promotion, transfer and training policies in general. The Commission believed that the practice of requiring employees to be mobile was widespread throughout industry and that the investigation would shed light on it.

Also in 1979, the Commission's first non-discrimination notice was issued, against Electrolux Ltd, requiring the company not to commit any further breach of the Equal Pay Act. Electrolux protested forcefully against the notice, saying that it was not a recalcitrant employer, that it had made many attempts to change its wage structure, that it had co-operated in every way during the investigation and had even made back-payments to female employees when not legally obliged to do so. Nevertheless, the

EOC felt the notice to be necessary so that it could monitor the new job evaluation based pay structure to ensure that it did not again drift towards discrimination. The sex discrimination aspects of the Electrolux investigation were later abandoned.

Despite these signs of a more robust attitude to enforcement, 1980 saw only one new formal investigation,[99] that into the redundancy provisions applied by the British Steel Corporation at its Shotton Works. At the root of this investigation was the (now well-accepted) notion that the different state retirement ages for men and women have an unavoidable knock-on effect into other areas, such as redundancy. Although it provided useful research material, it is today doubtful on two counts whether the British Steel investigation was legitimate. First, it is not clear that the investigation was directed towards any of the three purposes permitted by the legislation: the Commission was not alleging that illegal discrimination had occurred, so that the investigation could not be said to be for the elimination of discrimination or for the promotion of equality of opportunity;[100] and if it were to be justified as being with a view to proposing amendments to legislation, the legislation primarily under attack was that fixing the state retirement age rather than the Sex Discrimination Act. Secondly, it would appear that this was a general investigation into the activities of a named person, a type of investigation subsequently outlawed by the House of Lords in the *Hillingdon* and *Prestige* cases.[101]

An investigation was also proposed in 1980 into the policy and procedures of the Provincial Building Society in dealing with joint applications for mortgages. The Society sought judicial review of the decision to hold the investigation, but the action was settled after Webster J in the Divisional Court had severely criticised the EOC, in particular because it appeared to have been acting on the basis of stale complaints, to be determined to begin the investigation come what may, and not to have given the Society a fair chance to present its defence. In fairness to the Commission, it should be pointed out that the proceedings were compromised before it had any significant opportunity of stating its side of the case and there was no judgment setting out whether or not the charges against the Commission were justified. Instead of a formal investigation, the Commission thereupon conducted a collaborative review with the Society.

A new general investigation was begun in 1983 into the provision of craft, design and technology (CDT) courses in colleges of further education and, four years after its commencement, the Sidney Stringer investigation was also completed in that year. The latter concluded that there had, in fact, been no unlawful discrimination although normal appointment and promotion procedures had been ignored. The Commission recommended that such procedures should on all occasions be formally and properly followed and that a full and adequate record of proceedings should be kept. The Director of Education and Headteacher promised to do this and the Commission believed that the investigation had overall been valuable in raising issues of relevance to all concerned with the provision of education.

1984 saw some developments with respect to the long-running SOGAT investigation. A meeting took place between the leadership of the union and the investigating Commissioners at which it became clear that the union was not prepared voluntarily to make the changes necessary to break down job segregation. The whole Commission then considered and accepted the Report of the investigating Commissioners, which indicated unlawful discrimination. It was decided to serve non-discrimination notices and, in the course of making the statutory representations, the union promised to take informal steps to remedy the situation by amalgamating the two branches. On this basis, the Commission decided to defer service of the notices.

The Leeds Permanent Building Society investigation came to an end in 1984, five years after its launch. The Commission found that the Society had *never* appointed a woman during the five years its Management Trainee scheme was in operation; in 1978, the year investigated, it had recruited about 150 men to the scheme. It was found that the Society had discriminated directly against women applicants by refusing them interviews and, where interviews were granted, by interviewing them in a different and less favourable way than men, and by refusing them employment on the ground of their sex. In addition, the Commission surveyed the 1800 applicants for Traineeships in 1978 to determine whether the mobility requirement had had a disproportionately adverse impact on women. It found that women were less able to comply with the mobility requirement *as presented to them by the Society*. However, the Society operated the requirement in respect of its existing male managers in a flexible way, and it was such that women would have been no less able than men to comply with it. It appeared that the Society's actual mobility requirements were not made clear to women applicants. The EOC considered the argument that the mobility requirement was essential to the Society's business, but concluded that its retention in the unexplained form applied could not be justified. The Society then voluntarily changed its practices to the satisfaction of the EOC, so no non-discrimination notice was served. The Commission later concentrated on circulating its findings in this investigation to other bodies which might be discriminating in a similar fashion.

The North Gwent investigation also finished around the same time, again five years after its inception. The Commission found evidence of some unlawful discrimination and it made consequential recommendations. It commented in its Ninth Annual Report (1984) that the importance of this investigation lay 'not just in the Commission's final recommendation and findings but also in the fact that during the course of the investigation substantial improvements were made to the appointments and promotion procedures at the College by the College authorities themselves. These improvements made the issue of a non-discrimination notice unnecessary'.

The investigation into the training of CDT teachers, begun in 1983, was also completed in 1984. No unlawful acts had been alleged and the Commission's purpose in mounting this investigation was to examine the reasons why so few women train to become CDT teachers. The Commission commented in its 1984 Annual Report that

> Design and Technology has been identified by the Department of Education and Science as a key subject within the curriculum of children aged 5–16, and the Commission, having campaigned for many years to encourage schools to teach CDT to all their pupils, is concerned by the fact that many girls are still not offered the opportunity to study CDT on the same terms as are boys. The Commission's CDT working party concluded in 1982 that the very small number of women CDT teachers was one of several disincentives to the study of CDT by girls. The CDT teacher training institutions shared many of these concerns and enabled the Commission to produce a report which will be of interest to all those involved in the teaching of CDT.

The Report makes a number of practical suggestions to encourage women into the area of CDT teaching and has been widely circulated.

In 1984, the Commission also proposed a formal investigation into Barclays Bank plc. It had received a complaint from a school that the Bank had interviewed a male candidate of A-level standard but had not offered an interview to a female applicant with similar qualifications from the same school. The Bank was told of the Commission's concern and made representations. The Commission then produced a report on the Bank's recruitment policy and the Bank indicated that it was willing to introduce the necessary changes. In the end, it was decided not to proceed with the formal investigation but informally instead, the Bank promising not to breach the legislation and to provide the Commission with annual statistics for four years on numbers of applicants, interviewees and recruits by reference to their sex, qualifications, age, status and locations.

By 1985 it had become clear that the required SOGAT amalgamation was not going to be completed within the time envisaged. However, yet another deferment was granted, until January 1986, because the union was 'experiencing difficulties over issues which fell outside the Commission's terms of reference and in view of the fact that some agreement had been reached over the issues referred to in the draft non-discrimination notices'.[102]

The Commission began a formal investigation in 1985 into Dan Air Services' recruitment policy, after receiving a complaint that men were denied opportunities for employment as cabin staff. It turned out that this was a practice that Dan Air had operated throughout its 30 years in existence. The Commission found that the airline had directly discriminated against males and it served a non-discrimination notice, requiring it to stop discriminating and to provide the Commission with recruitment monitoring statistics for the next five years.

The Commission's patience with SOGAT finally ran out in September 1986, by which time it had become quite clear that there was no imminent prospect of the union mending its ways, so the Commission then issued non-discrimination notices in a form almost unchanged from those prepared in 1984. These require the parties not to discriminate in the provision of information about job vacancies to members of both branches, and, where seniority is relevant to the allocation of vacancies, to recognise that seniority acquired as a member of one branch has equal weight with seniority acquired as a member of the other branch. The notices enable the Commission to monitor the situation until January 1989.

At the end of 1986, a new investigation was begun into the segregation of children according to sex in relation to particular aspects of the curriculum in West Glamorgan, a practice which is known to the Commission to be prevalent throughout the country and which has been of concern to it for many years.

This account of the law enforcement activities of the Commission would be incomplete without a mention of the alternative strategies adopted by it in this area. The obvious legal limitations on the scope of formal investigations led it to try alternative proceedings when it discovered that there was a serious imbalance in the number of places provided for girls and boys in the City of Birmingham's remaining selective schools. In particular, a formal investigation would not have resulted in an authoritative judgment and no non-discrimination notice could have been issued in these circumstances.[103] The Commission therefore made a successful application by way of judicial review for a declaration that the City's practice constituted unlawful discrimination.[104] In addition, formal investigations appear to represent the tip of an iceberg only, because the EOC is constantly engaged in negotiations with persons whose behaviour and practices have been brought to its attention. Its own estimate is that, at any given moment, there are between 12 and 15 such situations on its books, any one of which could develop into a formal investigation if a satisfactory settlement is not reached. In practice, the vast majority of such potential respondents comply with the Commission's requirements, so that no further enforcement action is needed.

*Criticism of the use made by the EOC of its powers to conduct formal investigations and issue non-discrimination notices*

In assessing the use to which the EOC has put its enforcement powers, it is vital to remember the strategic importance ascribed to these powers by the framers of the anti-discrimination legislation: they were really to be the Commission's most significant function, since they aim at the elimination of widescale discriminatory conduct and the uncovering of patterns of behaviour which disadvantage women.

It has been seen that the EOC has embarked on eleven formal investigations in as many years. Of these, it has discontinued one completely and another partially. Two were general investigations, not involving allegations of unlawful discrimination. Of the remainder, five resulted in findings of unlawful discrimination. In only three cases to date has the Commission exercised its power to issue non-discrimination notices. Four of the investigations took four years or more to complete; the SOGAT investigation in fact took eight years, all told. By contrast, even though it has been in operation for one year less than the EOC, the CRE (admittedly on much larger funds) has undertaken 62 formal investigations and issued 19 non-discrimination notices.

Writing in 1983, the present author was highly critical of the EOC's record in this field.[105] At that time, it appeared that the EOC had failed to plan and conduct investigations thoroughly and there was little evidence, despite its repeated assertions to the contrary, that it had a coherent strategy with respect to the targeting of investigations. For its very first investigation, it chose a factually most unusual situation, to which scrutiny of the report shows that it applied poor methodology. The Electrolux investigation then turned out to be so unwieldy in its scope that it had to be abandoned in part. Two of the EOC's investigations (Electrolux and SOGAT) were clearly thrust on it as a result of outside pressures. Furthermore, the EOC seemed at that time remarkably reluctant to use its enforcement powers at all. In part, this was attributable to the fact that the EOC was an entirely new enterprise in 1975 and, unlike the CRE, had no predecessor whose experience it could inherit. It was also attributable to the Commission's lack, for the first few years of its life, of in-house legal advice (for which the blame must lie squarely with the government). Most importantly, though, it did appear in 1983 that the EOC's little use of its enforcement powers was at least partly attributable to a serious lack of direction within the Commission itself. Some Commissioners appeared to believe that enforcement was merely one of a number of functions entrusted to the Commission, whilst others considered it to be of overriding importance. Even amongst those who considered investigations to be of overriding importance, there seemed to be a split of opinion over policy in selecting and conducting investigations; and as mentioned earlier, there were indications that the six Commissioners from the two sides of industry, on occasion at least, operated a tacit pact to obstruct the launching of investigations which might have significant repercussions in terms of industrial relations.

Can the situation be said to have improved in recent years, in particular with the advent of a new Chairman and management team? The last four years have witnessed the final wrapping up of the SOGAT investigation, the launch and completion of two investigations, together with the launch of a third, and two out of the three cases in which non-discrimination notices have been served have occurred within this period. The Commission has been at pains to explain the perceived significance of the CDT investigation and of the new West Glamorgan investigation, which suggests a higher degree of strategising than in the past; and it appears to have reached a satisfactory compromise with Barclays Bank.[106] The Leeds Permanent Building Society investigation can, with the benefit of hindsight, be criticised on methodological grounds for having analysed too many applications, but there is little doubt that its ultimate findings are extremely useful. The Dan Air investigation seems at first sight a curious choice, in part because the cheaper alternative of assisting an individual complaint might have been equally effective, and in part because it is unclear why the non-recruitment of men should have been seen as a priority for the Commission; in retrospect, however, the investigation was probably of considerable value since it attracted a good deal of media coverage, whose effect was to focus public attention on the undesirability of job segregation and gender stereotyping. Furthermore, a new resolve appears from the Commission's most recent pronouncements in this area; in its *Eleventh Annual Report* (1986) it stated:

No instrument is more important than the Commission's own power to take enforcement action through formal investigations. We have this year demonstrated that, however much procedures could be improved, investigations can be effective. Where necessary, we are ready and willing to proceed to the ultimate sanction of a Non-Discrimination Notice. The issue of a notice to SOGAT '82 and two of its branches in October at the end of a most protracted investigation was speedily followed by the amalgamation of the branches, a course of action recognised by the Commission as the most effective way of eliminating the discrimination that had been found to exist. By contrast the investigation into Dan Air Services Ltd was completed in about 15 months from the initial steps, but it was not until we had become minded to issue a Non-Discrimination Notice that the company showed itself willing to make the necessary changes. We attached particular importance to the rights given by a notice to monitor compliance for five years. We shall continue to use this instrument for change where necessary. . . . On the other hand, we are delighted that many organisations are willing to move forward on their own initiative.

The outlook for a more forceful use of the Commission's enforcement powers thus seems more hopeful now than for a number of years passed. However, two further points must be made in this connection. First, the Commission ought to provide a proper and detailed explanation to its funding public of its strategy for the future: what does it regard as the key strongholds of sex discrimination which it will investigate? And how has it arrived at its priorities? Secondly, it is clear that the Commission has opted (whether by deliberate policy or in default thereof) to adopt as conciliatory as possible an approach in these situations. This remains its policy today, even though it is now demonstrating more clearly than in the early days its willingness to resort to legal action in the last resort. Can such a policy be justified? There is no doubt that, taking each case on its own, such a course is cheaper than launching a formal investigation; and there is no reason for the Commission to settle for anything less than it could have demanded at the end of an investigation. The disadvantage, however, lies in the absence of publicity when an informal settlement is reached: without publicity, the exercise – even though effective *vis-à-vis* the particular organisation involved – has no deterrent or educative value for the public at large. Conversely, a formal investigation will attract media attention and will focus many people's minds on, for example, a practice which had never before struck them as inequitable.

The EOC has played down the existence of informal settlements and even its Annual Reports make little reference to them, not linking them directly to the Commission's law enforcement role. This is regrettable. In the present author's view, the Commission's policy could only be justified if it involved a much greater degree of publicity. 'Publicity' needs only to take an anonymous form, outlining merely the general nature of the organisation involved and the practice under scrutiny. This would serve to educate and deter others, without actully identifying the organisation involved in the settlement. Such a procedure would in no way undermine the Commission's negotiating position, since if the organisation is unco-operative, as for example Dan Air was, the Commission will not hesitate to use its legal powers. The Commission ought, therefore, to ensure a far greater degree of public awareness of its activities in this field, so that there can be absolutely no doubt that certain practices and procedures are unlawful and, if not voluntarily altered, will become the subject matter of legal action.

**Enforcement of the legislation in cases of persistent discrimination, discriminatory practices, discriminatory advertisements, and instructions and pressure to discriminate.**

*Persistent discrimination*

The very complex procedure for obtaining an injunction where a respondent threatens to breach a non-discrimination notice or to commit a subsequent act of unlawful discrimination has been noted earlier in the present Chapter and in Chapter 3.[107] Despite its early avowed determination to make use of this provision,[108] the Commission has never actually done so, although it has begun the process in a handful of cases which were subsequently settled. The reason for this appears to be that the Commission does not monitor the after-effects of successful claims, so that it remains largely unaware of cases where discrimination persists. It is in reality restricted to those cases where the complainant comes back to the Commission with a subsequent complaint. This gap in the enforcement mechanism is especially regrettable in the light of the recent research evidence of Leonard demonstrating the recalcitrance of unsuccessful respondents in sex discrimination cases.[109] The ease with which the law can be flouted here makes it essential that this problem is tackled. Since only the EOC possesses the power to act in these cases, it ought to reallocate resources to enable itself to monitor all successful claims for a period of at least a year.

*Discriminatory practices*

The definition of a discriminatory practice[110] was noted in Chapter 3 (see p. 140). The chief way in which proceedings may be brought in respect of such practices is by the EOC launching a formal investigation.[111] This has occurred in two cases to date: the SOGAT investigation and the Leeds Permanent Building Society investigation.[112] The same general comments apply here as in relation to all other types of formal investigation. In particular, the Commission claims to be dealing with a very much larger number of discriminatory practices annually by conciliation, but far more publicity needs to be forthcoming from it to demonstrate publicly that this is happening.

*Discriminatory advertisements*

The Commission's power in relation to discriminatory advertisements was noted in Chapter 3 (see pp. 151–2). It will be recalled that the Commission (alone) can bring proceedings against those who, in advertisements, indicate an intention to commit an unlawful act of discrimination. This power does not extend to the prosecution of sexist or stereotyped advertising.

In the early days of the Act's operation, the Commission both received a large number of inquiries in relation to advertising[113] and was subjected to a good deal of facetious press comment about this aspect of its job. It therefore decided to place on record its policy in this area and to state publicly its view of the significance of this matter. Accordingly, in its *First Annual Report* (1976), it stated:

> The principal reason for the importance attached to this subject by the Commission is that, by its nature, advertising is the first public indicator of many of the attitudes and practices which the Sex Discrimination Act required to be modified; overnight, previously familiar forms of advertisment, particularly in relation to jobs and careers, became unlawful. Meanwhile the Commission – and only the Commission – has the power to institute proceedings if unlawful advertisements appear. While this means that if the Commission does not take the initiative no-one else can, because no individual has the authority to do so, the Commission has nevertheless chosen to adopt an advisory and explanatory approach, seeking from the outset as much voluntary co-operation as possible from advertisers and publishers and keeping its powers in reserve to deal if necessary with persistent or deliberate flouting of the law. In so doing, the Commission has consciously followed the intention of Parliament, which was that its approach should be constructive and preventive rather than merely punitive.

The Commission has pursued its 'constructive and preventive' approach by issuing a series of guidance documents on employment advertising practice. It has circulated these widely and believes them to be well-received and helpful. The Advertising Unit of the Commission also organises a wide range of seminars to educate advertisers in the requirements of the law. By 1977, the Commission already believed that this approach had paid off and that the elimination of sex discrimination from job advertising had become generally accepted as part of sound employment practice.[114] It reiterated this sentiment in 1978, commenting in its Annual Report of that year that requests for advice from publishers before advertisements were put forward for the client's approval were more than three times as numerous as complaints received about published advertising.

In consequence of its conciliatory policy in this area, it was not until 1979 that the Commission took any legal proceedings at all in repect of an advertisement. To this day only two cases,[115] both involving very blatant and deliberate disobedience of the legislation, have ever been bought by the EOC under the advertising provisions.[116]

In 1983, the Commission took part in research being undertaken by a Brussels-based voluntary organisation of professional women, 'Solidarité Femmes Emploi'. This research sought to establish the progress made in eight Member States of the EEC towards equality of opportunity as reflected in newspaper advertisements. During the relevant weeks, six hundred UK recruitment advertisements appearing in the *Guardian* and the *Manchester Evening News* were monitored. The British sample revealed 96 per cent compliance with the Sex Discrimination Act, the highest figure recorded. Eire and Denmark came next, with 92 per cent and 87 per cent. There was a much lower level of compliance in Belguim (31 per cent) and France (32 per cent). It was also noted that in Britain 38 per cent of the relevant advertisements went beyond the minimum requirements of the law, by making it explicit that the jobs in question were open to both sexes.

The Commission is clearly proud of its record in this field and this independent evidence is support of its achievements. However, it is important that it does not become complacent. In 1984 it reported an increase in the number of complaints it had received about apparently unlawful advertisements; and the total number of inquiries about advertising in general remains high: 1,914 in 1986 out of a total of 6,602. The Commission itself believes that this is due to a steadily growing public awareness of the requirements of the legislation, and not to any deterioration in the standards of advertisers. However, an alternative view might be that growing public knowledge of the legislation would fuel better informed complaints and that the high level of inquiries in this area is in fact prompted by increased disobedience of the law on the part of advertisers (itself perhaps a consequence of increased commercial competition in the current economic climate). There is a real danger, against which the Commission must guard by showing that it is prepared on occasion to use its legal powers, that it will settle into a policy not just of concilation but of inertia.

*Instructions and pressure to discriminate*

The Commissions's legal power to proceed in respect of discriminatory instructions[117] and pressure to discriminate[118] was described in Chapter 3 (see pp. 151–2).

In practice, the Commission has only recently brought its first cases in respect of instructions to discriminate, although it has relied on the existence of the power in the background before when negotiating with employers. This is in part because it has been constrained by the decision in *CRE* v. *Imperial Society of Teachers of Dancing*[119] to look for a prior course of dealing between the instructor and the person to whom the instructions are given.[120] However, the Commission has recently engaged in a project with the Manpower Services Commission, designed to alert the staff at Job Centres to the possibility of unlawful instructions to discriminate. This strategy has paid off and the Commission won its first three industrial tribunal cases under this provision in 1987.[121] At the time of writing, more cases are in the pipeline and the Commission is now determined to make much fuller use of this part of the Act.

The Commission has never brought proceedings in respect of pressure to discriminate. The statute deliberately entrusted these powers to the Commission because, even if an actual victim of discrimination subsequently emerges and brings successful individual proceedings, it will not necessarily follow that the original instigator of the discrimination is identified or proceeded against. Unless it is truly satisfied that these situations are not occurring, which is unlikely, the Commission is therefore at the very least under a moral obligation to use its powers in this area. This means that it should publicise its powers more widely and identify the key areas in which pressure to discriminate may be being exerted, investigate these situations and then, if necessary, take proceedings.

## The provision of assistance to complainants and prospective complainants

S.75 provides for the Commission to grant 'assistance' to complainants or prospective complainants under both the Sex Discrimination and the Equal Pay Acts. The Commission may grant assistance if it thinks fit to do so either because the case raises a question of principle or because it is unreasonable to expect the applicant to deal with the case unaided or by reason of any other special consideration.[122] Assistance can take the form of giving advice, trying to procure a settlement, arranging for advice to be given by a solicitor or counsel, or arranging representation.[123] If the Commission incurs expenses in providing assistance, the recovery of those expenses constitutes a first charge for the benefit of the Commission on any costs or expenses obtained by the applicant.[124] The Act requires the Commission to consider all applications for assistance, but the decision whether or not actually to grant it is, of course, discretionary.

The perceived significance of this power to the Commission was revealed as early as its *First Annual Report* (1976), in which it stated that 'in the absence of legal aid for proceedings before industrial tribunals, and given the general problem of proving discrimination, the s.75 powers of assistance are in fact part of the Commission's strategic role of helping to clarify the law'. The Commission also sees s.75 as useful in helping it to monitor the working of the legislation and providing evidence on which to base its proposals for reform. But it is important to remember that the drafters of the legislation never intended this to be a replacement for the formal investigative power; that they considered to be the Commission's major role, since it would lead to the uncovering of widescale instances of discrimination and inequality and, moreover, could be the subject matter of strategic planning.

The Commission has delegated its functions in this area, for the sake of speed and efficiency, to its Legal Committee. This Committee, which meets every month, monitors general trends in the caselaw as well as individual cases in which appeals are desirable. Its policy is to grant assistance whenever an important point of principle is involved or where a point of law needs clarifying.

Over the years, there has been a fairly steady increase in the number of cases in which assistance and advice have been granted, with a sharp increase evident since 1984. This is so despite the fact that the number of actual applications to industrial tribunals has shown a substantial decline. It is evidence of a growing authority on the part of the EOC and also attributable to the increasing complexity of discrimination cases now that concepts such as indirect discrimination are becoming better known and understood. Some part of the recent growth of assisted cases is also a consequence of the introduction of the concept of equal pay for work of equal value; not only do these cases raise important issues of law, but they frequently involve a large number of people so that technically there are many sets of proceedings. The Commission normally grants assistance in somewhere between 50 and 60 per cent of the cases in which formal applications are made to it each year.

1979 saw the first use of s.75 to enable preliminary references to be made to the European Court of Justice, as well as an appeal to the House of Lords. The EOC has clearly adopted a strategy of test-cases and there can be little doubt that many of the most important principles of sex discrimination law could not have been established without its assistance, since the cost to an individual would have been prohibitive. It should also be noted that, coincidentally, at least three of the cases supported by the EOC before the European Court, *Macarthys Ltd* v. *Smith*,[125] *Garland* v. *British Rail*[126] and *Marshall* v. *Southampton and SW Hants Area Health Authority*,[127] established very important 'constitutional' aspects of EEC law and probably thus conveyed an awareness of the field of anti-discrimination law to many who otherwise would have paid no regard to it.

## The production of codes of practice

S.56A[128] provides that the EOC may issue Codes of Practice containing such practical guidance as the Commission thinks fit for the elimination of discrimination and the promotion of equality of opportunity in employment. The Commission must consider representations made to it in respect of any draft code and must consult with whatever organisations it thinks appropriate. The draft code has to be transmitted to the Secretary of State who, if he approves of it, must lay it before both Houses of Parliament subject to the negative resolution procedure. A code of practice may include such practical guidance as the Commission thinks fit as to what steps it is reasonably practical for employers to take for the purpose of preventing their employees from committing acts of unlawful discrimination in the course of their employment.

The significance of such codes of practice derives from subsection (10) which states that a failure on the part of any person to observe any provision of a Code shall not of itself render him liable to any proceedings; but in any proceedings under the Sex Discrimination Act[129] before an industrial tribunal the Code is admissible in evidence and if any provision of the Code appears relevant to the tribunal it must be taken into account.

The EOC acted with scrupulous regard to the terms of the statute in preparing its Code of Practice. It first tested the waters by issuing a guidance booklet, entitled *Equal Opportunity Policies and Practices in Employment*, from which it derived some experience of the drafting problems involved. Then it produced a *Public Consultative Draft Code of Practice* in 1980 and a wide variety of organisations from both sides of industry commented on it during 1981. Over 80 responses were analysed in detail, following further discussions with a number of bodies. That draft was then amended in the light of the replies and a *Revised Consultative Draft* published in 1982. More limited consultations then took place on this revised draft, and a submission was finally made to the Secretary of State in April 1984. The *Code of Practice for the Elimination of Discrimination on the Grounds of Sex and Marriage and the Promotion of Equality of Opportunity in Employment* finally came into operation in April 1985. Although the drafting and other textual difficulties involved should certainly not be underestimated, the Code is not (and was never expected to be) a radical restatement of the law, so that it is unfortunate that it took nearly a decade to come into effect. During this time, industrial tribunals have become accustomed to finding their own way through the sex discrimination legislation and may now be somewhat reluctant to change their ways and make full use of the Code.

The Code is divided into an introduction and two main sections. The first section states the basic requirements of the anti-discrimination law and the second gives employers more practical guidance on such matters as monitoring of the workforce and the circumstances in which positive action is permissible. Annexed to the Code is a short summary of the main legal provisions. The Commission also produces a series of booklets expanding at greater length on specific subjects dealt with in the Code; these, of course, have no statutory evidentiary value.

The Code is sold,[130] rather than being distributed free.[131] The Commission believes that employers are more likely to pay serious regard to its terms if they have paid for it.

Ironically, in view of the length of time taken for its production, the present Code is in need of updating in order to take into account the provisions of the Sex Discrimination Act 1986. The Commission is to produce an explanatory leaflet for this purpose and does not intend in the immediate future to reopen the statutory procedure for the approval of a new Code.

## Review of the anti-discrimination laws

It was seen earlier in the present chapter that review of the anti-discrimination legislation is one of the primary duties cast on the EOC by s.53(1). To date, it has carried out two reviews of the legislation. The first was in 1980 and the Commission's proposals for reform were annexed to its Annual Report for that year. In making these proposals, the Commission clearly drew heavily on its (then) five year experience of operating the legislation and, in particular, on the experience it had gained through assisting individual cases under s.75. Some of the proposals it made at that time have since been incorporated in new legislation, in particular the recommendation that it should be possible to demand equal pay for work of equal value, although the impetus for this and other reforms came in the end from the EEC rather than from the EOC directly.[132]

It was regrettable that wider consultations did not take place before the Commission published its 1980 proposals, since a broad measure of public backing would have lent them greater support. However, the Commission in October 1986 did launch a consultative process with the issue of *Legislating for Change? Review of the Sex Discrimination Legislation*, to which extensive reference has been made elsewhere in the present work. The Commission, which has received a large number of comments on this document, intends to publish firm proposals for amendments to the legislation during 1988.

## NOTES

1. 'Equality for Women', Cmnd. 5724 (1974). The background to this White Paper is discussed in the EOC's *First Annual Report* (1976).
2. Ibid., paras 27–9.
3. Ibid., para. 108.
4. Ibid., para. 108.
5. Hereafter, unless otherwise stated, the notes in this chapter making reference to statutory sections refer to the Sex Discrimination Act 1975.
6. The Secretary of State has power to alter the number of Commissioners: s.53(3).
7. S.53(1). The Commission came formally into existence on 29 December 1975.
8. See *infra*, p. 239 *et seq*.
9. See Jackson, 'Policies and Implementation of Anti-discrimination Strategies', in Schmid and Weitzel (eds), *Sex Discrimination and Equal Opportunity* (1984, Gower).
10. See for example 'Women's Rights: the Missed Opportunity', *The Sunday Times*, 20 February 1977.
11. Schedule 3, para 2(1).
12. Ibid., para 2(2)(b). This means that they cannot transfer directly into the

Civil Service and that their loyalty is to the Commission. However, they enjoy broadly the same contractual terms and conditions as civil servants.

13. This latter provision has never been utilised. Schedule 3, para 3.
14. S.57(2).
15. S.53(2) and Schedule 3, para 4.
16. The Act after all uses the female pronoun for the purpose of defining discrimination and the circumstances in which it occurs.
17. Baroness Lockwood, Baroness Platt and Ms Joanna Foster.
18. Schedule 3, para 8.
19. The Glasgow Office deals with employment casework up to the stage of submission to the Commission for a decision on whether assistance should be granted by it, as to which see *infra*, p. 273 *et seq.*
20. For further discussion of this issue, see Sacks, 'The Equal Opportunities Commission – Ten Years On' (1986) 49 *MLR* 560.
21. Schedule 3, para 14.
22. Ibid., para 15.
23. In 1986, the CRE's budget was £10,530,039. Even taking into account the £2,836,308 paid by the CRE to the Community Relations Councils, this still means that its remaining 'free' budget is over twice that of the EOC. The CRE is based in London so that its staff costs are inevitably higher than those of the EOC, but this cannot explain the whole of the discrepancy. Even taking staff size as the indicator rather than annual grant, the CRE is over a third as large again as the EOC.
24. Schedule 3, para 11(2) provides for the delegation of any of the Commission's functions to a committee or to two or more Commissioners.
25. 'Equality for Women' Cmnd. 5724 (1974).
26. Ibid., para 109.
27. S.53(1).
28. The recent works of Leonard in relation to industrial tribunals, *Pyrrhic Victories* (1987, HMSO) and *Judging Inequality* (1987, Cobden Trust), provide good examples.
29. See, for example, Sacks, 'The Equal Opportunities Commission – Ten Years On' (1986) 49 *MLR* 560.
30. S.55
31. EOC, *Health and Safety Legislation: Should We Distinguish Between Men and Women* (1979).
32. *Eleventh Annual Report* (1986).
33. See Chapter 4, pp. 206–7 *et seq.* As a consequence of this threat, the Government has recently announced that it will introduce legislation to repeal many of these provisions: see *Consultative Document on the Restrictions on the Employment of Young People and the Removal of Sex Discrimination in Legislation* (1988, Department of Employment).
34. The substance of this section is also to be found in Applebey and Ellis, 'Formal investigations: the CRE and EOC as Law Enforcement Agencies' (1984) *Public Law* 236. It is reproduced here by kind permission of the publishers, Sweet and Maxwell/Stevens.
35. S.57(1). In practice, no formal investigation has been conducted at the instigation of the Secretary of State.
36. Unfortunately, in *Home Office* v. *CRE* [1982] 1 QB 385, Woolf J interpreted this expression extremely narrowly, saying that the phrase 'promotion of equality of opportunity' just expresses the obverse of 'the elimination of discrimination' and therefore only encompasses those areas ccovered by the anti-discrimination legislation. It is, of course, strongly arguable that equality

of opportunity is a much broader concept than this and refers to the removal of all obstacles, legal and illegal.

37. See s.53(1), discussed *supra*, p. 243. The Race Relations Act 1976, whose provisions in this field are otherwise substantially identical to those of the Sex Discrimination Act, permits a formal investigation 'to promote . . . good relations between persons of different racial groups generally' (s.43(1)). This provision enabled the CRE to carry out a formal investigation into acts done by the Home Office in the administration of the Immigration Act 1971: *Home Office* v. *CRE* [1982] 1 QB 385. The Sex Discrimination Act, for obvious reasons, omits any reference to the promotion of good relations between the sexes, so that a parallel investigation into sex discrimination in immigration would on this basis have been *ultra vires*.
38. See Griffiths LJ in *R* v. *CRE, Ex p. Hillingdon LBC* [1982] 1QB 276, at p. 292.
39. As amended by the Race Relations Act 1976, Schedule 4, para 2.
40. S.58(3A).
41. *R. v. CRE, Ex p. Hillingdon LBC* [1982] 1 QB 276.
42. The subsection had a curious legislative history, as Lord Denning MR explained. It first appeared at the Report Stage of the Race Relations Bill in the House of Lords, after an amendment had been moved by Lord Hailsham. His aim was secure for a person named the right to be heard during the course of an investigation, so he wished it to become a separate section. However, when the government finally accepted his amendment, they apparently accidentally had it incorporated into the preceding section and an identical arrangement was adopted for the Sex Discimination Act. The difficulties which this has caused have been considerable.
43. *R. v. CRE, Ex p. Hillingdon LBC* [1982] AC 779.
44. *R. v. CRE, Ex p. Prestige Group plc* [1984] 1 WLR 335. See also Applebey and Ellis, 'Blackening the Prestige Pot? Formal Investigations and the CRE' (1984) 100 *LQR* 349.
45. The power to subpoena information is discussed *infra*, p. 251 *et seq.*
46. For example, the EOC's formal investigation into British Steel, see *infra*, p. 262.
47. Judicial review proceedings are undoubtedly available if the Commission exceeds its statutory powers: *R* v. *CRE, Ex p. Hillingdon LBC* [1982] AC 779.
48. See *infra*, p. 266.
49. House of Commons Home Affairs Committee First Report (1981–2) HC 46–1.
50. EOC, *Legislating for Change? Review of the Sex Discrimination Legislation* (1986); CRE, *Review of the Race Relations Act 1976: Proposals for change* (1985).
51. *R. v. CRE, Ex p. Hillingdon LBC* [1982] AC 779, at p. 786.
52. And likewise the Race Relations Act 1976, s.49(3).
53. Emphasis supplied.
54. *R. v. CRE, Ex p. Hillingdon LBC* [1982] AC 779, at p. 791.
55. *R. v. CRE, Ex p. Prestige Group plc* [1984] 1 WLR 335.
56. Ibid., at p. 342.
57. *R. v. CRE, Ex p. Hillingdon LBC* [1982] AC 799, at p. 791.
58. *R. v. CRE, Ex p. Hillingdon LBC* [1982] 1QB 276, at pp. 301–2.
59. Ibid., especially Lord Denning MR at p. 286 and Griffiths LJ at p. 296.
60. See Chapter 3, p. 157 *et seq.* for discussion of discovery of documents in sex discrimination cases.
61. S.59(2).
62. And which will be discussed *infra*,. p. 256 *et seq.*
63. S.60(1).
64. S.60(2).
65. S.60(3) and (4).

66. *CRE* v. *Amari Plastics Ltd* [1982] 1 QB 1194. On the facts of this case, a delay of three years in publishing the report was held not to be excessive.
67. See *infra*, p. 254 *et seq.*
68. S.61.
69. This is the chief way in which proceedings may be brought in respect of a discriminatory practice. S.71(1)(b) provides another possible route for the enforcement by the Commission of the law on discriminatory practices, in the particular circumstances set out in that section.
70. Ss.67(1) and (2).
71. *R.* v. *CRE, Ex p. Hillingdon LBC* [1982] AC 779.
72. *R.* v. *CRE, Ex p. Prestige Group plc* [1984] 1 WLR 335.
73. S.67(6).
74. S.67(3).
75. S.67(4).
76. S.67(7).
77. S.60(1).
78. S.67(5).
79. *R* v. *CRE, Ex p. Cottrell and Rothon* [1980] 1 WLR 1580.
80. Per Lord Diplock in the *Hillingdon* case [1982] AC 779, at p. 791.
81. S.68(1).
82. Ss.68(2) and (3).
83. *CRE* v. *Amari Plastics Ltd* [1982] 1 QB 1194.
84. See Pardoe, 'Investigation by the CRE' (1982) 132 *NLJ* 670.
85. S.70.
86. See also Chapter 3, p. 151 *et seq.*
87. S.71(1).
88. S.71(2).
89. *R.* v. *CRE, Ex p. Hillingdon LBC* [1982] 1 QB 276, at p. 287.
90. Cf. the procedure for investigations conducted by the Fair Employment Agency into religious discrimination under the Fair Employment (Northern Ireland) Act 1976.
91. EOC, *Legislating for Change: Review of the Sex Discrimination Legislation* (1986).
92. The Commission would also like to be given a power, similar to that possessed by individual complainants (and discussed in Chapter 3, p. 157 *et seq.*) to administer a questionnaire to potential respondents, when it believes discrimination has occurred.
93. CRE *Review of the Race Relations Act 1976: Proposals for Change* (1985).
94. See also the very informative account of the EOC's activities in this field in Gregory, *Sex, Race and the Law* (1987, Sage).
95. See its *First Annual Report* (1976).
96. *Electrolux Ltd* v. *Hutchinson* [1977] ICR 252.
97. See, for example, its *Fifth Annual Report* (1980).
98. ACAS Report 'Industrial Relations in the Newspaper Industry', Cmnd. 6680 (1976), para 127, and Royal Commission on the Press 'Final Report', Cmnd. 6810 (1977) para 21.14.
99. In part, this can be attributed to the fact that staff resources were heavily committed to the investigations begun in the previous year.
100. See *supra*, n. 36, for the interpretation of the latter expression by the courts. The EOC itself stated in the report of the investigation that it considered it authorised by the duty to promote equality of opportunity between men and women generally.
101. [1982] AC 779 and [1984] 1 WLR 335.
102. See the *Tenth Annual Report* (1985).
103. See *supra*, p. 253.

104. R. v. *Birmingham City Council, Ex p. EOC* (1988) 18 *EOR* 45.
105. See Applebey and Ellis, 'Formal Investigations: the CRE and EOC as Law Enforcement Agencies' (1984) *Public Law* 236.
106. See the 'Interim Report of the Commission's agreement with Barclay's Bank plc' (1987); and (1987) 16 *EOR* 21.
107. S.71.
108. See, for example, the EOC's *Second Annual Report* (1977).
109. Leonard, *Pyrrhic Victories* (1987,HMSO). See also Chapter 3, p. 146.
110. By s.37.
111. S.37(3).
112. See *supra*, p. 261.
113. 30 per cent of total inquiries in 1976.
114. See the *Second Annual Report* (1977).
115. *EOC* v. *Robertson* [1980] IRLR 44 and *EOC* v. *Girling, Wilson and Harvie*, unreported at time of writing.
116. Proceedings were also begun but later settled in a case in 1980.
117. S.39.
118. S.40.
119. *CRE* v. *Imperial Society of Teachers of Dancing* [1983] ICR 473.
120. See Chapter 3, p. 141.
121. *EOC* v. *British Car Auctions Ltd, EOC* v. *Adams* and *EOC* v. *Foulds and Ridings Ltd*, all briefly reported in (1987) 14 *EOR* 2.
122. S.75(1).
123. S.75(2).
124. S.75(3).
125. *Macarthys Ltd* v. *Smith* [1980] IRLR 209.
126. *Garland* v. *British Rail* [1982] 2 WLR 918.
127. *Marshall* v. *Southampton and SW Hants Area Health Authority* [1986] 2 WLR 780.
128. Which was inserted into the Sex Discrimination Act 1975 by the Race Relations Act 1976, Schedule 4, para 1.
129. It is presumably a drafting slip that proceedings under the Equal Pay Act 1970 are not also included.
130. The current price at the time of writing is £1.60 per copy, or £8 for 10 copies.
131. At the time of writing, approximately 80,000 copies had been sold.
132. See Chapter 2 and 3.

# 6  Maternity rights

## THE IMPORTANCE OF MATERNITY RIGHTS

In 1985, there were estimated to be 11.1 million women in the
civilian labour force of Great Britain, accounting for 41.7 per cent
of that labour force.[1] The Department of Employment's projections
indicate a continuing rise in female economic activity rates, particularly during the late 1980s.[2] Every year, approximately 3.6 per cent
of these working women give birth to babies.[3] Some 15 per cent of
mothers now return to work very quickly, in other words by the
time the baby is eight months old, and another 9 per cent are
looking for work at this stage.[4] The proportion of immediate retur-
ners appears to be growing: only 9 per cent of women giving birth
to a first child during the period 1945–9 returned to work within
six months of the birth[5] and a similar proportion were found by
the Census in 1971 to be economically active twelve months after
giving birth.[6] A much larger number of women return to work after
their children have reached school age. As seen in Chapter 1, only
some quarter of married women with children aged under four are
in employment, whereas, in families where the youngest child is
aged between five and nine, the number of employed wives jumps
to over 50 per cent. When the youngest child is over 10, slightly
more than two-thirds of wives are back at work and in a quarter of
all families in this group both parents work full-time.[7]

Irrespective of any alterations in these statistics which might be
produced by varying our system of statutory maternity rights, it is
clear that a great many women today combine motherhood with
employment outside the home. For these women, there is no such
thing as equality of opportunity without adequate recognition by
the law of the physical and other demands being placed upon them
around the time of childbirth. Furthermore, the special responsibilities of parenthood do not, of course, end with infancy. It remains
true that as a society we entrust the primary role of caring for our
dependents to women [8] and, given this fact, the panoply of rights

embodied in the Sex Discrimination and Equal Pay Acts are meaningless in real terms unless accompanied by special provision in
the employment laws to reflect the obligations of mothers to their
children of all ages. However, it is a philosophy which is central
to this book that the provision of equal rights for men and women
should mean just that and that a greater penetration of women
into the world of work ought to go hand in hand with enhanced
opportunities for men to take an active role in their homes and in
caring for their families. This means that any law making special
provision for parental obligations ought to be cast in sex-neutral
terms and ought positively to encourage fathers as well as mothers
to play their part.[9]

Apart from the interest which working mothers themselves have
in adequate laws to guarantee their physical well-being and their
position as employees around the time of childbirth, their families
also often have a real interest in the matter of maternity rights. For
many families it is a financial necessity to have a working mother.
It has been estimated that the number of 'poor families' (that is to
say, those with an income below 140 per cent of supplementary
benefit level or what is today called income support) would increase
threefold were it not for the earnings of married women.[10] In
addition, the community as a whole has a right to demand that the
law makes appropriate concessions to working mothers, for the
health and well-being of future generations depend to a high degree
upon proper perinatal care.

The law of this country today provides five basic rights to
employed mothers. These are: the right not to be dismissed on
account of pregnancy; the right to time off work for ante-natal care;
the right to a period of leave of absence, and to reinstatement after
this leave; and the right to certain payments during absence from
employment. These rights will be discussed in the following section
and the argument advanced that they are cast in such complex and
restrictive terms as to be incapable of achieving the vital objectives
which provide their *raison d'être*.

## MATERNITY RIGHTS CONFERRED BY THE PRESENT LEGISLATION

### The right not to be dismissed on account of pregnancy

S.60 of the Employment Protection (Consolidation) Act 1978[11]
provides that a woman is automatically to be treated as unfairly
dismissed if the whole or principal reason for her dismissal is her
pregnancy or is any other reason connected with her pregnancy.

Examples of reasons connected with pregnancy include where the woman develops a medical condition, such as high blood pressure, which arises out of the pregnancy and which makes it advisable for her to rest,[12] and where the woman is temporarily absent from work because of a miscarriage.[13] In order to be able to rely on s.60, the woman must establish that her employer has either knowledge of or belief in her pregnancy, or knowledge of the facts and their connection with the pregnancy.[14]

The employer is provided with a defence where the woman is, because of her pregnancy, incapable of adequately doing her work; and also where, because of her pregnancy, it would be unlawful for her to continue with her work. In either instance, the employer must first offer the woman any other comparable and suitable job for which he has a vacancy.[15] The burden of proving these defences lies on the employer once the woman has shown that the dismissal was on account of pregnancy or a related reason.[16] In *Elegbede* v. *The Wellcome Foundation Ltd.*[17] an industrial tribunal ruled that, in order for the employer to make out the first defence, he must prove that the incapacity to do the job arises out of the fact of pregnancy itself, and not out of some associated illness from which the particular woman in question is suffering: Ms Elegbede's job was a sedentary one which a normally healthy pregnant woman would have been able to do. It was, accordingly, no defence for her employer to argue that she personally was incapable of performing it because she was suffering from high blood pressure resulting from her pregnancy. However, the Employment Appeal Tribunal disapproved of this analysis in *Grimsby Carpet Co. Ltd* v. *Bedford*.[18] They held that because Parliament made a distinction in the first part of s.60(1) between 'pregnancy' and 'reasons connected with pregnancy', but did not make the same distinction further on in the section in relation to defences, it did not follow that that distinction was not also to be considered in relation to defences. The part of the section dealing with defences speaks of incapability 'because of her pregnancy' and this must be taken to include, for reasons also of 'industrial common sense', cases where the incapability results from a pregnancy-related illness.

A complaint of a breach of s.60 must normally be made within three months of the dismissal,[19] a quite inappropriately short period given that the employee will either be in an advanced state of pregnancy or will recently have given birth at the time it expires.

The woman's claim is expressed by the statute to be for unfair dismissal. This means that the usual qualifying period for unfair dismissal complaints applies;[20] before June 1985, this period was one year, but since this date it has been increased to two years.[21] For the many employees who are unable to make a claim under s.60 because they have not worked for the employer for two years, a claim under the Sex Discrimination Act now provides a possible avenue of redress. As discussed in Chapter 3 (see p. 92 *et seq.*), if a woman is dismissed for a reason connected with her pregnancy, in circumstances in which an indisposed male employee would be more favourably treated, the Employment Appeal Tribunal has ruled that she may make out a complaint of unlawful sex discrimination.[22] Nevertheless, such a claim may still prove unsatisfactory from the woman's point of view, since the remedies available do not include reinstatement and this is very likely to be what she seeks. The law in this area is in substantial need of reform if justice is to be served and equality of opportunity is to be extended to all women; the answer must be to remove the qualifying period for unfair dismissal claims under s.60, so that *all* pregnant employees fall within its scope. A remedy under the Sex Discrimination Act is also, however, necessary to cover cases where the discrimination takes a form other than dismissal, for example, a refusal to appoint or to promote.[23]

S.60 also contains another very important limitation. The Court of Appeal has ruled that the section provides no protection for the employee who is dismissed by reason of redundancy, even where the reason that she has been selected for redundancy is that she is pregnant and her colleagues are not. In such a case, the fairness or otherwise of the dismissal has to be judged according to the criteria contained in s.57 of the 1978 Act: the dismissal is not automatically presumed to be unfair.[24] However, if the redundancy occurs after the employee has begun her period of maternity leave, then she is rather better placed by the legislation than other employees, since the Employment Appeal Tribunal has held that she will be treated as automatically unfairly dismissed if she is not offered a suitable alternative vacancy, even where it is unreasonable or uneconomic for the employer to offer the available vacancy;[25] this is because s.45(3) of the 1978 Act provides that:

> If an employee is entitled to return to work in accordance with subsection (1) but it is not practicable by reason of redundancy for the employer to permit her so to return to work she shall be entitled, where there is a suitable alternative vacancy, to be offered alternative employment with her employer

and paragraph 2(2) of Schedule 2 to the Act goes on to state that:

> If in the circumstances described in s.45(3) no offer is made of such alternative employment as is referred to in that subsection, then the dismissal which by virtue of s.56 is treated as taking place shall, notwithstanding anything in s.57 or 58, be treated as an unfair dismissal for the purposes of Part V of this Act.

## The right to time off work for ante-natal care

This right was introduced as recently as 1980, by the Employment Act of that year,[26] in response to evidence that the UK had at that date one of the worst perinatal mortality rates in the Western world.[27] s.13 of the 1980 Act provides that a pregnant employee is entitled not to be unreasonably refused time off work in order to keep an ante-natal appointment, certainly a necessary reform since research had shown that in some 42 per cent of larger manufacturing plants such leave had hitherto been denied.[28] The employer is entitled to demand from the employee (for all appointments except her first) a certificate from a registered medical practitioner, registered midwife or registered health visitor, stating that the employee is pregnant, together with an appointment card or other document showing that the appointment has been made.[29] There is no need for any qualifying period of service in order to rely on this right; nor need the employee be full-time, although it would, of course, affect the reasonableness of the employer's refusal to allow time off if the part-time employee could easily attend her appointment during non-working hours.[30]

An employee who is allowed to take time off during her working hours under this provision is entitled to be paid by her employer for her period of absence at the appropriate hourly rate.[31] If the employer allows the employee time off for an ante-natal visit, he implicitly agrees that it is reasonable that she should have this time off, and he cannot thereafter escape having to pay her remuneration in respect of the period.[32]

The limitation period for an action before an industrial tribunal alleging a breach of this provision is again only three months.[33]

## The right to leave of absence

To be entitled to leave of absence around the time of childbirth, an employee is required to fulfil stringent conditions. First, she must continue to be employed by her employer (whether or not she remains at work,[34] until immediately before the beginning of the eleventh week before her expected date of confinement.[35] This virtually inflexible[36] requirement is potentially harmful, since it may force the woman into continuing at work even against her doctor's advice.[37] There is also the risk that, through the woman's own ignorance of the law in this matter – and this is not an area in which she is likely to seek expert legal advice – or because of deception by her employer,[38] she may terminate her contract of employment before the required date and so lose her statutory rights.

Secondly, she must work at least 16 hours a week and have been continuously employed by the same employer for two years by the beginning of the eleventh week before her expected week of confinement.[39] Alternatively, she qualifies for leave if she works between eight and 16 hours a week and has worked for her present employer for five years.[40] Those working for less than eight hours a week have no statutory rights. The effect of these provisions, of which there is no equivalent elsewhere in the EEC, is certainly to deny maternity rights to many working women, either because they have not been employed for long enough in total or because they have not worked continuously for the same employer.[41] There is particular danger to women in short-term contracts of employment. In addition, the qualifying periods are based on the notion of women's 'jobs', rather than women's 'careers'. For many women pursuing careers, for example, in teaching, medicine or management, movement from one job to another will be necessary in order to make progress within the hierarchy of the profession, and such moves are especially likely to take place while the woman is young and so to coincide with the childbearing years. The requirement of continuity of service with a single employer represents a serious obstacle to career development for such women. The statutory scheme would far more closely approach the ideal of conferring equal employment opportunities on men and women if it dispensed with the qualifying periods altogether, or at least (in recognition of the genuine difficulties of employers) relaxed them very considerably. The National Council for Civil Liberties advocates a qualifying period of six months employment full or part-time with any employer. Collective agreements and individual contracts of employment may grant maternity rights after a shorter service period than the statute prescribes.[42]

Unfortunately, the government, far from being receptive to calls to abolish or relax the qualifying periods, has proposed that they should be made more stringent. In the White Paper 'Building Businesses, not Barriers'[43] it proposes that employees should be required to work a minimum of 20 hours a week for two years, or else 12 hours a week for five years, before qualifying for maternity leave. This proposal was immediately condemned by the EOC (which had not been consulted in advance by the government); it pointed out that women make up 87 per cent of those working less than 20 hours a week[44] and that many would, as a consequence of this proposal, lose their maternity rights.

In order to preserve her eventual right to return to work, the employee must also inform her employer in writing at least 21 days before her absence begins or, if that is not reasonably practicable, as soon as reasonably practicable, that she will be away because of pregnancy and that she intends to return to work, and she must inform him of the expected week of confinement.[45]

This statutory right is to leave of absence only. Again this ignores a basic philosophy which should underlie the legislation. The woman's physical and other well-being, and that of her baby, may require that other concessions be extended to her at this time, too; for example, she might need to be transferred from physically strenuous work to lighter work during her pregnancy, or to work shorter or more social hours. However, any such concessions have to be negotiated separately as the law stands at the moment.[46]

## The right to reinstatement after maternity leacve

An employee who is absent from work wholly or partly because of pregnancy or confinement[47] is entitled to return to work at any time up to 29 weeks after the birth.[48] In practice, this is a fairly short time in which to adapt to life with a baby and in which to make the necessary arrangements for its care whilst the parents are at work.[49] It is a less than generous period of leave by comparison with leave provided by many other Western European countries. S.48 of the 1978 Act is important in this context since it provides that an employee who has a right both under the Act and under a contract of employment to return to work may not exercise the two rights separately but may take advantage of whichever right is in any particular respect the more favourable. If, therefore, a woman's contract of employment provides for reinstatement at any time up to, say, a year after confinement, then she may rely on this aspect of her contract even if she wishes to claim statutory entitlement as regards other aspects of her return to work.[50] In practice, however, few employers today provide contractual maternity rights going far beyond the statutory minimum in this respect; a 1980 survey found that only 18 per cent of employers gave more generous maternity rights than the legislation and drew the conclusion that progress to improve benefits through collective bargaining had been slow.[51] The Labour Research Department reported in 1984 that, in a survey of 65 workplaces, it had found that only 32 had maternity schemes above the statutory norm; since the survey was mainly circulated amongst organised trade unions, it was assumed that even this figure represented a far higher level of provision than existed generally. The 32 agreements which did provide more than the statutory minimum ranged from those which gave only slight improvements over the state scheme to the best, which not only gave generous leave and pay but also followed this up with provisions making a return to work a more realistic prospect, such as providing the possibility of working part-time or job-sharing. The best maternity provisions it found were in the public sector.[52]

In this context, it will be recalled from Chapter 3 (see especially pp. 82–3) that the Sex Discrimination Act may sometimes be of assistance to a mother returning to work after giving birth; in *Home Office* v. *Holmes*,[53] the Employment Appeal Tribunal ruled that there was unlawful indirect discrimination on the ground of sex where the employer refused to allow the employee, a single parent, to transfer from full-time to part-time employment, in order to cope with her domestic responsibilities.

The employee's right is to return to the 'job' in which she was employed under her original contract of employment.[54] 'Job' is defined[55] to mean 'the nature of the work which [the employee] is employed to do in accordance with his contract and the capacity and place in which he is employed'. However, in *Edgell* v. *Lloyd's Register of Shipping*,[56] an industrial tribunal held that the statute does not mean that the woman is entitled to have 'exactly the same job back again'. The tribunal also held that, during maternity leave, the employer might undertake 'a certain amount of reorganisation. It is not our duty as a tribunal to question the right of management to manage. All we are here to do is to be quite certain that an employer when carrying out those changes acts justly or fairly to the employee'.[57]

The Act goes on to provide that the employee is entitled to return 'on terms and conditions not less favourable than those which would have been applicable to her if she had not been so absent',[58] which appears to mean that she can take advantage of any improvement in conditions, such as a general pay rise, which occurred whilst she was away. Unfortunately, the following subsection,[59] which purports to elucidate the meaning of its predecessor, causes difficulties of interpretation; it states that 'as regards seniority, pension rights and other similar rights, . . . the period or periods of employment prior to the employee's absence shall be regarded as continuous with her employment following that absence'.In other words, it preserves the continuity of the woman's employment, notwithstanding her absence. The problem is to know whether the period of absence itself counts in determining her length of service. For statutory purposes, for example, in computing redundancy pay, compensation for unfair dismissal or notice, the absence certainly counts.[60] For contractual purposes, however, the position is not so simple. The contract of employment may or may not subsist during the absence.[61] If the contract does so subsist, then there will be no problem and the period of absence will count in determining the employee's seniority (unless this is expressly excluded by the contract itself). But what happens where the contract does not subsist during the period of absence? Bercusson[62] considers that the absence nevertheless is to be counted 'as regards seniority, pension rights and other similar rights', whilst Rideout takes the opposite view.[63] Rideout's view unfortunately coincides more closely with the wording of the statute, although it produces greater complication and is less generous to the employee.

In order to exercise her right to return, the employee must give the relevant notices to her employer. The notice requirements contained in the earlier legislation were made considerably more stringent by the Employment Act 1980,[64] the government justifying the changes on the ground that employers and temporary substitute employees needed to know the woman's plans with respect to her return to work with greater accuracy.[65] However, the effectiveness of the means chosen to attain this result is doubtful because, even where women give notice of intended return, only a proportion of them in fact do return;[66] the explanation for this is thought to be that fear of miscarriage or stillbirth prompts the woman to ensure her position even where she does not intend to return to work if all goes well with the birth. In addition, the alleged inconvenience of this to employers is really very slight.[67] The result of the statutory changes has been to provide an obstacle course for the employee, which is accompanied by the very real danger that if she accidentally fails to comply with even the most minor element of it she will lose her statutory maternity rights.

The first notice required has already been mentioned;[68] it must be given in writing, usually 21 days before leave begins.[69] The second notice is at the employer's option; not earlier than 49 days after the expected week of confinement, he is entitled to write to the woman asking her for written confirmation that she intends to return to work. It is noteworthy that the Act permits this calculation to be made with respect to the expected, rather than the actual, week of confinement. This means that if, as frequently happens, the baby is born, say, two weeks late, the employer's letter can arrive when the child is only five weeks old and the mother's state of mind has by no means had a chance to return to its usual condition. The employee will not be entitled to return to work unless she sends her employer the required confirmation within 14 days of receiving the request for it or, if that is not reasonably practicable, as soon as reasonably practicable, and the employer's letter must explain this to her.[70] The government justified this new intermediate notification on the ground that, without it, there was too long a gap between the pre-leaving and pre-returning notices, and because the woman's intentions might change after the birth.

On the other hand, it can well be argued that the amended provisions pay too much attention to these matters and too little to the mother who, in the hectic early weeks following the birth, may not have articulated clearly to herself what she will want to do when the child is older and may even inadvertently overlook replying to her employer. The third notice must be given in writing to the employer at least 21 days before the day on which the employee proposes to return.[71]

An anomalous aspect of these notice requirements is that if the employee complies with them she is placed under absolutely no legal obligation to return (so that advice to a woman in this situation ought always be to give the required notice), whereas if she fails to observe them in the smallest detail she wholly forfeits her statutory rights. This was amply demostrated by *Lavery* v. *Plessey Telecommunications Ltd.*[72]. Ms Lavery attempted to exercise her right to return to work after having a baby by giving five days' notice of her intended day of return. Under the then-existing legislation, she was required to give seven days' notice of her intended day of return.[73] Her employers refused to take her back on the ground that she had failed to comply with the statute. A curious twist occurred in the case because, as has been seen, the statutory period of 29 weeks' maternity leave is calculated by reference to the week in which the birth actually occurs; Ms Lavery and her employers, perhaps unaware of this, had calculated her necessary date of return by reference to the week in which the baby was due. Since the baby had arrived 18 days late, Ms Lavery actually had several more days of leave entitlement and so could still have acted within the terms of the legislation by giving seven days' notice. The industrial tribunal rejected Ms Lavery's claim for unfair dismissal, saying that she was to blame for not informing her employers of the actual date of her confinement. The Employment Appeal Tribunal held that blame was not a relevant factor, but both it and the Court of Appeal dismissed Ms Lavery's appeal. The main ground for the decision was that Ms Lavery had failed to comply with the precise letter of the statute. It was held that the legislation provides expressly for a particular 'notified day of return' and all the provisions dealing with the right to return are geared to this 'notified date of return'. So, for example, the remedy of an employee for the refusal of an employer to give effect to the statutory right to return is to complain of unfair dismissal under s.56 of the 1978 Act; however, s.56 provides that she is to be treated as having been continuously employed until her notified day of return and as having been dismissed as from that day. This means that, if there is no notified day of return, there is no way in which the machinery of s.56 can operate. This led the Employment Appeal Tribunal, with whom the Court of Appeal agreed on this point, to conclude: it is

> clear that the giving of the seven days notice under s.47(1) is of critical importance, since all the employee's other rights flow from it. Unless the requisite notice is given under s.47, there are no remedies available to her. No notice complying with s.47(1) has been given by Ms Lavery. It is in our view irrelevent that she could have given such notice within the 29 weeks period. Although we sympathise with Ms Lavery, there is no escaping the fact that she has not given the statutory notice upon which her statutory right to return to work depends.[74]

The Employment Appeal Tribunal did, however, express itself highly dissatisfied with the statutory maternity provisions in general, Browne-Wilkinson J saying that they 'are of inordinate complexity exceeding the worst excesses of a taxing statute; we find that especially regrettable bearing in mind that they are regulating the everyday rights of ordinary employers and employees'.[75] The Court of Appeal associated itself with these comments. Nevertheless, it might be thought that the courts came to a less than generous conclusion in this case. If the 'notified day of return' was really so crucial, one might have expected that that day could have been deemed to have occurred seven days after Ms Lavery gave her defective notice. The argument that this might be unfair to the employer, who would not realise that she could still return on that date, can be countered since this situation arises in any case where the baby arrives later than expected and the employer does not discover this. In more general terms, hard cases such as Ms Lavery's tend to bring the law into disrespect. In the absence of more radical reform of the present qualifying requirements for maternity rights, greater justice would be done if a new statutory discretion were introduced, giving the tribunal power to allow a claim to maternity rights where there has been substantial compliance with the terms of the statute on the part of the employee, provided only that serious detriment would not result thereby to the employer.[76]

Another route open to an employee who has not complied with every detail of the statutory requirements may be to allege a term of her contract granting her maternity rights. The Court of Appeal was prepared to accept such an approach in *Lavery* v. *Plessey Telecommunications Ltd*, although ultimately it proved unsuccessful on the facts of that case. In *Lucas* v. *Norton of London Ltd*[77] although Ms Lucas failed to comply with the statutory notice requirement before beginning her maternity leave, the Employment Appeal Tribunal was prepared to spell out from discussions she had had with her employer an implied alteration in her original contract of employment. The result of this implied alteration was that she was given permission to be away from work for whatever reasonable time was involved in her having her baby; she would not be paid in respect of this period above the sum to which she was entitled under the statute; there was an obligation on the employer to take her back to her previous job at a reasonable time after her confinement and on reasonable notice; and she was under an obligation to return to her job after such a time. It followed, therefore, that when her employer refused to take her back after her leave, she was entitled to claim that she had been unfairly dismissed.[78]

There are certain statutory restrictions on the right to return to work.[79] Particularly important are the two which were created by the Employment Act 1980. The first is where, immediately before the woman's absence, the number of employees employed by her employer, added to the number employed by an associated[80] employer of his, did not exceed five; in addition, the employer must show that it is not reasonably practicable for him to permit her to return, or for him or an associated employer to offer her a new contract of employment on terms not substantially less favourable than those of her original contract.[81] The newly elected Conservative government promoted this exclusion in line with its policy of exempting small firms from certain of the more exacting aspects of employment legislation,[82] on the ground that small employers might encounter special difficulty in reinstating returning employees. However, this view is not supported by evidence, according to both the EOC[83] and W W Daniel. The latter found that the majority of women who work for small employers are not entitled to statutory maternity rights anyway, either because they only work part-time or because they have not worked for the necessary qualifying period; in any case, of those actually entitled to claim reinstatement only about 10 per cent of them in fact claimed the right and, more than any other group of employees, they tended to carry out their notification and return to work.[84] This exclusion is also open to criticism in that it discriminates against women working for smaller organisations, who are probably specially in need of statutory protection since they are correspondingly unlikely to be covered by more beneficial collective agreements. Nevertheless, undeterred by such arguments, the government has proposed in its recent White Paper, 'Building Businesses, not Barriers'[85], that this exclusion be expanded to cover firms with fewer than ten employees.

The second exclusion created by the Employment Act 1980 applies where it is not reasonably practicable for a reason other than redundancy[86] for the employer to permit the woman's return and he or an associated employer offers her employment on terms not substantially less favourable than those of her original contract.[87] The EOC objected strongly to this provision before the legislation was enacted, pointing out that in practice tribunals did not interpret the old rule, that the woman had a right to return to her original job, as strictly meaning the 'same' job; for example, the employee could be transferred to a different department so long as the duties of the post were within the terms of the original contract, and therefore the pre-existing law provided sufficient flexibility from the employer's point of view.[88] The rule introduced by the 1980 Act makes a very serious inroad into the woman's rights.[89] It is extremely difficult to disprove the employer's arguments in this type of situation, since the circumstances relate to his own business and so are peculiarly within his own knowledge. And once again the legislation is cast in terms of women's 'jobs' rather than 'careers'; for a woman trying to make her way up an established career structure, an alternative job to her original one may well represent an irremediable setback to her prospects.

The burden of proving each of the two exclusions is on the employer[90], who is not obliged to tell the employee that he intends to rely on them until she attempts to return to work, despite the protection afforded to the employer by all the notification requirements.

## The Right to Statutory Maternity Pay or Maternity Allowance

The Social Security Act 1986 introduced a new statutory maternity pay scheme which came into operation in April 1987. Prior to this date, an employee who satisfied the length of service requirements for maternity leave and who also gave the appropriate statutory notices to her employer was entitled to six weeks of maternity pay from her employer during her period of leave; this maternity pay consisted of 90 per cent of the employee's normal wage, reduced by the amount of the state maternity 'allowance', whether or not the employee was actually entitled to receive that allowance (the contribution conditions being different for the two payments).[91] The employer paying maternity pay was entitled to state reimbursement from the Maternity Pay Fund. In addition, the employee might also receive the flat-rate maternity 'allowance' from the Department of Health and Social Security; this was payable from the eleventh week before the expected week of confinement for a maximum of 18 weeks but, since its objective was to improve the health of mothers and babies by encouraging mothers to give up work in plenty of time before the birth, it was not payable until the mother had stopped working. In addition, all mothers physically present in the UK at the time of giving birth were entitled to a lump sum maternity 'grant' of £25, payable by the state. This figure had remained unchanged since 1969 and many people in latter years doubted whether it was worth the cost of administering it.

These financial provisions for maternity were the subject of considerable criticism, in particular on the ground of their complexity and technicality, both for employees and employers. In 1980, the Department of Health and Social Security proposed reform of the system,[92] but its ideas were based on a refusal to increase overall expenditure so that the improvement in the position of some women would only have been bought at the expense of others and, furthermore, the proposals were based exclusively on flat-rate and not earnings-related payments. These proposals met with general hostility and were abandoned. However, in 1985, the Green Paper 'Reform of Social Security: Programme for Change'[93] was presented to Parliament and out of its slightly more radical proposals there emerged the new scheme for 'statutory maternity pay'.

The essence of the new scheme is the bringing together of the two old payments, maternity pay and maternity allowance, with the aim of simplifying things, at least from the employer's point of view (although it is doubtful whether even this limited objective has, in fact, been achieved.) From the employee's perspective, the changes are fairly undramatic, the only real difference being that payments are now all claimable from a single source, the employer.

There are two elements of the new scheme: an earnings-related element, which is equivalent to 90 per cent of the woman's earnings and is payable for six weeks provided that certain qualifying conditions are met, and a flat-rate payment at the same rate as statutory sick pay which is either payable for the whole of the 18 week maternity pay period or else for 12 weeks additional to the period during which the higher rate is payable. Both payments are taxable and subject to national insurance contributions. In order to qualify for the flat-rate payment, the employee must have worked for the same employer for at least six months by the week preceding the *fourteenth* week before her expected week of confinement.[94] In order, additionally, to receive the earnings-related element, the employee must have worked full-time[95] for two years[96] for the same employer by the week preceding the fourteenth week before her expected week of confinement.[97] In order to receive either the flat-rate or the earnings-related elements, the employee must be able to show that she has become pregnant and reached the eleventh week before her expected week of confinement or else given birth prematurely.[98] She must also have been receiving normal weekly earnings at or above the lower earnings limit for national insurance contributions for the last eight weeks before the week preceding the fourteenth week before her expected week of confinement.[99]

As in the case of maternity leave, a woman is only entitled to statutory maternity pay if she gives her employer 21 days notice, in writing if he so requires, that she is going to be absent from work wholly or partly because of pregnancy or confinement.[100]

Statutory maternity pay is payable for a maximum period of 18 weeks.[101] However, there is a degree of flexibility as to when it may be paid, subject to an inflexible core period of 13 weeks, starting six weeks before the expected week of confinement. The woman can choose whether she takes the other five weeks before or after the 13 weeks, or some before and some after. If the woman is eligible for the higher rate, this is payable for the first six weeks of the payment period.[102] Statutory maternity pay cannot be paid before the eleventh week before the expected week of confinement[103] and it is not payable for any weeks that the mother works[104], but she will only lose benefit if she works during the 13-week core period; if she loses benefit in this way, the loss is first deductible from her flat-rate payments and not from her higher-rate payments.

Liability to make statutory maternity payments is placed squarely on the shoulders of the employer.[105] It is to be hoped that the courts will continue to take the same firm line here as with respect to the old system of maternity pay and hold that the right to statutory maternity pay is absolute and not defeated by the employer's insolvency during the pay period[106]. The employer recovers his payments of statutory maternity pay by deducting the appropriate amount from his remittance of national insurance contributions and tax to the Inland Revenue[107]. The need to make a special claim to the Department of Employment out of the Maternity Pay Fund, which was a feature of the old system, has thus been dispensed with.[108]

If a woman does not qualify for statutory maternity pay through her employer, she is still eligible for a maternity allowance from the Department of Health and Social Security if she has worked as an employed or self-employed person and paid full-rate national insurance contributions for at least 26 out of the 52 weeks ending in the week preceding the fourteenth week before the expected week of confinement. The rate of this maternity allowance is the same as sickness benefit. Like statutory maternity pay, it runs for 18 weeks: a core period of 13 weeks and a flexible five weeks.[109]

The old maternity grant has now been abolished[110]. Instead, under the new Social Fund, payments may be made 'to meet, in prescribed circumstances, maternity expenses':[111] 'the questions whether such a payment is to be awarded and how much it is to be shall be determined by a social fund officer'.[112] The legislation thus does not specify amounts but the government Green Paper suggested a figure of £75 payable to all mothers on income support. In fact, at the time of writing, the sum of £80 was being paid to all mothers on income support. This measure has been criticised on the ground that, in reality, it will mean smaller payments to many mothers on small incomes than hitherto.[113]

## CRITICISM OF THE STATUTORY SCHEME OF MATERNITY RIGHTS

The basic scheme of maternity rights described in the preceding section was first introduced into the law by the Employment Protection Act of 1975, and became operative in 1976 and 1977. It is thus of quite recent origin and at the time of its introduction it certainly represented an extremely important advance in the rights afforded to women in employment; perhaps above all, it gave social respectibility to the practice of mothers returning to work after bearing children. However, given the significance of the matter from the mother's and her family's points of view, as well as from the point of view of the community at large, the present system is seriously deficient. These deficiencies have in part been mentioned in discussion of the particular rights conferred, but the issue is so important that it merits discussion in its own right.

First, it has been seen that in many respects the law is so narrowly based that large numbers of female employees, whom in theory the legislation ought to protect, cannot actually take advantage of it at all. Fortunately for the health of the community, the right to time off for ante-natal care is not based on inflexible service qualifications, but, of course, the rights to leave, reinstatement and pay are. It has been seen that many pregnant employees simply fail to qualify because of the length of service necessary. Even if it is admitted that there is force in the argument that some commitment to work ought to have to be demonstrated before the employee acquires maternity rights, there is no justification for the requirement of continuity of service with the same employer which excludes significant numbers of women and represents a serious obstacle to career progression. Again, although theoretically a mother can take 29 weeks' leave after her child is born, in practice the amount of income provided for her during this period is so small that the maximum term is little more than a luxury open only to the wealthy; the best the woman can hope for under the statutory scheme is, as has been seen, 90 per cent of her ordinary pay over a period of six weeks, plus 12 weeks of the flat-rate maternity payment which may be very much less than her normal wage. If the right to 29 weeks' leave is really to mean anything at all, the legislation governing payments must be substantially reformed so as to produce a normal pay packet over a greatly extended period of time.

Secondly, the sheer complication of the law in this area is thoroughly undesirable. In some places, it is positively obscure[114] and even the judges have several times remarked on its extraordinary technicality.[115] The recently introduced statutory maternity pay scheme has certainly done nothing to alleviate this problem and indeed, in introducing a new critical date (the week preceding the fourteenth week before the expected week of confinement) it has added yet another bewildering detail. The woman has to comply exactly with the notification requirements which operate at three separate stages of the procedure, and she must remain employed until the eleventh week before her expected confinement. If she fails to comply with any of these requirements in the least detail, it has been seen that she may well lose all her maternity rights, and yet on such matters she is most unlikely to obtain proper legal advice. Her employer, if unscrupulous or even if just hard-pressed financially, may decide to take advantage of this.[116] Even where her contract of employment provides expressly or impliedly for some variation from the normal statutory system, the woman is faced with extreme technicality and will often be far from sure – with or without legal advice – what her rights really are. The inter-relation between statutory and contractual schemes is dealt with inadequately by the legislation, and has not yet been elaborated on fully by the courts.

And thirdly, the legislation does not pursue the right priorities.[117] Where it is so narrow as to exclude large numbers of working women (in particular, those working part-time), some of those excluded will be obliged for financial reasons to remain at work throughout pregnancy, relying on sick leave when the child is born and returning to work as soon as possible thereafter; such a practice may endanger the health of mother and child and, far from encouraging it, the law ought to provide positive disincentives to it. Even where the woman is within the statutory scheme, the legislation encourages her to take the shortest practicable leave, since she may well only be paid at anything like her normal wage level for six weeks. It also fails to recognise that on medical grounds some women require special treatment during pregnancy, such as lighter work or fewer purely sedentary duties or more rest-times, but all that the legislation provides, of course, is for leave of absence. Again, scant regard is paid in reality to the principle of equality of opportunity, despite the apparent aim of the legislation to provide a necessary complement to the Sex Discrimination and Equal Pay

Acts; in particular, career development for women (which is also in the longterm interests of employers) is hindered by the requirement of continuous service with one employer and by providing the employer with an easily proven excuse for not giving the woman her original job back. Empirical evidence supports the view that the present statutory maternity rights do not provide women with equality of employment opportunity: a recent survey found that 45 per cent of women who had returned to work part-time after having a baby returned to a job in a lower occupational category and that having a family had the effect of reducing the lifetime earnings of a woman by between a quarter and a half.[118] Such statistics also, of course, demonstrate considerable, although avoidable, economic losses to employers.

In a way, the most important social priority which is ignored by the present legislation is the need to involve fathers in childcare. Like positive action programmes in employment, this is an essential aspect of any legislative scheme which is seriously attempting to break down gender stereotyping since the statistics show us that, despite changes in the employment pattern of women in recent years, child-rearing remains a predominantly maternal occupation.

Our law can be distinguished from that of many other Western European countries in its complete disregard of the position of fathers in the context of employment. On the birth of their children, fathers can at present have leave from work only if their employer gratuituously grants this or if they have unused holiday entitlement. Such a situation is thoroughly unfair to fathers[119] and is also undesirable since it emphasises traditional role-playing from the first moment of the family's existence. If the mother is to return to work in due course then it is only sensible to expect that some of the work of caring for their family will be shouldered by the father and this partial restructuring of family life is only likely to be accomplished if the father is given an early opportunity to involve himself. The legislation requires immediate reform so as to guarantee a substantial period (two weeks is suggested) of paternity leave for all fathers engaged in paid work.

No less a body than the House of Lords' Select Committee on the European Communities, when examining the draft Directive on Parental Leave and Leave for Family Reasons,[120] commented on the niggardly nature of the UK's maternity rights legislation.[121] In particular, they pointed out that there is no equivalent in any other EEC country of the continuous service qualification; they also noted that all other then-EEC countries made earnings-related payments (at 75 per cent or higher, except in Greece) throughout the main leave period. Although the UK appears to offer a relatively generous period of maternity leave as compared with other EEC countries, this is in reality offset by the provisions in those other countries as to parental leave, which will be discussed later in the present chapter (see p. 303 *et seq.*).[122]

## THE EFFECT OF EEC LAW

The provisions of EEC law in the field of sex equality were discussed in Chapter 4. It will be recalled that EEC law creates no special régime of maternity rights, although it does except provisions in respect of pregnancy and maternity from the principle of equal treatment. For example, Article 2(3) of the Equal Treatment Directive[123] excepts from the scope of that Directive 'provisions concerning the protection of women, particularly as regards pregnancy and maternity'.[124] The width of this exception was put to the test in *Commission* v. *Italy*.[125] The Commission accused Italy of not giving full effect to the Equal Treatment Directive, in particular, with respect to its legislation governing maternity leave following the adoption of a child. The adoptive mother in this situation was entitled to three months' paid leave; the father was not so entitled and this disparity was alleged to be discriminatory on the ground of sex. Rozès AG submitted that this was a matter relating to 'working conditions' and so fell within the general scope of the Directive; furthermore, she considered that it could not be excused by means of the exception for maternity. Leave after giving birth to a natural child, granted in order to allow the mother to rest, ought, she considered, rightly tò be regarded as a provision designed to protect women in relation to maternity; but, on the other hand, leave after adoption has a different underlying rationale. It is intended to benefit primarily the child rather than the mother, by helping to foster the emotional ties necessary to settle it with its adopting family. Therefore, concluded the Advocate General, adoptive fathers must be entitled to this leave on exactly the same basis as their working wives. Such an analysis is attractive, despite the fact that it produces a relatively strict interpretation of the exception for pregnancy and maternity, because it actually examines the reasons for having special protective legislation for mothers, instead of merely assuming that this should be the case; such unquestioning assumptions carry with them the risk of assigning to women exclusively roles which neither need nor ought to be played by them alone, with corresponding disadvantages, both legal and practical, for both men and women. Unfortunately, the European Court did not follow the Advocate General's lead. It held instead that the distinction between adoptive mothers and fathers made by the Italian legislation was justified 'by the legit-

imate concern to assimilate as far as possible the conditions of entry
of the child into the adoptive family to those of the arrival of a
newborn child in the family during the very delicate initial
period'.[126] The Court therefore concluded that the situation could
not be regarded as discriminatory within the meaning of the Directive. This is a far less perceptive ruling than that of the (female)
Advocate General and could be taken to imply that there are aspects
of parenting (as distinct from giving birth) which are sex-specific.
Such a suggestion, as has been argued earlier, is unfair to fathers
as well as mothers.

Another retrogressive decision of the European Court came in
*Hofmann* v. *Barmer Ersatzkasse*.[127] Mr Hofmann, whose case was
supported by the European Commission, was the father of a baby.
He arranged for his employer to give him unpaid leave for the
period following the eight week 'protective' period of maternity
leave granted to mothers under Federal German law. His leave was
to extend until the date on which the child was six months old;
this meant that his leave was of the same duration as the optional
leave which the mother could have taken under German law. The
mother meanwhile returned to work. Mr Hofmann applied to the
social security authorities, claiming an allowance equal to that
which the mother would have received in the same circumstances.
In the course of the ensuing litigation, the case was referred to the
European Court for a ruling on the question of whether the Federal
German legislation conformed with the Equal Treatment Directive.
Mr Hofmann argued that the extra leave, after the protective eight
week period was over, was intended for the well-being of the child
and should be available equally to both parents as part of their
'working conditions'; the exception for maternity leave, he
contended, was designed to protect the health of the mother only
and could not lawfully be used to justify measures aimed at the
care of children. The European Court disagreed and held that an
analysis of the wording of the Equal Treatment Directive showed
that it was not intended to deal with matters of family organisation
nor to change the sharing of responsibilities as between mother
and father. A benefit such as maternity leave, granted to the mother
at the end of the protective period, fell within the scope of the
exception for pregnancy and maternity, since it was intended to
protect women with regard both to the consequences of pregnancy
and to the condition of motherhood; such leave could lawfully be
reserved to mothers only since only the mother could be subject to
undesirable pressures to resume work prematurely. Another
decision which highlights the weakness of the legal position of
fathers under the present law, this case is thought by some to
have strengthened considerably the arguments of the European

Commission for the adoption of the draft Directive on Parental Leave and Leave for Family Reasons, which is discussed in the next section.[128] The case itself was, of course, concerned with maternity leave for a time up to six months from the child's birth. It in no way answers the question of the legality of those returner schemes which allow only a mother the right to be reinstated in her old job one, two or even sometimes five years after her confinement. There would still appear to be considerable mileage in the argument that where the period of leave is as protracted as this it cannot be justified on the basis of the pregnancy and maternity exemption and so would have to be offered on identical terms to mothers and fathers.

## PARENTAL LEAVE AND LEAVE FOR FAMILY REASONS

### The Draft Directive

A draft Directive on Parental Leave and Leave for Family Reasons was published by the European Commission at the end of 1983.[129] This followed a Resolution of the European Parliament in February 1981, requesting a Community instrument on this subject; the Commission's Action Programme for 1982 to 1985[130] also included a call for a legal document 'to promote parental leave and leave for family reasons, while maintaining and extending public child-care facilities and services'.

Parental leave is an essentially different concept from maternity leave. The latter is confined to mothers since its rationale is primarily the physical protection of the mother (and, therefore, indirectly her child) during the period of time at which she is vulnerable on account of her pregnancy and confinement. Parental leave, on the other hand, is intended for the direct benefit of the child and the family unit as a whole; it is a period of time during which the child and its family can adapt to life together and during which the parent and child can establish a mutual relationship. It occurs after the protective period of maternity leave has come to an end. There is no reason for it to be confined to mothers and the Commission believes that it should be available on identical terms to both parents. Its importance is obvious in the light of the fact that today one-third of the UK's workforce are parents and more than two and a half million employees have children under the age of five. The case for parental leave, which is in essence a form of positive action, was cogently summed up in a paper presented to a CBI/EOC Conference in 1986.[131]

In our society, it is still women who are expected to take the main responsibility for raising the next generation. The demands imposed by this expectation detrimentally affect their employment and earnings capacity over a lifetime, a loss both to women and the economy as a whole. Because of childcare demands that women are expected to meet, the rapid postwar expansion in the employment of married women has been mainly concentrated in relatively poor, part-time jobs, and has made a very limited contribution to furthering equality for women in employment. To achieve significant advance in equality requires, among other things, that the demands of childcare are more equitably shared, and that they are recognised more fully in the way employment is structured. This requires a response from Government, employers and men. Parental leave is part of this response, though by no means a complete answer: it should not, for instance, be seen as a substitute for childcare provision such as nurseries and childminders, but rather as one of several childcare options open to parents. It does however have an important role to play – either in isolation or, preferably, as part of a package of measures which encourage and support a more equitable sharing of childcare and make employment more compatible with parenthood and other socially important commitments and work.

The draft Directive provides for an entitlement to parental leave from employment where there is nobody else available to look after the child in question. Such leave would be for a minimum period of three months per worker[132] per child; in other words, in a two-parent family in which both parents are employed, both mother and father could claim three months' leave each, after the statutory or contractual period of maternity leave had expired. Member States would be permitted to legislate for a longer period than three months if they so wished and the leave could also be taken part-time and extended proportionately if the parents chose to do this. Both parents would not be allowed to take the leave together and entitlement to the leave could not be transferred as between the parents. Leave would be extended for single-parent families or where the child was handicapped. It would be able to be taken at any time before the child was two years old (or five years in the case of a handicapped or adopted child). The draft leaves to the Member States the choice of whether parental leave should be paid or not; however, it does stipulate that if payment is made it should come out of public funds and must not be paid for by employers. Political pressure dictated this compromise over payment; although it would obviously be preferable from the parents' point of view for the leave to be paid, it was felt that to require this might jeopardise the whole draft and that it was of prime importance to see the principle of parental leave itself accepted.

The draft Directive also provides for leave for family reasons. In its original form, this would have entitled employees with 'family responsibilities' to 'short' periods of leave from work for 'pressing family reasons'. As examples of such pressing family reasons, the draft includes a child's or spouse's illness, the death of a near relative and, rather peculiarly, a child's wedding. Such leave would be open on identical terms to male and female workers. No minimum period is specified by the draft, so this would be a matter for individual Member States to decide. It would, unlike parental leave, be paid for directly by employers.

A year after the original draft Directive had appeared, the Commission published an amended draft.[133] This makes it clear that parental leave would not have to be taken immediately after maternity leave and that those eligible for it would include not only biological parents but also adoptive and step-parents and any other person acting in the place of parents in the event of such circumstances as the serious illness or death of the parents. Leave for family reasons would, under the amended draft, be for 'limited' rather than 'short' periods and extended to cover 'important' as well as 'pressing' family reasons.


## Parental Leave and Leave for Family Reasons in Other Member States of the EEC[134]

Both these forms of leave are now becoming increasingly available elsewhere in the EEC and, indeed, some of the relevant legislation extends beyond the provision envisaged in the draft Directive. Since January 1986, nine out of the 12 Member States of the EEC have had some statutory parental leave scheme. In France, either parent can take two years of unpaid leave or can work part-time. If there are three or more children in the family, the leave is paid at the rate of approximately £100 a month. In West Germany, a new law on parental leave came into operation in 1986, increasing the period of parental leave first to 10 months and then to 12 months from 1988; payment is at the rate of around £150 per month. Italy provides six months' leave at 30 per cent of earnings to either parent and Denmark has a 10 week period of parental leave, paid at the rate of 90 per cent of earnings. Belgium allows any worker to apply for between six and 12 months' leave for a number of purposes, one of which is to care for young children; this leave can be taken part-time and, if the employee's position is refilled by an unemployed person, a social security benefit is payable. In Greece, employees of companies with more than one hundred workers are entitled to three months' parental leave a year per child under two and a half.

The leave is unpaid but each parent has a separate right to it. In Luxembourg, public sector employees may take one year of unpaid leave after the maternity leave period is over. Spain and Portugal provide for three years' and six months' parental leave respectively.

As regards leave for family reasons, the other Member States of the EEC offer a variety of provisions. In Italy, all workers are entitled to indefinite, although unpaid, leave for the care of a sick child under the age of three. In Greece, employees of companies with more than one hundred workers may take up to six days leave for one dependant, eight days for two, and 10 days for three or more; 'dependants' include children under 16 and disabled or sick close relatives. In Belgium, there are collective agreements which give workers 10 days' unpaid leave a year for 'pressing family reasons', and in the public sector workers are entitled to four days' paid leave and two months' unpaid. In the public sector in France, a worker can have up to six days (or 12 in the case of a single parent) for the care of a sick child and in West Germany collective agreements provide five days' leave a year per child under the age of six to care for sick children, covered by sickness insurance benefits. Portugal provides up to 30 days' leave to care for sick children, covered by a social security benefit, and Spain allows up to 29 days' leave for family reasons.

## Developments with Respect to the Draft Directive

The draft Directive is based on Article 100 of the EEC Treaty[135] and therefore requires the unanimous approval of the Council of Ministers before it acquires the force of law. Such approval had not at the time of writing been given, largely on account of the intransigence of the British government which has vetoed the draft Directive on several occasions. Its reasons no doubt stem essentially from the Conservative government's desire to deregulate employment relations, but more particularly the government has argued that the introduction of parental leave along the lines proposed in the draft Directive would be prohibitively expensive. A 'guesstimate' of 3 per cent of industry's wage and salary bill was given to the House of Lords Select Committee on the European Communities; that Committee rather acidly pointed out the undesirability of the government objecting to the scheme on financial grounds when it had taken no methical steps to obtain a proper costing for it. The EOC has, however, commissioned a study of the cost of implementing the draft Directive. This was carried out in 1986 by Sally Holterman, a former Senior Economic Adviser with the Government Economic Service.[136] The report finds that the costs of parental leave would be small by comparison with the other social welfare costs connected with employment. It was estimated that leave would be taken, once the scheme was established, by between 120,000 and 170,000 parents. The women taking leave would account for about 1–1.5 per cent of all female employees, while the men would represent 0.1–0.15 per cent of all male employees. The annual net exchequer cost for unpaid parental leave is estimated at between £4 million and £8 million. If a flat-rate allowance was also paid to parents on leave this would cost between £31 million and £45 million. The real cost to employers resulting from disruption and recruitment is estimated at between £10 and £15 million, but Holtermann points out that these amounts are very small compared to employers' total wage bills (£152,710 million in the UK in 1984) or their total national insurance contributions (£11,391 million in the UK in 1984): the introduction of parental leave would increase the total wage bill by less than a 0.01 per cent. The EOC points out[137] that the Holtermann study was not a cost-benefit exercise and did not, therefore, attempt to value the benefits to family life which would flow from parental leave. It did, however, investigate the financial implications for women's lifetime earnings and it concludes that the benefits to women of parental leave might be worth an aggregate £16 million to £26 million a year. The study also points out (as has been the experience in West Germany and Belguim) that parental leave would create jobs; it estimates that between 6,000 and 9,000 people a year could be removed from the unemployment register as a result of parental leave, yielding an annual saving to the Exchequer of between £15 million and £25 million.

Despite the negative attitude of the British government towards parental and family leave, not all parts of the 'establishment' in this country have reacted similarly. In particular, the House of Lords' Select Committee on the European Communities has given its blessing to substantial parts of the draft.[138] Passages of its Report provide forthright and very welcome support for the principle of equality of opportunity, although in other respects it can be argued that the Committee settled for somewhat weak compromises. It concluded that there should be EEC legislation making parental leave mandatory, both because this will promote equal opportunities for women in employment and also because it will improve childcare. It felt that there was no convincing evidence one way or the other that parental leave would increase costs in industry; all sorts of indirect benefits for employers were seen as possible results, in particular, that parental leave might mean that employers would more often than at present be able to retain skilled and valued members of staff. On the other hand, temporary replacements for parents on leave would have to be paid for. The Committee concluded that, since parental leave would achieve such important social objectives, any increased costs to employers which it did, in fact, generate should be paid for in part by government.

On the question of which employees should qualify for parental leave, the Select Committee accepted a concession which might well remove from the benefits of the proposed Directive a substantial number of employees. It considered that the possibility of increased costs and disruption might turn out to be severe in the case of small employers, so it recommended that those employing fewer than 20 people should be exempt from the legislation. It also raised, but did not answer, the question of what, if any, service qualification should be required. The draft Directive proposes that parental leave should be conditional on a service qualification of, at the most, one year. However, this is of course more generous than the UK's present scheme of maternity rights, which is based on two years' service. The Select Committee considered it unsatisfactory that maternity and parental entitlements, which should be part of an integrated approach, should have different qualifying conditions. The CBI had submitted in evidence that the qualification for parental leave ought to be two years' service, but the EOC had suggested that the maternity qualification should be reduced. The Select Committee pointed out that consideration would have to be given to the whole issue of the alignment of maternity and parental leaves and it drew attention to the point of view expressed by the EOC, but without actually recommending it. The EOC had argued that a period of 16–20 weeks following the birth ought to be sufficient to allow the mother's complete physical recovery and to enable her to breast-feed the baby, so that maternity leave should be reduced from the present 29 weeks to this period; any leave after this time should be regarded as relating to the care of the child and should therefore be available to fathers as well as mothers. The EOC proposed two ways in which this narrower definition of maternity leave might be integrated with parental leave: either the entitlement to parental leave could run from the end of this shorter period of maternity leave, or else the last weeks of the existing maternity leave could be made available to either parent, with parental leave proper starting at 29 weeks after the birth.

The Select Committee opted for a considerable reduction in the period of mandatory parental leave, from the three months proposed in the draft Directive to one month. In arriving at this compromise, it commented that three months seemed 'too controversial to lead to easy acceptance among employers or early agreement in the Council of Ministers'. The principle of parental leave it considered 'more important than the fixing of any particular length of leave.'[139] And it was pointed out that only one month's leave would make it less necessary for firms to take on temporary replacements for workers on leave and would therefore help reduce employers' fears of increased costs.

However, the Select Committee did come down firmly in favour of parental leave being paid. It considered that many parents would not in practice be able to afford to take leave unless it was paid and that non-payment would act as a particular disincentive to fathers, because of their higher earnings, and to single parents, who would have no partner's earnings to fall back on. Furthermore, it was concluded that payment should come from public funds.

As far as leave for family reasons was concerned, unfortunately the Select Committee was unimpressed by this aspect of the draft Directive and it concluded that it was not a proper subject for legislation. The Committee commented that

> arguments which are convincing with regard to parental leave carry less conviction when applied to leave for family reasons. Parental leave can be seen as a bold social innovation bringing important benefits for childcare and equal opportunities at work. It is a proper subject for legislation. Legislation on leave for family reasons would merely acknowledge a widespread practice which 'pretty well any reasonable employer already gives'. The Committee do not believe that the need for family leave is great enough to require legislation which would in any case prove difficult to draft and implement.[140]

## NOTES

1. *Women and Men in Britain: A Statistical Profile* (EOC, 1986).
2. *Employment Gazette*, 93(7) (July 1985) p. 255.
3. W. W. Daniel, 'Womens's Experience of Maternity Rights Legislation', *Employment Gazette*, 88 (2) (May 1980) p. 468. This article was the first publication generated by a programme of research conducted at the request of the Department of Employment by W. W. Daniel at the Policy Studies Institute into the effects of statutory maternity rights. It was followed in June 1980 by 'Maternity Rights: the Experience of Women', PSI (hereafter referred to as 'The Experience of Women') and in August 1981 by 'Maternity Rights: the Experience of Employers', PSI (hereafter referred to as 'The Experience of Employers').
4. 'The Experience of Women', Chapter viii. Similarly, the 1984 Department of Employment 'Women and Employment' survey found that 17% of women giving birth to a first child during the mid–1970s had returned to work within six months of the birth.
5. Department of Employment 'Women and Employment' survey (1984).
6. See the Third Report of the House of Lords' Select Committee on the European Communities (Session 1984–85.)
7. These figures come from *Women and Men in Britain: a Statistical Profile* (EOC, 1985 and 1986) and are based on the General Household Survey. See also

Martin and Roberts, *Women and Employment: a Lifetime Perspective* (1984, HMSO). By comparison with other European countries, employment rates of women with young children in the UK are very low.

8.  See Martin and Roberts, *Women and Employment: A Lifetime Perspective* (1984, HMSO).

9.  See also Conaghan and Chudleigh, 'Women in Confinement: Can Labour Law Deliver the Goods?' (1987) *Journal of Law and Society*, Vol.14, p. 133.

10. McNay and Pond 'Low Pay and Family Poverty', Study Commission on the Family (1980).

11. Hereafter in this chapter referred to as the 1978 Act.

12. *Elegbede* v. *The Wellcome Foundation Ltd* [1977] IRLR 383.

13. *George* v. *Beecham Group Ltd* [1977] IRLR 43.

14. *Del Monte Ltd* v. *Mundon* [1980] ICR 694.

15. Ss.60(1), (2) and (3) of the 1978 Act.

16. *Brear* v. *Wright Hudson Ltd* [1977] IRLR 287; however, on the facts of this case the industrial tribunal was satisfied that incapacity had been proved on the unsubstantiated evidence of the employer.

17. *Elegbede* v. *The Wellcome Foundation Ltd* [1977] IRLR 383.

18. *Grimsby Carpet Co. Ltd.* v. *Bedford* (1987) 16 *EOR* 45.

19. S.67(2) of the 1978 Act.

20. See *Reaney* v. *Kanda Jean Products Ltd* [1978] IRLR 427; *Singer* v. *Millward Ladsky and Co* [1979] IRLR 217; and *Turley* v. *Allders Department Stores Ltd* [1980] IRLR 4. Bercusson in the Current Law Statutes Reprint of the 1978 Act disputes this approach on the ground that s.60 of the 1978 Act provides that dismissal on account of pregnancy is to be treated without more as unfair dismissal.

21. Unfair Dismissal (Variation of Qualifying Period) Order (S.I. 1985 No. 782). The qualifying period was originally only six months and W. W. Daniel in 'The Experience of Women' estimated that, when it was extended to one year, the number of women at risk of being dismissed for pregnancy but being unable to complain of unfair dismissal more than doubled. With the recent further increase in the qualifying period, this result will of course be greatly magnified.

22. *Hayes* v. *Malleable Working Men's Club* [1985] ICR 703. Cf. *Turley* v. *Allders Department Stores Ltd* [1980] IRLR 4. The *Hayes* ruling had, by the time of writing, been followed by at least four industrial tribunals and had resulted in the award to the women concerned of substantial damages: see *EOC News Release* 20 August 1987 and see also (1987) 16 *EOR* 46.

23. See also Chapter 3, particularly p. 94.

24. *Brown* v. *Stockton-on-Tees Borough Council* [1987] IRLR 230. At the time of writing an appeal against this decision had been heard by the House of Lords but the judgment was not yet available.

25. *Community Task Force* v. *Rimmer* (1986) ICR 491.

26. Most of the maternity rights discussed in this section were introduced by the Employment Protection Act 1975 and became operational in 1976 and 1977.

27. The TUC in particular had drawn Parliament's attention to the high incidence of complications affecting low-paid employees, as had the House of Commons Select Committee on Social Services. The clause was added to the Bill as it went through Parliament.

28. 'The Experience of Employers', especially p. 66. There is no definition provided by the Act of ante-natal care; presumably it may vary according to the medical condition of the woman and there seems no requirement that it should be provided exclusively by a doctor. In *Gregory* v. *Tudsbury Ltd*

[1982] IRLR 267, it was held that the term 'ante-natal care' was wide enough to cover relaxation classes.

29. Employment Act 1980, ss.13(2) and (3).
30. *Gregory* v. *Tudsbury Ltd* [1982] IRLR 267.
31. Employment Act 1980, ss.13(4) and (5).
32. *Gregory* v. *Tudsbury Ltd* [1982] IRLR 267.
33. Employment Act 1980, s.13(7).
34. So long as she continues to be employed by her employer, she may be physically absent from work for any reason, for example sickness, whether connected with the pregnancy or not, holiday or special leave: *Satchwell Sunvic Ltd* v. *Secretary of State for Employment* [1979] IRLR 455.
35. S.33(3)(a) of the 1978 Act. However, she cannot be obliged by contract to begin her leave at this date and no later: *ILEA* v. *Nash* [1979] ICR 229.
36. The only exception to it is where the employee has been dismissed for a reason contained in s.60 (incapability of doing her work or contravention of a statutory duty in her continuing to do it) and not re-engaged by the employer, whether the dismissal is fair or unfair.
37. Bercusson, in his comments in the Current Law Statutes Reprint of the 1978 Act, points out that, although absence from *work* by itself does not operate to deny the woman her rights, there is a temptation for tribunals and employers to regard absence for reasons of pregnancy as tantamount to resignation by the woman.
38. 'The Experience of Women' reported some evidence of informal pressure being put on the pregnant employee by her boss to leave prior to the eleventh week before the expected date of confinement.
39. S.33(3)(b), s.151 and Schedule 13 paragraph 3 of the 1978 Act.
40. S.151 and Schedule 13 paragraph 6 of the 1978 Act.
41. W. W. Daniel found that only about 54% of the employees in his sample satisfied the hours and service requirements. In particular, very few women indeed (five out of 1100) qualified by having worked for the same employer for five years for between eight and 16 hours a week; this represented less than half a percent of the total. It was also found that about 5% of the women who were otherwise qualified lost their maternity rights through having left work before the eleventh week before their expected confinement. In addition, amongst women in their sample, the majority who had less than two years continuous service with the same employer ('specific service') did have two years or more of continuous service with different employers ('general service'). If the service qualification for maternity rights had been general, rather than specific, the number of women fulfilling that requirement would have increased from 58% to 73%: 'The Experience of Women', especially Chapter IV.
42. The statutory terms for qualification cannot however be made more stringent by express provision in the contract of employment: *Hanson* v. *Fashion Industries (Hartlepool) Ltd* [1981] ICR 35.
43. 'Building Businesses, Not Barriers' Cmnd. 9794 (1986).
44. EOC News Release 16 July 1986.
45. S.33(3)(d) of the 1978 Act, added by the Employment Act 1980 s.11(1).
46. The same point applies on the woman's return to work after maternity leave, when she may well in practice require nursing breaks and more flexible hours whilst the baby is very young.
47. Query whether this wording precludes the employee from undertaking part-time employment during her maternity leave; it is arguable that if she is engaged in such work then her absence from her main job is attributable to this fact and not to the pregnancy or confinement.

48. S.45(1) of the 1978 Act.
49. The House of Lords Select Committee on the European Communities commented as follows in its Third Report (Session 1984–85): 'There has been little official response to [the] increase in the numbers of working mothers. Childcare provision geared to the needs of working parents is limited. The only relevant provision for children under five is in local authority day nurseries. After the War, day nursery places – which had been greatly expanded to encourage women to join the labour force during the War – were reduced. In 1983, there were 28,650 places in local authority day nurseries, less than one place for every 100 children under five. These places are not available to children from two parent families where both parents work. Although working single parents are a priority admission category, they compete for limited places with other priority groups. So in 1983 nearly 16,000 children were on waiting lists for places at these nurseries. For children over five some local authorities provide after-school or holiday play-schemes. But provision is patchy, with relatively few places' (at paragraph 25). Conaghan and Chudleigh, in 'Women in Confinement: Can Labour Law Deliver the Goods?' (1987) 14 *Journal of Law and Society* 133, comment: 'When the state needs women in the labour force it is more than able to provide the facilities to accommodate them as the greater number of public day-care and nursery facilities during the Second World War demonstrated. On the other hand, when the state wishes to shed labour it adopts a policy which assigns to women a primary domestic role; hence, the reduction in day-care facilities which accompanies a post-war policy which regarded women's rightful place as in the home. Thus it is arguable that the emergence of the maternity provisions were a product of the changing gender composition of the labour market which accompanied the entry of married women into the labour force in the 1960's. Likewise, with the onset of recession and the high rate of inflation, the need to shed labour focused on women as an obvious target particularly because . . . their return to the home disguised the true extent of unemployment.' See also *Women and Men in Britain: 'Statistical Profile'* (EOC 1986).
50. See *Kolfer Plant Ltd* v. *Wright* [1982] IRLR 311; *Lavery* v. *Plessey Telecommunications Ltd* [1983]) 1 A11 ER 849; and *Dowuona* v. *John Lewis plc* [1987] IRLR 310. But note the restrictive interpretation placed on s.48 by the Employment Appeal Tribunal in *Bovey* v. *Board of Governors of the Hospital for Sick Children* [1978] ICR 934, where Phillips J held that 'there must be a limit to the extent to which the right in question, to return to work, can be subdivided so as to identify the particular respects in which it is more favourable' (at p. 938).
51. 'Maternity Leave Survey, Part Two: Company Maternity Provisions' IRRR No. 218, February 1980.
52. Bargaining Report January/February 1984, p. 4.
53. *Home Office* v. *Holmes* [1985] 1 WLR 71.
54. S.45(1) of the 1978 Act.
55. By s.153(1) of the 1978 Act.
56. *Edgell* v. *Lloyd's Register of Shipping* [1977] IRLR 463.
57. Ibid., at p. 465.
58. S.45(1) of the 1978 Act.
59. S.45(2) of the 1978 Act.
60. Schedule 13 paragraphs 10 and 9 of the 1978 Act; paragraph 9 was applied in *Mitchell* v. *British Legion Club* [1981] ICR 18.
61. This is implicit in the wording of s.33(3) of the 1978 Act.
62. In his comments on s.45(2) in the Current Law Statutes Reprint of the 1978 Act.

63. Rideout, *Principles of Labour Law* (4th edn, 1983, Sweet and Maxwell) p. 106.
64. For comments on the general effects of this Act on maternity rights, see Pitt, 'Individual Rights under the New Legislation' (1980) 9 *ILJ* 233.
65. Employers' interest groups had criticised the employment protection legislation generally, and the Employment Bill was one of the first steps of the then newly-elected Conservative Government by way of response. However, W. W. Daniel's research project (which had not been concluded when the Employment Bill came before Parliament) found that nearly half of the employers in their survey reported that no aspect of employment legislation had had any noteworthy effect for them: 'The Experience of Employers', especially Chapter II.
66. In a study conducted by the EOC of employees of the Federation of Scottish Bank Employers, it was found that only one in three women declaring an intention to return to work after maternity leave actually did so. Barclays Bank told the commission that of 724 women who preserved reinstatement rights in 1977, only 112 returned to work: EOC's *Response to Working Papers Proposing Amendments to the Employment Protection Legislation* (1979). W. W. Daniel also found that women who gave notice of return fell into three groups of similar size: just over one third had returned as notified; 27% had planned to return but failed to do so; and the remaining approximate one-third had no real intention of returning: 'The Experience of Women', especially Chapter V.
67. Of all the women leaving an employer to have a baby, only about one in six is likely to give notice of return but fail to return; the proportion for small firms seems to be even smaller: 'The Experience of Women', especially Chapter V.
68. In relation to the right to leave of absence.
69. S.33(3)(d) of the 1978 Act, added by the Employment Act 1980, s.11(1).
70. Ss.33(3A) and 3B) of the 1978 Act, added by the Employment Act 1980, s.11(2).
71. S.49(1) of the 1978 Act, as amended by the Employment Act 1980, s.11(3). The notification period was only seven days under the 1978 Act, but the Government considered that this did not give the employer sufficient time to make the necessary arrangements for the woman's return.
72. *Lavery* v. *Plessey Telecommunications Ltd* [1983] 1 All ER 849. See also Ellis, 'Reinstatement after Confinement: an Obstacle Race for Mothers' (1984) 47 *MLR* 107.
73. See *supra*, n. 71.
74. *Lavery* v. *Plessey Telecommunications Ltd* [1982] IRLR 180, at p. 182.
75. Ibid, at p. 182.
76. See also *Dowuona* v. *John Lewis plc* [1987] IRLR 310.
77. *Lucas* v. *Norton of London Ltd* [1984] IRLR 86.
78. Some doubt was cast on the correctness of this decision by Balcombe LJ in *Dowuona* v. *John Lewis plc* [1987] IRLR 310. See also *McKnight* v. *Addlestones (Jewellers) Ltd* [1984] IRLR 453.
79. For example, it is illegal to employ a woman in a factory or workshop within four weeks of her giving birth: Public Health Act 1936, s. 205, and Factories Act 1961, Schedule 5.
80. 'Associated' is defined by s.153(4) of the 1978 Act as follows: 'any two employers are to be treated as associated if one is a company of which the other (directly or indirectly) has control, or if both are companies of which a third person (directly or indirectly) has control'. It was seen in Chapter 2, p. 42, that the same definition of 'associated' applies in the context of the Equal Pay Act 1970.

81. Ss.56A(1) and (3) of the 1978 Act, added by the Employment Act 1980, s.12.
82. See, for example, the Employment Act 1980, s.8.
83. See EOC's *Response to the Working Papers Proposing Amendments to the Employment Protection Legislation* (1979).
84. 'The Experience of Women, especially Chapter V. W. W. Daniel concluded that the employment protection legislation had made less impact on smaller firms than on larger ones. Only 18% of the establishments he sampled (all of whom had recently employed a pregnant woman) reported any problem over maternity rights (these difficulties chiefly concerned reinstatement,) and only 6% of smaller firms: 'The Experience of Employers,' especially Chapter II. An earlier survey, Clifton, 'The Impact of Employment Legislation on Small Firms' (Department of Employment Research Paper no. 6) had found that the effects of the legislation on small firms had not been very pronounced but that a significant proportion of them had been sufficiently affected by it for it to influence their behaviour. Of the firms surveyed who had actual experience of the legislation, the provision most often selected as likely to be troublesome (by 26%) was unfair dismissal; maternity leave came second (mentioned by 16%).
85. 'Building Business, Not Barriers', Cmnd. 9794 (1986).
86. In the case of redundancy, the returning employee is entitled, where there is a suitable alternative vacancy, to be offered alternative employment under the conditions laid down in ss.45(3) and (4) of the 1978 Act, see *supra*, p. 284.
87. Ss.56A(2) and (3) of the 1978 Act, added by the Employment Act 1980, s.12.
88. EOC's 'Response to Working Papers Proposing Amendments to the Employment Protection Legislation' (1979). See also *Edgell* v. *Lloyd's Register of Shipping* [1977] IRLR 463, discussed *supra*, p. 288.
89. The justification for it, namely that employers find the right to reinstatement burdensome, is not supported by the evidence. W. W. Daniel found that in practice employers concede the right to reinstatement, or else voluntarily grant mothers the opportunity to return to work, substantially more often than the law requires. Despite the fact that criticisms of reinstatement by employer-interest groups have centred on the difficulties of keeping open responsible and expert jobs, he in fact found that it was people doing just those types of jobs who were most likely to have been accorded the right or opportunity to return when they did not meet the statutory requirements: 'The Experience of Women', especially Chapter XII. The survey of employers found that public employers have had much more experience than private employers have had in specialised qualified women stopping work to have a baby; whatever problems they might have in covering such jobs during maternity leave, the evidence showed that those difficulties were very much less than the ones they faced if the woman left permanently: 'The Experience of Employers', especially Chapter VIII.
90. S.56A(4) of the 1978 Act, added by the Employment Act 1980, s.1
91. For a particularly harsh application of this rule, see *Cullen* v. *Creasey Hotels (Limbury) Ltd* [1980] ICR 236.
92. In a Consultative Document entitled 'A Fresh Look at Maternity Benefits'.
93. 'Reform of Social Security: Programme for Change' Cmnd. 9518.
94. Social Security Act 1986, s.46(2)(a). Note that the crucial date for this purpose is *not* the same as in the case of the right to maternity leave, where it is the *eleventh* week before the expected week of confinement on which the calculations have to be based, see *supra*, p. 285.
95. This means for at least 16 hours a week: Social Security Act 1986, s.48(5).

96. Or five years where the woman works between eight and 16 hours a week: ibid., s.48(5).
97. Ibid., s.48(4).
98. Ibid., s.46(2)(c).
99. Ibid., s.46(1)(b).
100. Ibid., ss.46(4) and (5).
101. Ibid., s.47(1).
102. Ibid., s.48(4).
103. Ibid., s.47(2).
104. Ibid., ss.47(4) and (6).
105. Ibid., s.46(3).
106. See the decision of the Employment Appeal Tribunal in *Secretary of State for Employment* v. *Cox* [1984] IRLR 437.
107. Social Security Act 1986, Schedule 4.
108. Ibid., Schedule 4.
109. Ibid., Schedule 4.
110. Ibid., s.38.
111. Ibid., s.32(2)(a).
112. Ibid., s.33(2).
113. See Conaghan, 'Statutory Maternity Pay under the Social Security Act 1986' (1987) 16 *ILJ* 125.
114. For example, ss.33(3) and 45(2) of the 1978 Act.
115. See in particular *Lavery* v. *Plessey Telecommunications Ltd* [1982] IRLR 180 and [1983] 1 All ER 849; *Secretary of State for Employment* v. *Cox* [1984] IRLR 437; and *Dowuona* v. *John Lewis plc* [1987] IRLR 310.
116. W. W. Daniel found that many women employees were unaware of the length of time for which they were entitled to leave of absence and there appeared to be a substantial number, particularly in small firms, who had the formal qualifications for maternity pay but had not received their entitlement: 'The Experience of Women', especially Chapters V and VI.
117. See also Winch, 'Maternity Rights Provisions – a New Approach' (1981) *JSWL* 321.
118. Martin and Roberts, *Women and Employment: a Lifetime Perspective* (1984, HMSO).
119. The great majority of whom wish for a formal scheme of paid paternity leave, according to Bell, McKee and Priestley, *Fathers, Childbirth and Work* (1983, EOC).
120. Draft Directive on Parental Leave and Leave for Family Reasons, Session 1984–85, Third Report, discussed in more detail *infra*, p. 301 *et seq*.
121. Especially in paragraphs 26 and 27.
122. For further details of maternity rights in other EEC countries, see *Parenthood in the Balance* (1982, EOC).
123. EEC Directive 76/207, OJ No L 39/40.
124. See also the Social Security Directive 79/7, 1979 OJ No L 6/24, Article 4(2); the Occupational Social Security Directive 86/378, 1986 OJ No L 225/40, Article 5(2); and the Directive on the Self-Employed 86/613, 1986 OJ No L 359, Preamble and Article 8.
125. *Commission* v. *Italy* Case 163/82 [1984] 3 CMLR 169.
126. Ibid., at p. 184.
127. *Hofmann* v. *Barmer Ersatzkasse* Case 184/83 [1984] ECR 3047.
128. See for example CREW Reports (1984) vol. 4, no. 8/9.
129. COM (83) 686 final, 22 November 1983.
130. As to which see Chapter 4, p. 220 *et seq*.

131.  Peter Moss, 'Why Parental Leave', in EOC Conference entitled *Parental Leave: an Employers' Guide*, 20 November 1986.
132.  The draft Directive does not extend to the self-employed.
133.  COM (84) 631 final, 9 November 1984.
134.  Sweden, not of course a member of the EEC, was the Western European country which pioneered such leave, introducing the initial provision in 1974.
135.  See Chapter 4, n. 128.
136.  Holtermann, *The Costs of Implementing Parental Leave in Great Britain* (1986, EOC).
137.  See EOC Briefing, 'Parental Leave – the Proposed EC Directive' (May 1986).
138.  In its Third Report for the Session 1984–85, February 1985.
139.  Ibid., at paragraph 105.
140.  Ibid., at paragraph 83.

# Index